P9-BIJ-930

HBase in Action

NICK DIMIDUK
AMANDEEP KHURANA

TECHNICAL EDITOR
MARK HENRY RYAN

MANNING
Shelter Island

For online information and ordering of this and other Manning books, please visit www.manning.com. The publisher offers discounts on this book when ordered in quantity. For more information, please contact

> Special Sales Department
> Manning Publications Co.
> 20 Baldwin Road
> PO Box 261
> Shelter Island, NY 11964
> Email: orders@manning.com

©2013 by Manning Publications Co. All rights reserved.

No part of this publication may be reproduced, stored in a retrieval system, or transmitted, in any form or by means electronic, mechanical, photocopying, or otherwise, without prior written permission of the publisher.

Many of the designations used by manufacturers and sellers to distinguish their products are claimed as trademarks. Where those designations appear in the book, and Manning Publications was aware of a trademark claim, the designations have been printed in initial caps or all caps.

♾ Recognizing the importance of preserving what has been written, it is Manning's policy to have the books we publish printed on acid-free paper, and we exert our best efforts to that end. Recognizing also our responsibility to conserve the resources of our planet, Manning books are printed on paper that is at least 15 percent recycled and processed without the use of elemental chlorine.

Manning Publications Co.
20 Baldwin Road
PO Box 261
Shelter Island, NY 11964

Development editors:	Renae Gregoire, Susanna Kline
Technical editor:	Mark Henry Ryan
Technical proofreaders:	Jerry Kuch, Kristine Kuch
Copyeditor:	Tiffany Taylor
Proofreaders:	Elizabeth Martin, Alyson Brener
Typesetter:	Gordan Salinovic
Cover designer:	Marija Tudor

ISBN 9781617290527
Printed in the United States of America
1 2 3 4 5 6 7 8 9 10 – MAL – 17 16 15 14 13 12

brief contents

contents

foreword

At a high level, HBase is like the atomic bomb. Its basic operation can be explained on the back of a napkin over a drink (or two). Its deployment is another matter.

HBase is composed of multiple moving parts. The distributed HBase application is made up of client and server processes. Then there is the Hadoop Distributed File System (HDFS) to which HBase persists. HBase uses yet another distributed system, Apache ZooKeeper, to manage its cluster state. Most deployments throw in Map-Reduce to assist with bulk loading or running distributed full-table scans. It can be tough to get all the pieces pulling together in any approximation of harmony.

Setting up the proper environment and configuration for HBase is critical. HBase is a general data store that can be used in a wide variety of applications. It ships with defaults that are conservatively targeted at a common use case and a generic hardware profile. Its ergonomic ability—its facility for self-tuning—is still under development, so you have to match HBase to the hardware and loading, and this configuration can take a couple of attempts to get right.

But proper configuration isn't enough. If your HBase data-schema model is out of alignment with how the data store is being queried, no amount of configuration can compensate. You can achieve huge improvements when the schema agrees with how the data is queried. If you come from the realm of relational databases, you aren't used to modeling schema. Although there is some overlap, making a columnar data store like HBase hum involves a different bag of tricks from those you use to tweak, say, MySQL.

If you need help with any of these dimensions, or with others such as how to add custom functionality to the HBase core or what a well-designed HBase application should look like, this is the book for you. In this timely, very practical text, Amandeep and Nick explain in plain language how to use HBase. It's the book for those looking to get a leg up in deploying HBase-based applications.

Nick and Amandeep are the lads to learn from. They're both long-time HBase practitioners. I recall the time Amandeep came to one of our early over-the-weekend Hackathons in San Francisco—a good many years ago now—where a few of us huddled around his well-worn ThinkPad trying to tame his RDF on an early version of an HBase student project.

He has been paying the HBase community back ever since by helping others on the project mailing lists. Nick showed up not long after and has been around the HBase project in one form or another since that time, mostly building stuff on top of it. These boys have done the HBase community a service by taking the time out to research and codify their experience in a book.

You could probably get by with this text and an HBase download, but then you'd miss out on what's best about HBase. A functional, welcoming community of developers has grown up around the HBase project and is all about driving the project forward. This community is what we—members such as myself and the likes of Amandeep and Nick—are most proud of. Although some big players contribute to HBase's forward progress—Facebook, Huawei, Cloudera, and Salesforce, to name a few—it's not the corporations that make a community. It's the participating individuals who make HBase what it is. You should consider joining us. We'd love to have you.

MICHAEL STACK
CHAIR OF THE APACHE HBASE
PROJECT MANAGEMENT COMMITTEE

letter to the HBase community

Before we examine the current situation, please allow me to flash back a few years and look at the beginnings of HBase.

In 2007, when I was faced with using a large, scalable data store at literally no cost—because the project's budget would not allow it—only a few choices were available. You could either use one of the free databases, such as MySQL or PostgreSQL, or a pure key/value store like Berkeley DB. Or you could develop something on your own and open up the playing field—which of course only a few of us were bold enough to attempt, at least in those days.

These solutions might have worked, but one of the major concerns was scalability. This feature wasn't well developed and was often an afterthought to the existing systems. I had to store billions of documents, maintain a search index on them, and allow random updates to the data, while keeping index updates short. This led me to the third choice available that year: Hadoop and HBase.

Both had a strong pedigree, and they came out of Google, a Valhalla of the best talent that could be gathered when it comes to scalable systems. My belief was that if these systems could serve an audience as big as the world, their underlying foundations must be solid. Thus, I proposed to built my project with HBase (and Lucene, as a side note).

Choices were easy back in 2007. But as we flash forward through the years, the playing field grew, and we saw the advent of many competing, or complementing, solutions. The term *NoSQL* was used to group the increasing number of distributed databases under a common umbrella. A long and sometimes less-than-useful discussion arose around that name alone; to me, what mattered was that the available choices increased rapidly.

The next attempt to frame the various nascent systems was based on how their features compared: strongly consistent versus eventual consistent models, which were built to fulfill specific needs. People again tried to put HBase and its peers into this perspective: for example, using Eric Brewer's CAP theorem. And yet again a heated discussion ensued about what was most important: being strongly consistent or being able to still serve data despite catastrophic, partial system failures.

And as before, to me, it was all about choices—but I learned that you need to fully understand a system before you can use it. It's *not* about slighting other solutions as inferior; today we have a plentiful selection, with overlapping qualities. You have to become a specialist to distinguish them and make the best choice for the problem at hand.

This leads us to HBase and the current day. Without a doubt, its adoption by well-known, large web companies has raised its profile, proving that it can handle the given use cases. These companies have an important advantage: they employ very skilled engineers. On the other hand, a lot of smaller or less fortunate companies struggle to come to terms with HBase and its applications. We need someone to explain in plain, no-nonsense terms how to build easily understood and reoccurring use cases on top of HBase.

How do you design the schema to store complex data patterns, to trade between read and write performance? How do you lay out the data's access patterns to saturate your HBase cluster to its full potential? Questions like these are a dime a dozen when you follow the public mailing lists. And that is where Amandeep and Nick come in. Their wealth of real-world experience at making HBase work in a variety of use cases will help you understand the intricacies of using the right data schema and access pattern to successfully build your next project.

What does the future of HBase hold? I believe it holds great things! The same technology is still powering large numbers of products and systems at Google, naysayers of the architecture have been proven wrong, and the community at large has grown into one of the healthiest I've ever been involved in. Thank you to all who have treated me as a fellow member; to those who daily help with patches and commits to make HBase even better; to companies that willingly sponsor engineers to work on HBase full time; and to the PMC of HBase, which is the absolutely most sincere group of people I have ever had the opportunity know—you rock.

And finally a big thank-you to Nick and Amandeep for writing this book. It contributes to the value of HBase, and it opens doors and minds. We met before you started writing the book, and you had some concerns. I stand by what I said then: this is the best thing you could have done for HBase and the community. I, for one, am humbled and proud to be part of it.

LARS GEORGE
HBASE COMMITTER

preface

I got my start with HBase in the fall of 2008. It was a young project then, released only in the preceding year. As early releases go, it was quite capable, although not without its fair share of embarrassing warts. Not bad for an Apache subproject with fewer than 10 active committers to its name! That was the height of the NoSQL hype. The term *NoSQL* hadn't even been presented yet but would come into common parlance over the next year. No one could articulate why the idea was important—only that it *was* important—and everyone in the open source data community was obsessed with this concept. The community was polarized, with people either bashing relational databases for their foolish rigidity or mocking these new technologies for their lack of sophistication.

The people exploring this new idea were mostly in internet companies, and I came to work for such a company—a startup interested in the analysis of social media content. Facebook still enforced its privacy policies then, and Twitter wasn't big enough to know what a Fail Whale was yet. Our interest at the time was mostly in blogs. I left a company where I'd spent the better part of three years working on a hierarchical database engine. We made extensive use of Berkeley DB, so I was familiar with data technologies that didn't have a SQL engine. I joined a small team tasked with building a new data-management platform. We had an MS SQL database stuffed to the gills with blog posts and comments. When our daily analysis jobs breached the 18-hour mark, we knew the current system's days were numbered.

After cataloging a basic set of requirements, we set out to find a new data technology. We were a small team and spent months evaluating different options while maintaining current systems. We experimented with different approaches and learned firsthand the pains of manually partitioning data. We studied the CAP theorem and eventual consistency—and the tradeoffs. Despite its warts, we decided on HBase, and we convinced our manager that the potential benefits outweighed the risks he saw in open source technology.

I'd played a bit with Hadoop at home but had never written a real MapReduce job. I'd heard of HBase but wasn't particularly interested in it until I was in this new position. With the clock ticking, there was nothing to do but jump in. We scrounged up a couple of spare machines and a bit of rack, and then we were off and running. It was a .NET shop, and we had no operational help, so we learned to combine bash with rsync and managed the cluster ourselves.

I joined the mailing lists and the IRC channel and started asking questions. Around this time, I met Amandeep. He was working on his master's thesis, hacking up HBase to run on systems other than Hadoop. Soon he finished school, joined Amazon, and moved to Seattle. We were among the very few HBase-ers in this extremely Microsoft-centric city. Fast-forward another two years...

The idea of *HBase in Action* was first proposed to us in the fall of 2010. From my perspective, the project was laughable. Why should we, two community members, write a book about HBase? Internally, it's a complex beast. *The Definitive Guide* was still a work in progress, but we both knew its author, a committer, and were well aware of the challenge before him. From the outside, I thought it's just a "simple key-value store." The API has only five concepts, none of which is complex. We weren't going to write another internals book, and I wasn't convinced there was enough going on from the application developer's perspective to justify an entire book.

We started brainstorming the project, and it quickly became clear that I was wrong. Not only was there enough material for a user's guide, but our position as community members made us ideal candidates to write such a book. We set out to catalogue the useful bits of knowledge we'd each accumulated over the couple of years we'd used the technology. That effort—this book—is the distillation of our eight years of combined HBase experience. It's targeted to those brand new to HBase, and it provides guidance over the stumbling blocks we encountered during our own journeys. We've collected and codified as much as we could of the tribal knowledge floating around the community. Wherever possible, we prefer concrete direction to vague advice. Far more than a simple FAQ, we hope you'll find this book to be a complete manual to getting off the ground with HBase.

HBase is now stabilizing. Most of the warts we encountered when we began with the project have been cleaned up, patched, or completely re-architected. HBase is approaching its 1.0 release, and we're proud to be part of this community as we approach this milestone. We're proud to present this manuscript to the community in hopes that it will encourage and enable the next generation of HBase users. The single strongest component of HBase is its thriving community—we hope you'll join us in that community and help it continue to innovate in this new era of data systems.

NICK DIMIDUK

If you're reading this, you're presumably interested in knowing how I got involved with HBase. Let me start by saying thank you for choosing this book as your means to learn about HBase and how to build applications that use HBase as their underlying storage system. I hope you'll find the text useful and learn some neat tricks that will help you build better applications and enable you to succeed.

I was pursuing graduate studies in computer science at UC Santa Cruz, specializing in distributed systems, when I started working at Cisco as a part-time researcher. The team I was working with was trying to build a data-integration framework that could integrate, index, and allow exploration of data residing in hundreds of heterogeneous data stores, including but not limited to large RDBMS systems. We started looking for systems and solutions that would help us solve the problems at hand. We evaluated many different systems, from object databases to graph databases, and we considered building a custom distributed data-storage layer backed by Berkeley DB. It was clear that one of the key requirements was scalability, and we didn't want to build a full-fledged distributed system. If you're in a situation where you think you need to build out a custom distributed database or file system, think again—try to see if an existing solution can solve part of your problem.

Following that principle, we decided that building out a new system wasn't the best approach and to use an existing technology instead. That was when I started playing with the Hadoop ecosystem, getting my hands dirty with the different components in the stack and going on to build a proof-of-concept for the data-integration system on top of HBase. It actually worked and scaled well! HBase was well-suited to the problem, but these were young projects at the time—and one of the things that ensured our success was the community. HBase has one of the most welcoming and vibrant open source communities; it was much smaller at the time, but the key principles were the same then as now.

The data-integration project later became my master's thesis. The project used HBase at its core, and I became more involved with the community as I built it out. I asked questions, and, with time, answered questions others asked, on both the mailing lists and the IRC channel. This is when I met Nick and got to know what he was working on. With each day that I worked on this project, my interest and love for the technology and the open source community grew, and I wanted to stay involved.

After finishing grad school, I joined Amazon in Seattle to work on back-end distributed systems projects. Much of my time was spent with the Elastic MapReduce team, building the first versions of their hosted HBase offering. Nick also lived in Seattle, and we met often and talked about the projects we were working on. Toward the end of 2010, the idea of writing *HBase in Action* for Manning came up. We initially scoffed at the thought of writing a book on HBase, and I remember saying to Nick, "It's gets, puts, and scans—there's not a lot more to HBase from the client side. Do you want to write a book about three API calls?"

But the more we thought about this, the more we realized that building applications with HBase was challenging and there wasn't enough material to help people get off the ground. That limited the adoption of the project. We decided that more material on how to effectively use HBase would help users of the system build the applications they need. It took a while for the idea to materialize; in fall 2011, we finally got started.

Around this time, I moved to San Francisco to join Cloudera and was exposed to many applications that were built on top of HBase and the Hadoop stack. I brought what I knew, combined it with what I had learned over the last couple of years working with HBase and pursuing my master's, and distilled that into concepts that became part of the manuscript for the book you're now reading. HBase has come a long way in the last couple of years and has seen many big players adopt it as a core part of their stack. It's more stable, faster, and easier to operationalize than it has ever been, and the project is fast approaching its 1.0 release.

Our intention in writing this book was to make learning HBase more approachable, easier, and more fun. As you learn more about the system, we encourage you to get involved with the community and to learn beyond what the book has to offer—to write blog posts, contribute code, and share your experiences to help drive this great open source project forward in every way possible. Flip open the book, start reading, and welcome to HBaseland!

AMANDEEP KHURANA

acknowledgments

Working on this book has been a humbling reminder that we, as users, stand on the shoulders of giants. HBase and Hadoop couldn't exist if not for those papers published by Google nearly a decade ago. HBase wouldn't exist if not for the many individuals who picked up those papers and used them as inspiration to solve their own challenges. To every HBase and Hadoop contributor, past and present: we thank you. We're especially grateful to the HBase committers. They continue to devote their time and effort to one of the most state-of-the-art data technologies in existence. Even more amazing, they give away the fruit of that effort to the wider community. Thank you.

This book would not have been possible without the entire HBase community. HBase enjoys one of the largest, most active, and most welcoming user communities in NoSQL. Our thanks to everyone who asks questions on the mailing list and who answers them in kind. Your welcome and willingness to answer questions encouraged us to get involved in the first place. Your unabashed readiness to post questions and ask for help is the foundation for much of the material we distill and clarify in this book. We hope to return the favor by expanding awareness of and the audience for HBase.

We'd like to thank specifically the many HBase committers and community members who helped us through this process. Special thanks to Michael Stack, Lars George, Josh Patterson, and Andrew Purtell for the encouragement and the reminders of the value a user's guide to HBase could bring to the community. Ian Varley, Jonathan Hsieh, and Omer Trajman contributed in the form of ideas and feedback. The chapter on OpenTSDB and the section on asynchbase were thoroughly reviewed by Benoît Sigoure; thank you for your code and your comments. And thanks to Michael for contributing the foreword to our book and to Lars for penning the letter to the HBase community.

We'd also like to thank our respective employers (Cloudera, Inc., and The Climate Corporation) not just for being supportive but also for providing encouragement, without which finishing the manuscript would not have been possible.

At Manning, we thank our editors Renae Gregoire and Susanna Kline. You saw us through from a rocky start to the successful completion of this book. We hope your other projects aren't as exciting as ours! Thanks also to our technical editor Mark Henry Ryan and our technical proofreaders Jerry Kuch and Kristine Kuch.

The following peer reviewers read the manuscript at various stages of its development and we would like to thank them for their insightful feedback: Aaron Colcord, Adam Kawa, Andy Kirsch, Bobby Abraham, Bruno Dumon, Charles Pyle, Cristofer Weber, Daniel Bretoi, Gianluca Righetto, Ian Varley, John Griffin, Jonathan Miller, Keith Kim, Kenneth DeLong, Lars Francke, Lars Hofhansl, Paul Stusiak, Philipp K. Janert, Robert J. Berger, Ryan Cox, Steve Loughran, Suraj Varma, Trey Spiva, and Vinod Panicker.

Last but not the least—no project is complete without recognition of family and friends, because such a project can't be completed without the support of loved ones. Thank you all for your support and patience throughout this adventure.

about this book

HBase sits at the top of a stack of complex distributed systems including Apache Hadoop and Apache ZooKeeper. You need not be an expert in all these technologies to make effective use of HBase, but it helps to have an understanding of these foundational layers in order to take full advantage of HBase. These technologies were inspired by papers published by Google. They're open source clones of the technologies described in these publications. Reading these academic papers isn't a prerequisite for using HBase or these other technologies; but when you're learning a technology, it can be helpful to understand the problems that inspired its invention. This book doesn't assume you're familiar with these technologies, nor does it assume you've read the associated papers.

HBase in Action is a user's guide to HBase, nothing more and nothing less. It doesn't venture into the bowels of the internal HBase implementation. It doesn't cover the broad range of topics necessary for understanding the Hadoop ecosystem. *HBase in Action* maintains a singular focus on *using HBase*. It aims to educate you enough that you can build an application on top of HBase and launch that application into production. Along the way, you'll learn some of those HBase implementation details. You'll also become familiar with other parts of Hadoop. You'll learn enough to understand why HBase behaves the way it does, and you'll be able to ask intelligent questions. This book won't turn you into an HBase committer. It *will* give you a practical introduction to HBase.

Roadmap

HBase in Action is organized into four parts. The first two are about using HBase. In these six chapters, you'll go from HBase novice to fluent in writing applications on HBase. Along the way, you'll learn about the basics, schema design, and how to use the most advanced features of HBase. Most important, you'll learn how to *think in* HBase. The two chapters in part 3 move beyond sample applications and give you a taste of HBase in real applications. Part 4 is aimed at taking your HBase application from a development prototype to a full-fledged production system.

Chapter 1 introduces the origins of Hadoop, HBase, and NoSQL in general. We explain what HBase is and isn't, contrast HBase with other NoSQL databases, and describe some common use cases. We'll help you decide if HBase is the right technology choice for your project and organization. Chapter 1 concludes with a simple HBase install and gets you started with storing data.

Chapter 2 kicks off a running sample application. Through this example, we explore the foundations of using HBase. Creating tables, storing and retrieving data, and the HBase data model are all covered. We also explore enough HBase internals to understand how data is organized in HBase and how you can take advantage of that knowledge in your own applications.

Chapter 3 re-introduces HBase as a distributed system. This chapter explores the relationship between HBase, Hadoop, and ZooKeeper. You'll learn about the distributed architecture of HBase and how that translates into a powerful distributed data system. The use cases for using HBase with Hadoop MapReduce are explored with hands-on examples.

Chapter 4 is dedicated to HBase schema design. This complex topic is explained using the example application. You'll see how table design decisions affect the application and how to avoid common mistakes. We'll map any existing relational database knowledge you have into the HBase world. You'll also see how to work around an imperfect schema design using server-side filters. This chapter also covers the advanced physical configuration options exposed by HBase.

Chapter 5 introduces coprocessors, a mechanism for pushing computation out to your HBase cluster. You'll extend the sample application in two different ways, building new application features into the cluster itself.

Chapter 6 is a whirlwind tour of alternative HBase clients. HBase is written in Java, but that doesn't mean your application must be. You'll interact with the sample application from a variety of languages and over a number of different network protocols.

Part 3 starts with Chapter 7, which opens a real-world, production-ready application. You'll learn a bit about the problem domain and the specific challenges the application solves. Then we dive deep into the implementation and don't skimp on the technical details. If ever there was a front-to-back exploration of an application built on HBase, this is it.

Chapter 8 shows you how to map HBase onto a new problem domain. We get you up to speed on that domain, GIS, and then show you how to tackle domain-specific challenges in a scalable way with HBase. The focus is on a domain-specific schema design and making maximum use of scans and filters. No previous GIS experience is expected, but be prepared to use most of what you've learned in the previous chapters.

In part 4, chapter 9 bootstraps your HBase cluster. Starting from a blank slate, we show you how to tackle your HBase deployment. What kind of hardware, how much hardware, and how to allocate that hardware are all fair game in this chapter. Considering the cloud? We cover that too. With hardware determined, we show you how to configure your cluster for a basic deployment and how to get everything up and running.

Chapter 10 rolls your deployment into production. We show you how to keep an eye on your cluster through metrics and monitoring tools. You'll see how to further tune your cluster for performance, based on your application workloads. We show you how to administer the needs of your cluster, keep it healthy, diagnose and fix it when it's sick, and upgrade it when the time comes. You'll learn to use the bundled tools for managing data backups and restoration, and how to configure multi-cluster replication.

Intended audience

This book is a hands-on user's guide to a database. As such, its primary audience is application developers and technology architects interested in coming up to speed on HBase. It's more practical than theoretical and more about consumption than internals. It's probably more useful as a developer's companion than a student's textbook. It also covers the basics of deployment and operations, so it will be a useful starting point for operations engineers. (Honestly, though, the book for that crowd, as pertains to HBase, hasn't been written yet.)

HBase is written in Java and runs on the JVM. We expect you to be comfortable with the Java programming language and with JVM concepts such as class files and JARs. We also assume a basic familiarity with some of the tooling around the JVM, particularly Maven, as it pertains to the source code used in the book. Hadoop and HBase are run on Linux and UNIX systems, so experience with UNIX basics such as the terminal are expected. The Windows operating systems aren't supported by HBase and aren't supported with this book. Hadoop experience is helpful, although not mandatory. Relational databases are ubiquitous, so concepts from those technologies are also assumed.

HBase is a distributed system and participates in distributed, parallel computation. We expect you to understand basic concepts of concurrent programs, both multi-threaded and concurrent processes. We don't expect you know how to program a concurrent program, but you should be comfortable with the idea of multiple simultaneous threads of execution. This book isn't heavy in algorithmic theory, but anyone working with terabytes or petabytes of data should be familiar with asymptotic computational complexity. Big-O notation does play a role in the schema design chapter.

Code conventions

In line with our aim of producing a practical book, you'll find that we freely mix text and code. Sometimes as little as two lines of code are presented between paragraphs. The idea is to present as little as necessary before showing you how to use the API;

then we provide additional detail. Those code snippets evolve and grow over the course of a section or chapter. We always conclude a chapter that contains code with a complete listing that provides the full context. We occasionally employ pseudo-code in a Python-like style to assist with an explanation. This is done primarily where the pure Java contains so much boilerplate or other language noise that it confuses the intended point. Pseudo-code is always followed by the real Java implementation.

Because this is a hands-on book, we also include many commands necessary to demonstrate aspects of the system. These commands include both what you type into the terminal and the output you can expect from the system. Software changes over time, so it's entirely possible that this output has changed since we printed the output of the commands. Still, it should be enough to orient you to the expected behavior.

In commands and source code, we make extensive use of **bold text**; and annotations draw your attention to the important aspects of listings. Some of the command output, particularly when we get into the HBase shell, can be dense; use the bold text and annotations as your guide. Code terms used in the body of the text appear in a monotype font like this.

Code downloads

All of our source code, both small scripts and full applications, is available and open source. We've released it under the Apache License, Version 2.0—the same as HBase. You can find the source code on the GitHub organization dedicated to this book at www.github.com/hbaseinaction. Each project contained therein is a complete, self-contained application. You can also download the code from the publisher's website at www.manning.com/HBaseinAction.

In the spirit of open source, we hope you'll find our example code useful in your applications. We encourage you to play with it, modify it, fork it, and share it with others. If you find bugs, please let us know in the form of issues, or, better still, pull requests. As they often say in the open source community: patches welcome.

Author Online

Purchase of *HBase in Action* includes free access to a private web forum run by Manning Publications where you can make comments about the book, ask technical questions, and receive help from the authors and from other users. To access the forum and subscribe to it, go to www.manning.com/HelloHBaseinAction. This page provides information on how to get on the forum once you're registered, what kind of help is available, and the rules of conduct on the forum.

Manning's commitment to our readers is to provide a venue where a meaningful dialogue between individual readers and between readers and the authors can take place. It's not a commitment to any specific amount of participation on the part of the authors, whose contribution to the book's forum remains voluntary (and unpaid). We suggest you try asking the authors some challenging questions, lest their interest stray!

The Author Online forum and the archives of previous discussions will be accessible from the publisher's website as long as the book is in print.

about the authors

 NICK DIMIDUK stumbled into HBase in 2008 when his nightly ETL jobs started taking 20+ hours to complete. Since then, he has applied Hadoop and HBase to projects in social media, social gaming, click-stream analysis, climatology, and geographic data. Nick also helped establish Seattle's Scalability Meetup and tried his hand at entrepreneurship. His current passion is distributed, scalable, online access to scientific data.

AMANDEEP KHURANA is a Solutions Architect at Cloudera, Inc., where he works with customers on their Hadoop and HBase adoption lifecycle—from planning to building and deploying applications built to scale. Prior to Cloudera, Amandeep worked with Amazon Web Services as a part of the Elastic MapReduce team. Amandeep's background is in large-scale distributed systems and information management.

about the cover illustration

The figure on the cover of *HBase in Action* is captioned a "Liburnian Fisherwoman." The Liburnians were an ancient Illyrian tribe inhabiting a district called Liburnia, a coastal region of the northeastern Adriatic in what is now Croatia. This illustration is taken from a recent reprint of Balthasar Hacquet's *Images and Descriptions of Southwestern and Eastern Wenda, Illyrians, and Slavs* published by the Ethnographic Museum in Split, Croatia, in 2008. Hacquet (1739–1815) was an Austrian physician and scientist who spent many years studying the botany, geology, and ethnography of many parts of the Austrian Empire, as well as the Veneto, the Julian Alps, and the western Balkans, inhabited in the past by peoples of many different tribes and nationalities. Hand-drawn illustrations accompany the many scientific papers and books that Hacquet published.

The rich diversity of the drawings in Hacquet's publications speaks vividly of the uniqueness and individuality of Alpine and Balkan regions just 200 years ago. This was a time when the dress codes of two villages separated by a few miles identified people uniquely as belonging to one or the other, and when members of an ethnic tribe, social class, or trade could be easily distinguished by what they were wearing. Dress codes have changed since then and the diversity by region, so rich at the time, has faded away. It is now often hard to tell the inhabitant of one continent from another and the residents of the picturesque towns and villages on the Adriatic coast are not readily distinguishable from people who live in other parts of the world.

We at Manning celebrate the inventiveness, the initiative, and the fun of the computer business with book covers based on costumes from two centuries ago brought back to life by illustrations such as this one.

Part 1

HBase fundamentals

The first three chapters of *HBase in Action* introduce the basics of HBase. In chapter 1, we provide an overview of databases in general and give specific context for HBase.

Chapter 2 teaches the foundations of HBase as you build an example application: TwitBase. Through this application, you'll see how to interact with HBase and how to design a schema for HBase, and you'll get a glimpse of how to make efficient use of HBase in your own applications.

HBase is a distributed system, and we explore that architecture in chapter 3. You'll see how HBase manages your data across the cluster and how to interact with HBase from MapReduce. Upon completion of part 1, you'll have the basic knowledge you need to begin building your own HBase application.

Introducing HBase

This chapter covers

- The origins of Hadoop, HBase, and NoSQL
- Common use cases for HBase
- A basic HBase installation
- Storing and querying data with HBase

HBase is a database: the Hadoop database. It's often described as a sparse, distributed, persistent, multidimensional sorted map, which is indexed by rowkey, column key, and timestamp. You'll hear people refer to it as a key value store, a column family-oriented database, and sometimes a database storing versioned maps of maps. All these descriptions are correct. But fundamentally, it's a platform for storing and retrieving data with random access, meaning you can write data as you like and read it back again as you need it. HBase stores structured and semistructured data naturally so you can load it with tweets and parsed log files and a catalog of all your products right along with their customer reviews. It can store unstructured data too, as long as it's not too large. It doesn't care about types and allows for a dynamic and flexible data model that doesn't constrain the kind of data you store.

HBase isn't a relational database like the ones to which you're likely accustomed. It doesn't speak SQL or enforce relationships within your data. It doesn't allow interrow transactions, and it doesn't mind storing an integer in one row and a string in another for the same column.

HBase is designed to run on a cluster of computers instead of a single computer. The cluster can be built using commodity hardware; HBase scales horizontally as you add more machines to the cluster. Each node in the cluster provides a bit of storage, a bit of cache, and a bit of computation as well. This makes HBase incredibly flexible and forgiving. No node is unique, so if one of those machines breaks down, you simply replace it with another. This adds up to a powerful, scalable approach to data that, until now, hasn't been commonly available to mere mortals.

Join the community

Unfortunately, no official public numbers specify the largest HBase clusters running in production. This kind of information easily falls under the realm of *business confidential* and isn't often shared. For now, the curious must rely on footnotes in publications, bullets in presentations, and the friendly, unofficial chatter you'll find at user groups, meet-ups, and conferences.

So participate! It's good for you, and it's how we became involved as well. HBase is an open source project in an extremely specialized space. It has well-financed competition from some of the largest software companies on the planet. It's the community that created HBase and the community that keeps it competitive and innovative. Plus, it's an intelligent, friendly group. The best way to get started is to join the mailing lists.[1] You can follow the features, enhancements, and bugs being currently worked on using the JIRA site.[2] It's open source and collaborative, and users like yourself drive the project's direction and development.

Step up, say hello, and tell them we sent you!

Given that HBase has a different design and different goals as compared to traditional database systems, building applications using HBase involves a different approach as well. This book is geared toward teaching you how to effectively use the features HBase has to offer in building applications that are required to work with large amounts of data. Before you set out on the journey of learning how to use HBase, let's get historical perspective about how HBase came into being and the motivations behind it. We'll then touch on use cases people have successfully solved using HBase. If you're like us, you'll want to play with HBase before going much further. We'll wrap up by walking through installing HBase on your laptop, tossing in some data, and pulling it out. Context is important, so let's start at the beginning.

---

[1] HBase project mailing lists: http://hbase.apache.org/mail-lists.html.
[2] HBase JIRA site: https://issues.apache.org/jira/browse/HBASE.

1.1 Data-management systems: a crash course

Relational database systems have been around for a few decades and have been hugely successful in solving data storage, serving, and processing problems over the years. Several large companies have built their systems using relational database systems, online transactional systems, as well as back-end analytics applications.

Online transaction processing (OLTP) systems are used by applications to record transactional information in real time. They're expected to return responses quickly, typically in milliseconds. For instance, the cash registers in retail stores record purchases and payments in real time as customers make them. Banks have large OLTP systems that they use to record transactions between users like transferring of funds and such. OLTP systems aren't limited to money transactions. Web companies like LinkedIn also have such applications—for instance, when users connect with other users. The term *transaction* in OLTP refers to transactions in the context of databases, not financial transactions.

Online analytical processing (OLAP) systems are used to answer analytical queries about the data stored in them. In the context of retailers, these would mean systems that generate daily, weekly, and monthly reports of sales and slice and dice the information to allow analysis of it from several different perspectives. OLAP falls in the domain of business intelligence, where data is explored, processed, and analyzed to glean information that could further be used to drive business decisions. For a company like LinkedIn, where the establishing of connections counts as transactions, analyzing the connectedness of the graph and generating reports on things like the number of average connections per user falls in the category of business intelligence; this kind of processing would likely be done using OLAP systems.

Relational databases, both open source and proprietary, have been successfully used at scale to solve both these kinds of use cases. This is clearly highlighted by the balance sheets of companies like Oracle, Vertica, Teradata, and others. Microsoft and IBM have their share of the pie too. All such systems provide full ACID[3] guarantees. Some scale better than others; some are open source, and others require you to pay steep licensing fees.

The internal design of relational databases is driven by relational math, and these systems require an up-front definition of schemas and types that the data will thereafter adhere to. Over time, SQL became the standard way of interacting with these systems, and it has been widely used for several years. SQL is arguably a lot easier to write and takes far less time than coding up custom access code in programming languages. But it might not be the best way to express the access patterns in every situation, and that's where issues like object-relational mismatch arose.

---

[3] For those who don't know (or don't remember), ACID is an acronym standing for *atomicity, consistency, isolation,* and *durability*. These are fundamental principles used to reason about data systems. See http://en.wikipedia.org/wiki/ACID for an introduction.

Any problem in computer science can be solved with a level of indirection. Solving problems like object-relational mismatch was no different and led to frameworks being built to alleviate the pain.

1.1.1 Hello, Big Data

Let's take a closer look at the term *Big Data*. To be honest, it's become something of a loaded term, especially now that enterprise marketing engines have gotten hold of it. We'll keep this discussion as grounded as possible.

What is Big Data? Several definitions are floating around, and we don't believe that any of them explains the term clearly. Some definitions say that Big Data means the data is large enough that you have to think about it in order to gain insights from it. Others say it's Big Data when it stops fitting on a single machine. These definitions are accurate in their own respect but not necessarily complete. Big Data, in our opinion, is a fundamentally different way of thinking about data and how it's used to drive business value. Traditionally, there were transaction recording (OLTP) and analytics (OLAP) on the recorded data. But not much was done to understand the reasons behind the transactions or what factors contributed to business taking place the way it did, or to come up with insights that could drive the customer's behavior directly. In the context of the earlier LinkedIn example, this could translate into finding missing connections based on user attributes, second-degree connections, and browsing behavior, and then prompting users to connect with people they may know. Effectively pursuing such initiatives typically requires working with a large amount of varied data.

This new approach to data was pioneered by web companies like Google and Amazon, followed by Yahoo! and Facebook. These companies also wanted to work with different kinds of data, and it was often unstructured or semistructured (such as logs of users' interactions with the website). This required the system to process several orders of magnitude more data. Traditional relational databases were able to scale up to a great extent for some use cases, but doing so often meant expensive licensing and/or complex application logic. But owing to the data models they provided, they didn't do a good job of working with evolving datasets that didn't adhere to the schemas defined up front. There was a need for systems that could work with different kinds of data formats and sources without requiring strict schema definitions up front, and do it at scale. The requirements were different enough that going back to the drawing board made sense to some of the internet pioneers, and that's what they did. This was the dawn of the world of *Big Data systems* and *NoSQL*. (Some might argue that it happened much later, but that's not the point. This did mark the beginning of a different way of thinking about data.)

As part of this innovation in data management systems, several new technologies were built. Each solved different use cases and had a different set of design assumptions and features. They had different data models, too.

How did we get to HBase? What fueled the creation of such a system? That's up next.

1.1.2   Data innovation

As we now know, many prominent internet companies, most notably Google, Amazon, Yahoo!, and Facebook, were on the forefront of this explosion of data. Some generated their own data, and others collected what was freely available; but managing these vastly different kinds of datasets became core to doing business. They all started by building on the technology available at the time, but the limitations of this technology became limitations on the continued growth and success of these businesses. Although data management technology wasn't core to the businesses, it became essential for *doing* business. The ensuing internal investment in technical research resulted in many new experiments in data technology.

Although many companies kept their research closely guarded, Google chose to talk about its successes. The publications that shook things up were the Google File System[4] and MapReduce papers.[5] Taken together, these papers represented a novel approach to the storage and processing of data. Shortly thereafter, Google published the Bigtable paper,[6] which provided a complement to the storage paradigm provided by its file system. Other companies built on this momentum, both the ideas and the habit of publishing their successful experiments. As Google's publications provided insight into indexing the internet, Amazon published Dynamo,[7] demystifying a fundamental component of the company's shopping cart.

It didn't take long for all these new ideas to begin condensing into open source implementations. In the years following, the data management space has come to host all manner of projects. Some focus on fast key-value stores, whereas others provide native data structures or document-based abstractions. Equally diverse are the intended access patterns and data volumes these technologies support. Some forego writing data to disk, sacrificing immediate persistence for performance. Most of these technologies don't hold ACID guarantees as sacred. Although proprietary products do exist, the vast majority of the technologies are open source projects. Thus, these technologies as a collection have come to be known as *NoSQL*.

Where does HBase fit in? HBase does qualify as a NoSQL store. It provides a *key-value API*, although with a twist not common in other key-value stores. It promises *strong consistency* so clients can see data immediately after it's written. HBase runs on *multiple nodes* in a cluster instead of on a single machine. It doesn't expose this detail to its clients. Your application code doesn't know if it's talking to 1 node or 100, which makes things simpler for everyone. HBase is designed for *terabytes to petabytes* of data, so it optimizes for this use case. It's a part of the *Hadoop ecosystem* and depends on some

---

[4] Sanjay Ghemawat, Howard Gobioff, and Shun-Tak Leung, "The Google File System," Google Research Publications, http://research.google.com/archive/gfs.html.

[5] Jeffrey Dean and Sanjay Ghemawat, "MapReduce: Simplified Data Processing on Large Clusters," Google Research Publications, http://research.google.com/archive/mapreduce.html.

[6] Fay Chang et al., "Bigtable: A Distributed Storage System for Structured Data," Google Research Publications, http://research.google.com/archive/bigtable.html.

[7] Werner Vogels, "Amazon's Dynamo," All Things Distributed, www.allthingsdistributed.com/2007/10/amazons_dynamo.html.

key features, such as data redundancy and batch processing, to be provided by other parts of Hadoop.

Now that you have some context for the environment at large, let's consider specifically the beginnings of HBase.

1.1.3   *The rise of HBase*

Pretend that you're working on an open source project for searching the web by crawling websites and indexing them. You have an implementation that works on a small cluster of machines but requires a lot of manual steps. Pretend too that you're working on this project around the same time Google publishes papers about its data-storage and -processing frameworks. Clearly, you would jump on these publications and spearhead an open source implementation based on them. Okay, maybe you wouldn't, and we surely didn't; but Doug Cutting and Mike Cafarella did.

Built out of Apache Lucene, Nutch was their open source web-search project and the motivation for the first implementation of Hadoop.[8] From there, Hadoop began to receive lots of attention from Yahoo!, which hired Cutting and others to work on it full time. From there, Hadoop was extracted out of Nutch and eventually became an Apache top-level project. With Hadoop well underway and the Bigtable paper published, the groundwork existed to implement an open source Bigtable on top of Hadoop. In 2007, Cafarella released code for an experimental, open source Bigtable. He called it HBase. The startup Powerset decided to dedicate Jim Kellerman and Michael Stack to work on this Bigtable analog as a way of contributing back to the open source community on which it relied.[9]

HBase proved to be a powerful tool, especially in places where Hadoop was already in use. Even in its infancy, it quickly found production deployment and developer support from other companies. Today, HBase is a top-level Apache project with thriving developer and user communities. It has become a core infrastructure component and is being run in production at scale worldwide in companies like StumbleUpon, Trend Micro, Facebook, Twitter, Salesforce, and Adobe.

HBase isn't a cure-all of data management problems, and you might include another technology in your stack at a later point for a different use case. Let's look at how HBase is being used today and the types of applications people have built using it. Through this discussion, you'll gain a feel for the kinds of data problems HBase can solve and has been used to tackle.

1.2   *HBase use cases and success stories*

Sometimes the best way to understand a software product is to look at how it's used. The kinds of problems it solves and how those solutions fit into a larger application architecture can tell you a lot about a product. Because HBase has seen a number of

---

[8] A short historical summary was published by Doug Cutting at http://cutting.wordpress.com/2009/08/10/joining-cloudera/.

[9] See Jim Kellerman's blog post at http://mng.bz/St47.

publicized production deployments, we can do just that. This section elaborates on some of the more common use cases that people have successfully used HBase to solve.

> **NOTE** Don't limit yourself to thinking that HBase can solve only these kinds of use cases. It's a nascent technology, and innovation in terms of use cases is what drives the development of the system. If you have a new idea that you think can benefit from the features HBase offers, try it. The community would love to help you during the process and also learn from your experiences. That's the spirit of open source software.

HBase is modeled after Google's Bigtable, so we'll start our exploration with the canonical Bigtable problem: storing the internet.

1.2.1 *The canonical web-search problem: the reason for Bigtable's invention*

Search is the act of locating information you care about: for example, searching for pages in a textbook that contain the topic you want to read about, or for web pages that have the information you're looking for. Searching for documents containing particular terms requires looking up indexes that map terms to the documents that contain them. To enable search, you have to build these indexes. This is precisely what Google and other search engines do. Their document corpus is the entire internet; the search terms are whatever you type in the search box.

Bigtable, and by extension HBase, provides storage for this corpus of documents. Bigtable supports row-level access so crawlers can insert and update documents individually. The search index can be generated efficiently via MapReduce directly against Bigtable. Individual document results can be retrieved directly. Support for all these access patterns was key in influencing the design of Bigtable. Figure 1.1 illustrates the critical role of Bigtable in the web-search application.

> **NOTE** In the interest of brevity, this look at Bigtable doesn't do the original authors justice. We highly recommend the three papers on Google File System, MapReduce, and Bigtable as required reading for anyone curious about these technologies. You won't be disappointed.

With the canonical HBase example covered, let's look at other places where HBase has found purchase. The adoption of HBase has grown rapidly over the last couple of years. This has been fueled by the system becoming more reliable and performant, due in large part to the engineering effort invested by the various companies backing and using it. As more commercial vendors provide support, users are increasingly confident in using the system for critical applications. A technology designed to store a continuously updated copy of the internet turns out to be pretty good at other things internet-related. HBase has found a home filling a variety of roles in and around social-networking companies. From storing communications between individuals to communication analytics, HBase has become a critical infrastructure at Facebook, Twitter, and StumbleUpon, to name a few.

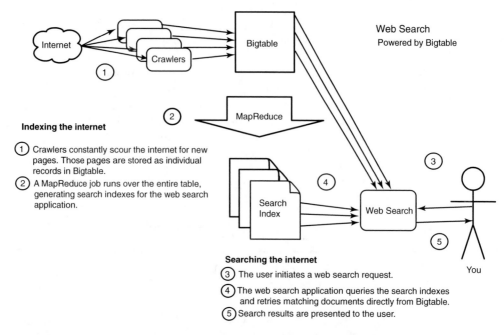

Indexing the internet

① Crawlers constantly scour the internet for new pages. Those pages are stored as individual records in Bigtable.

② A MapReduce job runs over the entire table, generating search indexes for the web search application.

Searching the internet

③ The user initiates a web search request.

④ The web search application queries the search indexes and retries matching documents directly from Bigtable.

⑤ Search results are presented to the user.

Figure 1.1   Providing web-search results using Bigtable, simplified. The crawlers—applications collecting web pages—store their data in Bigtable. A MapReduce process scans the table to produce the search index. Search results are queried from Bigtable to display to the user.

HBase has been used in three major types of use cases but it's not limited to those. In the interest of keeping this chapter short and sweet, we'll cover the major use cases here.

1.2.2 *Capturing incremental data*

Data often trickles in and is added to an existing data store for further usage, such as analytics, processing, and serving. Many HBase use cases fall in this category—using HBase as the data store that captures incremental data coming in from various data sources. These data sources can be, for example, web crawls (the canonical Bigtable use case that we talked about), advertisement impression data containing information about which user saw what advertisement and for how long, or time series data generated from recording metrics of various kinds. Let's talk about a few successful use cases and the companies that are behind these projects.

CAPTURING METRICS: OPENTSDB

Web-based products serving millions of users typically have hundreds or thousands of servers in their back-end infrastructure. These servers spread across various functions—serving traffic, capturing logs, storing data, processing data, and so on. To keep the products up and running, it's critical to monitor the health of the servers as well as the software running on these servers (from the OS right up to the application the user is interacting with). Monitoring the entire stack at scale requires systems that can collect and store metrics of all kinds from these different sources. Every company has its own way of achieving this. Some use proprietary tools to collect and visualize metrics; others use open source frameworks.

StumbleUpon built an open source framework that allows the company to collect metrics of all kinds into a single system. Metrics being collected over time can be thought of as basically time-series data: that is, data collected and recorded over time. The framework that StumbleUpon built is called OpenTSDB, which stands for Open Time Series Database. This framework uses HBase at its core to store and access the collected metrics. The intention of building this framework was to have an extensible metrics collection system that could store and make metrics be available for access over a long period of time, as well as allow for all sorts of new metrics to be added as more features are added to the product. StumbleUpon uses OpenTSDB to monitor all of its infrastructure and software, including its HBase clusters. We cover OpenTSDB in detail in chapter 7 as a sample application built on top of HBase.

CAPTURING USER-INTERACTION DATA: FACEBOOK AND STUMBLEUPON

Metrics captured for monitoring are one category. There are also metrics about user interaction with a product. How do you keep track of the site activity of millions of people? How do you know which site features are most popular? How do you use one page view to directly influence the next? For example, who saw what, and how many times was a particular button clicked? Remember the Like button in Facebook and the Stumble and +1 buttons in StumbleUpon? Does this smell like a counting problem? They increment a counter every time a user *likes* a particular topic.

StumbleUpon had its start with MySQL, but as the service became more popular, that technology choice failed it. The online demand of this increasing user load was too much for the MySQL clusters, and ultimately StumbleUpon chose HBase to replace those clusters. At the time, HBase didn't directly support the necessary features. StumbleUpon implemented atomic increment in HBase and contributed it back to the project.

Facebook uses the counters in HBase to count the number of times people *like* a particular page. Content creators and page owners can get near real-time metrics about how many users *like* their pages. This allows them to make more informed decisions about what content to generate. Facebook built a system called Facebook Insights, which needs to be backed by a scalable storage system. The company looked at various options, including RDBMS, in-memory counters, and Cassandra, before settling on HBase. This way, Facebook can scale horizontally and provide the service to millions of users as well as use its existing experience in running large-scale HBase clusters. The system handles tens of billions of events per day and records hundreds of metrics.

TELEMETRY: MOZILLA AND TREND MICRO

Operational and software-quality data includes more than just metrics. Crash reports are an example of useful software-operational data that can be used to gain insights into the quality of the software and plan the development roadmap. This isn't necessarily related to web servers serving applications. HBase has been successfully used to capture and store crash reports that are generated from software crashes on users' computers.

The Mozilla Foundation is responsible for the Firefox web browser and Thunderbird email client. These tools are installed on millions of computers worldwide and run on a wide variety of OSs. When one of these tools crashes, it may send a crash report back to Mozilla in the form of a bug report. How does Mozilla collect these reports? What use are they once collected? The reports are collected via a system called Socorro and are used to direct development efforts toward more stable products. Socorro's data storage and analytics are built on HBase.[10]

The introduction of HBase enabled basic analysis over far more data than was previously possible. This analysis was used to direct Mozilla's developer focus to great effect, resulting in the most bug-free release ever.

Trend Micro provides internet security and threat-management services to corporate clients. A key aspect of security is awareness, and log collection and analysis are critical for providing that awareness in computer systems. Trend Micro uses HBase to manage its web reputation database, which requires both row-level updates and support for batch processing with MapReduce. Much like Mozilla's Socorro, HBase is also used to collect and analyze log activity, collecting billions of records every day. The flexible schema in HBase allows data to easily evolve over time, and Trend Micro can add new attributes as analysis processes are refined.

ADVERTISEMENT IMPRESSIONS AND CLICKSTREAM

Over the last decade or so, online advertisements have become a major source of revenue for web-based products. The model has been to provide free services to users but have ads linked to them that are targeted to the user using the service at the time. This kind of targeting requires detailed capturing and analysis of user-interaction data to understand the user's profile. The ad to be displayed is then selected based on that profile. Fine-grained user-interaction data can lead to building better models, which in turn leads to better ad targeting and hence more revenue. But this kind of data has two properties: it comes in the form of a continuous stream, and it can be easily partitioned based on the user. In an ideal world, this data should be available to use as soon as it's generated, so the user-profile models can be improved continuously without delay—that is, in an online fashion.

> ### Online vs. offline systems
> The terms *online* and *offline* have come up a couple times. For the uninitiated, these terms describe the conditions under which a software system is expected to perform. Online systems have low-latency requirements. In some cases, it's better for these systems to respond with no answer than to take too long producing the correct answer. You can think of a system as online if there's a user at the other end impatiently tapping their foot. Offline systems don't have this low-latency requirement. There's a user waiting for an answer, but that response isn't expected immediately.

---

[10] Laura Thomson, "Moving Socorro to HBase," Mozilla WebDev, http://mng.bz/L2k9.

> **(continued)**
> The intent to be an online or an offline system influences many technology decisions when implementing an application. HBase is an online system. Its tight integration with Hadoop MapReduce makes it equally capable of offline access as well.

These factors make collecting user-interaction data a perfect fit for HBase, and HBase has been successfully used to capture raw clickstream and user-interaction data incrementally and then process it (clean it, enrich it, use it) using different processing mechanisms (MapReduce being one of them). If you look for companies that do this, you'll find plenty of examples.

1.2.3 Content serving

One of the major use cases of databases traditionally has been that of serving content to users. Applications that are geared toward serving different types of content are backed by databases of all shapes, sizes, and colors. These applications have evolved over the years, and so have the databases they're built on top of. A vast amount of content of varied kinds is available that users want to consume and interact with. In addition, accessibility to such applications has grown, owing to this burgeoning thing called the internet and an even more rapidly growing set of devices that can connect to it. The various kinds of devices lead to another requirement: different devices need the same content in different formats.

That's all about users *consuming* content. In another entirely different use case, users *generate* content: tweets, Facebook posts, Instagram pictures, and micro blogs are just a few examples.

The bottom line is that users consume and generate a lot of content. HBase is being used to back applications that allow a large number of users interacting with them to either consume or generate content.

A content management system (CMS) allows for storing and serving content, as well as managing everything from a central location. More users and more content being generated translates into a requirement for a more scalable CMS solution. Lily,[11] a scalable CMS, uses HBase as its back end, along with other open source frameworks such as Solr to provide a rich set of functionality.

Salesforce provides a hosted CRM product that exposes rich relational database functionality to customers through a web browser interface. Long before Google was publishing papers about its proto-NoSQL systems, the most reasonable choice to run a large, carefully scrutinized database in production was a commercial RDBMS. Over the years, Salesforce has scaled that approach to do hundreds of millions of transactions per day, through a combination of database sharding and cutting-edge performance engineering.

---

[11] Lily Content Management System: www.lilyproject.org.

When looking for ways to expand its database arsenal to include distributed database systems, Salesforce evaluated the full spectrum of NoSQL technologies before deciding to implement HBase.[12] The primary factor in the choice was consistency. Bigtable-style systems are the only architectural approach that combines seamless horizontal scalability with strong record-level consistency. Additionally, Salesforce already used Hadoop for doing large offline batch processing, so the company was able to take advantage of in-house expertise in running and administering systems on the Hadoop stack.

URL SHORTENERS

URL shorteners gained a lot of popularity in the recent past, and many of them cropped up. StumbleUpon has its own, called su.pr. Su.pr uses HBase as its back end, and that allows it to scale up—shorten URLs and store tons of short URLs and their mapping to the longer versions.

SERVING USER MODELS

Often, the content being served out of HBase isn't consumed directly by users, but is instead used to make decisions about what should be served. It's metadata that is used to enrich the user's interaction.

Remember the user profiles we talked about earlier in the context of ad serving? Those profiles (or models) can also be served out of HBase. Such models can be of various kinds and can be used for several different use cases, from deciding what ad to serve to a particular user, to deciding price offers in real time when users shop on an e-commerce portal, to adding context to user interaction and serving back information the user asked for while searching for something on a search engine. There are probably many such use cases that aren't publicly talked about, and mentioning them could get us into trouble.

Runa[13] serves user models that are used to make real-time price decisions and make offers to users during their engagement with an e-commerce portal. The models are fine-tuned continuously with the help of new user data that comes in.

1.2.4   *Information exchange*

The world is becoming more connected by the day, with all sorts of social networks cropping up.[14] One of the key aspects of these social networks is the fact that users can interact using them. Sometimes these interactions are in groups (small and large alike); other times, the interaction is between two individuals. Think of hundreds of millions of people having conversations over these networks. They aren't happy with just the ability to communicate with people far away; they also want to look at the history of all their communication with others. Luckily for social network companies, storage is cheap, and innovations in Big Data systems allow them to use the cheap storage to their advantage.[15]

---

[12] This statement is based on personal conversations with some of the engineers at Salesforce.

[13] www.runa.com.

[14] Some might argue that connecting via social networks doesn't mean being more social. That's a philosophical discussion, and we'll stay out of it. It has nothing to do with HBase, right?

[15] Plus all those ad dollars need to be put to use somehow.

One such use case that is often publicly discussed and is probably a big driver of HBase development is Facebook messages. If you're on Facebook, you've likely sent or received messages from your Facebook friends at some point. That feature of Facebook is entirely backed by HBase. All messages that users write or read are stored in HBase.[16] The system supporting Facebook messages needs to deliver high write throughput, extremely large tables, and strong consistency within a datacenter. In addition to messages, other applications had requirements that influenced the decision to use HBase: read throughput, counter throughput, and automatic sharding are necessary features. The engineers found HBase to be an ideal solution because it supports all these features, it has an active user community, and Facebook's operations teams had experience with other Hadoop deployments. In "Hadoop goes realtime at Facebook,"[17] Facebook engineers provide deeper insight into the reasoning behind this decision and their experience using Hadoop and HBase in an online system.

Facebook engineers shared some interesting scale numbers at HBaseCon 2012. Billions of messages are exchanged every day on this platform, translating to about 75 billion operations per day. At peak time, this can involve up to 1.5 million operations per second on Facebook's HBase clusters. From a data-size perspective, Facebook is adding 250 TB of new data to its clusters every month.[18] This is likely one of the largest known HBase deployments out there, both in terms of the number of servers and the number of users the application in front of it serves.

These are just a few examples of how HBase is solving interesting problems new and old. You may have noticed a common thread: using HBase for both online services and offline processing over the same data. This is a role for which HBase is particularly well suited. Now that you have an idea how HBase can be used, let's get started using it.

1.3   Hello HBase

HBase is built on top of Apache Hadoop and Apache ZooKeeper. Like the rest of the Hadoop ecosystem components, it's written in Java. HBase can run in three different modes: *standalone, pseudo-distributed,* and *full-distributed.* The standalone mode is what we'll work with through the book. That means you're running all of HBase in just one Java process. This is how you'll interact with HBase for exploration and local development. You can also run in pseudo-distributed mode, a single machine running many Java processes. The last deployment configuration is fully distributed across a cluster of machines. The other modes required dependency packages to be installed and HBase to be configured properly. These topics are covered in chapter 9.

---

[16] Kannan Muthukkaruppan, "The Underlying Technology of Messages," Facebook, https://www.facebook.com/note.php?note_id=454991608919.

[17] Dhruba Borthakur et al., "Apache Hadoop goes realtime at Facebook," ACM Digital Library, http://dl.acm.org/citation.cfm?id=1989438.

[18] This statistic was shared during a keynote at HBaseCon 2012. We don't have a document to cite, but you can do a search for more info.

HBase is designed to run on *nix systems, and the code and hence the commands throughout the book are designed for *nix systems. If you're running Windows, the best bet is to get a Linux VM.

> **A note about Java**
>
> HBase is essentially written in Java, barring a couple of components, and the only language that is currently supported as a first-class citizen is Java. If you aren't a Java developer, you'll need to learn some Java skills along with learning about HBase. The intention of this book is to teach you how to use HBase effectively, and a big part of that is learning how to use the API, which is all Java. So, brace up.

1.3.1   Quick install

To run HBase in the standalone mode, you don't need to do a lot. You'll work with the Apache 0.92.1 release and install it using the tarball. Chapter 9 talks more about the various distributions. If you'd like to work with a different distribution than the stock Apache 0.92.1, feel free to install that. The examples are based on 0.92.1 (and Cloudera's CDH4), and any version that has compatible APIs should work fine.

HBase needs the Java Runtime Environment (JRE) to be installed and available on the system. Oracle's Java is the recommended package for use in production systems. The Hadoop and HBase communities have tested some of the JRE versions, and the recommended one for HBase 0.92.1 or CDH4 at the time of writing this manuscript is Java 1.6.0_31.[19] Java 7 hasn't been tested with HBase so far and therefore isn't recommended. Go ahead and install Java on your system before diving into the installation of HBase.

Download the tarball from the Apache HBase website's download section (http://hbase.apache.org/):

```
$ mkdir hbase-install
$ cd hbase-install
$ wget http://apache.claz.org/hbase/hbase-0.92.1/hbase-0.92.1.tar.gz
$ tar xvfz hbase-0.92.1.tar.gz
```

These steps download and untar the HBase tarball from the Apache mirror. As a convenience, create an environment variable pointing at this location; it'll make life easier later. Put it in your environment file so you don't have to set it every time you open a new shell. You'll use HBASE_HOME later in the book:

```
$ export HBASE_HOME=`pwd`/hbase-0.92.1
```

Once that's done, you can spin up HBase using the provided scripts:

```
$ $HBASE_HOME/bin/start-hbase.sh
starting master, logging to .../hbase-0.92.1/bin/../logs/...-master out
```

---

[19] Installing the recommended Java versions: http://mng.bz/Namq.

If you want, you can also put $HBASE_HOME/bin in your PATH so you can simply run hbase rather than $HBASE_HOME/bin/hbase next time.

That's all there is to it. You just installed HBase in *standalone* mode. The configurations for HBase primarily go into two files: hbase-env.sh and hbase-site.xml. These exist in the /etc/hbase/conf/ directory. By default in standalone mode, HBase writes data into /tmp, which isn't the most durable place to write to. You can edit the hbase-site.xml file and put the following configuration into it to change that location to a directory of your choice:

```
<property>
    <name>hbase.rootdir</name>
    <value>file:///home/user/myhbasedirectory/</value>
</property>
```

Your HBase install has a management console of sorts running on http://localhost:60010. It looks something like the screen in figure 1.2.

Now that you have everything installed and HBase fired up, let's start playing with it.

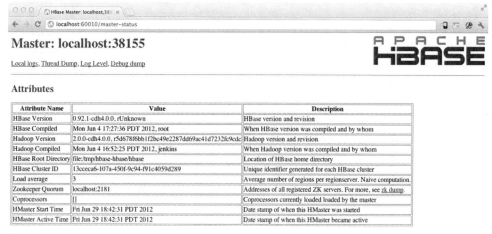

Figure 1.2 The HBase Master status page. From this interface, you can get a general sense of the health of your installation. It also allows you to explore the distribution of data and perform basic administrative tasks, but most administration isn't done through this interface. You'll learn more about HBase operations in chapter 10.

1.3.2 Interacting with the HBase shell

You use the HBase shell to interact with HBase from the command line. This works the same way for both local and cluster installations. The HBase shell is a JRuby application wrapping the Java client API. You can run it in either *interactive* or *batch* mode. Interactive is for casual inspection of an HBase installation; batch is great for programmatic interaction via shell scripts and or even loading small files. For this section, we'll keep to interactive mode.

> **JRuby and JVM languages**
>
> Those of you unfamiliar with Java may be confused by this JRuby concept. JRuby is an implementation of the Ruby programming language on top of the Java runtime. In addition to the usual Ruby syntax, JRuby provides support for interacting with Java objects and libraries. Java and Ruby aren't the only languages available on the JVM. Jython is an implementation of Python on the JVM, and there are entirely unique languages like Clojure and Scala as well. All of these languages can interact with HBase via the Java client API.

Let's start with interactive mode. Launch the shell from your terminal using `hbase shell`. The shell provides you with tab-completion of your commands and inline access to command documentation:

```
$ hbase shell
HBase Shell; enter 'help<RETURN>' for list of supported commands.
Type "exit<RETURN>" to leave the HBase Shell
Version 0.92.1-cdh4.0.0, rUnknown, Mon Jun  4 17:27:36 PDT 2012

hbase(main):001:0>
```

If you've made it this far, you've confirmed the installation of both Java and the HBase libraries. For the final validation, let's ask for a listing of registered tables. Doing so makes a full-circle request from this client application to the HBase server infrastructure and back again. At the shell prompt, type `list` and press Enter. You should see zero results found as a confirmation and again be greeted with a prompt:

```
hbase(main):001:0> list
TABLE
0 row(s) in 0.5710 seconds

hbase(main):002:0>
```

With your installation complete and verified, let's create a table and store some data.

1.3.3 Storing data

HBase uses the *table* as the top-level structure for storing data. To write data into HBase, you need a table to write it into. To begin, create a table called `mytable` with a single *column family.* Yes, column family. (Don't worry; we'll explain later.) Create your table now:

```
hbase(main):002:0> create 'mytable', 'cf'
0 row(s) in 1.0730 seconds
hbase(main):003:0> list
TABLE
mytable
1 row(s) in 0.0080 seconds
```

Listing tables returns new table that was just created

Command to create table mytable; column family name is cf

WRITING DATA

With a table created, you can now write some data. Let's add the string hello HBase to the table. In HBase parlance, we say, "*Put* the *bytes* 'hello HBase' to a *cell* in 'mytable' in the 'first' *row* at the 'cf:message' *column*." Catch all that? Again, we'll cover all this terminology in the next chapter. For now, perform the write:

```
hbase(main):004:0> put 'mytable', 'first', 'cf:message', 'hello HBase'
0 row(s) in 0.2070 seconds
```

That was easy. HBase stores numbers as well as strings. Go ahead and add a couple more values, like so:

```
hbase(main):005:0> put 'mytable', 'second', 'cf:foo', 0x0
0 row(s) in 0.0130 seconds
hbase(main):006:0> put 'mytable', 'third', 'cf:bar', 3.14159
0 row(s) in 0.0080 second
```

You now have three cells in three rows in your table. Notice that you didn't define the columns before you used them. Nor did you specify what type of data you stored in each column. This is what the NoSQL crowd means when they say HBase is a *schema-less* database. But what good is writing data if you can't read it? No good at all. It's time to read your data back.

READING DATA

HBase gives you two ways to read data: get and scan. As you undoubtedly astutely noticed, the command you gave HBase to store the cells was put. get is the complement of put, reading back a single row. Remember when we mentioned HBase having a key-value API but with a twist? scan is that twist. Chapter 2 will explain how scan works and why it's important. In the meantime, focus on using it.

Start with get:

```
hbase(main):007:0> get 'mytable', 'first'
COLUMN                CELL
 cf:message           timestamp=1323483954406, value=hello HBase
1 row(s) in 0.0250 seconds
```

Just like that, you pulled out your first row. The shell shows you all the cells in the row, organized by column, with the value associated at each *timestamp*. HBase can store multiple versions of each cell. The default number of versions stored is three, but it's configurable. At read time, only the latest version is returned, unless otherwise specified. If you don't want multiple versions to be stored, you can configure HBase to store only one version. There is no way to disable this feature.

Use scan when you want values from multiple rows. Be careful! Unless you specify otherwise, it returns all rows in the table. Don't say we didn't warn you. Try it:

```
hbase(main):008:0> scan 'mytable'
ROW                   COLUMN+CELL
 first                column=cf:message, timestamp=1323483954406, value=hell
                      o HBase
 second               column=cf:foo, timestamp=1323483964825, value=0
 third                column=cf:bar, timestamp=1323483997138, value=3.14159
3 row(s) in 0.0240 seconds
```

All your data came back. Notice the order in which HBase returns rows. They're ordered by the row name; HBase calls this the *rowkey*. HBase has a couple other tricks up its sleeve, but everything else is built on the basic concepts you've just used. Let's wrap it up.

1.4   Summary

We covered quite a bit of material for an introductory chapter. Knowing where a technology comes from is always helpful when you're learning. By now you should understand the roots of HBase and have some context for the NoSQL phenomenon. You also understand the basics of the problem HBase is designed for as well as some of the problems HBase has solved. Not only that, but you're running HBase *right now* and using it to store some of your most precious "hello world" data.

No doubt we've raised more questions for you. Why is strong consistency important? How does the client find the right node for a read? What's so fancy about scans? What other tricks does HBase have waiting? We'll answer all these and more in the coming chapters. Chapter 2 will get you started on the path of building your own application that uses HBase as its back-end data store.

Getting started 2

This chapter covers

- Connecting to HBase and defining tables
- The basic commands for interacting with HBase
- Physical and logical data models of HBase
- Queries over compound rowkeys

The goal of the next couple of chapters is to teach you how to use HBase. First and foremost, you'll become comfortable with the features HBase provides you as an application developer. You'll gain a handle on the *logical data model* presented by HBase, the various modes of interacting with HBase, and the details of how to use those APIs. Our other goal is to teach you HBase schema design. HBase has a different *physical data model* from the relational data systems you're likely used to. We'll teach you the basics of that physical model so that you can take advantage of it while designing schemas optimized for your applications.

To accomplish all these goals, you'll build an application from scratch. Allow us to introduce TwitBase, a simplified clone of the social network Twitter, implemented entirely in HBase. We won't cover all the features of Twitter and this isn't intended to be a production-ready system. Instead, think of TwitBase as an early Twitter prototype. The key difference between this system and the early versions of

Twitter is that TwitBase is designed with *scale* in mind and hence is backed by a data store that can help achieve that.

This chapter starts with the basics. You'll see how to create HBase tables, populate them with data, and read it back again. We'll introduce the basic operations HBase provides for working with data as well as the fundamental components of the data model. Along the way, you'll learn a little about how HBase works under the hood. This knowledge is fundamental to making good decisions in your schema designs. This chapter is the launch-point for your study of HBase and the rest of this book.

All the code used in this chapter and throughout the book is available at https://github.com/hbaseinaction/twitbase.

2.1   *Starting from scratch*

At its core, TwitBase stores three simple data elements: *users, twits,* and *relationships.* Users are the center of TwitBase. They log into the application, maintain a profile, and interact with other users by posting twits. Twits are short messages written publicly by the users of TwitBase. Twits are the primary mode of interaction between users. Users have conversations by twitting between themselves. Relationships are the glue for all this interaction. A relationship connects one user to another, making it easy to read twits from other users. This chapter will focus on users and twits. We'll save relationships for a later chapter.

> ### A word about Java
>
> The vast majority of code used in this book is written in Java. We use pseudo-code here and there to help teach concepts, but the working code is Java. Java is a practical reality of using HBase. The entire Hadoop stack, including HBase, is implemented in Java. The HBase client library is Java. The MapReduce library is Java. An HBase deployment requires tuning the JVM for optimal performance. But there are means for interacting with Hadoop and HBase from non-Java and non-JVM languages. We cover many of these options in chapter 6.

2.1.1   *Create a table*

You'll start building TwitBase by laying the foundations for storing its users. HBase is a database that stores data in tables, so you'll begin by creating a `users` table. To do that, you'll pick up where you left off, at the HBase shell:

```
$ hbase shell
HBase Shell; enter 'help<RETURN>' for list of supported commands.
Type "exit<RETURN>" to leave the HBase Shell
Version 0.92.0, r1231986, Mon Jan 16 13:16:35 UTC 2012

hbase(main):001:0>
```

The shell opens a connection to HBase and greets you with a prompt. With the shell prompt ahead of you, create your first table:

```
hbase(main):001:0> create 'users', 'info'
0 row(s) in 0.1200 seconds

hbase(main):002:0>
```

Presumably 'users' is the name of the table, but what about this 'info' business? Just like tables in a relational database, tables in HBase are organized into *rows* and *columns*. HBase treats columns a little differently than a relational database. Columns in HBase are organized into groups called *column families*. info is a column family in the users table. A table in HBase must have at least one column family. Among other things, column families impact physical characteristics of the data store in HBase. For this reason, at least one column family must be specified at table creation time. You can alter column families after the table is created, but doing so is a little tedious. We'll discuss column families in more detail later. For now, know that your users table is as simple as it gets—a single column family with default parameters.

2.1.2 *Examine table schema*

If you're familiar with relational databases, you'll notice right away that the table creation didn't involve any columns or types. Other than the column family name, HBase doesn't require you to tell it anything about your data ahead of time. That's why HBase is often described as a *schema-less* database.

You can verify that your users table was created by asking HBase for a listing of all registered tables:

```
hbase(main):002:0> list
TABLE
users
1 row(s) in 0.0220 seconds

hbase(main):003:0>
```

The list command proves the table exists, but HBase can also give you extended details about your table. You can see all those default parameters using the describe command:

```
hbase(main):003:0> describe 'users'
DESCRIPTION                                    ENABLED
 {NAME => 'users', FAMILIES => [{NAME => 'info', true
  BLOOMFILTER => 'NONE', REPLICATION_SCOPE => '0
 ', COMPRESSION => 'NONE', VERSIONS => '3', TTL
 => '2147483647', BLOCKSIZE => '65536', IN_MEMOR
 Y => 'false', BLOCKCACHE => 'true'}]}
1 row(s) in 0.0330 seconds

hbase(main):004:0>
```

The shell describes your table as a map with two properties: the table name and a list of column families. Each column family has a number of associated configuration details. These are the physical characteristics we mentioned earlier. For now, don't worry about these details; we'll examine them all in due course.

> ### HBase shell
> The HBase shell exposes a wealth of features, though it's primarily used for administrative purposes. Being implemented in JRuby, it has access to the entire Java client API. You can further explore the shell's capabilities using the `help` command.

2.1.3 *Establish a connection*

The shell is well and good, but who wants to implement TwitBase in shell commands? Those wise HBase developers thought of this and equipped HBase with a complete Java client library. A similar API is exposed to other languages too; we'll cover those in chapter 6. For now, we'll stick with Java. The Java code for opening a connection to the `users` table looks like this:

```
HTableInterface usersTable = new HTable("users");
```

The `HTable` constructor reads the default configuration information to locate HBase, similar to the way the shell did. It then locates the `users` table you created earlier and gives you a handle to it.

You can also pass a custom configuration object to the `HTable` object:

```
Configuration myConf = HBaseConfiguration.create();
HTableInterface usersTable = new HTable(myConf, "users");
```

This is equivalent to letting the `HTable` object create the configuration object on its own. To customize the configuration, you can define parameters like this:

```
myConf.set("parameter_name", "parameter_value");
```

> ### HBase client configuration
> HBase client applications need to have only one configuration piece available to them to access HBase—the ZooKeeper quorum address. You can manually set this configuration like this:
>
> myConf.set("hbase.zookeeper.quorum", "serverip");
>
> Both ZooKeeper and the exact interaction between client and the HBase cluster are covered in the next chapter where we go into details of HBase as a distributed store. For now, all you need to know is that the configuration parameters can be picked either by the Java client from the hbase-site.xml file in their classpath or by you setting the configuration explicitly in the connection. When you leave the configuration completely unspecified, as you do in this sample code, the default configuration is read and localhost is used for the ZooKeeper quorum address. When working in local mode, as you are here, that's exactly what you want.

2.1.4 *Connection management*

Creating a table instance is a relatively expensive operation, requiring a bit of network overhead. Rather than create a new table handle on demand, it's better to use a connection pool. Connections are allocated from and returned to the pool. Using an `HTablePool` is more common in practice than instantiating `HTables` directly:

```
HTablePool pool = new HTablePool();
HTableInterface usersTable = pool.getTable("users");
... // work with the table
usersTable.close();
```

Closing the table when you're finished with it allows the underlying connection resources to be returned to the pool.

What good is a table without data in it? No good at all. Let's store some data.

2.2 Data manipulation

Every row in an HBase table has a unique identifier called its *rowkey*. Other coordinates are used to locate a piece of data in an HBase table, but the rowkey is primary. Just like a primary key in a table in a relational database, rowkey values are distinct across all rows in an HBase table. Every interaction with data in a table begins with the rowkey. Every user in TwitBase is unique, so the user's name makes a convenient rowkey for the `users` table; that's what you'll use.

The HBase API is broken into operations called *commands*. There are five primitive commands for interacting with HBase: Get, Put, Delete, Scan, and Increment. The command used to store data is Put. To store data in a table, you'll need to create a Put instance. Creating a Put instance from a rowkey looks like this:

```
Put p = new Put(Bytes.toBytes("Mark Twain"));
```

Why can't you store the user's name directly? All data in HBase is stored as raw data in the form of a byte array, and that includes the rowkeys. The Java client library provides a utility class, `Bytes`, for converting various Java data types to and from `byte[]` so you don't have to worry about doing it yourself. Note that this Put instance has not been inserted into the table yet. You're only building the object right now.

2.2.1 Storing data

Now that you've staged a command for adding data to HBase, you still need to provide data to store. You can start by storing basic information about Mark, such as his email address and password. What happens if another person comes along whose name is also Mark Twain? They'll conflict, and you won't be able to store data about them in TwitBase. Instead of using the person's real name as the rowkey, let's use a unique username and store their real name in a column. Putting (no pun intended!) it all together:

```
Put p = new Put(Bytes.toBytes("TheRealMT"));
p.add(Bytes.toBytes("info"),
  Bytes.toBytes("name"),
  Bytes.toBytes("Mark Twain"));
p.add(Bytes.toBytes("info"),
  Bytes.toBytes("email"),
  Bytes.toBytes("samuel@clemens.org"));
```

Into the cell "info:name" store "Mark Twain"

Into the cell "info:email" store "samuel@clemens.org"

```
p.add(Bytes.toBytes("info"),
   Bytes.toBytes("password"),
   Bytes.toBytes("Langhorne"));
```

> Into the cell "info:password"
> store "Langhorne"

Remember, HBase uses coordinates to locate a piece of data within a table. The rowkey is the first coordinate, followed by the column family. When used as a data coordinate, the column family serves to group columns. The next coordinate is the *column qualifier*, often called simply *column*, or *qual*, once you're versed in HBase vernacular. The column qualifiers in this example are name, email, and password. Because HBase is schema-less, you never need to predefine the column qualifiers or assign them types. They're dynamic; all you need is a name that you give them at write time. These three coordinates define the location of a *cell*. The cell is where HBase stores data as a *value*. A cell is identified by its [rowkey, column family, column qualifier] coordinate within a table. The previous code stores three values in three cells within a single row. The cell storing Mark's name has the coordinates [TheRealMT, info, name].

The last step in writing data to HBase is sending the command to the table. That part is easy:

```
HTableInterface usersTable = pool.getTable("users");
Put p = new Put(Bytes.toBytes("TheRealMT"));
p.add(...);
usersTable.put(p);
usersTable.close();
```

2.2.2   Modifying data

Changing data in HBase is done the same way you store new data: create a Put object, give it some data at the appropriate coordinates, and send it to the table. Let's update Mark's password to something more secure.

```
Put p = new Put(Bytes.toBytes("TheRealMT"));
p.add(Bytes.toBytes("info"),
   Bytes.toBytes("password"),
   Bytes.toBytes("abc123"));
usersTable.put(p);
```

2.2.3   Under the hood: the HBase write path

Whether you use Put to record a new row in HBase or to modify an existing row, the internal process is the same. HBase receives the command and persists the change, or throws an exception if the write fails. When a write is made, by default, it goes into two places: the write-ahead log (WAL), also referred to as the HLog, and the MemStore (figure 2.1). The default behavior of HBase recording the write in both places is in order to maintain data durability. Only after the change is written to and confirmed in both places is the write considered complete.

The MemStore is a write buffer where HBase accumulates data in memory before a permanent write. Its contents are flushed to disk to form an HFile when the MemStore fills up. It doesn't write to an existing HFile but instead forms a new file on every flush. The HFile is the underlying storage format for HBase. HFiles belong to a column family,

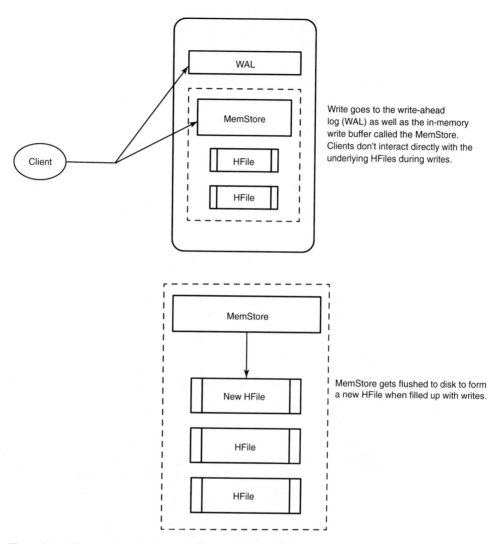

Write goes to the write-ahead log (WAL) as well as the in-memory write buffer called the MemStore. Clients don't interact directly with the underlying HFiles during writes.

MemStore gets flushed to disk to form a new HFile when filled up with writes.

Figure 2.1 **HBase write path. Every write to HBase requires confirmation from both the WAL and the MemStore. The two steps ensure that every write to HBase happens as fast as possible while maintaining durability. The MemStore is flushed to a new HFile when it fills up.**

and a column family can have multiple HFiles. But a single HFile can't have data for multiple column families. There is one MemStore per column family.[1]

Failures are common in large distributed systems, and HBase is no exception. Imagine that the server hosting a MemStore that has not yet been flushed crashes. You'll lose the data that was in memory but not yet persisted. HBase safeguards against that by writing to the WAL before the write completes. Every server that's part of the

---

[1] The size of the MemStore is defined by the system-wide property in hbase-site.xml called `hbase.hregion.memstore.flush.size`. You'll learn more about the various configurations in chapter 9.

HBase cluster keeps a WAL to record changes as they happen. The WAL is a file on the underlying file system. A write isn't considered successful until the new WAL entry is successfully written. This guarantee makes HBase as durable as the file system backing it. Most of the time, HBase is backed by the Hadoop Distributed Filesystem (HDFS).

If HBase goes down, the data that was not yet flushed from the MemStore to the HFile can be recovered by replaying the WAL. You don't have to do this manually. It's all handled under the hood by HBase as a part of the recovery process. There is a single WAL per HBase server, shared by all tables (and their column families) served from that server.

As you can imagine, skipping the WAL during writes can help improve write performance. There's one less thing to do, right? We don't recommend disabling the WAL unless you're willing to lose data when things fail. In case you want to experiment, you can disable the WAL like this:

```
Put p = new Put();
p.setWriteToWAL(false);
```

> **NOTE** Not writing to the WAL comes at the cost of increased risk of losing data in case of RegionServer failure. Disable the WAL, and HBase *can't* recover your data in the face of failure. Any writes that haven't flushed to disk will be lost.

2.2.4 *Reading data*

Reading data back out of HBase is as easy as writing. Make a `Get` command instance, tell it what cells you're interested in, and send it to the table:

```
Get g = new Get(Bytes.toBytes("TheRealMT"));
Result r = usersTable.get(g);
```

The table gives you back a `Result` instance containing your data. This instance contains all the columns from all the column families that exist for the row. That's potentially far more data than you need. You can limit the amount of data returned by placing restrictions on the `Get` instance. To retrieve only the `password` column, execute `addColumn()`. The same can be done per column family using `addFamily()`, in which case it'll return all the columns in the specified column family:

```
Get g = new Get(Bytes.toBytes("TheRealMT"));
g.addColumn(
  Bytes.toBytes("info"),
  Bytes.toBytes("password"));
Result r = usersTable.get(g);
```

Retrieve the specific value and convert it back from bytes like so:

```
Get g = new Get(Bytes.toBytes("TheRealMT"));
g.addFamily(Bytes.toBytes("info"));
byte[] b = r.getValue(
  Bytes.toBytes("info"),
  Bytes.toBytes("email"));
String email = Bytes.toString(b); // "samuel@clemens.org"
```

2.2.5   *Under the hood: the HBase read path*

As a general rule, if you want fast access to data, keep it ordered and keep as much of it as possible in memory. HBase accomplishes both of these goals, allowing it to serve millisecond reads in most cases. A read against HBase must be reconciled between the persisted HFiles and the data still in the MemStore. HBase has an LRU cache for reads. This cache, also called the BlockCache, sits in the JVM heap alongside the MemStore. The BlockCache is designed to keep frequently accessed data from the HFiles in memory so as to avoid disk reads. Each column family has its own BlockCache.

Understanding the BlockCache is an important part of understanding how to run HBase at optimal performance. The "Block" in BlockCache is the unit of data that HBase reads from disk in a single pass. The HFile is physically laid out as a sequence of blocks plus an index over those blocks. This means reading a block from HBase requires only looking up that block's location in the index and retrieving it from disk. The block is the smallest indexed unit of data and is the smallest unit of data that can be read from disk. The block size is configured per column family, and the default value is 64 KB. You may want to tweak this value larger or smaller depending on your use case. If you primarily perform random lookups, you likely want a more granular block index, so a smaller block size is preferred. Having smaller blocks creates a larger index and thereby consumes more memory. If you frequently perform sequential scans, reading many blocks at a time, you can afford a larger block size. This allows you to save on memory because larger blocks mean fewer index entries and thus a smaller index.

Reading a row from HBase requires first checking the MemStore for any pending modifications. Then the BlockCache is examined to see if the block containing this row has been recently accessed. Finally, the relevant HFiles on disk are accessed. There are more things going on under the hood, but this is the overall outline. Figure 2.2 illustrates the read path.

Note that HFiles contain a snapshot of the MemStore at the point when it was flushed. Data for a complete row can be stored across multiple HFiles. In order to read

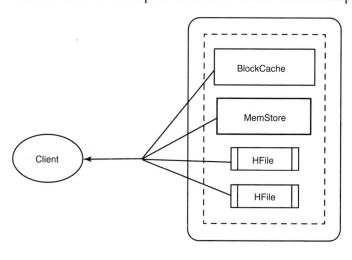

Figure 2.2   HBase read path. Data is reconciled from the BlockCache, the Mem-Store, and the HFiles to give the client an up-to-date view of the row(s) it asked for.

a complete row, HBase must read across all HFiles that might contain information for that row in order to compose the complete record.

2.2.6   *Deleting data*

Deleting data from HBase works just like storing it. You make an instance of the Delete command, constructed with a rowkey:

```
Delete d = new Delete(Bytes.toBytes("TheRealMT"));
usersTable.delete(d);
```

You can delete only part of a row by specifying additional coordinates:

```
Delete d = new Delete(Bytes.toBytes("TheRealMT"));
d.deleteColumns(
  Bytes.toBytes("info"),
  Bytes.toBytes("email"));
usersTable.delete(d);
```

The method deleteColumns() removes a cell entirely from the row. This is a distinct method from deleteColumn() (notice the missing *s* at the end of the method name), which operates on the content of a cell.

2.2.7   *Compactions: HBase housekeeping*

The Delete command doesn't delete the value immediately. Instead, it marks the record for deletion. That is, a new "tombstone" record is written for that value, marking it as deleted. The tombstone is used to indicate that the deleted value should no longer be included in Get or Scan results. Because HFiles are immutable, it's not until a *major compaction* runs that these tombstone records are reconciled and space is truly recovered from deleted records.

Compactions come in two flavors: minor and major. Both types result in a consolidation of the data persisted in HFiles. A minor compaction folds HFiles together, creating a larger HFile from multiple smaller HFiles, as shown in figure 2.3. Restricting the number of HFiles is important for read performance, because all of them must be referenced to read a complete row. During the compaction, HBase reads the content of the existing HFiles, writing records into a new one. Then, it swaps in the new HFile as the current active one and deletes the old ones that formed the new one.[2] HBase decides which HFiles to compact based on their number and relative sizes. Minor compactions are designed to be minimally detrimental to HBase performance, so there is an upper limit on the number of HFiles involved. All of these settings are configurable.

When a compaction operates over all HFiles in a column family in a given region, it's called a major compaction. Upon completion of a major compaction, all HFiles in the column family are merged into a single file. Major compactions can also be triggered

---

[2] As you can imagine, this process can require a lot of disk IO. What's less clear is that it can also cause network IO. See appendix B for an explanation of the HDFS write path for further details.

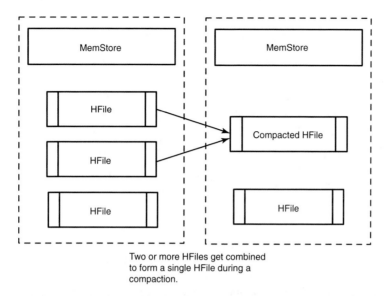

Two or more HFiles get combined to form a single HFile during a compaction.

Figure 2.3   Minor compaction. Records are read from the existing HFiles and combined into a single, merged HFile. That new HFile is then marked as the new canonical data on disk, and the old HFiles are deleted. When a compaction is run simultaneously over all HFiles in a column family, it's called a major compaction.

for the entire table (or a particular region) manually from the shell. This is a relatively expensive operation and isn't done often. Minor compactions, on the other hand, are relatively lightweight and happen more frequently. Major compactions are the only chance HBase has to clean up deleted records. Resolving a delete requires removing both the deleted record and the deletion marker. There's no guarantee that both the record and marker are in the same HFile. A major compaction is the only time when HBase is guaranteed to have access to both of these entries at the same time.

The compaction process is described in greater detail, along with incremental illustrations, in a post on the NGDATA blog.[3]

2.2.8   *Versioned data*

In addition to being a schema-less database, HBase is also *versioned*. For example, you can look back in time for the original password:

```
List<KeyValue> passwords = r.getColumn(
  Bytes.toBytes("info"),
  Bytes.toBytes("password"));
b = passwords.get(0).getValue();
String currentPasswd = Bytes.toString(b); // "abc123"
b = passwords.get(1).getValue();
String prevPasswd = Bytes.toString(b); // "Langhorne"
```

---

[3]   Bruno Dumon, "Visualizing HBase Flushes and Compactions," NGDATA, www.ngdata.com/site/blog/74-ng.html.

Every time you perform an operation on a cell, HBase implicitly stores a new version. Creating, modifying, and deleting a cell are all treated identically; they're all new versions. `Get` requests reconcile which version to return based on provided parameters. The version is used as the final coordinate when accessing a specific cell value. HBase uses the current time[4] in milliseconds when a version isn't specified, so the version number is represented as a `long`. By default, HBase stores only the last three versions; this is configurable per column family. Each version of data within a cell contributes one `KeyValue` instance to the `Result`. You can inspect the version information in a `KeyValue` instance with its `getTimestamp()` method:

```
long version =
  passwords.get(0).getTimestamp(); // 1329088818321
```

When a cell exceeds the maximum number of versions, the extra records are dropped during the next major compaction.

Instead of deleting an entire cell, you can operate on a specific version or versions within that cell. The `deleteColumns()` method (with the *s*) described previously operates on all `KeyValues` with a version less than the provided version. If no version is provided, the default of *now* is used. The `deleteColumn()` method (without the *s*) deletes a specific version of a cell. Be careful which method you call; they have identical calling signatures and only subtly different semantics.

2.2.9 *Data model recap*

This section covers a lot of ground, both in terms of data model and implementation details. Let's pause momentarily to recap what we've discussed thus far. The logical entities in an HBase schema are as follows:

- *Table*—HBase organizes data into *tables*. Table names are `Strings` and composed of characters that are safe for use in a file system path.
- *Row*—Within a table, data is stored according to its *row*. Rows are identified uniquely by their *rowkey*. Rowkeys don't have a data type and are always treated as a `byte[]`.
- *Column family*—Data within a row is grouped by *column family*. Column families also impact the physical arrangement of data stored in HBase. For this reason, they must be defined up front and aren't easily modified. Every row in a table has the same column families, although a row need not store data in all its families. Column family names are `Strings` and composed of characters that are safe for use in a file system path.
- *Column qualifier*—Data within a column family is addressed via its *column qualifier*, or *column*. Column qualifiers need not be specified in advance. Column qualifiers need not be consistent between rows. Like rowkeys, column qualifiers don't have a data type and are always treated as a `byte[]`.

---

[4] That is, the current time in milliseconds of the RegionServer that received the operation. Thus it's important to keep the clocks on all machines in your HBase cluster in sync. You'll learn more about these concerns in chapter 9.

- *Cell*—A combination of rowkey, column family, and column qualifier uniquely identifies a *cell*. The data stored in a cell is referred to as that cell's *value*. Values also don't have a data type and are always treated as a `byte[]`.
- *Version*—Values within a cell are versioned. Versions are identified by their timestamp, a `long`. When a version isn't specified, the current timestamp is used as the basis for the operation. The number of cell value versions retained by HBase is configured via the column family. The default number of cell versions is three.

These six concepts form the foundation of HBase. They're exposed to the user via the logical view presented by the API. They're the building blocks on which the implementation manages data physically on disk. Keeping these six concepts straight in your mind will take you a long way in understanding HBase.

A unique data value in HBase is accessed by way of its coordinates. The complete coordinates to a value are rowkey, column family, column qualifier, and version. These coordinates are covered in more detail in the next section.

2.3 Data coordinates

In the logical data model, the version number is also part of the coordinates of a piece of data. You can think of a relational database as storing a piece of data in a table in a 2D coordinate system based first on row and second on column. By that analogy, HBase stores a piece of data in a table based on a 4D coordinate system. The coordinates used by HBase, in order, are rowkey, column family, column qualifier, and version. Figure 2.4 illustrates these coordinates in our `users` table.

Considering the full set of coordinates as a unit, you can think of HBase as a *key-value* store. With this abstraction of the logical data model in mind, you can consider the coordinates as a key and the cell data as the value (see figure 2.5).

The HBase API is built such that you aren't required to provide the entire coordinate path when requesting data. If you omit the version in your `Get` request, HBase

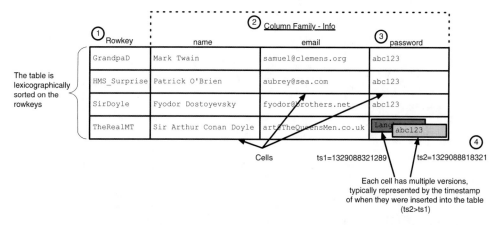

Figure 2.4   The coordinates used to identify data in an HBase table are ❶ rowkey, ❷ column family, ❸ column qualifier, and ❹ version.

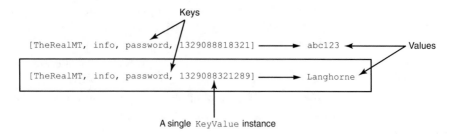

Figure 2.5   HBase can be considered a key-value store, where the four coordinates to a cell act as a key. In the API, the complete coordinates to a value, plus the value itself, are packaged together by the KeyValue class.

provides you with a map of version to value. By providing decreasingly specific coordinates in your request, HBase allows you to request more data in a single operation. In that way, you can think of HBase as a key-value store where the value is a map, or a map of maps. Figure 2.6 illustrates this idea.

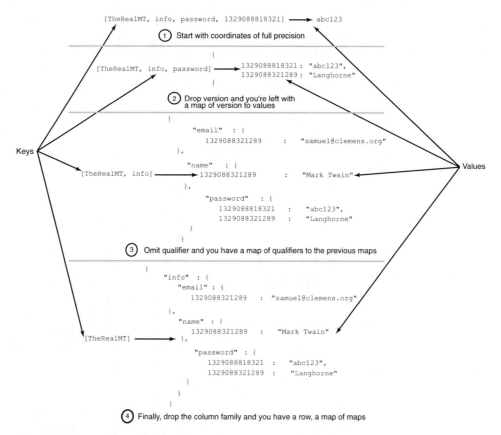

Figure 2.6   Alternate views of HBase as a key-value data store. Decreasing the precision of your cell coordinates results in larger groups of KeyValues as the resulting values.

We'll discuss this concept in more detail when we explain the HBase data models, later in this chapter.

2.4 Putting it all together

Now that you've seen how to interact with HBase, let's assemble what you know into a working example. To start, define a simple model object for the User instances, as in the next listing.

Listing 2.1 User data model

```
package HBaseIA.TwitBase.model;

public abstract class User {

  public String user;
  public String name;
  public String email;
  public String password;

  @Override
  public String toString() {
    return String.format("<User: %s, %s, %s>", user, name, email);
  }
}
```

Let's wrap all the user-centric HBase interactions in a single class. Start by declaring the commonly used byte[] constants. Then define some helper methods to encapsulate command creation. Follow that with the public interfaces and a private implementation of the User model, as shown next.

Listing 2.2 CRUD operations in UsersDAO.java

```
package HBaseIA.TwitBase.hbase;

//...                                          ⟵──┐ Import details
                                                   │ omitted
public class UsersDAO {

  public static final byte[] TABLE_NAME =
    Bytes.toBytes("users");
  public static final byte[] INFO_FAM =
    Bytes.toBytes("info");

  private static final byte[] USER_COL =
    Bytes.toBytes("user");
  private static final byte[] NAME_COL =           Declare commonly
    Bytes.toBytes("name");                         used byte[]s once
  private static final byte[] EMAIL_COL =
    Bytes.toBytes("email");
  private static final byte[] PASS_COL =
    Bytes.toBytes("password");
  public static final byte[] TWEETS_COL =
    Bytes.toBytes("tweet_count");

  private HTablePool pool;
```

```
public UsersDAO(HTablePool pool) {
  this.pool = pool;
}
```
> Let calling environment
> manage connection pool

```
private static Get mkGet(String user) {
  Get g = new Get(Bytes.toBytes(user));
  g.addFamily(INFO_FAM);
  return g;
}

private static Put mkPut(User u) {
  Put p = new Put(Bytes.toBytes(u.user));
  p.add(INFO_FAM, USER_COL, Bytes.toBytes(u.user));
  p.add(INFO_FAM, NAME_COL, Bytes.toBytes(u.name));
  p.add(INFO_FAM, EMAIL_COL, Bytes.toBytes(u.email));
  p.add(INFO_FAM, PASS_COL, Bytes.toBytes(u.password));
  return p;
}

private static Delete mkDel(String user) {
  Delete d = new Delete(Bytes.toBytes(user));
  return d;
}
```
> Use helper methods to
> encapsulate routine
> command work

```
public void addUser(String user,
                    String name,
                    String email,
                    String password)
  throws IOException {

  HTableInterface users = pool.getTable(TABLE_NAME);

  Put p = mkPut(new User(user, name, email, password));
  users.put(p);

  users.close();
}

public HBaseIA.TwitBase.model.User getUser(String user)
  throws IOException {
  HTableInterface users = pool.getTable(TABLE_NAME);

  Get g = mkGet(user);
  Result result = users.get(g);
  if (result.isEmpty()) {
    return null;
  }

  User u = new User(result);
  users.close();
  return u;
}

public void deleteUser(String user) throws IOException {
  HTableInterface users = pool.getTable(TABLE_NAME);

  Delete d = mkDel(user);
  users.delete(d);

  users.close();
}
```

```
        private static class User
          extends HBaseIA.TwitBase.model.User {
          private User(Result r) {                          ◁── ┐  Construct model.User
            this(r.getValue(INFO_FAM, USER_COL),                 │  instance from Result
                 r.getValue(INFO_FAM, NAME_COL),
                 r.getValue(INFO_FAM, EMAIL_COL),
                 r.getValue(INFO_FAM, PASS_COL),
                 r.getValue(INFO_FAM, TWEETS_COL) == null
                   ? Bytes.toBytes(0L)
                   : r.getValue(INFO_FAM, TWEETS_COL));
          }

          private User(byte[] user,
                       byte[] name,
                       byte[] email,
                       byte[] password,
                       byte[] tweetCount) {
            this(Bytes.toString(user),
                 Bytes.toString(name),                            Convenience
                 Bytes.toString(email),                           constructors from
                 Bytes.toString(password));                       Strings and byte[]s
            this.tweetCount = Bytes.toLong(tweetCount);
          }

          private User(String user,
                       String name,
                       String email,
                       String password) {
            this.user = user;
            this.name = name;
            this.email = email;
            this.password = password;
          }
        }
      }
    }
```

The last piece of this puzzle is a main() method. Let's make a UsersTool, shown in the next listing, to simplify interaction with the users table in HBase.

Listing 2.3 UsersTool, a command-line interface to the users table

```
package HBaseIA.TwitBase;                       ┐  Import details
                                                 │  omitted
//...                                       ◁────┘

public class UsersTool {

  public static final String usage =
        "UsersTool action ...\n" +
        "  help - print this message and exit.\n" +
        "  add user name email password" +
        "  - add a new user.\n" +
        "  get user - retrieve a specific user.\n" +
        "  list - list all installed users.\n";

  public static void main(String[] args)
      throws IOException {
```

```
if (args.length == 0 || "help".equals(args[0])) {
  System.out.println(usage);
  System.exit(0);
}

HTablePool pool = new HTablePool();
UsersDAO dao = new UsersDAO(pool);

if ("get".equals(args[0])) {
  System.out.println("Getting user " + args[1]);
  User u = dao.getUser(args[1]);
  System.out.println(u);
}

if ("add".equals(args[0])) {
  System.out.println("Adding user...");
  dao.addUser(args[1], args[2], args[3], args[4]);
  User u = dao.getUser(args[1]);
  System.out.println("Successfully added user " + u);
}

if ("list".equals(args[0])) {
  for(User u : dao.getUsers()) {
    System.out.println(u);
  }
}

pool.closeTablePool(UsersDAO.TABLE_NAME);
  }
}
```

UsersDAO leaves connection pool management up to consuming environment

Don't forget to close remaining connections

With all the code available, you can try the whole thing. In the root directory of this book's source code, compile the application jar:

```
$ mvn package
...
[INFO] --------------------------------------------------------
[INFO] BUILD SUCCESS
[INFO] --------------------------------------------------------
[INFO] Total time: 20.467s
```

This produces a twitbase-1.0.0.jar file in the target directory.

Using UsersTool to add Mark to the users table is easy:

```
$ java -cp target/twitbase-1.0.0.jar \
  HBaseIA.TwitBase.UsersTool \
  add \
  TheRealMT \
  "Mark Twain" \
  samuel@clemens.org \
  abc123
Successfully added user <User: TheRealMT>
```

You can list the contents of your table:

```
$ java -cp target/twitbase-1.0.0.jar \
  HBaseIA.TwitBase.UsersTool \
```

```
list
21:49:30 INFO cli.UsersTool: Found 1 users.
<User: TheRealMT>
```

Now that you've seen a little of how to interact with HBase, let's better understand the logical and physical data models present in HBase.

2.5 Data models

As you've seen, the way HBase models data is a little different from the relational systems with which you're familiar. These systems require strict rules around tables, columns, and data types—the *shape* of your data. Data conforming to these strict requirements is called *structured* data. HBase is designed for data without such a strict shape. Records can have divergent columns, variance in field size, and so on. This kind of data is said to have a *semistructured* shape.

The propensity of a data system toward structured or semistructured data at the logical model influences decisions in the physical model. Relational systems assume all records in a table to be structured and highly regular. They use this to their advantage in physical implementations, optimizing on-disk formats and in-memory structures accordingly. Likewise, HBase takes advantage of the semistructured shape of the data it stores. As systems evolve, these assumptions in the physical model influence the logical. Because of this tight relationship, a strong understanding of both logical and physical models is required to make optimal use of a data system.

In addition to focusing on semistructured data, HBase has another primary concern: scale. The loose coupling of data components in a semistructured logical model has the benefit of being easier to physically distribute. The physical model in HBase is designed with physical distribution in mind and that decision also influences the logical model. On the other hand, this physical model forces HBase to give up some features provided by relational systems. In particular, HBase can't enforce relational constraints or provide multirow transactions.[5] These next couple topics are influenced by this relationship.

2.5.1 Logical model: sorted map of maps

There are a number of valid descriptions for the logical data model used in HBase. Figure 2.6 illustrated that model as a key-value store. The next model we'll consider is a *sorted map of maps*. Presumably you're familiar with a map or dictionary structure from your favorite programming language. Think of HBase as an unlimited, persisted, nested version of that structure.

We'll start with this *map of maps* idea. You've seen the coordinate system HBase uses to identify data in a cell: [rowkey, column family, column qualifier, version]. For an example, take Mark's record from the users table (figure 2.7).

---

[5] Not yet, anyway. Rudimentary support for multirow transactions over data on a single host is provided by a future HBase release. You can track the progress of this feature via https://issues.apache.org/jira/browse/HBASE-5229.

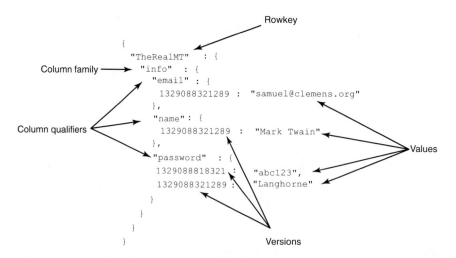

Figure 2.7 Sorted map of maps. HBase logically organizes data as a nested map of maps. Within each map, data is physically sorted by that map's key. In this example, `"email"` comes before `"name"` and more recent versions come before older ones.

While thinking of this map of maps, consider those coordinates from the inside out. You can think of a cell as a map keyed on version with the stored data as the value. One layer up, a column family is a map keyed on column qualifier with the cell as the value. At the top, a table is a map keyed on rowkey to the column family. Described in Java, you'd have this monstrosity: Map<RowKey, Map<ColumnFamily, Map<ColumnQualifier, Map<Version, Data>>>>. It's not pretty, but it's simple.

Notice also we said it's a *sorted* map of maps. The example shows only a single record, but even there the sorting is present. Notice the two versions in the password cell. The newest version is sorted before the later versions. HBase sorts the version timestamp in descending order so the newest data is always on top. This physical design decision results in slightly faster access to recent versions. The other map keys are sorted in ascending order. The current example doesn't display this behavior, so let's insert a couple records and see what it looks like:

```
$ java -cp target/twitbase-1.0.0.jar \
  HBaseIA.TwitBase.UsersTool \
  add \
  HMS_Surprise \
  "Patrick O'Brian" \
  aubrey@sea.com \
  abc123
Successfully added user <User: HMS_Surprise>

$ java -cp target/twitbase-1.0.0.jar \
  HBaseIA.TwitBase.UsersTool \
  add \
  GrandpaD \
  "Fyodor Dostoyevsky" \
```

```
    fyodor@brothers.net \
    abc123
Successfully added user <User: GrandpaD>

$ java -cp target/twitbase-1.0.0.jar \
    HBaseIA.TwitBase.UsersTool \
    add \
    SirDoyle \
    "Sir Arthur Conan Doyle" \
    art@TheQueensMen.co.uk \
    abc123
Successfully added user <User: SirDoyle>
```

Now you can list the users table again and see:

```
$ java -cp target/twitbase-1.0.0.jar \
    HBaseIA.TwitBase.UsersTool \
    list
21:54:27 INFO TwitBase.UsersTool: Found 4 users.
<User: GrandpaD>
<User: HMS_Surprise>
<User: SirDoyle>
<User: TheRealMT>
```

This sorting business turns out to be a critical consideration when designing HBase table schema in practice. This is another point where the physical data model influences the logical. Understanding this detail allows you to design your schema to take advantage of this feature.

2.5.2 *Physical model: column family oriented*

Like a relational database, tables in HBase consist of rows and columns. In HBase, the columns are grouped together in column families. This grouping is expressed logically as a layer in the map of maps. Column families are also expressed physically. Each column family gets its own set of HFiles on disk. This physical isolation allows the underlying HFiles of one column family to be managed in isolation of the others. As far as compactions are concerned, the HFiles for each column family are managed independently.

Records in HBase are stored in the HFiles as key-value pairs. The HFile itself is a binary file and isn't human-readable. Mark's user data stored on disk in an HFile looks something like figure 2.8.

Notice that Mark's row consumes multiple records in the HFile. Each column qualifier and version gets its own record. Also, notice there are no unused or *null* records. HBase doesn't need to store anything to indicate the absence of data. For this reason,

```
"TheRealMT" , "info" , "email" ,      1329088321289 ,  "samuel@clemens.org"
"TheRealMT" , "info" , "name" ,       1329088321289 ,  "Mark Twain"
"TheRealMT" , "info" , "password" ,   1329088818321 ,  "abc123",
"TheRealMT" , "info" , "password" ,   1329088321289 ,  "Langhorne"
```

Figure 2.8   HFile data for the `info` column family in the `users` table. Each record is a complete entry in the HFile.

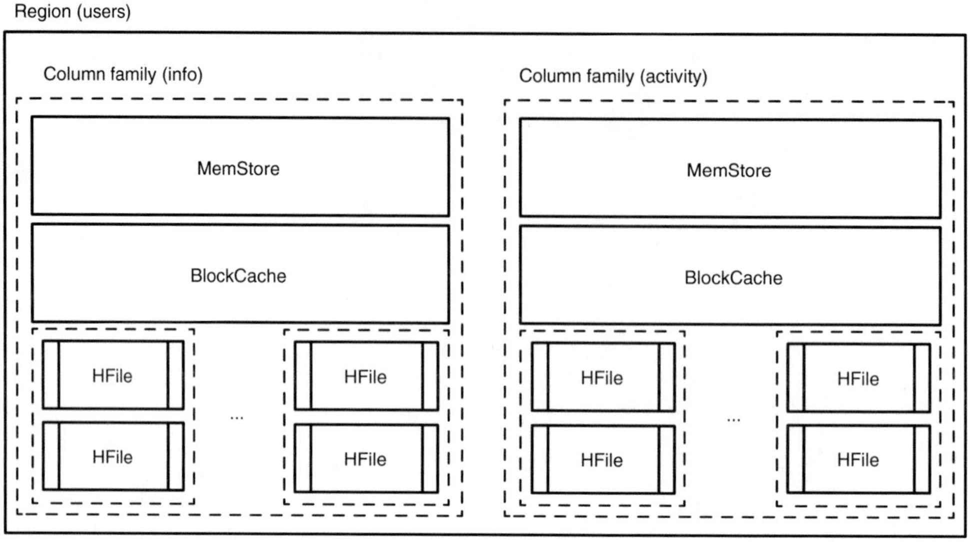

Region (users)

Figure 2.9   A region in the `users` table. All data for a given row in the table is managed together in a region.

storage in the column family is column-oriented, just like in any other column-oriented database. Data from a single column family for a single row need not be stored in the same HFile. Mark's `info` data could be spread across any number of HFiles. The only requirement is that within an HFile, data for a row's column family is stored together.

If the `users` table had another column family *and* Mark had data in those columns, Mark's row would have records in those HFiles as well. Using separate HFiles for each column family means HBase doesn't need to read all the data for a row when performing a read. It need only retrieve data for the requested column families. Being column-oriented means HBase need not read over *placeholder* entries when looking for a specific cell. These two physical details make for efficient storage and fast reads of particularly sparse datasets.

Let's say you add another column family to the `users` table for storing activity on the TwitBase site; it will result in more HFiles. The complete set of tooling that allows HBase to host a single row is illustrated in figure 2.9. For reasons we'll cover in the next chapter, HBase refers to this machinery as a *region*.

As you can see in figure 2.9, interacting with data in different column families involves completely separate MemStores and HFiles. This allows data in the `activity` column family to grow without adversely affecting performance of the `info` column family.

2.6   *Table scans*

You likely noticed the lack of a `query` command of any kind. You won't find one, at least not today. The only way to access records containing a specific value is by using the `Scan` command to read across some portion of the table, applying a *filter* to retrieve only the relevant records. As you might imagine, the records returned while scanning are presented in sorted order. HBase is designed to support this kind of behavior so it's fast.

To scan the entire contents of a table, use the bare `Scan` constructor:

```
Scan s = new Scan();
```

Often, however, you're only interested in a subset of the entire table. Perhaps you only want users with IDs starting with the letter *T.* Provide the `Scan` constructor with start and end rows:

```
Scan s = new Scan(
  Bytes.toBytes("T"),
  Bytes.toBytes("U"));
```

This is a contrived example, perhaps, but you get the idea. How about a practical example? You need to store twits. Further, you know you'll want to access the most recent twits from a particular user. Let's start there.

2.6.1 *Designing tables for scans*

Just as you would when designing a relational schema, designing schema for HBase tables requires that you consider the data shape and access patterns. Twits are a different kind of data with different access patterns than users, so let's put them in their own table. For kicks, you'll create the new table using the Java API instead of the shell. Table manipulation is performed using an instance of the `HBaseAdmin` object:

```
Configuration conf = HBaseConfiguration.create();
HBaseAdmin admin = new HBaseAdmin(conf);
```

Making an `HBaseAdmin` instance explicitly requires a `Configuration` instance, a detail hidden from you by the default `HTable` and `HTablePool` constructors. That's simple enough. Now you can define a new table and create it:

```
HTableDescriptor desc = new HTableDescriptor("twits");
HColumnDescriptor c = new HColumnDescriptor("twits");
c.setMaxVersions(1);
desc.addFamily(c);
admin.createTable(desc);
```

The `HTableDescriptor` object lets you build up the description of the new table, starting with its name: `twits`. Likewise, you build up the column family, also named `twits`, using the `HColumnDescriptor`. As with the users table, you only need one column family here. You don't need twit versioning, so you'll limit the retained versions to one.

With a fancy new `twits` table, you can begin storing twits. A twit consists of a message and the date and time it was posted. You'll need a unique value for the rowkey, so let's try the username plus the timestamp. Easy enough; let's store twits like this:

```
Put put = new Put(
  Bytes.toBytes("TheRealMT" + 1329088818321L));
put.add(
  Bytes.toBytes("twits"),
```

```
  Bytes.toBytes("dt"),
  Bytes.toBytes(1329088818321L)));
put.add(
  Bytes.toBytes("twits"),
  Bytes.toBytes("twit"),
  Bytes.toBytes("Hello, TwitBase!"));
```

Well, almost like this. First, notice that the user ID is a variable-length string. This can cause you some hassle when using a compound rowkey because you need to split on a delimiter of some kind. An alternative approach is to hash the portion of the rowkey that is of variable length. Choose a hashing algorithm that produces values of constant size. MD5 is a good choice because you want twits to be stored in groups by user. Those groups can be stored in any order. Within the group, appending the postdate orders the twits chronologically. MD5 is a one-way hash; don't forget to also store the unencoded user ID in a column if you need it later. Writing to the twits table looks something like this:

```
int longLength = Long.SIZE / 8;
byte[] userHash = Md5Utils.md5sum("TheRealMT");
byte[] timestamp = Bytes.toBytes(-1 * 1329088818321L);
byte[] rowKey = new byte[Md5Utils.MD5_LENGTH + longLength];
int offset = 0;
offset = Bytes.putBytes(rowKey, offset, userHash, 0, userHash.length);
Bytes.putBytes(rowKey, offset, timestamp, 0, timestamp.length);
Put put = new Put(rowKey);
put.add(
  Bytes.toBytes("twits"),
  Bytes.toBytes("user"),
  Bytes.toBytes("TheRealMT");
put.add(
  Bytes.toBytes("twits"),
  Bytes.toBytes("twit"),
  Bytes.toBytes("Hello, TwitBase!"));
```

You know you'll want the most recent twits first. You know that HBase stores rows in sorted order by rowkey in its physical data model. You take advantage of that feature. By including the timestamp of the twit in the rowkey and multiplying it by -1, you have the most recent twits first.

Rowkey design is critical in HBase schema
This point we can't stress enough: HBase rowkeys are the number one most important thing to think about when designing a table. We cover this in much greater detail in chapter 4. We mention it now so you can keep it in mind as you pursue the examples. The first question you should always ask yourself when looking at an HBase schema is, "What's in the rowkey?" The next question should be, "How can I use the rowkey more effectively?"

2.6.2 *Executing a scan*

Using the user as the first portion of the twits rowkey turns out to be useful. It effectively creates *buckets* of data by user in the natural ordering of rows. All data from one user is in continuous rows. What does the Scan look like? More or less the same as before, just with more complexity in calculating the stop key:

```
byte[] userHash = Md5Utils.md5sum(user);
byte[] startRow = Bytes.padTail(userHash, longLength); // 212d...866f00...
byte[] stopRow = Bytes.padTail(userHash, longLength);
stopRow[Md5Utils.MD5_LENGTH-1]++;                      // 212d...867000...
Scan s = new Scan(startRow, stopRow);
ResultsScanner rs = twits.getScanner(s);
```

In this case, you create the stop key by incrementing the value of the last byte of the user ID portion of the rowkey. Scanners return records *inclusive* of the start key and *exclusive* of the end key, so this gives you twits for only the matching user.

Reading twits off the ResultScanner is a simple loop:

```
for(Result r : rs) {
  // extract the username
  byte[] b = r.getValue(
    Bytes.toBytes("twits"),
    Bytes.toBytes("user"));
  String user = Bytes.toString(b);
  // extract the twit
  b = r.getValue(
    Bytes.toBytes("twits"),
    Bytes.toBytes("twit"));
  String message = Bytes.toString(b);
  // extract the timestamp
  b = Arrays.copyOfRange(
    r.getRow(),
    Md5Utils.MD5_LENGTH,
    Md5Utils.MD5_LENGTH + longLength);
  DateTime dt = new DateTime(-1 * Bytes.toLong(b));
}
```

The only work done in the loop is fixing the timestamp value and converting byte[] values back to their proper data types. Voila! You'll have something like this:

```
<Twit: TheRealMT 2012-02-20T00:13:27.931-08:00 Hello, TwitBase!>
```

2.6.3 *Scanner caching*

A scan can be configured to retrieve a batch of rows in every RPC call it makes to HBase. This configuration can be done at a per-scanner level by using the setCaching(int) API on the scan object. This configuration can also be set in the hbase-site.xml configuration file using the hbase.client.scanner.caching property. If the caching value is set to *n*, the scanner will return *n* rows with every RPC call and they will be cached at the client side while it works through them. The default value of this configuration is 1, which basically means that when you scan through a table, only one row is returned per RPC call that the client makes to HBase. That's a conservative number, and you can tune it for better performance. But setting the value too high would mean that the client's interaction with HBase would have longer pauses, and this could result in timeouts on HBase's side.

The `ResultScanner` interface also has a `next(int)` call that you can use to ask it to return the next *n* rows from the scan. This is an API convenience that doesn't have any relation to the number of RPC calls the client makes to HBase to get those *n* rows. Under the hood, `ResultScanner` makes as many RPC calls as necessary to satisfy the request; the number of rows returned per RPC call is solely dependent on the caching value you configure for the scanner.

2.6.4   *Applying filters*

It's not always possible to design a rowkey to perfectly match your access patterns. Sometimes you'll have use cases where you need to scan through a set of data in HBase but return only a subset of it to the client. This is where *filters* come in. Add a filter to your `Scan` object like this:

```
Filter f = ...
Scan s = new Scan();
s.setFilter(f);
```

A filter is a predicate that executes in HBase instead of on the client. When you specify a `Filter` in your `Scan`, HBase uses it to determine whether a record should be returned. This can avoid a lot of unnecessary data transfer. It also keeps the filtering on the server instead of placing that burden on the client.

The filter applied is anything implementing the `org.apache.hadoop.hbase.filter.Filter` interface. HBase provides a number of filters, but it's easy to implement your own.

To filter all twits that mention TwitBase, you can use a `ValueFilter` in combination with a `RegexStringComparator`:

```
Scan s = new Scan();
s.addColumn(Bytes.toBytes("twits"), Bytes.toByes("twit"));
Filter f = new ValueFilter(
  CompareOp.EQUAL,
  new RegexStringComparator(".*TwitBase.*"));
s.setFilter(f);
```

HBase also provides a class for filter construction. The `ParseFilter` object implements a kind of query language used to construct a `Filter` instance for you. The same TwitBase filter can be constructed from an expression:

```
Scan s = new Scan();
s.addColumn(TWITS_FAM, TWIT_COL);
String expression = "ValueFilter(=,'regexString:.*TwitBase.*')";
ParseFilter p = new ParseFilter();
Filter f = p.parseSimpleFilterExpression(Bytes.toBytes(expression));
s.setFilter(f);
```

In either case, your regular expression is compiled and applied in the region before data ever reaches the client.

This is a simple example of using a filter in your applications. Filters in HBase can be applied to rowkeys, column qualifiers, or data values. You can also compose multiple filters together using the `FilterList` and `WhileMatchFilter` objects. Filters also allow you to page over data, limiting the number of rows returned by the scanner. We cover the bundled filters in more depth in chapter 4.

2.7 *Atomic operations*

The last command in the HBase arsenal is the *Increment Column Value (ICV)*. It's exposed as both the `Increment` command object like the others but also as a method on the `HTableInterface`. Let's use the `HTableInterface` version because it offers slightly more intuitive semantics. Using it to keep count of the number of twits per user looks like this:

```
long ret = usersTable.incrementColumnValue(
  Bytes.toBytes("TheRealMT"),
  Bytes.toBytes("info"),
  Bytes.toBytes("tweet_count"),
  1L);
```

This command allows you to change an integral value stored in an HBase cell without reading it back first. The data manipulation happens in HBase, not in your client application, which makes it fast. It also avoids a possible race condition where some other client is interacting with the same cell. You can think of the ICV as identical to Java's `AtomicLong.addAndGet()` method. The increment value can be any Java `Long` value, positive or negative. We'll cover atomic operations in more detail in the next section.

Notice also that you're not storing this data in the `twits` table but instead in the users table. You store it there because you don't want this information as part of a scan. Keeping it in the `twits` table would upset the common access pattern of that table.

Like Java's Atomic family of classes, the `HTableInterface` also provides `checkAndPut()` and `checkAndDelete()` methods. They allow for more fine-grained control while maintaining the atomic semantics. You could implement the `incrementColumnValue()` method using `checkAndPut()`:

```
Get g = new Get(Bytes.toBytes("TheRealMT"));
Result r = usersTable.get(g);
long curVal = Bytes.toLong(
  r.getColumnLatest(
    Bytes.toBytes("info"),
    Bytes.toBytes("tweet_count")).getValue());
long incVal = curVal + 1;
Put p = new Put(Bytes.toBytes("TheRealMT"));
p.add(
  Bytes.toBytes("info"),
  Bytes.toBytes("tweet_count"),
  Bytes.toBytes(incVal));
usersTable.checkAndPut(
  Bytes.toBytes("TheRealMT"),
```

```
Bytes.toBytes("info"),
Bytes.toBytes("tweet_count"),
Bytes.toBytes(curVal),
p);
```

This implementation is quite a bit longer, but you can do it. Using `checkAndDelete()` looks much the same.

Following the same patterns as before, you can now easily build a `TwitsTool`. The model, DAO, and command-line implementations look similar to what you've seen for the `users` table. An implementation is provided in the source code accompanying this book.

2.8   ACID semantics

If you've worked with database systems, you've heard about the ACID semantics that various systems provide. ACID is a set of properties that are important to be aware of when building applications that use database systems for storage. Using these properties, you can reason the behavior of your application when it comes to interacting with the underlying store. For the sake of simplicity, let's again define ACID. Keep in mind that ACID is different from CAP, which we briefly touched on earlier:

- *Atomicity*—Atomicity is the property of an operation being *atomic,* or, in other words, *all or nothing.* If the operation succeeds, the entire operation succeeds. If the operation fails, it fails in its entirety and the system is left in exactly the same state as it was in before the operation started.
- *Consistency*—Consistency is the property of an operation taking the system from one valid state to another. If the operation makes the system inconsistent, it won't be performed or it will be rolled back.
- *Isolation*—Isolation means that no operation interferes with any other operation in the system. For instance, no two writes to a single object will happen at the same time. The writes will happen one after the other, but not at the exact same moment.
- *Durability*—Durability is something we talked about earlier. It means that once data is written, it's guaranteed to be read back and not lost in due course of normal operation of the system.

2.9   Summary

In case you missed something along the way, here is a quick overview of the material covered in this chapter.

HBase is a database designed for *semistructured* data and *horizontal scalability.* It stores data in *tables.* Within a table, data is organized over a four-dimensional coordinate system: *rowkey, column family, column qualifier,* and *version.* HBase is *schema-less,* requiring only that column families be defined ahead of time. It's also *type-less,* storing all data as uninterpreted arrays of bytes. There are five basic *commands* for interacting with data in HBase: `Get`, `Put`, `Delete`, `Scan`, and `Increment`. The only way to *query* HBase based on non-rowkey values is by a *filtered scan.*

HBase is *not* an ACID-compliant database[6]

HBase isn't an ACID-compliant database. But HBase provides some guarantees that you can use to reason about the behavior of your application's interaction with the system. These guarantees are as follows:

1. Operations are row-level atomic. In other words, any Put() on a given row either succeeds in its entirety or fails and leaves the row the way it was before the operation started. There will never be a case where part of the row is written and some part is left out. This property is regardless of the number of column families across which the operation is being performed.
2. Interrow operations are *not* atomic. There are no guarantees that all operations will complete or fail together in their entirety. All the individual operations are atomic as listed in the previous point.
3. checkAnd* and increment* operations are atomic.
4. Multiple write operations to a given row are always independent of each other in their entirety. This is an extension of the first point.
5. Any Get() operation on a given row returns the complete row as it exists at that point in time in the system.
6. A scan across a table is *not* a scan over a snapshot of the table at any point. If a row R is mutated after the scan has started but before R is read by the scanner object, the updated version of R is read by the scanner. But the data read by the scanner is consistent and contains the complete row at the time it's read.

From the context of building applications with HBase, these are the important points you need to be aware of.

The *data model* is *logically* organized as either a *key-value store* or as a *sorted map of maps*. The *physical data model* is *column-oriented* along column families and individual records are stored in a *key-value* style. HBase persists data records into *HFiles*, an immutable file format. Because records can't be modified once written, new values are persisted to new HFiles. Data view is reconciled on the fly at read time and during compactions.

The HBase Java client API exposes tables via the HTableInterface. Table connections can be established by constructing an HTable instance directly. Instantiating an HTable instance is expensive, so the preferred method is via the HTablePool because it manages connection reuse. Tables are created and manipulated via instances of the HBaseAdmin, HTableDescriptor, and HColumnDescriptor classes. All five commands are exposed via their respective command objects: Get, Put, Delete, Scan, and Increment. Commands are sent to the HTableInterface instance for execution. A variant of Increment is also available using the HTableInterface.incrementColumnValue() method. The results of executing Get, Scan, and Increment commands are returned in instances of Result and ResultScanner objects. Each record returned is represented

---

[6] HBase's ACID semantics are described in the HBase manual: http://hbase.apache.org/acid-semantics.html.

by a `KeyValue` instance. All of these operations are also available on the command line via the HBase shell.

Schema designs in HBase are heavily influenced by anticipated data-access patterns. Ideally, the tables in your schema are organized according to these patterns. The rowkey is the only fully indexed coordinate in HBase, so queries are often implemented as rowkey scans. Compound rowkeys are a common practice in support of these scans. An even distribution of rowkey values is often desirable. Hashing algorithms such as MD5 or SHA1 are commonly used to achieve even distribution.

Distributed HBase, HDFS, and MapReduce

This chapter covers

- HBase as a distributed storage system
- When to use MapReduce instead of the key-value API
- MapReduce concepts and workflow
- How to write MapReduce applications with HBase
- How to use HBase for map-side joins in MapReduce
- Examples of using HBase with MapReduce

As you've realized, HBase is built on Apache Hadoop. What may not yet be clear to you is why. Most important, what benefits do we, as application developers, enjoy from this relationship? HBase depends on Hadoop for two separate concerns. Hadoop MapReduce provides a distributed computation framework for high-throughput *data access*. The Hadoop Distributed File System (HDFS) gives HBase a storage layer providing *availability* and *reliability*. In this chapter, you'll see how Twit-Base is able to take advantage of this data access for bulk processing and how HBase uses HDFS to guarantee availability and reliability.

To begin this chapter, we'll show you why MapReduce is a valuable alternative access pattern for processing data in HBase. Then we'll describe Hadoop MapReduce in general. With this knowledge, we'll tie it all back into HBase as a distributed system. We'll show you how to use HBase from MapReduce jobs and explain some useful tricks you can do with HBase from MapReduce. Finally, we'll show you how HBase provides availability, reliability, and durability for your data. If you're a seasoned Hadooper and know a bunch about MapReduce and HDFS, you can jump straight to section 3.3 and dive into learning about distributed HBase.

The code used in this chapter is a continuation of the TwitBase project started in the previous chapter and is available at https://github.com/hbaseinaction/twitbase.

3.1 A case for MapReduce

Everything you've seen so far about HBase has a focus on *online* operations. You expect every Get and Put to return results in milliseconds. You carefully craft your Scans to transfer as little data as possible over the wire so they'll complete as quickly as possible. You emphasize this behavior in your schema designs, too. The twits table's rowkey is designed to maximize physical data locality and minimize the time spent scanning records.

Not all computation must be performed online. For some applications, *offline* operations are fine. You likely don't care if the monthly site traffic summary report is generated in four hours or five hours, as long as it completes before the business owners are ready for it. Offline operations have performance concerns as well. Instead of focusing on individual request latency, these concerns often focus on the entire computation in aggregate. MapReduce is a computing paradigm built for offline (or batch) processing of large amounts of data in an efficient manner.

3.1.1 Latency vs. throughput

The concept of this duality between online and offline concerns has come up a couple times now. This duality exists in traditional relational systems too, with Online Transaction Processing (OLTP) and Online Analytical Processing (OLAP). Different database systems are optimized for different access patterns. To get the best performance for the least cost, you need to use the right tool for the job. The same system that handles fast real-time queries isn't necessarily optimized for batch operations on large amounts of data.

Consider the last time you needed to buy groceries. Did you go to the store, buy a single item, and return it to your pantry, only to return to the store for the next item? Well sure, you may do this sometimes, but it's not ideal, right? More likely you made a shopping list, went to the store, filled up your cart, and brought everything home. The entire trip took longer, but the time you spent away from home was shorter per item than taking an entire trip per item. In this example, the time in transit dominates the time spent shopping for, purchasing, and unpacking the groceries. When buying multiple things at once, the average time spent per item purchased is much lower. Making the shopping list results in higher throughput. While in the store, you'll need a bigger cart to accommodate that long shopping list; a small hand basket won't cut it. Tools that work for one approach aren't always sufficient for another.

We think about data access in much the same way. Online systems focus on minimizing the time it takes to access one piece of data—the round trip of going to the store to buy a single item. Response latency measured on the 95th percentile is generally the most important metric for online performance. Offline systems are optimized for access in the aggregate, processing as much as we can all at once in order to maximize throughput. These systems usually report their performance in number of units processed per second. Those units might be requests, records, or megabytes. Regardless of the unit, it's about overall processing time of the task, not the time of an individual unit.

3.1.2 *Serial execution has limited throughput*

You wrapped up the last chapter by using `Scan` to look at the most recent twits for a user of TwitBase. Create the start rowkey, create the end rowkey, and execute the scan. That works for exploring a single user, but what if you want to calculate a statistic over all users? Given your user base, perhaps it would be interesting to know what percentage of twits are about Shakespeare. Maybe you'd like to know how many users have mentioned *Hamlet* in their twits.

How can you look at all the twits from all the users in the system to produce these metrics? The `Scan` object will let you do that:

```
HTableInterface twits = pool.getTable(TABLE_NAME);
Scan s = new Scan();
ResultScanner results = twits.getScanner(s);
for(Result r : results) {
   ... // process twits
}
```

This block of code asks for *all* the data in the table and returns it for your client to iterate through. Does it have a bit of code-smell to you? Even before we explain the inner workings of iterating over the items in the `ResultScanner` instance, your intuition should flag this as a bad idea. Even if the machine running this loop could process 10 MB/sec, churning through 100 GB of twits would take nearly 3 hours!

3.1.3 *Improved throughput with parallel execution*

What if you could parallelize this problem—that is, split your gigabyte of twits into pieces and process all the pieces in parallel? You could turn 3 hours into 25 minutes by spinning up 8 threads and running them all in parallel. A laptop has 8 cores and can easily hold 100 GB of data, so assuming it doesn't run out of memory, this should be pretty easy.

Embarrassingly parallel

Many problems in computing are inherently parallel. Only because of incidental concerns must they be written in a serial fashion. Such concerns could be any of programming language design, storage engine implementation, library API, and so on. The challenge falls to you as an algorithm designer to see these situations for what they are. Not all problems are easily parallelizable, but you'll be surprised by how many are once you start to look.

The code for distributing the work over different threads might look something like this:

```
int numSplits = 8;
Split[] splits = split(startrow, endrow, numSplits);              Split
List<Future<?>> workers = new ArrayList<Future<?>>(numSplits);    work
ExecutorService es = Executors.newFixedThreadPool(numSplits);
for (final Split split : splits) {
  workers.add(es.submit(new Runnable() {                          Distribute
    public void run() {                                           work
      HTableInterface twits = pool.getTable(TABLE_NAME);
      Scan s = new Scan(split.start, split.end);
      ResultScanner results = twits.getScanner(s);
      for(Result r : results) {
        ...                                  Do
      }                                      work
    }
  }));
}
for(Future<?> f : workers) {
  f.get();
  ...                          Aggregate
}                              work
es.shutdownNow();
```

That's not bad, but there's one problem. People are using TwitBase, and before long you'll have 200 GB of twits—and then 1 TB and then 50 TB! Fitting all that data on your laptop's hard drive is a serious challenge, and it's running desperately low on cores. What do you do? You can settle for waiting longer for the computation to finish, but that solution won't last forever as hours quickly turn into days. Parallelizing the computation worked well last time, so you might as well throw more computers at it. Maybe you can buy 20 cheapish servers for the price of 10 fancy laptops.

Now that you have the computing power, you still need to deal with splitting the problem across those machines. Once you've solved that problem, the aggregation step will require a similar solution. And all this while you've assumed everything works as expected. What happens if a thread gets stuck or dies? What if a hard drive fails or the machine suffers random RAM corruption? It would be nice if the workers could restart where they left off in case one of the splits kills the program. How does the aggregation keep track of which splits have finished and which haven't? How do the results get shipped back for aggregation? Parallelizing the problem was pretty easy, but the rest of this distributed computation is painful bookkeeping. If you think about it, the bookkeeping would be required for every algorithm you write. The solution is to make that into a framework.

3.1.4 *MapReduce: maximum throughput with distributed parallelism*

Enter Hadoop. Hadoop gives us two major components that solve this problem. The *Hadoop Distributed File System (HDFS)* gives all these computers a common, shared file system where they can all access the data. This removes a lot of the pain from farming out the data to the workers and aggregating the work results. Your workers can access the input data from HDFS and write out the processed results to HDFS, and all the others can see them. *Hadoop MapReduce* does all the bookkeeping we described, splitting up the workload and making sure it gets done. Using MapReduce, all you write are the *Do Work* and *Aggregate Work* bits; Hadoop handles the rest. Hadoop refers to the Do Work part as the *Map Step*. Likewise, Aggregate Work is the *Reduce Step*. Using Hadoop MapReduce, you have something like this instead:

```
public class Map
   extends Mapper<LongWritable, Text, Text, LongWritable> {

   protected void map(LongWritable key,
                      Text Value,
                      Context context) {
       . . .                 <──┐  Do
   }                            │  work
}
```

This code implements the `map` task. This function expects `long` keys and `Text` instances as input and writes out pairs of `Text` to `LongWritable`. `Text` and `LongWritable` are Hadoop-speak for `String` and `Long`, respectively.

   Notice all the code you're not writing. There are no split calculations, no Futures to track, and no thread pool to clean up after. Better still, this code can run anywhere on the Hadoop cluster! Hadoop distributes your worker logic around the cluster according to resource availability. Hadoop makes sure every machine receives a unique slice of the `twits` table. Hadoop ensures no work is left behind, even if workers crash.

   Your Aggregate Work code is shipped around the cluster in a similar fashion. The Hadoop harness looks something like this:

```
public class Reduce
   extends Reducer<Text, LongWritable, Text, LongWritable> {

   protected void reduce(Text key,
                         Iterable<LongWritable> vals,
                         Context context) {
       . . .                 <──┐  Aggregate
   }                            │  work
}
```

Here you see the `reduce` task. The function receives the `[String,Long]` pairs output from `map` and produces new `[String,Long]` pairs. Hadoop also handles collecting the output. In this case, the `[String,Long]` pairs are written back to the HDFS. You could have just as easily written them back to HBase. HBase provides `TableMapper` and `TableReducer` classes to help with that.

You've just seen when and why you'll want to use MapReduce instead of programming directly against the HBase client API. Now let's take a quick look at the MapReduce framework. If you're already familiar with Hadoop MapReduce, feel free to skip down to section 3.3: "HBase in distributed mode."

3.2   *An overview of Hadoop MapReduce*

In order to provide you with a general-purpose, reliable, fault-tolerant distributed computation harness, MapReduce constrains how you implement your program. These constraints are as follows:

- All computations are implemented as either `map` or `reduce` tasks.
- Each task operates over a portion of the total input data.
- Tasks are defined primarily in terms of their input data and output data.
- Tasks depend on their input data and don't communicate with other tasks.

Hadoop MapReduce enforces these constraints by requiring that programs be implemented with `map` and `reduce` functions. These functions are composed into a *Job* and run as a unit: first the mappers and then the reducers. Hadoop runs as many simultaneous tasks as it's able. Because there are no runtime dependencies between concurrent tasks, Hadoop can run them in any order as long as the `map` tasks are run before the `reduce` tasks. The decisions of how many tasks to run and which tasks to run are up to Hadoop.

Exceptions to every rule

As far as Hadoop MapReduce is concerned, the points outlined previously are more like guidelines than rules. MapReduce is *batch-oriented*, meaning most of its design principles are focused on the problem of distributed *batch processing of large amounts* of data. A system designed for the distributed, real-time processing of an event stream might take a different approach.

On the other hand, Hadoop MapReduce can be abused for any number of other workloads that fit within these constraints. Some workloads are I/O heavy, others are computation heavy. The Hadoop MapReduce framework is a reliable, fault-tolerant job execution framework that can be used for both kinds of jobs. But MapReduce *is* optimized for I/O intensive jobs and makes several optimizations around minimizing network bottlenecks by reducing the amount of data that needs to be transferred over the wire.

3.2.1 MapReduce data flow explained

Implementing programs in terms of Map and Reduce Steps requires a change in how you tackle a problem. This can be quite an adjustment for developers accustomed to other common kinds of programming. Some people find this change so fundamental that they consider it a *change of paradigm*. Don't worry! This claim may or may not be true. We'll make it as easy as possible to think in MapReduce. MapReduce is all about processing large amounts of data in parallel, so let's break down a MapReduce problem in terms of the flow of data.

For this example, let's consider a log file from an application server. Such a file contains information about how a user spends time using the application. Its contents look like this:

```
Date       Time   UserID Activity     TimeSpent

01/01/2011 18:00  user1  load_page1   3s
01/01/2011 18:01  user1  load_page2   5s
01/01/2011 18:01  user2  load_page1   2s
01/01/2011 18:01  user3  load_page1   3s
01/01/2011 18:04  user4  load_page3   10s
01/01/2011 18:05  user1  load_page3   5s
01/01/2011 18:05  user3  load_page5   3s
01/01/2011 18:06  user4  load_page4   6s
01/01/2011 18:06  user1  purchase     5s
01/01/2011 18:10  user4  purchase     8s
01/01/2011 18:10  user1  confirm      9s
01/01/2011 18:10  user4  confirm      11s
01/01/2011 18:11  user1  load_page3   3s
```

Let's calculate the amount of time each user spends using the application. A basic implementation might be to iterate through the file, summing the values of TimeSpent for each user. Your program could have a single HashMap (or dict, for you Pythonistas) with UserID as the key and summed TimeSpent as the value. In simple pseudo-code, that program might look like this:

```
agg = {}
for line in file:
  record = split(line)                              Do work
  agg[record["UserID"]] += record["TimeSpent"]
report(agg)                                         Aggregate
                                                    work
```

This looks a lot like the serial example from the previous section, doesn't it? Like the serial example, its throughput is limited to a single thread on a single machine. MapReduce is for distributed parallelism. The first thing to do when parallelizing a problem is break it up. Notice that each line in the input file is processed independently from all the other lines. The only time when data from different lines is seen together is during the aggregation step. That means this input file can be parallelized by any number of lines, processed independently, and aggregated to produce exactly the same result. Let's split it into four pieces and assign those pieces to four different machines, as per figure 3.1.

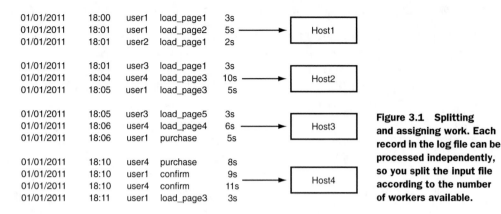

Figure 3.1 Splitting and assigning work. Each record in the log file can be processed independently, so you split the input file according to the number of workers available.

Look closely at these divisions. Hadoop doesn't know anything about this data other than that it's line-oriented. In particular, there's no effort made to group according to UserID. This is an important point we'll address shortly.

Now the work is divided and assigned. How do you rewrite the program to work with this data? As you saw from the map and reduce stubs, MapReduce operates in terms of key-value pairs. For line-oriented data like this, Hadoop provides pairs of [line number:line]. While walking through the MapReduce workflow, we refer in general to this first set of key-value pairs as [k1,v1]. Let's start by writing the Map Step, again in pseudo-code:

```
def map(line_num, line):          ┐ Do work
  record = split(line)          ⟵─┘
  emit(record["UserID"], record["TimeSpent"])
```

The Map Step is defined in terms of the lines from the file. For each line in its portion of the file, this Map Step splits the line and produces a new key-value pair of [UserID:TimeSpent]. In this pseudo-code, the function emit handles reporting the produced pairs back to Hadoop. As you likely guessed, we'll refer to the second set of key-value pairs as [k2,v2]. Figure 3.2 continues where the previous figure left off.

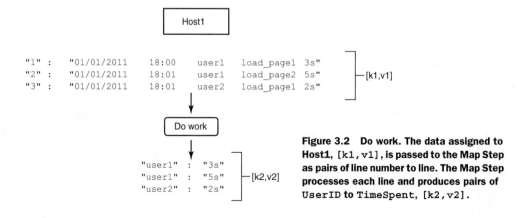

Figure 3.2 Do work. The data assigned to Host1, [k1,v1], is passed to the Map Step as pairs of line number to line. The Map Step processes each line and produces pairs of UserID to TimeSpent, [k2,v2].

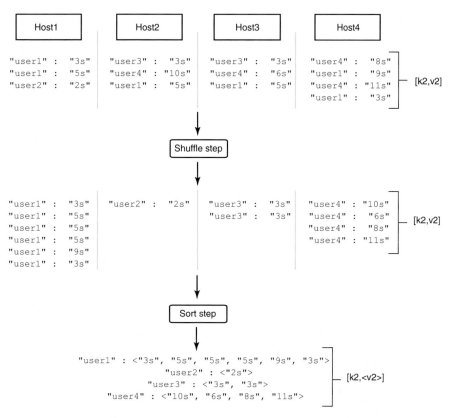

Figure 3.3 Hadoop performs the Shuffle and Sort Step automatically. It serves to prepare the output from the Map Step for aggregation in the Reduce Step. No values are changed by the process; it serves only to reorganize data.

Before Hadoop can pass the values of [k2,v2] on to the Reduce Step, a little book-keeping is necessary. Remember that bit about grouping by UserID? The Reduce Step expects to operate over all TimeSpent by a given UserID. For this to happen correctly, that grouping work happens now. Hadoop calls these the *Shuffle and Sort Steps*. Figure 3.3 illustrates these steps.

MapReduce takes [k2,v2], the output from all four Map Steps on all four servers, and assigns it to reducers. Each reducer is assigned a set of values of UserID and it copies those [k2,v2] pairs from the mapper nodes. This is called the Shuffle Step. A reduce task expects to process all values of k2 at the same time, so a sort on key is necessary. The output of that Sort Step is [k2,<v2>], a list of Times for each UserID. With the grouping complete, the reduce tasks run. The aggregate work function looks like this:

```
def reduce(user, times):
    for time in times:            ┐  Aggregate
        sum += time          ◁────┘  work
    emit(user, sum)
```

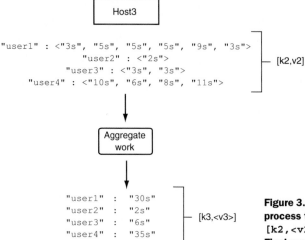

Figure 3.4   **Aggregate work. Available servers process the groups of `UserID` to `Times`, `[k2,<v2>]`, in this case, summing the values. Final results are emitted back to Hadoop.**

The Reduce Step processes the `[k2,<v2>]` input and produces aggregated work as pairs of `[UserID:TotalTime]`. These sums are collected by Hadoop and written to the output destination. Figure 3.4 illustrates this final step.

You can run this application if you'd like; the source is bundled with the TwitBase code. To do so, compile the application JAR and launch the job like this:

```
$ mvn clean package
[INFO] Scanning for projects...
[INFO]
[INFO] ------------------------------------------------------------------
[INFO] Building TwitBase 1.0.0
[INFO] ------------------------------------------------------------------
...
[INFO] ------------------------------------------------------------------
[INFO] BUILD SUCCESS
[INFO] ------------------------------------------------------------------
$ java -cp target/twitbase-1.0.0.jar \
  HBaseIA.TwitBase.mapreduce.TimeSpent \
  src/test/resource/listing\ 3.3.txt ./out
...
22:53:15 INFO mapred.JobClient: Running job: job_local_0001
22:53:15 INFO mapred.Task:  Using ResourceCalculatorPlugin : null
22:53:15 INFO mapred.MapTask: io.sort.mb = 100
22:53:15 INFO mapred.MapTask: data buffer = 79691776/99614720
22:53:15 INFO mapred.MapTask: record buffer = 262144/327680
22:53:15 INFO mapred.MapTask: Starting flush of map output
22:53:15 INFO mapred.MapTask: Finished spill 0
22:53:15 INFO mapred.Task: Task:attempt_local_0001_m_000000_0 is done. And is
      in the process of commiting
22:53:16 INFO mapred.JobClient:  map 0% reduce 0%
...
```

```
22:53:21 INFO mapred.Task: Task 'attempt_local_0001_r_000000_0' done.
22:53:22 INFO mapred.JobClient:  map 100% reduce 100%
22:53:22 INFO mapred.JobClient: Job complete: job_local_0001
$ cat out/part-r-00000
user1    30
user2    2
user3    6
user4    35
```

That's MapReduce as the data flows. Every MapReduce application performs this sequence of steps, or most of them. If you can follow these basic steps, you've successfully grasped this new paradigm.

3.2.2 MapReduce under the hood

Building a system for general-purpose, distributed, parallel computation is nontrivial. That's precisely why we leave that problem up to Hadoop! All the same, it can be useful to understand how things are implemented, particularly when you're tracking down a bug. As you know, Hadoop MapReduce is a distributed system. Several independent components form the framework. Let's walk through them and see what makes MapReduce tick.

A process called the JobTracker acts as an overseer application. It's responsible for managing the MapReduce applications that run on your cluster. Jobs are submitted to the JobTracker for execution and it manages distributing the workload. It also keeps tabs on all portions of the job, ensuring that failed tasks are retried. A single Hadoop cluster can run multiple MapReduce applications simultaneously. It falls to the Job-Tracker to oversee resource utilization, and job scheduling as well.

The work defined by the Map Step and Reduce Step is executed by another process called the TaskTracker. Figure 3.5 illustrates the relationship between a Job-Tracker and its TaskTrackers. These are the actual worker processes. An individual TaskTracker isn't specialized in any way. Any TaskTracker can run any task, be it a map or reduce, from any job. Hadoop is smart and doesn't randomly spray work across the

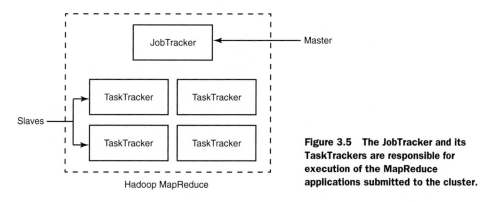

Figure 3.5   The JobTracker and its TaskTrackers are responsible for execution of the MapReduce applications submitted to the cluster.

nodes. As we mentioned, Hadoop is optimized for minimal network I/O. It achieves this by bringing computation as close as possible to the data. In a typical Hadoop, HDFS DataNodes and MapReduce TaskTrackers are collocated with each other. This allows the map and reduce tasks to run on the same physical node where the data is located. By doing so, Hadoop can avoid transferring the data over the network. When it isn't possible to run the tasks on the same physical node, running the task in the same rack is a better choice than running it on a different rack. When HBase comes into the picture, the same concepts apply, but in general HBase deployments look different from standard Hadoop deployments. You'll learn about deployment strategies in chapter 10.

3.3 HBase in distributed mode

By now you know that HBase is essentially a database built on top of HDFS. It's also sometimes referred to as the *Hadoop Database*, and that's where it got its name. Theoretically, HBase can work on top of any distributed file system. It's just that it's tightly integrated with HDFS, and a lot more development effort has gone into making it work well with HDFS as compared to other distributed file systems. Having said that, from a theoretical standpoint, there is no reason that other file systems can't support HBase. One of the key factors that makes HBase scalable (and fault tolerant) is that it persists its data onto a distributed file system that provides it a single namespace. This is one of the key factors that allows HBase to be a fully consistent data store.

HDFS is inherently a scalable store, but that's not enough to scale HBase as a low-latency data store. There are other factors at play that you'll learn about in this section. Having a good understanding of these is important in order to design your application optimally. This knowledge will enable you to make smart choices about how you want to access HBase, what your keys should look like, and, to some degree, how HBase should be configured. Configuration isn't something you as an application developer should be worried about, but it's likely that you'll have some role to play when bringing HBase into your stack initially.

3.3.1 Splitting and distributing big tables

Just as in any other database, tables in HBase comprise rows and columns, albeit with a different kind of schema. Tables in HBase can scale to billions of rows and millions of columns. The size of each table can run into terabytes and sometimes even petabytes. It's clear at that scale that the entire table can't be hosted on a single machine. Instead, tables are split into smaller chunks that are distributed across multiple servers. These smaller chunks are called *regions* (figure 3.6). Servers that host regions are called *RegionServers*.

RegionServers are typically collocated with HDFS DataNodes (figure 3.7) on the same physical hardware, although that's not a requirement. The only requirement is that RegionServers should be able to access HDFS. They're essentially clients and

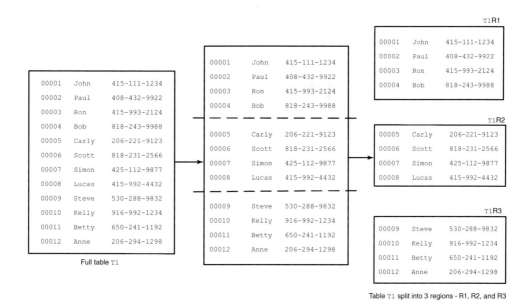

Figure 3.6 **A table consists of multiple smaller chunks called regions.**

store/access data on HDFS. The *master* process does the distribution of regions among RegionServers, and each RegionServer typically hosts multiple regions.

Given that the underlying data is stored in HDFS, which is available to all clients as a single namespace, all RegionServers have access to the same persisted files in the file system and can therefore host any region (figure 3.8). By physically collocating Data-Nodes and RegionServers, you can use the data locality property; that is, RegionServers can theoretically read and write to the local DataNode as the primary DataNode.

You may wonder where the TaskTrackers are in this scheme of things. In some HBase deployments, the MapReduce framework isn't deployed at all if the workload is primarily random reads and writes. In other deployments, where the MapReduce processing is also a part of the workloads, TaskTrackers, DataNodes, and HBase Region-Servers can run together.

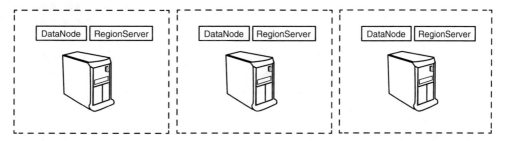

Figure 3.7 **HBase RegionServer and HDFS DataNode processes are typically collocated on the same host.**

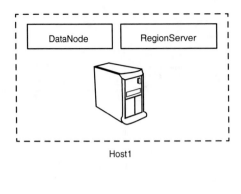

T1R1

00001	John	415-111-1234
00002	Paul	408-432-9922
00003	Ron	415-993-2124
00004	Bob	818-243-9988

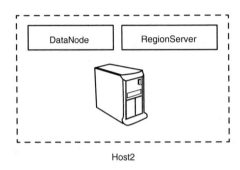

T1R2

00005	Carly	206-221-9123
00006	Scott	818-231-2566
00007	Simon	425-112-9877
00008	Lucas	415-992-4432

T1R3

00009	Steve	530-288-9832
00010	Kelly	916-992-1234
00011	Betty	650-241-1192
00012	Anne	206-294-1298

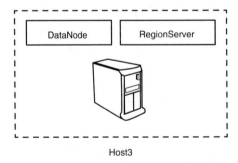

Host3

Figure 3.8 Any RegionServer can host any region. RegionServers 1 and 2 are hosting regions, whereas RegionServer 3 isn't.

The size of individual regions is governed by the configuration parameter hbase.hregion.max.filesize, which can be configured in the hbase-site.xml file of your deployment. When a region becomes bigger than that size (as you write more data into it), it gets split into two regions.

3.3.2   *How do I find my region?*

You've learned that tables are split into regions and regions are assigned to Region-Servers without any predefined assignment rules. In case you're wondering, regions don't keep moving around in a running system! Region assignment happens when regions split (as they grow in size), when RegionServers die, or when new RegionServers are added to the deployment. An important question to ask here is, "When a region is assigned to a RegionServer, how does my client application (the one doing reads and writes) know its location?"

Two special tables in HBase, -ROOT- and .META., help find where regions for various tables are hosted. Like all tables in HBase, -ROOT- and .META. are also split into regions. -ROOT- and .META. are both special tables, but -ROOT- is more special than .META.; -ROOT- never splits into more than one region. .META. behaves like all other tables and can split into as many regions as required.

When a client application wants to access a particular row, it goes to the -ROOT- table and asks it where it can find the region responsible for that particular row. -ROOT- points it to the region of the .META. table that contains the answer to that question. The .META. table consists of entries that the client application uses to determine which RegionServer is hosting the region in question. Think of this like a distributed B+Tree of height 3 (see figure 3.9). The -ROOT- table is the -ROOT- node of the B+Tree. The .META. regions are the children of the -ROOT- node (-ROOT- region)n and the regions of the user tables (leaf nodes of the B+Tree) are the children of the .META. regions.

Let's put -ROOT- and .META. into the example; see figure 3.10. Note that the region assignments shown here are arbitrary and don't represent how they will happen when such a system is deployed.

3.3.3 How do I find the -ROOT- table?

You just learned how the -ROOT- and .META. tables help you find out other regions in the system. At this point, you might be left with a question: "Where is the -ROOT- table?" Let's figure that out now.

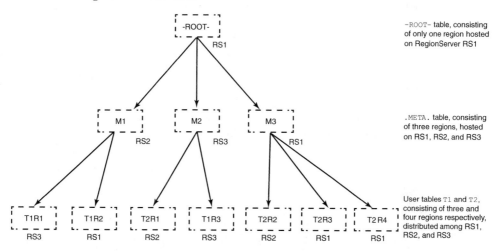

Figure 3.9 -ROOT-, .META., and user tables viewed as a B+Tree

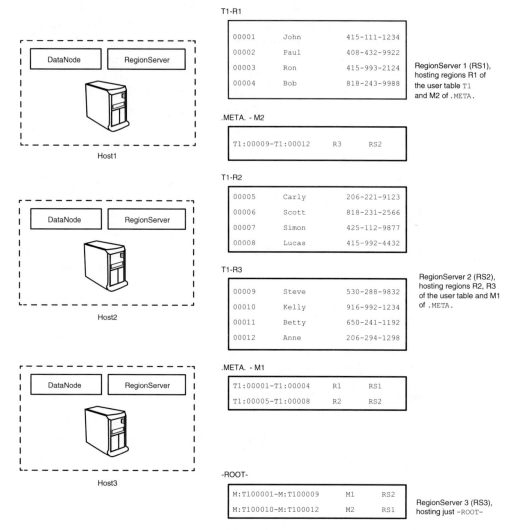

Figure 3.10   User table `T1` in HBase, along with `-ROOT-` and `.META.`, distributed across the various RegionServers

The entry point for an HBase system is provided by another system called ZooKeeper (http://zookeeper.apache.org/). As stated on ZooKeeper's website, ZooKeeper is a centralized service for maintaining configuration information, naming, providing distributed synchronization, and providing group services. It's a highly available, reliable distributed configuration service. Just as HBase is modeled after Google's BigTable, ZooKeeper is modeled after Google's Chubby.[1]

The client interaction with the system happens in steps, where ZooKeeper is the point of entry, as mentioned earlier. These steps are highlighted in figure 3.11.

---

[1] Mike Burrow, "The Chubby Lock Service for Loosely-Coupled Distributed Systems," Google Research Publications, http://research.google.com/archive/chubby.html.

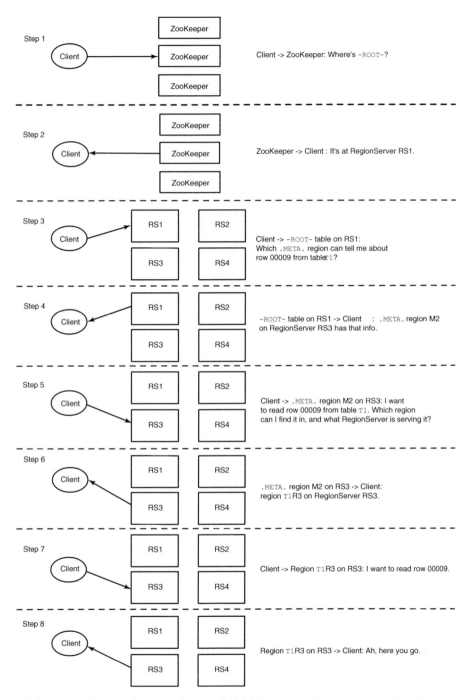

Figure 3.11 **Steps that take place when a client interacts with an HBase system. The interaction starts with ZooKeeper and goes to the RegionServer serving the region with which the client needs to interact. The interaction with the RegionServer could be for reads or writes. The information about `-ROOT-` and `.META.` is cached by the client for future interactions and is refreshed if the regions it's expecting to interact with based on that information don't exist on the node it thinks they should be on.**

This section gave you an overview of the implementation of HBase's distributed architecture. You can see all these details for yourself on your own cluster. We show you exactly how to explore ZooKeeper, -ROOT-, and .META. in appendix A.

3.4 HBase and MapReduce

Now that you have an understanding of MapReduce and HBase in distributed mode, let's look at them together. There are three different ways of interacting with HBase from a MapReduce application. HBase can be used as a *data source* at the beginning of a job, as a *data sink* at the end of a job, or as a *shared resource* for your tasks. None of these modes of interaction are particularly mysterious. The third, however, has some interesting use cases we'll address shortly.

All the code snippets used in this section are examples of using the Hadoop MapReduce API. There are no HBase client HTable or HTablePool instances involved. Those are embedded in the special input and output formats you'll use here. You will, however, use the Put, Delete, and Scan objects with which you're already familiar. Creating and configuring the Hadoop Job and Configuration instances can be messy work. These snippets emphasize the HBase portion of that work. You'll see a full working example in section 3.5.

3.4.1 HBase as a source

In the example MapReduce application, you read lines from log files sitting in the HDFS. Those files, specifically the directory in HDFS containing those files, act as the data source for the MapReduce job. The schema of that data source describes [k1,v1] tuples as [line number:line]. The TextInputFormat class configured as part of the job defines this schema. The relevant code from the TimeSpent example looks like this:

```
Configuration conf = new Configuration();
Job job = new Job(conf, "TimeSpent");
...
job.setInputFormatClass(TextInputFormat.class);
job.setOutputFormatClass(TextOutputFormat.class);
```

TextInputFormat defines the [k1,v1] type for line number and line as the types LongWritable and Text, respectively. LongWritable and Text are serializable Hadoop wrapper types over Java's Long and String. The associated map task definition is typed for consuming these input pairs:

```
public void map(LongWritable key, Text value,
Context context) {
  ...
}
```

HBase provides similar classes for consuming data out of a table. When mapping over data in HBase, you use the same Scan class you used before. Under the hood, the row-range defined by the Scan is broken into pieces and distributed to all the workers (figure 3.12).

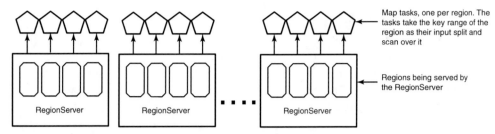

Map tasks, one per region. The tasks take the key range of the region as their input split and scan over it

Regions being served by the RegionServer

Figure 3.12 MapReduce job with mappers taking regions from HBase as their input source. By default, one mapper is created per region.

This is identical to the splitting you saw in figure 3.1. Creating a `Scan` instance for scanning over all rows in a table from MapReduce looks like this:

```
Scan scan = new Scan();
scan.addColumn(Bytes.toBytes("twits"), Bytes.toBytes("twit"));
```

In this case, you're asking the scanner to return only the text from the `twits` table.

Just like consuming text lines, consuming HBase rows requires a schema. All jobs reading from an HBase table accept their `[k1,v1]` pairs in the form of `[rowkey:scan result]`. That's the same scanner result as when you consume the regular HBase API. They're presented using the types `ImmutableBytesWritable` and `Result`. The provided `TableMapper` wraps up these details for you, so you'll want to use it as the base class for your Map Step implementation:

```
protected void map(
    ImmutableBytesWritable rowkey,
    Result result,
    Context context) {
    ...
}
```

Define types for input [kl,vl] the map task receives, in this case from scanner

The next step is to take your `Scan` instance and wire it into MapReduce. HBase provides the handy `TableMapReduceUtil` class to help you initialize the `Job` instance:

```
TableMapReduceUtil.initTableMapperJob(
    "twits",
    scan,
    Map.class,
    ImmutableBytesWritable.class,
    Result.class,
    job);
```

This takes your job-configuration object and sets up the HBase-specific input format (`TableInputFormat`). It then configures MapReduce to read from the table using your `Scan` instance. It also wires in your `Map` and `Reduce` class implementations. From here, you write and run the MapReduce application as normal.

When you run a MapReduce job as described here, one `map` task is launched for every region in the HBase table. In other words, the map tasks are partitioned such that each `map` task reads from a region independently. The JobTracker tries to schedule map tasks as close to the regions as possibly and take advantage of data locality.

3.4.2   *HBase as a sink*

Writing to an HBase table from MapReduce (figure 3.13) as a data sink is similar to reading from a table in terms of implementation.

HBase provides similar tooling to simplify the configuration. Let's first make an example of sink configuration in a standard MapReduce application.

In `TimeSpent`, the values of `[k3,v3]` generated by the aggregators are `[UserID:TotalTime]`. In the MapReduce application, they're of the Hadoop serializable types `Text` and `LongWritable`, respectively. Configuring output types is similar to configuring input types, with the exception that the `[k3,v3]` output types can't be inferred by the `OutputFormat`:

```
Configuration conf = new Configuration();
Job job = new Job(conf, "TimeSpent");
job.setOutputKeyClass(Text.class);
job.setOutputValueClass(LongWritable.class);
...
job.setInputFormatClass(TextInputFormat.class);
job.setOutputFormatClass(TextOutputFormat.class);
```

In this case, no line numbers are specified. Instead, the `TextOuputFormat` schema creates a tab-separated output file containing first the `UserID` and then the `TotalTime`. What's written to disk is the `String` representation of both types.

The `Context` object contains the type information. The reduce function is defined as

```
public void reduce(Text key, Iterable<LongWritable> values,
Context context) {
    ...
}
```

When writing to HBase from MapReduce, you're again using the regular HBase API. The types of `[k3,v3]` are assumed to be a rowkey and an object for manipulating HBase. That means the values of v3 must be either `Puts` or `Deletes`. Because both of these object types include the relevant rowkey, the value of k3 is ignored. Just as the `TableMapper` wraps up these details for you, so does the `TableReducer`:

```
protected void reduce(
    ImmutableBytesWritable rowkey,
    Iterable<Put> values,
    Context context) {
    ...
}
```

> **Define input types for reducer [k2,{v2}].**
> **These are intermediate key-value pairs**
> **that the map tasks are outputting.**

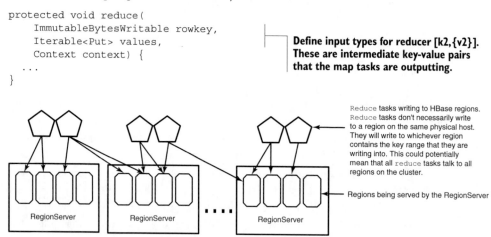

Reduce tasks writing to HBase regions. Reduce tasks don't necessarily write to a region on the same physical host. They will write to whichever region contains the key range that they are writing into. This could potentially mean that all reduce tasks talk to all regions on the cluster.

Regions being served by the RegionServer

Figure 3.13   HBase as a sink for a MapReduce job. In this case, the reduce tasks are writing to HBase.

The last step is wiring your reducer into the job configuration. You need to specify the destination table along with all the appropriate types. Once again, it's `TableMapReduceUtil` to the rescue; it sets up the `TableOutputFormat` for you! You use `IdentityTableReducer`, a provided class, because you don't need to perform any computation in the Reduce Step:

```
TableMapReduceUtil.initTableReducerJob(
  "users",
  IdentityTableReducer.class,
  job);
```

Now your job is completely wired up, and you can proceed as normal. Unlike the case where map tasks are reading from HBase, tasks don't necessarily write to a single region. The writes go to the region that is responsible for the rowkey that is being written by the reduce task. The default partitioner that assigns the intermediate keys to the `reduce` tasks doesn't have knowledge of the regions and the nodes that are hosting them and therefore can't intelligently assign work to the reducers such that they write to the local regions. Moreover, depending on the logic you write in the `reduce` task, which doesn't have to be the identity reducer, you might end up writing all over the table.

3.4.3   *HBase as a shared resource*

Reading from and writing to HBase using MapReduce is handy. It gives us a harness for batch processing over data in HBase. A few predefined MapReduce jobs ship with HBase; you can explore their source for more examples of using HBase from Map-Reduce. But what else can you do with HBase?

One common use of HBase is to support a large map-side join. In this scenario, you're reading from HBase as an indexed resource accessible from all `map` tasks. What is a map-side join, you ask? How does HBase support it? Excellent questions!

Let's back up a little. A *join* is common practice in data manipulation. Joining two tables is a fundamental concept in relational databases. The idea behind a join is to combine records from the two different sets based on like values in a common attribute. That attribute is often called the *join key.*

For example, think back to the `TimeSpent` MapReduce job. It produces a dataset containing a `UserID` and the `TotalTime` they spent on the TwitBase site:

```
UserID   TimeSpent

Yvonn66  30s
Mario23   2s
Rober4    6s
Masan46  35s
```

You also have the user information in the TwitBase table that looks like this:

```
UserID   Name             Email                        TwitCount

Yvonn66  Yvonne Marc      Yvonn66@unmercantile.com     48
Masan46  Masanobu Olof    Masan46@acetylic.com         47
Mario23  Marion Scott     Mario23@Wahima.com           56
Rober4   Roberto Jacques  Rober4@slidage.com            2
```

You'd like to know the ratio of how much time a user spends on the site to their total twit count. Although this is an easy question to answer, right now the relevant data is split between two different datasets. You'd like to join this data such that all the information about a user is in a single row. These two datasets share a common attribute: UserID. This will be the join key. The result of performing the join and dropping unused fields looks like this:

```
UserID    TwitCount    TimeSpent

Yvonn66    48            30s
Mario23    56             2s
Rober4      2             6s
Masan46    47            35s
```

Joins in the relational world are a lot easier than in MapReduce. Relational engines enjoy many years of research and tuning around performing joins. Features like indexing help optimize join operations. Moreover, the data typically resides on a single physical server. Joining across multiple relational servers is far more complicated and isn't common in practice. A join in MapReduce means joining on data spread across multiple servers. But the semantics of the MapReduce framework make it easier than trying to do a join across different relational database systems. There are a couple of different variations of each type, but a join implementation is either *map-side* or *reduce-side*. They're referred as map- or reduce-side because that's the task where records from the two sets are linked. Reduce-side joins are more common because they're easier to implement. We'll describe those first.

REDUCE-SIDE JOIN

A reduce-side join takes advantage of the intermediate Shuffle Step to collocate relevant records from the two sets. The idea is to map over both sets and emit tuples keyed on the join key. Once together, the reducer can produce all combinations of values. Let's build out the algorithm.

Given the sample data, the pseudo-code of the map task for consuming the TimeSpent data looks like this:

```
map_timespent(line_num, line):
  userid, timespent = split(line)
  record = {"TimeSpent" : timespent,         Producing compound records as
           "type" : "TimeSpent"}             v2 is common in MapReduce jobs
  emit(userid, record)
```

This map task splits the k1 input line into the UserID and TimeSpent values. It then constructs a dictionary with type and TimeSpent attributes. As [k2,v2] output, it produces [UserID:dictionary].

A map task for consuming the Users data is similar. The only difference is that it drops a couple of unrelated fields:

```
map_users(line_num, line):
  userid, name, email, twitcount = split(line)
  record = {"TwitCount" : twitcount,         Name and email aren't
           "type" : "TwitCount"}             carried along for the ride
  emit(userid, record)
```

Both `map` tasks use `UserID` as the value for k2. This allows Hadoop to group all records for the same user. The `reduce` task has everything it needs to complete the join:

```
reduce(userid, records):
  timespent_recs = []
  twitcount_recs = []

  for rec in records:
    if rec.type == "TimeSpent":
      rec.del("type")
      timespent_recs.push(rec)
    else:
      rec.del("type")
      twitcount_recs.push(rec)

  for timespent in timespent_recs:
    for twitcount in twitcount_recs:
      emit(userid, merge(timespent, twitcount))
```

Group by type — Once grouped, type attribute is no longer needed

Produce all possible combinations of twitcount and timespent for user; for this example, should be a single value

The `reduce` task groups records of identical type and produces all possible combinations of the two types as k3. For this specific example, you know there will be only one record of each type, so you can simplify the logic. You also can fold in the work of producing the ratio you want to calculate:

```
reduce(userid, records):
  for rec in records:
    rec.del("type")
  merge(records)
  emit(userid, ratio(rec["TimeSpent"], rec["TwitCount"]))
```

This new and improved `reduce` task produces the new, joined dataset:

```
UserID    ratio

Yvonn66   30s:48
Mario23    2s:56
Rober4     6s:2
Masan46   35s:47
```

There you have it: the reduce-side join in its most basic glory. One big problem with the reduce-side join is that it requires all [k2,v2] tuples to be shuffled and sorted. For our toy example, that's no big deal. But if the datasets are very, very large, with millions of pairs per value of k2, the overhead of that step can be huge.

Reduce-side joins require shuffling and sorting data between `map` and `reduce` tasks. This incurs I/O costs, specifically network, which happens to be the slowest aspect of any distributed system. Minimizing this network I/O will improve join performance. This is where the map-side join can help.

MAP-SIDE JOIN

The map-side join is a technique that isn't as general-purpose as the reduce-side join. It assumes the `map` tasks can look up random values from one dataset while they iterate over the other. If you happen to want to join two datasets where at least one of them can fit in memory of the map task, the problem is solved: load the smaller dataset into a hash-table so the map tasks can access it while iterating over the other dataset. In these cases, you can skip the Shuffle and Reduce Steps entirely and emit your final output from the Map Step. Let's go back to the same example. This time you'll put the Users dataset into memory. The new map_timespent task looks like this:

```
map_timespent(line_num, line):
  users_recs = read_timespent("/path/to/users.csv")
  userid, timespent = split(line)
  record = {"TimeSpent" : timespent}
  record = merge(record, users_recs[userid])
  emit(userid, ratio(record["TimeSpent"], record["TwitCount"]))
```

Compared to the last version, this looks like cheating! Remember, though, you can only get away with this approach when you can fit one of the datasets entirely into memory. In this case, your join will be much faster.

There are of course implications to doing joins like this. For instance, each map task is processing a single split, which is equal to one HDFS block (typically 64–128 MB), but the join dataset that it loads into memory is 1 GB. Now, 1 GB can certainly fit in memory, but the cost involved in creating a hash-table for a 1 GB dataset for every 128 MB of data being joined makes it not such a good idea.

MAP-SIDE JOIN WITH HBASE

Where does HBase come in? We originally described HBase as a giant hash-table, remember? Look again at the map-side join implementation. Replace users_recs with the Users table in TwitBase. Now you can join over the massive Users table and massive TimeSpent data set in record time! The map-side join using HBase looks like this:

```
map_timespent(line_num, line):
  users_table = HBase.connect("Users")
  userid, timespent = split(line)
  record = {"TimeSpent" : timespent}
  record = merge(record, users_table.get(userid, "info:twitcount"))
  emit(userid, ratio(record["TimeSpent"], record["info:twitcount"]))
```

Think of this as an external hash-table that each map task has access to. You don't need to create that hash-table object for every task. You also avoid all the network I/O involved in the Shuffle Step necessary for a reduce-side join. Conceptually, this looks like figure 3.14.

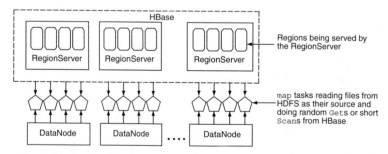

Figure 3.14   Using HBase as a lookup store for the map tasks to do a map-side join

There's a lot more to distributed joins than we've covered in this section. They're so common that Hadoop ships with a contrib JAR called `hadoop-datajoin` to make things easier. You should now have enough context to make good use of it and also take advantage of HBase for other MapReduce optimizations.

3.5   *Putting it all together*

Now you see the full power of Hadoop MapReduce. The JobTracker distributes work across all the TaskTrackers in the cluster according to optimal resource utilization. If any of those nodes fails, another machine is staged and ready to pick up the computation and ensure job success.

Idempotent operations

Hadoop MapReduce assumes your `map` and `reduce` tasks are idempotent. This means the `map` and `reduce` tasks can be run any number of times with the same input and produce the same output state. This allows MapReduce to provide fault tolerance in job execution and also take maximum advantage of cluster processing power. You must take care, then, when performing stateful operations. HBase's `Increment` command is an example of such a stateful operation.

For example, suppose you implement a row-counting MapReduce job that maps over every key in the table and increments a cell value. When the job is run, the JobTracker spawns 100 mappers, each responsible for 1,000 rows. While the job is running, a disk drive fails on one of the TaskTracker nodes. This causes the `map` task to fail, and Hadoop assigns that task to another node. Before failure, 750 of the keys were counted and incremented. When the new instance takes up that task, it starts again at the beginning of the key range. Those 750 rows are counted twice.

Instead of incrementing the counter in the mapper, a better approach is to emit `["count",1]` pairs from each mapper. Failed tasks are recovered, and their output isn't double-counted. Sum the pairs in a reducer, and write out a single value from there. This also avoids an unduly high burden being applied to the single machine hosting the incremented cell.

Another thing to note is a feature called *speculative execution*. When certain tasks are running more slowly than others and resources are available on the cluster, Hadoop schedules extra copies of the task and lets them compete. The moment any one of the copies finishes, it kills the remaining ones. This feature can be enabled/disabled through the Hadoop configuration and should be disabled if the MapReduce jobs are designed to interact with HBase.

This section provides a complete example of consuming HBase from a MapReduce application. Please keep in mind that running MapReduce jobs on an HBase cluster creates a significant burden on the cluster. You don't want to run MapReduce jobs on the same cluster that serves your low-latency queries, at least not when you expect to maintain OLTP-style service-level agreements (SLAs)! Your online access will suffer while the MapReduce jobs run. As food for thought, consider this: don't even run a JobTracker or TaskTrackers on your HBase cluster. Unless you absolutely must, leave the resources consumed by those processes for HBase.

3.5.1 Writing a MapReduce application

HBase is running on top of Hadoop, specifically the HDFS. Data in HBase is partitioned and replicated like any other data in the HDFS. That means running a MapReduce program over data stored in HBase has all the same advantages as a regular MapReduce program. This is why your MapReduce calculation can execute the same HBase scan as the multithreaded example and attain far greater throughput. In the MapReduce application, the scan is executing simultaneously on multiple nodes. This removes the bottleneck of all data moving through a single machine. If you're running MapReduce on the same cluster that's running HBase, it's also taking advantage of any collocation that might be available. Putting it all together, the Shakespearean counting example looks like the following listing.

Listing 3.1   A Shakespearean twit counter

```
package HBaseIA.TwitBase.mapreduce;

//...                                          Import details
                                               omitted
public class CountShakespeare {

  public static class Map
    extends TableMapper<Text, LongWritable> {

    public static enum Counters {ROWS, SHAKESPEAREAN};

    private boolean containsShakespeare(String msg) {
      //...                                     Natural language
    }                                           processing (NLP)
                                                magic happens here
    @Override
    protected void map(
        ImmutableBytesWritable rowkey,
        Result result,
        Context context) {
      byte[] b = result.getColumnLatest(
                      TwitsDAO.TWITS_FAM,
                      TwitsDAO.TWIT_COL).getValue();
      String msg = Bytes.toString(b);
      if (msg != null && !msg.isEmpty())        Counters are a cheap
        context.getCounter(Counters.ROWS).increment(1);   way to collect metrics
      if (containsShakespeare(msg))             in Hadoop jobs
        context.getCounter(Counters.SHAKESPEAREAN).increment(1);
    }
  }

  public static void main(String[] args) throws Exception {
    Configuration conf = HBaseConfiguration.create();
    Job job = new Job(conf, "TwitBase Shakespeare counter");
    job.setJarByClass(CountShakespeare.class);
```

```
      Scan scan = new Scan();
      scan.addColumn(TwitsDAO.TWITS_FAM, TwitsDAO.TWIT_COL);
      TableMapReduceUtil.initTableMapperJob(
        Bytes.toString(TwitsDAO.TABLE_NAME),
        scan,
        Map.class,
        ImmutableBytesWritable.class,
        Result.class,
        job);

      job.setOutputFormatClass(NullOutputFormat.class);
      job.setNumReduceTasks(0);
      System.exit(job.waitForCompletion(true) ? 0 : 1);
  }
}
```

Just like scan executed in multithreaded example

CountShakespeare is pretty simple; it packages a Mapper implementation and a main method. It also takes advantage of the HBase-specific MapReduce helper class TableMapper and the TableMapReduceUtil utility class that we talked about earlier in the chapter. Also notice the lack of a reducer. This example doesn't need to perform additional computation in the reduce phase. Instead, map output is collected via job counters.

3.5.2 *Running a MapReduce application*

Would you like to see what it looks like to run a MapReduce job? We thought so. Start by populating TwitBase with a little data. These two commands load 100 users and then load 100 twits for each of those users:

```
$ java -cp target/twitbase-1.0.0.jar \
  HBaseIA.TwitBase.LoadUsers 100
$ java -cp target/twitbase-1.0.0.jar \
  HBaseIA.TwitBase.LoadTwits 100
```

Now that you have some data, you can run the CountShakespeare application over it:

```
$ java -cp target/twitbase-1.0.0.jar \
  HBaseIA.TwitBase.mapreduce.CountShakespeare
...
19:56:42 INFO mapred.JobClient: Running job: job_local_0001
19:56:43 INFO mapred.JobClient:  map 0% reduce 0%
...
19:56:46 INFO mapred.JobClient:  map 100% reduce 0%
19:56:46 INFO mapred.JobClient: Job complete: job_local_0001
19:56:46 INFO mapred.JobClient: Counters: 11
19:56:46 INFO mapred.JobClient: CountShakespeare$Map$Counters
19:56:46 INFO mapred.JobClient:     ROWS=9695
19:56:46 INFO mapred.JobClient:     SHAKESPEAREAN=4743
...
```

According to our proprietary algorithm for Shakespearean reference analysis, just under 50% of the data alludes to Shakespeare!

Counters are fun and all, but what about writing back to HBase? We've developed a similar algorithm specifically for detecting references to *Hamlet*. The mapper is similar

to the Shakespearean example, except that its [k2,v2] output types are [Immutable-
BytesWritable,Put]—basically, HBase rowkey and an instance of the Put command
you learned in the previous chapter. Here's the reducer code:

```
public static class Reduce
    extends TableReducer<
            ImmutableBytesWritable,
            Put,
            ImmutableBytesWritable> {

    @Override
    protected void reduce(
        ImmutableBytesWritable rowkey,
        Iterable<Put> values,
        Context context) {
      Iterator<Put> i = values.iterator();
      if (i.hasNext()) {
        context.write(rowkey, i.next());
      }
    }
  }
}
```

There's not much to it. The reducer implementation accepts [k2,{v2}], the rowkey
and a list of Puts as input. In this case, each Put is setting the info:hamlet_tag column to true. A Put need only be executed once for each user, so only the first is emitted to the output context object. [k3,v3] tuples produced are also of type
[ImmutableBytesWritable,Put]. You let the Hadoop machinery handle execution of
the Puts to keep the reduce implementation idempotent.

3.6   *Availability and reliability at scale*

You'll often hear the terms *scalable, available,* and *reliable* in the context of distributed
systems. In our opinion, these aren't absolute, definite qualities of any system, but a
set of parameters that can have varied values. In other words, different systems scale to
different sizes and are available and reliable in certain scenarios but not others. These
properties are a function of the architectural choices that the systems make. This takes
us into the domain of the CAP theorem,[2] which always makes for an interesting discussion and a fascinating read.[3] Different people have their own views about it,[4] and we'd
prefer not to go into a lot of detail and get academic about what the CAP theorem
means for various database systems. Let's instead jump into understanding what *availability* and *reliability* mean in the context of HBase and how it achieves them. These
properties are useful to understand from the point of view of building your application so that you as an application developer can understand what you can expect from
HBase as a back-end data store and how that affects your SLAs.

---

[2] CAP theorem: http://en.wikipedia.org/wiki/CAP_theorem.
[3] Read more on the CAP theorem in Henry Robinson's "CAP Confusion: Problems with 'partition tolerance,'"
     Cloudera, http://mng.bz/4673.
[4] Learn how the CAP theorem is incomplete in Daniel Abadi's "Problems with CAP, and Yahoo's little known
     NoSQL system," DBMS Musings, http://mng.bz/j01r.

AVAILABILITY

Availability in the context of HBase can be defined as the ability of the system to handle failures. The most common failures cause one or more nodes in the HBase cluster to fall off the cluster and stop serving requests. This could be because of hardware on the node failing or the software acting up for some reason. Any such failure can be considered a network partition between that node and the rest of the cluster.

When a RegionServer becomes unreachable for some reason, the data it was serving needs to instead be served by some other RegionServer. HBase can do that and keep its availability high. But if there is a network partition and the HBase masters are separated from the cluster or the ZooKeepers are separated from the cluster, the slaves can't do much on their own. This goes back to what we said earlier: availability is best defined by the kind of failures a system can handle and the kind it can't. It isn't a binary property, but instead one with various degrees.

Higher availability can be achieved through defensive deployment schemes. For instance, if you have multiple masters, keep them in different racks. Deployment is covered in detail in chapter 10.

RELIABILITY AND DURABILITY

Reliability is a general term used in the context of a database system and can be thought of as a combination of data durability and performance guarantees in most cases. For the purpose of this section, let's examine the data durability aspect of HBase. Data durability, as you can imagine, is important when you're building applications atop a database. /dev/null has the fastest write performance, but you can't do much with the data once you've written it to /dev/null. HBase, on the other hand, has certain guarantees in terms of data durability by virtue of the system architecture.

3.6.1 *HDFS as the underlying storage*

HBase assumes two properties of the underlying storage that help it achieve the availability and reliability it offers to its clients.

SINGLE NAMESPACE

HBase stores its data on a single file system. It assumes all the RegionServers have access to that file system across the entire cluster. The file system exposes a single namespace to all the RegionServers in the cluster. The data visible to and written by one RegionServer is available to all other RegionServers. This allows HBase to make availability guarantees. If a RegionServer goes down, any other RegionServer can read the data from the underlying file system and start serving the regions that the first RegionServer was serving (figure 3.15).

At this point, you may be thinking that you could have a network-attached storage (NAS) that was mounted on all the servers and store the data on that. That's theoretically doable, but there are implications to every design and implementation choice. Having a NAS that all the servers read/write to means your disk I/O will be bottlenecked by the interlink between the cluster and the NAS. You can have fat interlinks, but they will still limit the amount you can scale to. HBase made a design choice to use

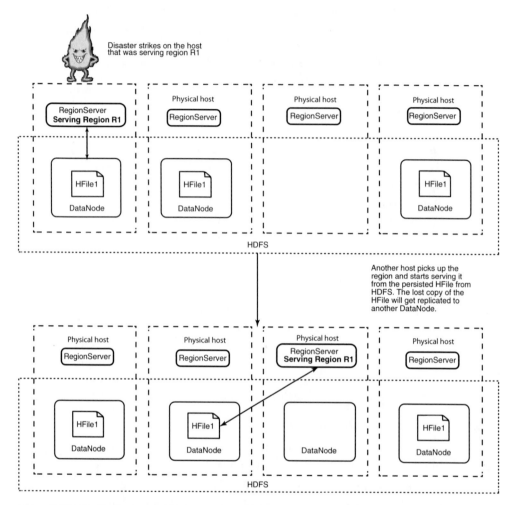

Figure 3.15   If a RegionServer fails for some reason (such as a Java process dying or the entire physical node catching fire), a different RegionServer picks up the regions the first one was serving and begins serving them. This is enabled by the fact that HDFS provides a single namespace to all the RegionServers, and any of them can access the persisted files from any other.

distributed file systems instead and was built tightly coupled with HDFS. HDFS provides HBase with a single namespace, and the DataNodes and RegionServers are collocated in most clusters. Collocating these two processes helps in that RegionServers can read and write to the local DataNode, thereby saving network I/O whenever possible. There is still network I/O, but this optimization reduces the costs.

You're currently using a standalone HBase instance for the TwitBase application. Standalone HBase isn't backed by HDFS. It's writing all data onto the local file system. Chapter 9 goes into details of deploying HBase in a fully distributed manner, backed by HDFS. When you do that, you'll configure HBase to write to HDFS in a prespecified location, which is configured by the parameter `hbase.rootdir`. In standalone mode, this is pointing to the default value, `file:///tmp/hbase-${user.name}/hbase`.

RELIABILITY AND FAILURE RESISTANCE

HBase assumes that the data it persists on the underlying storage system will be accessible even in the face of failures. If a server running the RegionServer goes down, other RegionServers should be able to take up the regions that were assigned to that server and begin serving requests. The assumption is that the server going down won't cause data loss on the underlying storage. A distributed file system like HDFS achieves this property by replicating the data and keeping multiple copies of it. At the same time, the performance of the underlying storage should not be impacted greatly by the loss of a small percentage of its member servers.

Theoretically, HBase could run on top of any file system that provides these properties. But HBase is tightly coupled with HDFS and has been during the course of its development. Apart from being able to withstand failures, HDFS provides certain write semantics that HBase uses to provide durability guarantees for every byte you write to it.

3.7   *Summary*

We covered quite a bit of ground this chapter, much of if at an elementary level. There's a lot more going on in Hadoop than we can cover with a single chapter. You should now have a basic understanding of Hadoop and how HBase uses it. In practice, this relationship with Hadoop provides an HBase deployment with many advantages. Here's an overview of what we discussed.

HBase is a database built on Hadoop. It depends on Hadoop for both *data access* and *data reliability*. Whereas HBase is an *online* system driven by *low latency*, Hadoop is an *offline* system optimized for *throughput*. These complementary concerns make for a powerful, flexible data platform for building horizontally scalable data applications.

Hadoop MapReduce is a distributed computation framework providing data access. It's a *fault-tolerant*, *batch-oriented* computing model. MapReduce programs are written by composing `map` and `reduce` operations into *Jobs*. Individual *tasks* are assumed to be *idempotent*. MapReduce takes advantage of the HDFS by assigning tasks to blocks on the file system and *distributing the computation to the data*. This allows for *highly parallel* programs with minimal distribution overhead.

HBase is designed for MapReduce interaction; it provides a `TableMapper` and a `TableReducer` to ease implementation of MapReduce applications. The `TableMapper` allows your MapReduce application to easily read data directly out of HBase. The `TableReducer` makes it easy to write data back to HBase from MapReduce. It's also possible to interact with the HBase key-value API from within the Map and Reduce Steps. This is helpful for situations where all your tasks need random access to the same data. It's commonly used for implementing distributed map-side joins.

If you're curious to learn more about how Hadoop works or investigate additional techniques for MapReduce, *Hadoop: The Definitive Guide* by Tom White (O'Reilly, 2009) and *Hadoop in Action* by Chuck Lam (Manning, 2010) are both great references.

Part 2

Advanced concepts

Wth the basics covered, part 2 explores more advanced topics. Chapter 4 covers, in detail, HBase schema design. It continues the example application established in chapter 2 and provides insight into how to model data in HBase for your application. This chapter will help you understand the trade-offs you'll make in your schema design choices. Chapter 5 shows how to build and use coprocessors, an advanced technique for pushing computational logic into your HBase cluster, close to where your data is stored. Chapter 6 explains how to interact with HBase with alternative client libraries, on and off the JVM. With this part of the book under your belt, you'll be ready to make effective use of HBase in your application and also build with HBase in non-Java applications.

HBase table design

This chapter covers

- HBase schema design concepts
- Mapping relational modeling knowledge to the HBase world
- Advanced table definition parameters
- HBase Filters to optimize read performance

In the first three chapters, you learned about interacting with HBase using the Java API and built a sample application to learn how to do so. As a part of building our TwitBase, you created tables in your HBase instance to store data in. The table definition was given to you, and you created the tables without going into the details of why you created them the way you did. In other words, we didn't talk about how many column families to have, how many columns to have in a column family, what data should go into the column names and what should go into the cells, and so on. This chapter introduces you to HBase schema design and covers things that you should think about when designing schemas and rowkeys in HBase. HBase schemas are different from relational database schemas. They're much simpler and provide a few things you can play with. Sometimes we refer to HBase as *schema-less* as well. But the simplicity gives you the ability to tweak it in order to extract optimal performance for your application's access patterns. Some schemas may be great for writes, but when reading the same data back, these schemas may not perform as well, or vice versa.

To learn about designing HBase schemas, you'll continue to build on the TwitBase application and introduce new features into it. Until now, TwitBase was pretty basic. You had users and twits. That's not nearly enough functionality for an application and won't drive user traffic unless users have the ability to be social and read other users' twits. Users want to follow other users, so let's build tables for that purpose.

> **NOTE** This chapter continues the approach that the book has followed so far of using a running example to introduce and explain concepts. You'll start with a simple schema design and iteratively improve it, and we'll introduce important concepts along the way.

4.1   How to approach schema design

TwitBase users would like to follow twits from other users, as you can imagine. To provide that ability, the first step is to maintain a list of everyone a given user follows. For instance, TheFakeMT follows both TheRealMT and HRogers. To populate all the twits that TheFakeMT should see when they log in, you begin by looking at the list {TheRealMT, HRogers} and reading the twits for each user in that list. This information needs to be persisted in an HBase table.

Let's start thinking about the schema for that table. When we say *schema*, we include the following considerations:

- How many column families should the table have?
- What data goes into what column family?
- How many columns should be in each column family?
- What should the column names be? Although column names don't have to be defined on table creation, you need to know them when you write or read data.
- What information should go into the cells?
- How many versions should be stored for each cell?
- What should the rowkey structure be, and what should it contain?

Some people may argue that a schema is only what you define up front on table creation. Others may argue that all the points in this list are part of schema design. Those are good discussions to engage in. NoSQL as a domain is relatively new, and clear definitions of terms are emerging as we speak. We feel it's important to encompass all of these points into a broad schema design topic because the schema impacts the structure of your table and how you read or write to it. That is what you'll do next.

4.1.1   Modeling for the questions

Let's return to the table, which will store data about what users a particular user follows. Access to this table follows two patterns: read the entire list of users, and query for the presence of a specific user in that list, "Does TheFakeMT follow TheRealMT?" That's a relevant question, given that TheFakeMT wants to know everything possible about the real one. In that case, you'd be interested in checking whether TheRealMT exists in the list of users TheFakeMT follows. A possible solution is to have a row for each user, with the user ID being the rowkey and each column representing a user they follow.

Remember column families? So far, you've used only a single column family because you haven't needed anything more. But what about this table? All users in the list of users TheFakeMT follows have an equal chance of being checked for existence, and you can't differentiate between them in terms of access patterns. You can't assume that one member of this list is accessed more often than any of the others. This bit of reasoning allows you to conclude that the entire list of followed users should go into the same column family.

How did we come to that conclusion? All data for a given column family goes into a single store on HDFS. A store may consist of multiple HFiles, but ideally, on compaction, you achieve a single HFile. Columns in a column family are all stored together on disk, and that property can be used to isolate columns with different access patterns by putting them in different column families. This is also why HBase is called a *column-family-oriented store*. In the table you're building, you don't need to isolate certain users being followed from others. At least, that's the way it seems right now. To store these relationships, you can create a new table called `follows` that looks like figure 4.1.

You can create this table using the shell or the Java client, as you learned in chapter 2. Let's look at it in a little more depth and make sure you have the optimal table design. Keep in mind that once the table is created, changing any of its column families will require that the table be taken offline.

Online migrations

HBase 0.92 has an experimental feature to do online schema migrations, which means you don't need to take tables offline to change column families. We don't recommend doing this as a regular practice. Designing your tables well up front goes a long way.

With a table design as shown in figure 4.1, a table with data looks like figure 4.2.

Now you need to validate that this table satisfies your requirements. To do so, it's important to define the access patterns—that is, how data in your HBase tables is accessed by the application. Ideally, you should do that as early in the process as possible.

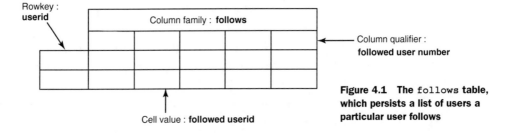

Figure 4.1 The `follows` table, which persists a list of users a particular user follows

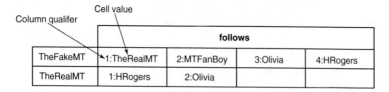

	\n*Cell value* Column qualifer			
	follows			
TheFakeMT	1:TheRealMT	2:MTFanBoy	3:Olivia	4:HRogers
TheRealMT	1:HRogers	2:Olivia		

Figure 4.2 The `follows` table with sample data. `1:TheRealMT` represents a cell in the column family `follows` with the column qualifier `1` and the value `TheRealMT`. The fake Mark Twain wants to know everything he can about the real one. He's following not only the real Mark Twain but also his fans, his wife, and his friends. Cheeky, huh? The real Mark Twain, on the other hand, keeps it simple and only wants to get twits from his dear friend and his wife.

> **NOTE** Define access patterns as early in the design process as possible so they can inform your design decisions.

You aren't too far along, so let's do it now. To define the access patterns, a good first step is to define the questions you want to answer using this table. For instance, in TwitBase, you want this table to answer, "Whom does TheFakeMT follow?" Thinking further along those lines, you can come up with the following questions:

1 Whom does TheFakeMT follow?
2 Does TheFakeMT follow TheRealMT?
3 Who follows TheFakeMT?
4 Does TheRealMT follow TheFakeMT?

Questions 2 and 4 are basically the same; just the names have swapped places. That leaves you with the first three questions. That's a great starting point!

"Whom does TheFakeMT follow?" can be answered by a simple `get()` call on the table you just designed. It gives you the entire row, and you can iterate over the list to find the users TheFakeMT follows. The code looks like this:

```
Get g = new Get(Bytes.toBytes("TheFakeMT"));
Result result = followsTable.get(g);
```

The result set returned can be used to answer questions 1 and 2. The entire list returned is the answer to question 1. You can create an array list like this:

```
List<String> followedUsers = new ArrayList<String>();
List<KeyValue> list = result.list();
Iterator<KeyValue> iter = list.iterator();
while(iter.hasNext()) {
    KeyValue kv = iter.next();
    followedUsers.add(Bytes.toString(kv.getValue()));
}
```

Answering question 2 means iterating through the entire list and checking for the existence of TheRealMT. The code is similar to the previous snippet, but instead of creating an array list, you compare at each step:

```
String followedUser = "TheRealMT";
List<KeyValue> list = result.list();
```

```
Iterator<KeyValue> iter = list.iterator();
while(iter.hasNext()) {
    KeyValue kv = iter.next();
    if(followedUser.equals(Bytes.toString(kv.getValue())));
        return true;
}
return false;
```

It doesn't get simpler than that, does it? Let's continue building on this and ensure that your table design is the best you can accomplish and is optimal for all expected access patterns.

4.1.2 Defining requirements: more work up front always pays

You now have a table design that can answer two out of the four questions on the earlier list. You haven't yet ascertained whether it answers the other two questions. Also, you haven't defined your write patterns. The questions so far define the read patterns for the table.

From the perspective of TwitBase, you expect data to be written to HBase when the following things happen:

- A user follows someone
- A user unfollows someone they were following

Let's look at the table and try to find places you can optimize based on these write patterns. One thing that jumps out is the work the client needs to do when a user follows someone new. This requires making an addition to the list of users the user is already following. When TheFakeMT follows one more user, you need to know that the user is number 5 in the list of users TheFakeMT follows. That information isn't available to your client code without asking the HBase table. Also, there is no concept of asking HBase to add a cell to an existing row without specifying the column qualifier. To solve that problem, you have to maintain a counter somewhere. The best place to do that is the same row. In that case, the table now looks like figure 4.3.

The count column gives you the ability to quickly display the number of users anyone is following. You can answer the question "How many people does TheFakeMT follow?" by getting the count column without having to iterate over the entire list. This is good progress! Also notice that you haven't needed to change the table definition so far. That's HBase's schema-less data model at work.

Adding a new user to the list of followed users involves a few steps, as outlined in figure 4.4.

	follows				
TheFakeMT	1:TheRealMT	2:MTFanBoy	3:Olivia	4:HRogers	count:4
TheRealMT	1:HRogers	2:Olivia	count:2		

Figure 4.3 The `follows` table with a counter in each row to keep track of the number of users any given user is following at the moment

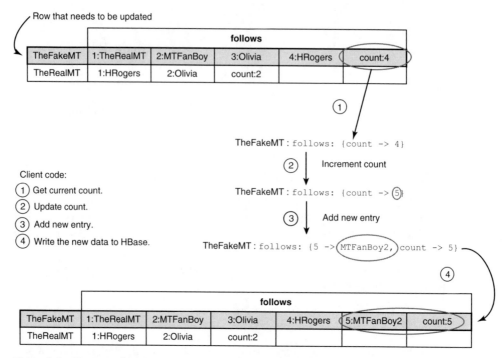

Figure 4.4   Steps required to add a new user to the list of followed users, based on the current table design

Code for adding a new user to the list of followed users looks like this:

```
Get g = new Get(Bytes.toBytes("TheFakeMT"));
g.addColumn(Bytes.toBytes("follows"),
          Bytes.toBytes("count");
Result r = followsTable.get(g);
byte[] count_bytes = r.getValue(Bytes.toBytes("follows"),
                                Bytes.toBytes("count"));
int count = Bytes.toInteger(count_bytes);
count++;
String newUserFolowed = "MTFanBoy2";
Put p = new Put(Bytes.toBytes("TheFakeMT"));
p.add(Bytes.toBytes("follows"),
    Bytes.toBytes(count),
    Bytes.toBytes(newUserFollowed));
p.add(Bytes.toBytes("follows"),
    Bytes.toBytes("count"),
    Bytes.toBytes(count));
followsTable.put(p);
```

Get current count from table

Increment count and put in new entry

As you can see, keeping a count makes the client code complicated. Every time you have to add a user to the list of users A is following, you have to first read back the count from the HBase table, add the next user, and update the count. This process smells a lot like a transaction from the relational database systems you've likely worked with.

follows				
TheFakeMT	TheRealMT:1	MTFanBoy:1	Olivia:1	HRogers:1
TheRealMT	HRogers:1	Olivia:1		

Figure 4.5   Cells now have the followed user's username as the column qualifier and an arbitrary string as the cell value.

Given that HBase doesn't have the concept of transactions, this process has a couple of issues you should be aware of. First, it isn't thread-safe. What if the user decides to follow two different users at the same time, maybe using two different browser windows or different devices? That's not a common occurrence, but a similar effect can happen when the user clicks the Follow button for two different users quickly, one after the other: the threads processing those requests may read back the same count, and one may overwrite the other's work. Second, what if the client thread dies halfway through that process? You'll have to build logic to roll back or repeat the write operation in your client code. That's a complication you'd rather avoid.

The only way you can solve this problem without making the client code complicated is to remove the counter. Again, you can use the schema-less data model to your advantage. One way to do it is to move the followed user ID into the column qualifier. Remember, HBase stores only `byte[]`, and you can have an arbitrary number of columns within a column family. Let's use those properties to your advantage and change the table to look like figure 4.5. You put the followed user's username in the column qualifier instead of their *position* on the list of followed users. The cell value now can be anything. You need something to put there because cells can't be empty, so you can enter the number 1. This is different from how you would design tables in relational systems.

> **TIP** Column qualifiers can be treated as data, just like values. This is different from relational systems, where column names are fixed and need to be defined up front at the time of table creation. The word *column* can be considered a misnomer. HBase tables are multidimensional maps.

The simplicity and flexibility of HBase's schema allows you to make such optimizations without a lot of work but gain significant simplicity in client code or achieve greater performance.

With this new table design, you're back to not having to keep a count, and the client code can use the followed user ID in the column qualifier. That value is always unique, so you'll never run into the problem of overwriting existing information. The code for adding new users to the followed list becomes much simpler:

```
String newUserFollowed = "MTFanBoy2";
Put p = new Put(Bytes.toBytes("TheFakeMT"));
p.add(Bytes.toBytes("follows"),                    New user ID in column
    Bytes.toBytes(newUserFollowed),                qualifier; cell value is I
    Bytes.toBytes(1));
followsTable.put(p);
```

The code for reading back the list changes a little. Instead of reading back the cell values, you now read back the column qualifiers. With this change in the design, you lose the count that was available earlier. Don't worry about it right now; we'll teach you how to implement that functionality in the next chapter.

> **TIP**   HBase doesn't have the concept of cross-row transactions. Avoid designs that require transactional logic in client code, because it leads to a complex client that you have to maintain.

4.1.3 *Modeling for even distribution of data and load*

TwitBase may have some users who follow many people. The implication is that the HBase table you just designed will have variable-length rows. That's not a problem per se. But it affects the read patterns. Think about the question, "Does TheFakeMT follow TheRealMT?" With this table, how can this question be answered? A simple `Get` request specifying TheRealMT in the rowkey and TheFakeMT as the column qualifier will do the trick. This is an extremely fast operation for HBase.

HBase access time complexity

Answering the question "What's a fast operation for HBase?" involves many considerations. Let's first define some variables:

- n = Number of `KeyValue` entries (both the result of `Puts` and the tombstone markers left by `Deletes`) in the table.
- b = Number of blocks in an HFile.
- e = Number of `KeyValue` entries in an average HFile. You can calculate this if you know the row size.
- c = Average number of columns per row.

Note that we're looking at this in the context of a single column family.

You begin by defining the time taken to find the relevant HFile block for a given rowkey. This work happens whether you're doing a `get()` on a single row or looking for the starting key for a scan.

First, the client library has to find the correct RegionServer and region. It takes three fixed operations to get to the right region—lookup ZK, lookup -ROOT-, lookup .META.. This is an O(1)[1] operation.

In a given region, the row can exist in two places in the read path: in the MemStore if it hasn't been flushed to disk yet, or in an HFile if it has been flushed. For the sake of simplicity, we're assuming there is only one HFile and either the entire row is contained in that file or it hasn't been flushed yet, in which case it's in the MemStore.

---

[1]   If you who don't have a computer science background, or if your CS is rusty, this O(n) business is called *asymptotic notation*. It's a way to talk about, in this case, the worst-case runtime complexity of an algorithm. O(n) means the algorithm grows *linearly* with the size of n. O(1) means the algorithm runs in *constant time*, regardless of the size of the input. We're using this notation to talk about the time it takes to access data stored in HBase, but it can also be used to talk about other characteristics of an algorithm, such as its memory footprint. For a primer on asymptotic notation, see http://mng.bz/4GMf.

(continued)

Let's use e as a reasonable proxy for the number of entries in the MemStore at any given time. If the row is in the MemStore, looking it up is O(log e) because the MemStore is implemented as a skip list.[2] If the row has been flushed to disk, you have to find the right HFile block. The block index is ordered, so finding the correct block is a O(log b) operation. Finding the KeyValue objects that make up the row you're looking for is a linear scan inside the block. Once you've found the first KeyValue object, it's a linear scan thereafter to find the rest of them. The scan is O(e/b), assuming that the number of cells in the row all fit into the same block. If not, the scan must access data in multiple sequential blocks, so the operation is dominated by the number of rows read, making it O(c). In other words, the scan is O(max($c,e/b$)).

To sum it up, the cost of getting to a particular row is as follows:

O(1) for region lookup

+ O(log e) to locate the KeyValue in the MemStore if it's in the MemStore or O(1) for region lookup

+ O(log b) to find the correct block in the HFile

+ O(max($c,e/b$)) to find the dominating component of the scan if it has been flushed to disk

When accessing data in HBase, the dominating factor is the time taken to scan the HFile block to get to the relevant KeyValue objects. Having wide rows increases the cost of traversing the entire row during a scan. All of this assumes that you know the rowkey of the row you're looking for.

If you don't know the rowkey, you're scanning an entire range of rows (possibly the entire table) to find the row you care about, and that is O(n). In this case, you no longer benefit from limiting your scan to a few HFile blocks.

We didn't talk about the disk-seek overhead here. If the data read from the HFile is already loaded into the block cache, this sidebar's analysis holds true. If the data needs to be read into the BlockCache from HDFS, the cost of reading the blocks from disk is much greater, and this analysis won't hold much significance, academically speaking.

The take-away is that accessing wider rows is more expensive than accessing smaller ones, because the rowkey is the dominating component of all these indexes. Knowing the rowkey is what gives you all the benefits of how HBase indexes under the hood.

Consider the schema design shown in figure 4.6 for the follows table. Until now, you've been working with a table that's designed to be a *wide table*. In other words, a single row contains lots of columns. The same information can be stored in the form of a *tall table*, which is the new schema in figure 4.6. The KeyValue objects in HFiles store the column family along with it. Keeping to short column family names makes a difference in reducing both disk and network I/O. This optimization also applies to

---

[2] Learn more about skip lists here: http://en.wikipedia.org/wiki/Skip_list.

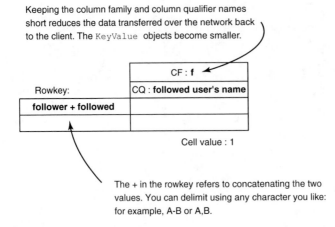

Keeping the column family and column qualifier names short reduces the data transferred over the network back to the client. The `KeyValue` objects become smaller.

Rowkey: follower + followed

CF : f

CQ : followed user's name

Cell value : 1

The + in the rowkey refers to concatenating the two values. You can delimit using any character you like: for example, A-B or A,B.

Figure 4.6   **New schema for the** `follows` **table with the follower as well as followed user IDs in the rowkey. This translates into a single follower-followed relationship per row in the HBase table. This is a tall table instead of a wide table like the previous ones.**

rowkeys, column qualifiers, and even cells! Store compact representations of your data to reduce I/O load.

A table with some sample data is shown in figure 4.7.

This new design for the table makes answering the second question, "Does The-FakeMT follow TheRealMT?" faster than it is with some of the previous designs. You can `get()` on a row with rowkey `TheFakeMT+TheRealMT` and get your answer. There's only one cell in the column family, so you don't need multiple `KeyValues` as in the previous design. In HBase, accessing a single narrow row resident in the BlockCache is the fastest possible read operation.

Answering the first question, "Whom does `TheFakeMT` follow?" becomes an index lookup to the first block with a prefix of `TheFakeMT` followed by a scan on subsequent rows with rowkeys starting with `TheFakeMT`. From an I/O standpoint, you're reading the same amount of data from the RegionServer when scanning those rows as compared to doing a `Get` on a single wide row and iterating over all the cells. Remember the HFile design? *The physical storage for both the table designs mentioned is essentially the same.* The physical indexing is what changed, as we'll discuss a little later.

	f
TheFakeMT+TheRealMT	Mark Twain:1
TheFakeMT+MTFanBoy	Amandeep Khurana:1
TheFakeMT+Olivia	Olivia Clemens:1
TheFakeMT+HRogers	Henry Rogers:1
TheRealMT+Olivia	Olivia Clemens:1
TheRealMT+HRogers	Henry Rogers:1

Figure 4.7   **The** `follows` **table designed as a tall table instead of a wide table. (And Amandeep is the fanboy we've been referring to so far.) Putting the user name in the column qualifier saves you from looking up the users table for the name of the user given an ID. You can simply list names or IDs while looking at relationships just from this table. The downside is that you need to update the name in all the cells if the user updates their name in their profile. This is classic de-normalization.**

The code for getting the list of followed users now looks like this:

```
Scan s = new Scan();
s.addFamily(Bytes.toBytes("f"));
s.setStartRow(Bytes.toBytes("TheFakeMT"));
s.setStopRow(Bytes.toBytes("TheFakeMT" + 1));
ResultScanner results = followsTable.getScanner(s);
List<String> followedList = new ArrayList<String>();
for(Result r : results) {
    String relation = Bytes.toString(r.getRow());
    String followedUser = relation.split("+")[1];
    followedList.add(followedUser);
}
```

Create new scanner to scan all relations for TheFakeMT. Start at TheFakeMT and stop at TheFakeMT+1. Includes all rows where TheFakeMT is first part of key.

Extract second half of rowkey. Code assumes + as delimiter.

The code for checking whether a relationship exists between two users looks like this:

```
Get g = new Get(Bytes.toBytes("TheFakeMT" + "+" + "TheRealMT"));
g.addFamily(Bytes.toBytes("f"));
Result r = followsTable.get(g);
if(!r.isEmpty())
    return true;
```

Get row for relation between TheFakeMT and TheRealMT

If row returned isn't empty, it means the relation exists.

To add to the list of followed users, you do a simple put() as follows:

```
Put p = new Put(Bytes.toBytes("TheFakeMT" + "+" + "TheRealMT"));
p.add(Bytes.toBytes("f"), Bytes.toBytes(newFollowedUser), Bytes.toBytes(1));
followsTable.put(p);
```

TIP The get() API call is internally implemented as a scan() operation scanning over a single row.

Tall tables aren't always the answer to table design. To gain the performance benefits of a tall table, you trade off atomicity for certain operations. In the earlier design, you could update the followed list for any user with a single Put operation on a row. Put operations at a row level are atomic. In the second design, you give up the ability to do that. In this case, it's okay because your application doesn't require that. But other use cases may need that atomicity, in which case wide tables make more sense.

NOTE You give up atomicity in order to gain performance benefits that come with a tall table.

A good question to ask here is, why put the user ID in the column qualifier? It isn't necessary to do that. Think about TwitBase and what users may be doing that translates into reading this table. Either they're asking for a list of all the people they follow or they're looking at someone's profile to see if they're following that user. Either way, the user ID isn't enough. The user's real name is more important. That information is stored in the users table at this point. In order to populate the real name for the end user, you have to fetch it from the user table for each row in the follows table that you'll return to the user. Unlike in a relational database system, where you do a join and can accomplish all this in a single SQL query, here you have to explicitly make your client read from two different tables to populate all the information you need. To simplify, you could *de-normalize*[3] and put the username in the column qualifier, or, for that matter, in the cell in this table. But it's not hunky-dory if you do this. This approach makes maintaining consistency across the users table and the follows table a little challenging. That's a trade-off you may or may not choose to make. The intention of doing it here is to expose you to the idea of de-normalizing in HBase and the reasoning behind it. If you expect your users to change their names frequently, de-normalizing may not be a good idea. We're assuming that their names are relatively static content and de-normalizing won't cost you much.

> **TIP**   De-normalize all you can without adding complexity to your client code. As of today, HBase doesn't provide the features that make normalization easy to do.

You can use another optimization to simplify things. In the twits table, you used MD5 as the rowkey. This gave you a fixed-length rowkey. Using hashed keys has other benefits, too. Instead of having userid1+userid2 as the rowkey in the follows table, you can instead have MD5(userid1)MD5(userid2) and do away with the + delimiter. This gives you two benefits. First, your rowkeys are all of consistent length, giving you more predictability in terms of read and write performance. That's probably not a huge win if you put a limit on the user ID length. The other benefit is that you don't need the delimiter any more; it becomes simpler to calculate start and stop rows for the scans.

Using hashed keys also buys you a more uniform distribution of data across regions. In the example you've been working with so far, distribution isn't a problem. It becomes a problem when your access patterns are skewed inherently and you're at risk of *hot-spotting* on a few regions rather than spreading the load across the entire cluster.

> **Hot-spotting**
>
> Hot-spotting in the context of HBase means there is a heavy concentration of load on a small subset of regions. This is undesirable because the load isn't distributed across the entire cluster. Overall performance becomes bottlenecked by the few hosts that are serving those regions and thereby doing a majority of the work.

For instance, if you're inserting time-series data, and the timestamp is at the beginning of the rowkey, you're always appending to the bottom of the table because the timestamp for any write is always greater than any timestamp that has already been written. So, you'll hot-spot on the *last* region of the table.

If you MD5 the timestamp and use that as the rowkey, you achieve an even distribution across all regions, but you lose the ordering in the data. In other words, you can no longer scan a small time range. You need either to read specific timestamps or scan

---

[3]   If this is the first time you've come across the term *de-normalization*, it will be useful to read up on it before you proceed. Essentially, you're increasing the replication of data, paying more in storage and update costs, to reduce the number of accesses required to answer a question and speed overall access times. A good place to start is http://en.wikipedia.org/wiki/Denormalization.

the entire table. You haven't lost getting access to records, though, because your clients can MD5 the timestamp before making the request.

Hashing and MD5[4]

Hash functions can be defined as functions that map a large value of variable length to a smaller value of fixed length. There are various types of hashing algorithms, and MD5 is one of them. MD5 produces a 128-bit (16-byte) hash value for any data you hash. It's a popular hash function that you're likely to come across in various places; you probably already have.

Hashing is an important technique in HBase specifically and in information-retrieval implementations in general. Covering these algorithms in detail is beyond the scope of this text. If you want to learn more about the guts of hashing and the MD5 algorithm, we recommend finding an online resource.

The `follows` table looks like figure 4.8 if you use MD5s in the rowkeys. By storing MD5s of the user IDs in the rowkey, you can't get back the user IDs when you read back. When you want the list of users Mark Twain follows, you get the MD5s of the user IDs instead of the user IDs. But the name of the user is stored in the column qualifier because you want to store that information as well. To make the user ID accessible, you can put it into the column qualifier and the name into the cell value.

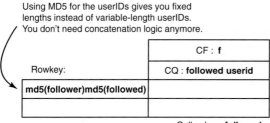

Using MD5 for the userIDs gives you fixed lengths instead of variable-length userIDs. You don't need concatenation logic anymore.

Rowkey:

	CF : f
	CQ : **followed userid**
md5(follower)md5(followed)	

Cell value : **followed users name**

Figure 4.8   Using MD5s as part of rowkeys to achieve fixed lengths and better distribution

The table looks like figure 4.9 with data in it.

	f
MD5(TheFakeMT) MD5(TheRealMT)	TheRealMT:Mark Twain
MD5(TheFakeMT) MD5(MTFanBoy)	MTFanBoy:Amandeep Khurana
MD5(TheFakeMT) MD5(Olivia)	Olivia:Olivia Clemens
MD5(TheFakeMT) MD5(HRogers)	HRogers:Henry Rogers
MD5(TheRealMT) MD5(Olivia)	Olivia:Olivia Clemens
MD5(TheRealMT) MD5(HRogers)	HRogers:Henry Rogers

Figure 4.9   Using MD5 in the rowkey lets you get rid of the + delimiter that you needed so far. The rowkeys now consist of fixed-length portions, with each user ID being 16 bytes.

---

[4]   Message-Digest Algorithm: http://en.wikipedia.org/wiki/MD5.

4.1.4 *Targeted data access*

At this point, you may wonder what kind of indexing is taking place in HBase. We've talked about it in the last two chapters, but it becomes important when thinking about your table designs. The tall table versus wide table discussion is fundamentally a discussion of what needs to be indexed and what doesn't. Putting more information into the rowkey gives you the ability to answer some questions in constant time. Remember the read path and block index from chapter 2? That's what's at play here, enabling you to get to the right row quickly.

Only the keys (the `Key` part of the `KeyValue` object, consisting of the rowkey, column qualifier, and timestamp) are indexed in HBase tables. Think of it as the primary key in a relational database system, but you can't change the column that forms the primary key, and the key is a compound of three data elements (rowkey, column qualifier, and timestamp). *The only way to access a particular row is through the rowkey.* Indexing the qualifier and timestamp lets you skip to the right column without scanning all the previous columns in that row. The `KeyValue` object that you get back is basically a row from the HFile, as shown in figure 4.10.

There are two ways to retrieve data from a table: `Get` and `Scan`. If you want a single row, you use a `Get` call, in which case you *have to* provide the rowkey. If you want to execute a `Scan`, you can choose to provide the start and stop rowkeys if you know them, and limit the number of rows the scanner object will scan.

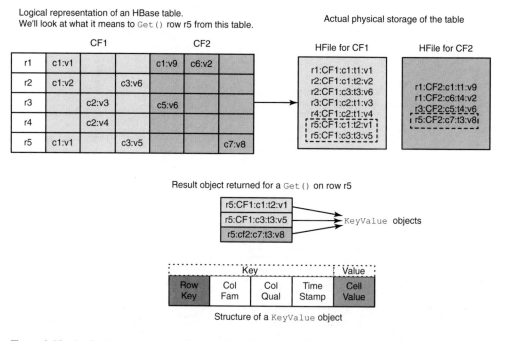

Figure 4.10   Logical to physical translation of an HBase table. The `KeyValue` object represents a single entry in the HFile. The figure shows the result of executing `get(r5)` on the table to retrieve row `r5`.

	Rowkey	Col fam	Col qual	Time stamp
		Key		
Limit rows	✓	X	X	X
Limit HFiles	✓	✓	X	✓
Limit disk I/O	✓	✓	X	✓
Limit network I/O	✓	✓	✓	✓

Figure 4.11 Depending on what part of the key you specify, you can limit the amount of data you read off the disk or transfer over the network. Specifying the rowkey lets you read just the exact row you need. But the server returns the entire row to the client. Specifying the column family lets you further specify what part of the row to read, thereby allowing for reading only a subset of the HFiles if the row spans multiple families. Further specifying the column qualifier and timestamp lets you save on the number of columns returned to the client, thereby saving on network I/O.

When you execute a Get, you can skip to the exact block that contains the row you're looking for. From there, it scans the block to find the relevant KeyValue objects that form the row. In the Get object, you can also specify the column family and the column qualifiers if you want. By specifying the column family, you can limit the client to accessing only the HFiles for the specified column families. Specifying the column qualifier doesn't play a role in limiting the HFiles that are read off the disk, but it does limit what's sent back over the wire. If multiple HFiles exist for a column family on a given region, all of them are accessed to find the components of the row you specify in the Get call. This access is regardless of how many HFiles contain data relevant to the request. Being as specific as possible in your Get is useful, though, so you don't transfer unnecessary data across the wire to the client. The only cost is potential disk I/O on the RegionServer. If you specify timestamps in your Get object, you can avoid reading HFiles that are older than that timestamp. Figure 4.11 illustrates this in a simple table.

You can use this information to inform your table design. Putting data into the cell value occupies the same amount of storage space as putting it into the column qualifier or the rowkey. But you can possibly achieve better performance by moving it up from the cell to the rowkey. The downside to putting more in the rowkey is a bigger block index, given that the keys are the only bits that go into the index.

You've learned quite a few things so far, and we'll continue to build on them in the rest of the chapter. Let's do a quick recap before we proceed:

- HBase tables are flexible, and you can store anything in the form of byte[].
- Store everything with similar access patterns in the same column family.
- Indexing is done on the Key portion of the KeyValue objects, consisting of the rowkey, qualifier, and timestamp in that order. Use it to your advantage.
- Tall tables can potentially allow you to move toward O(1) operations, but you trade atomicity.
- De-normalizing is the way to go when designing HBase schemas.

- Think how you can accomplish your access patterns in single API calls rather than multiple API calls. HBase doesn't have cross-row transactions, and you want to avoid building that logic in your client code.
- Hashing allows for fixed-length keys and better distribution but takes away ordering.
- Column qualifiers can be used to store data, just like cells.
- The length of column qualifiers impacts the storage footprint because you can put data in them. It also affects the disk and network I/O cost when the data is accessed. Be concise.
- The length of the column family name impacts the size of data sent over the wire to the client (in `KeyValue` objects). Be concise.

Having worked through an example table design process and learned a bunch of concepts, let's solidify some of the core ideas and look at how you can use them while designing HBase tables.

4.2   *De-normalization is the word in HBase land*

One of the key concepts when designing HBase tables is de-normalization. We'll explore it in detail in this section. So far, you've looked at maintaining a list of the users an individual user follows. When a TwitBase user logs in to their account and wants to see twits from the people they follow, your application fetches the list of followed users and their twits, returning that information. This process can take time as the number of users in the system grows. Moreover, if a user is being followed by lots of users, their twits are accessed every time a follower logs in. The region hosting the popular user's twits is constantly answering requests because you've created a read hot spot. The way to solve that is to maintain a twit stream for every user in the system and add twits to it the moment one of the users they follow writes a twit.

Think about it. The process for displaying a user's twit stream changes. Earlier, you read the list of users they follow and then combined the latest twits for each of them to form the stream. With this new idea, you'll have a persisted list of twits that make up a user's stream. You're basically de-normalizing your tables.

Normalization and de-normalization

Normalization is a technique in the relational database world where every type of repeating information is put into a table of its own. This has two benefits: you don't have to worry about the complexity of updating all copies of the given data when an update or delete happens; and you reduce the storage footprint by having a single copy instead of multiple copies. The data is recombined at query time using JOIN clauses in SQL statements.

De-normalization is the opposite concept. Data is repeated and stored at multiple locations. This makes querying the data much easier and faster because you no longer need expensive JOIN clauses.

(continued)

From a performance standpoint, normalization optimizes for writes, and de-normalization optimizes for reads.

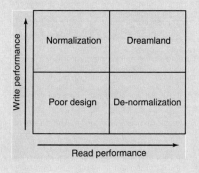

Normalization optimizes the table for writes; you pay the cost of combining data at read time. De-normalization optimizes for reads, but you pay the cost of writing multiple copies at write time.

In this case, you can de-normalize by having another table for twit streams. By doing this, you'll take away the read-scalability issue and solve it by having multiple copies of the data (in this case, a popular user's twits) available for all readers (the users following the popular user).

As of now, you have the `users` table, the `twits` table, and the `follows` table. When a user logs in, you get their twit stream by using the following process:

1 Get a list of people the user follows.
2 Get the twits for each of those followed users.
3 Combine the twits and order them by timestamp, latest first.

You can use a couple of options to de-normalize. You can add another column family to the `users` table and maintain a stream there for each user. Or you can have another table for twit streams. Putting the twit stream in the `users` table isn't ideal because the rowkey design of that table is such that it isn't optimal for what you're trying to do. Keep reading; you'll see this reasoning soon.

The access pattern for the twit stream table consists of two parts:

- Reading a list of twits to show to a given user when the user logs in, and displaying it in reverse order of creation timestamp (latest first)
- Adding to the list of twits for a user when any of the users they follow writes a twit

Another thing to think about is the retention policy for the twit stream. You may want to maintain a stream of the twits from only the last 72 hours, for instance. We talk about Time To Live (TTL) later, as a part of advanced column family configurations.

Using the concepts that we've covered so far, you can see that putting the user ID and the reverse timestamp in the rowkey makes sense. You can easily scan a set of rows in the table to retrieve the twits that form a user's twit stream. You also need the user ID of the person who created each twit. This information can go into the column qualifier. The table looks like figure 4.12.

Reverse timestamp = `Long.MAX_VALUE` - timestamp	info
md5(TheFakeMT) + reverse ts	TheRealMT:First twit
md5(TheFakeMT) + reverse ts	Olivia:Second twit
md5(TheFakeMT) + reverse ts	HRogers:Twit foo
md5(TheFakeMT) + reverse ts	TheRealMT:Twit bar
md5(TheRealMT) + reverse ts	Olivia:Second twit
md5(TheRealMT) + reverse ts	HRogers:Twit foo

Figure 4.12   A table to store twit streams for every user. Reverse timestamps let you sort the twits with the latest twit first. That allows for efficient scanning and retrieval of the n latest twits. Retrieving the latest twits in a user's stream involves scanning the table.

When someone creates a twit, all their followers should get that twit in their respective streams. This can be accomplished using coprocessors, which we talk about in the next chapter. Here, we can talk about what the process is. When a user creates a twit, a list of all their followers is fetched from the relationships table, and the twit is added to each of the followers' streams. To accomplish this, you need to first be able to find the list of users following any given user, which is the inverse of what you've solved so far in your relationships table. In other words, you want to answer the question, "Who follows me?" effectively.

With the current table design, this question can be answered by scanning the entire table and looking for rows where the second half of the rowkey is the user you're interested in. Again, this process is inefficient. In a relational database system, this can be solved by adding an index on the second column and making a slight change to the SQL query. Also keep in mind that the amount of data you would work with is much smaller. What you're trying to accomplish here is the ability to perform these kinds of operations with large volumes of data.

4.3   *Heterogeneous data in the same table*

HBase schemas are flexible, and you'll use that flexibility now to avoid doing scans every time you want a list of followers for a given user. The intent is to expose you to the various ideas involved in designing HBase tables. The relationships table as you have it now has the rowkey as follows:

```
md5(user) + md5(followed user)
```

You can add the relationship information to this key and make it look like this:

```
md5(user) + relationship type + md5(user)
```

That lets you store both kinds of relationships in the same table: *following* as well as *followed by*. Answering the questions you've been working with so far now involves checking for the relationship information from the key. When you're accessing all the followers for a particular user or all the users a particular user is following, you'll do scans over a set of rows. When you're looking for a list of users for the first case, you want to avoid having to read information for the other case. In other words, when you're looking for a list of followers for a user, you don't want a list of users that the user follows in the dataset returned to your client application. You can accomplish this by specifying the start and end keys for the scan.

Let's look at another possible key structure: putting the relationship information in the first part of the key. The new key looks like this:

```
relationship type + md5(user) + md5(user)
```

Think about how the data is distributed across the RegionServers now. Everything for a particular type of relationship is collocated. If you're querying for a list of followers more often than the followed list, the load isn't well distributed across the various regions. That is the downside of this key design and the challenge in storing heterogeneous data in the same table.

> **TIP** Isolate different access patterns as much as possible.

The way to improve the load distribution in this case is to have separate tables for the two types of relationships you want to store. You can create a table called `followedBy` with the same design as the `follows` table. By doing that, you avoid putting the relationship type information in the key. This allows for better load distribution across the cluster.

One of the challenges we haven't addressed yet is keeping the two relationship entries consistent. When Mark Twain decides to follow his fanboy, two entries need to be made in the tables: one in the `follows` table and the other in the `followedBy` table. Given that HBase doesn't allow inter-table or inter-row transactions, the client application writing these entries has to ensure that both rows are written. Failures happen all the time, and it will make the client application complicated if you try to implement transactional logic there. In an ideal world, the underlying database system should handle this for you; but design decisions are different at scale, and this isn't a solved problem in the field of distributed systems at this point.

4.4 Rowkey design strategies

By now, you may have seen a pattern in the design process you went through to come up with the two tables to store relationship information. The thing you've been tweaking is the rowkey.

> **TIP** In designing HBase tables, the rowkey is the single most important thing. You should model keys based on the expected access pattern.

Your rowkeys determine the performance you get while interacting with HBase tables. Two factors govern this behavior: the fact that regions serve a range of rows based on the rowkeys and are responsible for every row that falls in that range, and the fact that HFiles store the rows sorted on disk. These factors are interrelated. HFiles are formed when regions flush the rows they're holding in memory; these rows are already in

```
"TheRealMT",  "info",  "email",     1329088321289,  "samuel@clemens.org"

"TheRealMT",  "info",  "name",      1329088321289,  "Mark Twain"

"TheRealMT",  "info",  "password", 1329088818321,   "abc123"

"TheRealMT",  "info",  "password", 1329088321289,   "Langhorne"
```

HFile for the **info** column family in the `users` table

Figure 4.13   The conceptual structure of an HFile

sorted order and get flushed that way as well. This sorted nature of HBase tables and their underlying storage format allows you to reason about performance based on how you design your keys and what you put in your column qualifiers. To refresh your memory about HFiles, look at figure 4.13; it's the HFile you read about in chapter 2.

Unlike relational databases, where you can index on multiple columns, HBase indexes only on the key; the only way to access data is by using the rowkey. If you don't know the rowkey for the data you want to access, you'll end up scanning a chunk of rows, if not the entire table. There are various techniques to design rowkeys that are optimized for different access patterns, as we'll explore next.

4.5   I/O considerations

The sorted nature of HBase tables can turn out to be a great thing for your application—or not. For instance, when we looked at the twit stream table in the previous section, its sorted nature gave you the ability to quickly scan a small set of rows to find the latest twits that should show up in a user's stream. But the same sorted nature can hurt you when you're trying to write a bunch of time-series data into an HBase table (remember hot-spotting?). If you choose your rowkey to be the timestamp, you'll always be writing to a single region, whichever is responsible for the range in which the timestamp falls. In fact, you'll always be writing to the *end* of a table, because timestamps are monotonically increasing in nature. This not only limits your throughput to what a single region can handle but also puts you at risk of overloading a single machine where other machines in the cluster are sitting idle. The trick is to design your keys such that they're optimized for the access pattern you care about.

4.5.1   Optimized for writes

When you're writing lots of data into HBase tables, you want to optimize by distributing the load across RegionServers. This isn't all that hard to do, but you *may* have to make trade-offs in optimizing your read patterns: for instance, the time-series data example. If your data is such that you use the timestamp as the rowkey, you'll hot-spot on a single region during write time.

In many use cases, you don't need to access the data based on a single timestamp. You'll probably want to run a job that computes aggregates over a time range, and if that's not latency sensitive, you can afford to do a parallel scan across multiple regions to do that for you. The question is, how do you distribute that data across multiple regions? There are a few options to consider, and the answer depends on what kind of information you want your rowkeys to contain.

HASHING

If you're willing to lose the timestamp information from your rowkey (which may be okay in cases where you need to scan the entire table every time you want to do something, or you know the exact key every time you want to read data), making your rowkey a hash of the original data is a possible solution:

```
hash("TheRealMT") -> random byte[]
```

You need to know "TheRealMT" every time you want to access the row that is keyed by the hashed value of this function.

   With time-series data, that generally isn't the case. You most likely don't know the specific timestamp when you access data; you probably have a time range in mind. But there are cases like the `twits` table or the relationship tables you created earlier, where you know the user ID and can calculate the hash to find the correct row. To achieve a good distribution across all regions, you can hash using MD5, SHA-1, or any other hash function of your choice that gives you random distribution.

> ### Collisions
>
> Hashing algorithms have a non-zero probability of collision. Some algorithms have more than others. When working with large datasets, be careful to use a hashing algorithm that has lower probability of collision. For instance, SHA-1 is better than MD5 in that regard and may be a better option in some cases even though it's slightly slower in performance.

The way you use your hash function is also important. The relationship tables you built earlier in this chapter use MD5 hashes of the user IDs, but you can easily regenerate those when you're looking for a particular user's information. But note that you're concatenating the MD5 hashes of two user IDs (`MD5(user1) + MD5(user2)`) rather than concatenating the user IDs and then hashing the result (`MD5(user1 + user2)`). The reason is that when you want to scan all the relationships for a given user, you pass start and stop rowkeys to your `scanner` object. Doing that when the key is a hash of the combination of the two user IDs isn't possible because you lose the information for the given user ID from that rowkey.

SALTING

Salting is another trick you can have in your tool belt when thinking about rowkeys. Let's consider the same time-series example discussed earlier. Suppose you know the time range at read time and don't want to do full table scans. Hashing the timestamp and making the hash value the rowkey requires full table scans, which is highly inefficient, especially if you have the ability to limit the scan. Making the hash value the rowkey isn't your solution here. You can instead prefix the timestamp with a random number.

For example, you can generate a random salt number by taking the hash code of the timestamp and taking its modulus with some multiple of the number of Region-Servers:

```
int salt = new Integer(new Long(timestamp).hashCode()).shortValue() % <number
    of region servers>
```

This involves taking the salt number and putting it in front of the timestamp to generate your timestamp:

```
byte[] rowkey = Bytes.add(Bytes.toBytes(salt) \
+ Bytes.toBytes("|") + Bytes.toBytes(timestamp));
```

Now your rowkeys are something like the following:

```
0|timestamp1
0|timestamp5
0|timestamp6
1|timestamp2
1|timestamp9
2|timestamp4
2|timestamp8
```

These, as you can imagine, distribute across regions based on the first part of the key, which is the random salt number.

`0|timestamp1`, `0|timestamp5`, and `0|timestamp6` go to one region unless the region splits, in which case it's distributed to two regions. `1|timestamp2` and `1|timestamp9` go to a different region, and `2|timestamp4` and `2|timestamp8` go to the third. Data for consecutive timestamps is distributed across multiple regions.

But not everything is hunky-dory. Reads now involve distributing the scans to all the regions and finding the relevant rows. Because they're no longer stored together, a short scan won't cut it. It's about trade-offs and choosing the ones you need to make in order to have a successful application.

4.5.2 Optimized for reads

Optimizing rowkeys for reads was your focus while designing the twit stream table. The idea was to store the last few twits for a user's stream together so they could be fetched quickly without having to do disk seeks, which are expensive. It's not just the disk seeks but also the fact that if the data is stored together, you have to read a smaller number of HFile blocks into memory to read the dataset you're looking for; data is stored together, and every HFile block you read gives you more information per read than if the data were distributed all over the place. In the twit stream table, you used reverse timestamps (Long.MAX_VALUE - timestamp) and appended it to the user ID to form the rowkey. Now you need to scan from the user ID for the next *n* rows to find the *n* latest twits the user must see. The structure of the rowkey is important here. Putting the user ID first allows you to configure your scan so you can easily define your start rowkey. That's the topic we discuss next.

4.5.3 *Cardinality and rowkey structure*

The structure of the rowkey is of utmost importance. Effective rowkey design isn't just about what goes into the rowkey, but also about where elements are positioned in the rowkey. You've already seen two cases of how the structure impacted read performance in the examples you've been working on.

First was the relationship table design, where you put the relationship type between the two user IDs. It didn't work well because the reads became inefficient. You had to read (at least from the disk) all the information for both types of relationships for any given user even though you only needed information for one kind of relationship. Moving the relationship type information to the front of the key solved that problem and allowed you to read only the data you needed.

Second was the twit stream table, where you put the reverse timestamp as the second part of the key and the user ID as the first. That allowed you to scan based on user IDs and limit the number of rows to fetch. Changing the order there resulted in losing the information about the user ID, and you had to scan a time range for the twits, but that range contained twits for all users with something in that time range.

For the sake of creating a simple example, consider the reverse timestamps to be in the range 1..10. There are three users in the system: TheRealMT, TheFakeMT, and Olivia. If the rowkey contains the user ID as the first part, the rowkeys look like the following (in the order that HBase tables store them):

```
Olivia1
Olivia2
Olivia5
Olivia7
Olivia9
TheFakeMT2
TheFakeMT3
TheFakeMT4
TheFakeMT5
TheFakeMT6
TheRealMT1
TheRealMT2
TheRealMT5
TheRealMT8
```

But if you flip the order of the key and put the reverse timestamp as the first part, the rowkey ordering changes:

```
1Olivia
1TheRealMT
2Olivia
2TheFakeMT
2TheRealMT
3TheFakeMT
4TheFakeMT
5Olivia
5TheFakeMT
5TheRealMT
```

```
6TheFakeMT
7Olivia
8TheRealMT
9Olivia
```

Getting the last *n* twits for any user now involves scanning the entire time range because you can no longer specify the user ID as the start key for the scanner.

Now look back at the time-series data example, where you added a salt as a prefix to the timestamp to form the rowkey. That was done to distribute the load across multiple regions at write time. You had only a few ranges to scan at read time when you were looking for data from a particular time range. This is a classic example of using the placement of the information to achieve distribution across the regions.

> **TIP**   Placement of information in your rowkey is as important as the information you choose to put into it.

We have explored several concepts about HBase table design in this chapter thus far. You may be at a place where you understand everything and are ready to go build your application. Or you may be trying to look at what you just learned through the lens of what you already know in the form of relational database table modeling. The next section is to help you with that.

4.6   *From relational to non-relational*

You've likely used relational database systems while building applications and been involved in the schema design. If that's not the case and you don't have a relational database background, skip this section. Before we go further into this conversation, we need to emphasize the following point: *There is no simple way to map your relational database knowledge to HBase. It's a different paradigm of thinking.*

If you find yourself in a position to migrate from a relational database schema to HBase, our first recommendation is *don't do it* (unless you absolutely have to). As we have said on several occasions, relational databases and HBase are different systems and have different design properties that affect application design. A naïve migration from relational to HBase is tricky. At best, you'll create a complex set of HBase tables to represent what was a much simpler relational schema. At worst, you'll miss important but subtle differences steeped in the relational system's ACID guarantees. Once an application has been built to take advantage of the guarantees provided by a relational database, you're better off starting from scratch and rethinking your tables and how they can serve the same functionality to the application.

Mapping from relational to non-relational isn't a topic that has received much attention so far. There is a notable master's thesis[5] that explores this subject. But we can draw some analogies and try to make the learning process a little easier. In this section, we'll map relational database modeling concepts to what you've learned so far about modeling HBase tables. Things don't necessarily map 1:1, and these concepts are evolving and being defined as the adoption of NoSQL systems increases.

---

[5]   Ian Thomas Varley, "No Relation: The Mixed Blessing of Non-Relational Databases," Master's thesis, http://mng.bz/7avI.

4.6.1 Some basic concepts

Relational database modeling consists of three primary concepts:

- *Entities*—These map to *tables*.
- *Attributes*—These map to *columns*.
- *Relationships*—These map to *foreign-key* relationships.

The mapping of these concepts to HBase is somewhat convoluted.

ENTITIES

A table is just a table. That's probably the most obvious mapping from the relational database world to HBase land. In both relational databases and HBase, the default *container* for an entity is a table, and each row in the table should represent one instance of that entity. A *user* table has one user in each row. This isn't an iron-clad rule, but it's a good place to start. HBase forces you to bend the rules of normalization, so a lot of things that are full tables in a relational database end up being something else in HBase. Soon you'll see what we mean.

ATTRIBUTES

To map attributes to HBase, you must distinguish between (at least) two types:

- *Identifying attribute*—This is the attribute that *uniquely* identifies exactly one instance of an entity (that is, one row). In relational tables, this attribute forms the table's *primary key*. In HBase, this becomes part of the *rowkey*, which, as you saw earlier in the chapter, is the most important thing to get right while designing HBase tables.

  Often an entity is identified by multiple attributes. This maps to the concept of *compound keys* in relational database systems: for instance, when you define relationships. In the HBase world, the identifying attributes make up the rowkey, as you saw in the tall version of the `follows` table. The rowkey was formed by concatenating the user IDs of the users that formed the relationship. HBase doesn't have the concept of compound keys, so both identifying attributes had to be put into the rowkey.

  Using values of fixed length makes life much easier. Variable lengths mean you need delimiters and escaping logic in your client code to figure out the composite attributes that form the key. Fixed length also makes it easier to reason about start and stop keys. A way to achieve fixed length is to hash the individual attributes as you did in the `follows` table.

  NOTE It's common practice to take multiple attributes and make them a part of the rowkey, which is a `byte[]`. Remember, HBase doesn't care about types.

- *Non-identifying attribute*—Non-identifying attributes are easier to map. They basically map to column qualifiers in HBase. For the `users` table that you built earlier in the book, non-identifying attributes were things like the password and the email address. No uniqueness guarantees are required on these attributes.

As explained earlier in this chapter, each key/value (for example, the fact that user
TheRealMT has a state of Missouri) carries its entire set of coordinates around with it:
rowkey, column family name, column qualifier, and timestamp. If you have a relational database table with wide rows (dozens or hundreds of columns), you probably
don't want to store each of those columns as a column in HBase (particularly if most
operations deal with mutating the entire row at a time). Instead, you can serialize all
the values in the row into a single binary *blob* that you store as the value in a single cell.
This takes a lot less disk space, but it has downsides: the values in the row are now
opaque, and you can't use the structure that HBase tables have to offer. When the storage footprint (and hence the disk and network I/O) are important and the access patterns always involve reading entire rows, this approach makes sense.

RELATIONSHIPS

Logical relational models use two main varieties of relationships: one-to-many and
many-to-many. Relational databases model the former directly as *foreign keys* (whether
explicitly enforced by the database as constraints, or implicitly referenced by your
application as join columns in queries) and the latter as *junction tables* (additional
tables where each row represents one instance of a relationship between the two main
tables). There is no direct mapping of these in HBase, and often it comes down to de-
normalizing the data.

The first thing to note is that HBase, not having any built-in joins or constraints,
has little use for explicit relationships. You can just as easily place data that is one-to-
many in nature into HBase tables: one table for users and another for their twits. But
this is only a relationship in that some parts of the row in the former table happen to
correspond to parts of rowkeys in the latter table. HBase knows nothing of this relationship, so it's up to your application to do things with it (if anything). As mentioned
earlier, if the job is to return all the twits for all the users you follow, you can't rely on a
join or subquery to do this, as you can in SQL:

```
SELECT * FROM twit WHERE user_id IN
(SELECT user_id from followees WHERE follower = me)
ORDER BY date DESC limit 10;
```

Instead, you need to write code outside of HBase that iterates over each user and then
does a separate HBase lookup for that user to find their recent twits (or else, as
explained previously, de-normalize copies of the twits for each follower).

As you can see, outside of implicit relationships enforced by some external application, there's no way to physically connect disparate data records in HBase. At least not
yet!

4.6.2 *Nested entities*

One thing that's significantly different about HBase is that the *columns* (also known as
column qualifiers) aren't predefined at design time. They can be anything. And in an
earlier example, an early version of the `follows` table had one row for the user and
one column for each follower (first with an integer counter for the column qualifier,

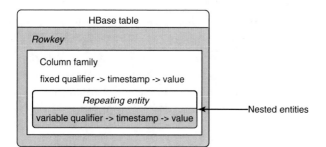

Figure 4.14 Nesting entities in an HBase table

then with the followed username as the qualifier). Note that far from being a *flexible schema row*, this represents the ability to *nest* another entity inside the row of a parent or primary entity (figure 4.14).

Nested entities are another tool in your relational-to-non-relational tool belt: if your tables exist in a parent-child, master-detail, or other strict one-to-many relationship, it's possible to model it in HBase as a single row. The rowkey will correspond to the parent entity. The nested values will contain the children, where each child entity gets one column qualifier into which *their* identifying attributes are stored, with the remainder of the non-identifying attributes stashed into the value (concatenated together, for example). The real HBase row defines the parent record (and can have some *normal* columns, too); records of the child entity are stored as individual columns (figure 4.15).

As an added bonus, in this pattern you *do* get transactional protection around the parent and child records, because in HBase, the row is the boundary of transactional protection. So you can do check and put operations and generally be sure that all your modifications are *wrapped up* and commit or fail together.

HBase table		
Rowkey		
	Key attr 1	byte[8]
	Key attr 2	timestamp
Columns		
	Column 1	string
	Column 2	byte[?]
	Entity	

Figure 4.15 HBase tables can contain regular columns along with nested entities.

You can put in nested entities by using HBase's flexibility because of the way columns are designed. HBase doesn't necessarily have special abilities to store nested entities.

There are some limitations to this, of course. First, this technique only works to one level deep: your nested entities can't themselves have nested entities. You can still have multiple different nested child entities in a single parent, and the column qualifier is their identifying attributes.

Second, it's not as efficient to access an individual value stored as a nested column qualifier inside a row, as compared to accessing a row in another table, as you learned earlier in the chapter.

Still, there are compelling cases where this kind of schema design is appropriate. *If the only way you get at the child entities is via the parent entity, and you'd like to have transactional protection around all children of a parent, this can be the right way to go.*

Things get a little trickier with many-to-many relationships. HBase doesn't help you with optimized joins or any such thing; but you don't get off easy by nesting an entity, because each relationship has two parents. This often translates to de-normalization, as it did in the case of the `follows` table earlier in the chapter. You de-normalized the follower relationship, which is a self-referential many-to-many relationship on users.

These are the basic foundations of mapping your relational modeling knowledge to concepts in the HBase world.

4.6.3 *Some things don't map*

So far, you've mapped a bunch of concepts from the relational world to HBase. We haven't talked about column families yet. It turns out there's no direct analogue in the relational world! Column families exist in HBase as a way for a single row to contain disjoint sets of columns in a way that's physically efficient but can be processed atomically. Unless you use a column-oriented database like Vertica, or special analytical features of the commercial relational databases, this isn't something relational databases do.

COLUMN FAMILIES

One way of thinking about column families is that they model yet another kind of relationship that we didn't talk about previously: the one-to-one relationship, where you have two tables with the same primary key, and each table has either 0 or 1 row with each primary key value. An example is user personal information (email address, birthday, and so on) versus user system preferences (background color, font size, and so on). It's common to model these as two separate physical tables in a relational database, with the thought that because your SQL statements nearly always hit one or the other, but not both, they may perform more optimally if you separate the tables. (This depends heavily on which database you're using and a million other factors, but it does happen.)

In HBase, this is a perfect case for using two column families in a single table. And, likewise, the *nested* entity relationships mentioned earlier can easily be partitioned into separate column families, on the assumption that you'd likely not access both together.

Generally speaking, using multiple column families in HBase is an advanced feature that you should only jump into if you're sure you understand the trade-offs.

(LACK OF) INDEXES

Another common question when migrating from a relational database to HBase is: what about indexes? In relational databases, the ability to easily declare indexes that are automatically maintained by the database engine is one of the most magical and helpful capabilities the software provides, and it's nowhere to be found in HBase. For now, the answer to this question is: tough luck.

You can make some approximation of this feature by de-normalizing data and writing it into multiple tables, but make no mistake: when you move to HBase, you're explicitly giving up the warm, comfortable world where a simple `CREATE INDEX` statement solves big performance problems and gets your boss off your back. In HBase, you have to work through all those questions up front and design your access patterns into your schema.

VERSIONING

There's one final interesting angle on the relationship between relational databases and non-relational ones: the time dimension. If, in your relational schema, there are places where you explicitly store timestamps, these can in many cases be subsumed into the timestamp that's stored in HBase cells. Beware that this is only a long, so if you need more than UNIX-era timestamps held in a 64-bit long, that's all you get in HBase timestamps (thus they're probably not right for storing the granules of time in atomic simulations).

Even better, if your application currently goes out of its way to store historical versions of values in a table (in a pattern often referred to as the *history table* pattern, where you use the same primary key from the main table coupled with a timestamp, in order to preserve all copies of rows over time): rejoice! You can dump that dumb idea and replace it with a single HBase entity, and set the number of versions to keep appropriately in the column family metadata. This is an area that's significantly easier in HBase; the original architects of relational models didn't want to consider time to be a special dimension outside of the relational model, but let's face it: it is.

We hope you now have a good sense of what all those years of studying relational database design bought you in the move to HBase. If you understand the basics of logical modeling and know what schema dimensions are available in HBase, you've got a fighting chance of preserving the intent of your designs.

4.7   *Advanced column family configurations*

HBase has a few advanced features that you can use when designing your tables. These aren't necessarily linked to the schema or the rowkey design but define aspects of the behavior of the tables. In this section, we'll cover these various configuration parameters and how you can use them to your advantage.

4.7.1   *Configurable block size*

The HFile block size can be configured at a column family level. This block is different from HDFS blocks that we talked about earlier. The default value is 65,536 bytes, or 64 KB. The block index stores the starting key of each HFile block. The block size configuration affects the size of the block index size. The smaller the block size, the larger the index, thereby yielding a bigger memory footprint. It gives you better random lookup performance because smaller blocks need to be loaded into memory. If you want good sequential scan performance, it makes sense to load larger chunks of the HFile into the memory at once, which means setting the block size to a larger value. The index size shrinks and you trade random read performance.

You can set the block size during table instantiation like this:

```
hbase(main):002:0> create 'mytable',
{NAME => 'colfam1', BLOCKSIZE => '65536'}
```

4.7.2   Block cache

Often, workloads don't benefit from putting data into a read cache—for instance, if a certain table or column family in a table is only accessed for sequential scans or isn't accessed a lot and you don't care if Gets or Scans take a little longer. In such cases, you can choose to turn off caching for those column families. If you're doing lots of sequential scans, you're churning your cache a lot and possibly polluting it for data that you can benefit by having in the cache. By disabling the cache, you not only save that from happening but also make more cache available for other tables and other column families in the same table.

By default, the block cache is enabled. You can disable it at the time of table creation or by altering the table:

```
hbase(main):002:0> create 'mytable',
{NAME => 'colfam1', BLOCKCACHE => 'false'}
```

4.7.3   Aggressive caching

You can choose some column families to have a higher priority in the block cache (LRU cache). This comes in handy if you expect more random reads on one column family compared to another. This configuration is also done at table-instantiation time:

```
hbase(main):002:0> create 'mytable',
{NAME => 'colfam1', IN_MEMORY => 'true'}
```

The default value for the IN_MEMORY parameter is false. Setting it to true isn't done a lot in practice because no added guarantees are provided except the fact that HBase will try to keep this column family in the block cache more aggressively than the other column families.

4.7.4   Bloom filters

The block index provides an effective way to find blocks of the HFiles that should be read in order to access a particular row. But its effectiveness is limited. The default size of an HFile block is 64 KB, and this size isn't tweaked much.

If you have small rows, indexing just the starting rowkey for an entire block doesn't give you indexing at a fine granularity. For example, if your rows have a storage footprint of 100 bytes, a 64 KB block contains $(64 * 1024)/100 = 655.53 = \sim700$ rows, for which you have only the start row as the indexed bit. The row you're looking for may fall in the range of a particular block but doesn't necessarily have to exist in that block. There can be cases where the row doesn't exist in the table or resides in a different HFile or even the MemStore. In that case, reading the block from disk brings with it I/O overhead and also pollutes the block cache. This impacts performance, especially when you're dealing with a large dataset and lots of concurrent clients trying to read it.

Bloom filters allow you to apply a negative test to the data stored in each block. When a request is made for a specific row, the bloom filter is checked to see whether that row is *not* in the block. The bloom filter says conclusively that the row isn't present, or says that it doesn't know. That's why we say it's a *negative test*. Bloom filters can also be applied to the cells within a row. The same negative test is made when accessing a specific column qualifier.

Bloom filters don't come for free. Storing this additional index layer takes more space. Bloom filters grow with the size of the data they index, so a row-level bloom filter takes up less space than a qualifier-level bloom filter. When space isn't a concern, they allow you to squeeze that much additional performance out of the system.

You enable bloom filters on the column family, like this:

```
hbase(main):007:0> create 'mytable',
{NAME => 'colfam1', BLOOMFILTER => 'ROWCOL'}
```

The default value for the BLOOMFILTER parameter is NONE. A row-level bloom filter is enabled with ROW, and a qualifier-level bloom filter is enabled with ROWCOL. The row-level bloom filter checks for the non-existence of the particular rowkey in the block, and the qualifier-level bloom filter checks for the non-existence of the row and column qualifier combination. The overhead of the ROWCOL bloom filter is higher than that of the ROW bloom filter.

4.7.5 *TTL*

Often, applications have the flexibility or requirement to delete old data from their databases. Traditionally, a lot of flexibility was built in because scaling databases beyond a certain point was hard. In TwitBase, for instance, you wouldn't want to delete any twits generated by users in the course of their use of the application. This is all human-generated data and may turn out to be useful at a future date when you want to do some advanced analytics. But it isn't a requirement to keep all those twits accessible in real time. Twits older than a certain period can be archived into flat files.

HBase lets you configure a TTL in seconds at the column family level. Data older than the specified TTL value is deleted as part of the next major compaction. If you have multiple versions on the same cell, the versions that are older than the configured TTL are deleted. You can disable the TTL, or make it *forever* by setting the value to INT.MAX_VALUE (2147483647), which is the default value. You can set the TTL while creating the table like this:

```
hbase(main):002:0> create 'mytable', {NAME => 'colfam1', TTL => '18000'}
```

This command sets the TTL on the column family colfam1 as 18,000 seconds = 5 hours. Data in colfam1 that is older than 5 hours is deleted during the next major compaction.

4.7.6 *Compression*

HFiles can be compressed and stored on HDFS. This helps by saving on disk I/O and instead paying with a higher CPU utilization for compression and decompression while writing/reading data. Compression is defined as part of the table definition, which is given at the time of table creation or at the time of a schema change. It's recommended that you enable compression on your tables unless you know for a fact that you won't benefit from it. This can be true in cases where either the data can't be compressed much or your servers are CPU bound for some reason.

Various compression codecs are available to be used with HBase, including LZO, Snappy, and GZIP. LZO[6] and Snappy[7] are among the more popular ones. Snappy was released by Google in 2011, and support was added into the Hadoop and HBase projects soon after its release. Prior to this, LZO was the codec of choice. The LZO native libraries that need to be used with Hadoop are GPLv2-licensed and aren't part of any of the HBase or Hadoop distributions; they must be installed separately. Snappy, on the other hand, is BSD-licensed, which makes it easier to bundle with the Hadoop and HBase distributions. LZO and Snappy have comparable compression ratios and encoding/decoding speeds.

You can enable compression on a column family when creating tables like this:

```
hbase(main):002:0> create 'mytable',
{NAME => 'colfam1', COMPRESSION => 'SNAPPY'}
```

Note that data is compressed only on disk. It's kept uncompressed in memory (MemStore or block cache) or while transferring over the network.

It shouldn't happen often, but if you want to change the compression codec being used for a particular column family, doing so is straightforward. You need to alter the table definition and put in the new compression scheme. The HFiles formed as a part of compactions thereafter will all be compressed using the new codec. There is no need to create new tables and copy data over. But you have to ensure that the old codec libraries aren't deleted from the cluster until all the old HFiles are compacted after this change.

4.7.7 *Cell versioning*

HBase by default maintains three versions of each cell. This property is configurable. If you care about only one version, it's recommended that you configure your tables to maintain only one. This way, it doesn't hold multiple versions for cells you may update. Versions are also configurable at a column family level and can be specified at the time of table instantiation:

```
hbase(main):002:0> create 'mytable', {NAME => 'colfam1', VERSIONS => 1}
```

You can specify multiple properties for column families in the same create statement, like this:

```
hbase(main):002:0> create 'mytable',
                   {NAME => 'colfam1', VERSIONS => 1, TTL => '18000'}
```

---

[6] Lempel-Ziv-Oberhumer compression algorithm: www.oberhumer.com/opensource/lzo/.
[7] Snappy compression library, by Google: http://code.google.com/p/snappy/.

You can also specify the minimum versions that should be stored for a column family like this:

```
hbase(main):002:0> create 'mytable', {NAME => 'colfam1', VERSIONS => 5,
                    MIN_VERSIONS => '1'}
```

This comes in handy in conjunction with setting the TTLs on the family. When all versions currently stored are older than the TTL, at least the MIN_VERSION number of last versions is kept around. This ensures that you don't get empty results if you query and the data is older than the TTL.

4.8   *Filtering data*

You've learned so far that HBase has a flexible schema and a simple disk layout, which allows applications to work closer to the disk and network and optimize at that level. Designing effective schemas is one aspect of it, and by now you have a bunch of concepts that you can apply to do that. You can design your keys such that data you access together is placed close on the disk so you can save on disk seeks while reading or writing. Often you have certain criteria, based on which you're reading data that you can use to further optimize access. Filters are a powerful feature that can come in handy in such cases.

We haven't come across many real-life use cases that use filters much; generally the access pattern can be optimized with tweaks to the table designs. But sometimes you've tweaked your table design as much as you can, and optimized it for as many different access patterns as possible. When you still need to reduce the data returned to clients, that's when you reach for a *filter*. Filters are sometimes called *push-down predicates*, allowing you to *push* data-filtering criteria down to the server (see figure 4.16). That logic is applied during reads and affects the data that is returned to the client. This saves network I/O by limiting the data transferred over the network. But data is still

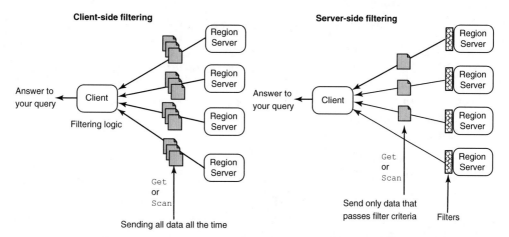

Figure 4.16   Filtering data can be done at the client side by reading data into the client application from the RegionServers and applying the filter logic there; or it can be done at the server side by pushing the filtering logic down to the RegionServers, thereby reducing the amount of data transferred over the network to the clients. Filters can essentially save on network I/O costs, and sometimes even on disk I/O.

read off the disk into the RegionServers, and filters are applied at the RegionServers. The network I/O savings can be significant because you're probably storing a large amount of data in HBase tables, and reading it all into the client application to filter out useful bits is expensive.

HBase provides an API you can use to implement custom filters. A bunch of filters come bundled as well. Filtering can be done based on the rowkeys, which happens the earliest in the read process. Thereafter, filtering can happen based on the `KeyValues` read off the HFiles. A filter has to implement the `Filter` interface that's part of the HBase JAR or extend one of the abstract classes that implement it. We recommend extending the `FilterBase` abstract class so you can avoid having to write boilerplate code. Extending other classes such as `CompareFilter` is also an option and works equally well. The interface has the following methods that are called at various points while reading a row (see figure 4.17 for the order). They're always executed in the sequence described next:

1 This method is the first one to be called and performs filtering based on the rowkey:

```
boolean filterRowKey(byte[] buffer, int offset, int length)
```

Based on the logic in there, it returns `true` if the row is to be filtered out (not included in the result set returned) or `false` if it's to be sent to the client.

2 If the row isn't filtered in the previous step, this method is invoked next for every `KeyValue` object that's part of the current row:

```
ReturnCode filterKeyValue(KeyValue v)
```

This method returns a `ReturnCode`, which is an enum defined as a part of the `Filter` interface. The `ReturnCode` returned determines what happens to that particular `KeyValue` object.

3 This method comes after the `KeyValues` are filtered based on step 2:

```
void filterRow(List<KeyValue> kvs)
```

This method is passed the list of `KeyValue` objects that made it after filtering. Given that this method has access to that list, you can perform any transformations or operations you want to on the elements in the list at this point.

4 At this point, the framework provides another chance to filter out the row if you choose to do so:

```
boolean filterRow()
```

Returning `true` filters out the row under consideration.

5 You can build logic in your filter to stop a scan early. This is the method into which you put that logic:

```
boolean filterAllRemaining()
```

This is handy in cases where you're scanning a bunch of rows, looking for something specific in the rowkey, column qualifier, or cell value, and you don't care about the remaining rows once you've found it. This is the last method to be called in the filtering process.

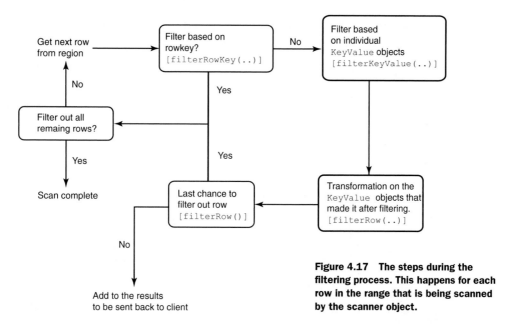

Figure 4.17   The steps during the filtering process. This happens for each row in the range that is being scanned by the scanner object.

Another useful method is reset(). It resets the filter and is called by the server after it has been applied to the entire row.

> **NOTE**   This API is powerful, but we aren't aware of it being used much in applications. In many cases, the requirement for using filters changes if the schema design is changed.

4.8.1   *Implementing a filter*

You've been building TwitBase, and as the application has matured and gained users, you realize that the password strength policy you have in place for new users doesn't ensure passwords that are secure enough. This brings about a new policy, albeit a simple one: TwitBase now requires all users to have a password that's at least four characters long. This will apply to new and old users alike. To enforce this policy on old users, you need to go through the entire list of users and check for password length. In cases where it's less than four characters, the password needs to be expired and a notification sent across informing the user of the new policy and the action they need to take: resetting their password to something that's at least six characters long.

You'll implement this using a custom filter that checks the length of the value in the cell. This filter can be applied to a scan (or to a MapReduce job), which outputs only the users to whom the password change notification has to be sent. The output is the user's name, user ID, and email address. You'll implement this using a scan, but you can easily convert it to a MapReduce job.

The filter you need to build is concerned only about the value in the password cell and not about anything else. The filtering logic goes in the filterKeyValue(..) method, where the password column is checked. If the password is shorter than the minimum required length, the row is included in the results; otherwise it's excluded. The inclusion/exclusion of the row is done by the `filterRow()` method.

Listing 4.1 Implementing a custom filter to check password length

```
public class PasswordStrengthFilter extends FilterBase {          ← Custom filter extending
  private int len;                                                   FilterBase abstract class
  private boolean filterRow = false;

  public PasswordStrengthFilter() {
    super();
  }                                             Constructor
                                                class takes
  public PasswordStrengthFilter(int len) {  ←  length as an     Check length: method
    this.len = len;                              argument        sets filterRow boolean
  }                                                              variable to true if row is
                                                                 to be filtered out, which
  public ReturnCode filterKeyValue(KeyValue v) {        ←        happens if password
    if (Bytes.toString(v.getQualifier()).equals(Bytes.toString(UsersDAO.    length is greater than
        PASS_COL))) {                                            min required length
      if(v.getValueLength() >= len)           Exclude password
        this.filterRow = true;                column from dataset
      return ReturnCode.SKIP;             ←   returned to client
    }
    return ReturnCode.INCLUDE;
  }                                           Tell whether row is
                                              to be filtered out
  public boolean filterRow() {          ←
    return this.filterRow;
  }                                     Reset state of filter
                                        once it's applied to
  public void reset() {            ←    a given row
    this.filterRow = false;
  }

  // Other methods that need implementation. See source code.
}
```

To install custom filters, you have to compile them into a JAR and put them in the HBase classpath so they get picked up by the RegionServers at startup time. In a running system, you have to restart your cluster. The custom filter you just wrote is available in the GitHub project in the package `HBaseIA.TwitBase.filters` by the name `PasswordStrengthFilter`. To compile the JAR, in the top-level directory of the project, do the following:

```
mvn install
cp target/twitbase-1.0.0.jar /my/folder/
```

Now, edit your hbase-env.sh file in $HBASE_HOME/conf and put the path of the created JAR into the classpath variable.

```
export HBASE_CLASSPATH=/my/folder/twitbase-1.0.0.jar
```

Restart the HBase process.

This filter can be used in a scan as follows:

```
HTable t = new HTable(UsersDAO.TABLE_NAME);
Scan scan = new Scan();
scan.addColumn(UsersDAO.INFO_FAM, UsersDAO.PASS_COL);
scan.addColumn(UsersDAO.INFO_FAM, UsersDAO.NAME_COL);
scan.addColumn(UsersDAO.INFO_FAM, UsersDAO.EMAIL_COL);
Filter f = new PasswordStrengthFilter(4);
scan.setFilter(f);
```

This usage filters out all rows where the password length is greater than or equal to four characters and returns rows with the names and emails of the users whose passwords don't match the minimum length requirement. The password field isn't returned because its KeyValue object is excluded in the filter.

This code is available in the PasswordStrengthFilterExample class in the same project. To run the code, you can do the following:

```
java -cp target/twitbase-1.0.0.jar \
 HBaseIA.TwitBase.filters.PasswordStrengthFilterExample
```

4.8.2 *Prebundled filters*

HBase ships with numerous filters bundled along, so you may not need to implement your own. To see a comprehensive list, we recommend that you look at the javadocs. We'll cover some of the more commonly used ones here.

ROWFILTER

RowFilter is a comparison filter that comes bundled and allows you to filter data based on rowkeys. You can do exact matches, substring matches, or regular-expression matches and filter out data that doesn't match. To instantiate RowFilter, you have to provide a comparison operator and the value you want to compare. The constructor is as follows:

```
public RowFilter(CompareOp rowCompareOp,
                 WritableByteArrayComparable rowComparator)
```

The comparison operators are defined in CompareOp, which is an enum defined in the CompareFilter abstract class and can have the following values:

- LESS–Checks whether the value is less than the one provided in the comparator
- LESS_OR_EQUAL–Checks whether the value is less than or equal to the comparator
- EQUAL–Checks whether the value is equal to the comparator
- NOT_EQUAL–Checks whether the value is not equal to the comparator
- GREATER_OR_EQUAL–Checks whether the value is greater than or equal to the comparator
- GREATER–Checks whether the value is greater than the comparator
- NO_OP–Returns false by default, thereby filtering out everything

The comparator has to extend the WritableByteArrayComparable abstract class. The prebundled comparator types available are as follows:

- BinaryComparator–Compares using the `Bytes.compareTo()` method
- BinaryPrefixComparator–Does a prefix-based bytewise comparison using `Bytes.compareTo()`, starting from the left
- NullComparator–Checks whether the given value is null
- BitComparator–Does a bitwise comparison
- RegexStringComparator–Compares the passed value with the regular expression provided at the time of instantiating the comparator
- SubstringComparator–Does a `contains()` check in the passed value for the substring provided as a part of the comparator

Here are some examples of how to use `RowFilter`:

```
Filter myFilter = new RowFilter(CompareFilter.CompareOp.EQUAL,        ◁─┐   Compare rowkey
                new RegexStringComparator(".*foo"));                         with regular
                                                                             expression

Filter myFilter = new RowFilter(CompareFilter.CompareOp.EQUAL,        ◁─┐   Check whether
                new SubstringComparator("foo"));                            rowkey
                                                                           contains given
                                                                           substring

Filter myFilter = new RowFilter(CompareFilter.CompareOp.GREATER_OR_EQUAL,  ◁─┐
                new BinaryComparator("row10"));
```

> Compare rowkey with regular expression
> Check whether rowkey contains given substring
> Check whether rowkey is greater than provided value

PREFIXFILTER

This is a special case of `RowFilter`. Use it to filter based on a prefix value of the rowkey. It's similar to providing an end key to the `Scan(byte[] startRow, byte[] stopRow)` constructor, except you don't need to calculate `stopRow` yourself. This is useful because calculating `stopRow` correctly can sometimes be tricky when taking `byte[]` overflow into account. `PrefixFilter` isn't smart enough to skip ahead to the first matching `startRow`, so be sure to provide it. It's smart enough to end the scan once it finds the first rowkey that doesn't match the prefix.

Use `PrefixFilter` like this:

```
String prefix = "a";                          ◁─┐   Return only rows that
Scan scan = new Scan(prefix.getBytes());            start with the letter a
scan.setFilter(new PrefixFilter(prefix.getBytes()));
```

QUALIFIERFILTER

`QualifierFilter` is a comparison filter like `RowFilter`, except it matches the column qualifier name rather than the rowkey. It uses the same comparison operators and comparator types as `RowFilter`. There is a filter to match the column family name as well, but it isn't as interesting as `QualifierFilter`. Besides, you can limit the `scan` or `get` operation to a particular column family.

You use `QualifierFilter` like this:

> Return KeyValue objects where column qualifier is less than or equal to colqual20

```
Filter myFilter = new QualifierFilter(CompareFilter.CompareOp.LESS_OR_EQUAL,   ◁─┐
                new BinaryComparator(Bytes.toBytes("colqual20")));
```

Like a scan, you can apply any filter to a Get object, but not all of them make sense. For instance, filtering a Get based on the rowkey isn't useful. But you can filter out columns being returned in a Get using QualifierFilter.

VALUEFILTER

ValueFilter provides the same functionality as RowFilter or QualifierFilter, but over cell values. Using this filter allows you to filter out all cells that don't match the provided criteria:

> **Filter out columns if cell value doesn't start with foo**

```
Filter myFilter = new ValueFilter(CompareFilter.CompareOp.EQUAL,
                new BinaryPrefixComparator(Bytes.toBytes("foo")));
```

TIMESTAMPFILTER

This filter allows much finer-grained control over the versions that are returned to the client. You provide a list of timestamps that should be returned, and only cells with a matching timestamp are returned.

If you want a time range when you're scanning or retrieving individual rows, you can use the setTimeRange(..) method on the Get or Scan object to enforce that. The filter, on the other hand, lets you specify a list of timestamps that should be matched:

```
List<Long> timestamps = new ArrayList<Long>();
timestamps.add(100L);
timestamps.add(200L);
timestamps.add(300L);
Filter myFilter = new TimestampsFilter(timestamps);
```

> **Return cells with timestamps 100, 200, and 300 only**

FILTERLIST

Often it's useful to combine multiple filters. Suppose you're looking to get back all rows that match a certain regular expression but are interested in cells that contain a particular word. In that case, you can combine filters into a FilterList object and pass it to the scanner. The FilterList class also implements the Filter interface and can be used to create filtering logic that combines multiple individual filters.

You can configure the filter list in two modes: MUST_PASS_ALL or MUST_PASS_ONE. As the names suggest, the modes include results in the final list if they pass all filters or if they pass only one filter, respectively:

> **Create list of filters**

> **Instantiate filter list with list of filters and config mode for list**

```
List<Filter> myList = new ArrayList<Filter>();
myList.add(myTimestampFilter);
myList.add(myRowFilter);
FilterList myFilterList =
new FilterList(FilterList.Operator.MUST_PASS_ALL, myList);
myFilterList.addFilter(myQualiFilter);
```

> **Add filter to filter list that wasn't part of original list**

The filters are applied in the order that the List object gives them back. So, you can choose to have finer control based on the type of list object you use or by inserting the filters in the list in a particular order.

The `Filtering` API is powerful and has features that allow you to optimize disk seeks. This not only saves network I/O but also saves on disk I/O. To see the usage of this feature, look at the `ColumnPrefixFilter`, which is one of the bundled filters that ships with HBase.

4.9   Summary

This chapter covered a lot of material. We're glad you made it to the end and hope you learned a few things along the way. In many ways, HBase provides a new approach to data management. That's true both in the capabilities of the system as well as in the best practices around using that system. With any luck, this chapter has opened your eyes to the considerations that must be addressed when designing HBase tables as well as the feature trade-offs you make when you decide to work with or without a relational system. We'll do our best to recap.

It's about the questions, not the relationships. When designing for HBase, it's about efficiently looking up the answer to a question, not purity of the entity model. You must make this trade-off because distributed transactions bottleneck concurrency and distributed joins are network-bound. Never in section 4.1.1 did we ask, "How can the data be modeled for efficient storage?" Instead we focused on answering queries efficiently.

Design is never finished. You have to put something on paper and run it through some scenarios to see where it breaks down. Allow your schema to evolve. De-normalization is both a powerful friend and a frightful foe. There's always a trade-off between the response time of reads and the complexity of writes. Maximize the number of questions you can answer with a given design, and then tweak it to support two new access patterns. Your users will thank you.

Scale is a first-class entity. When building on HBase or any other distributed system, distribution of workload is always a concern. These tools are designed to handle a huge volume of traffic spread across the cluster. A build-up of traffic, or hot spot, on any single member of the cluster is catastrophic. Because of that, you must always keep the even distribution of that load in the back of your mind. HBase gives you the ability to design that load into your schema. Use it wisely.

Every dimension is an opportunity. HBase has multiple indexes over multiple dimensions of the physical data model. Every one of them is exposed to you directly. This is as much a challenge as it is empowering. If you can't figure out how to answer that last question, step back and see if there's an index you haven't taken advantage of yet. Seeing these opportunities is a big part of why it's important to understand how HBase works under the hood.

Remember, designing your rowkey is the single most important decision you can make. Take full advantage of the flexibility of the logical data model. `Scans` are your friend, but use them wisely and for the right access patterns. And remember, when all else fails, you can always fall back on a custom filter.

Now that you're equipped with the tricks of the trade when it comes to designing HBase tables, the next two chapters are about extending HBase to add interesting functionality that you may want for your application. Chapters 7 and 8 are dedicated to exploring how HBase can be used to solve real-world problems; you'll learn practical use of some of the techniques covered in this chapter.

Extending HBase
with coprocessors

This chapter covers

- Coprocessors and how to use them effectively
- Types of coprocessors: observer and endpoint
- How to configure and validate coprocessor installation on your cluster

Everything you've seen of HBase as an online system is centered on data access. The five HBase commands introduced in chapter 2 are exclusively for reading or writing data. For the HBase cluster, the most computationally expensive portion of any of those operations occurs when applying server-side filters on Scan results. Even so, this computation is extremely specific to accessing the data. You can use custom filters to push application logic onto the cluster, but filters are constrained to the context of a single row. To perform computation over your data in HBase, you're forced to rely on Hadoop MapReduce or on custom client code that will read, modify, and write data back to HBase.

HBase coprocessors are an addition to our data-manipulation toolset that were introduced as a feature in HBase in the 0.92.0 release. With the introduction of coprocessors, we can push *arbitrary computation* out to the HBase nodes hosting our

126

data. This code is *run in parallel* across all the RegionServers. This transforms an HBase cluster from horizontally scalable storage to a highly capable, distributed, data-storage and *-processing* system.

> **WARNING** Coprocessors are a brand-new feature in HBase and are *untested* in production deployments. Their integration with HBase internals is *extremely invasive.* Think of them as akin to Linux kernel modules or RDBMS stored procedures implemented in C. Writing an observer coprocessor is tricky to get right, and such a coprocessor can be extremely difficult to debug when running at scale. Unlike client-side bugs, a buggy coprocessor *will* take down your cluster. The HBase community is still working out exactly how to use coprocessors effectively.[1] Caution is advised.

In this chapter, we'll introduce you to the two types of coprocessors and show examples of how to use each one. We hope this will open your mind to the possibilities so you'll be able to use coprocessors in your own applications. You never know: maybe you can be the one to write the blog post describing the canonical coprocessor example! Please make it more interesting than WordCount.

More inspiration from Google

As with much of the rest of the Hadoop ecosystem, coprocessors come to the open source community by way of Google. The idea for HBase coprocessors came from two slides[2] in a talk presented in 2009. Coprocessors are cited as crucial for a number of horizontally scalable, low-latency operations. These operations include machine translation, full-text queries, and scalable metadata management.

5.1 The two kinds of coprocessors

Coprocessors come in two flavors: *observers* and *endpoints*. Each serves a different purpose and is implemented according to its own API. Observers allow the cluster to behave differently during normal client operations. Endpoints allow you to extend the cluster's capabilities, exposing new operations to client applications.

5.1.1 Observer coprocessors

To understand observer coprocessors, it helps to understand the lifecycle of a request. A request starts with the client, creating a request object and invoking the appropriate method on the `HTableInterface` implementation. For example, a `Put` instance is created and the `put()` method called. The HBase client resolves the RegionServer that should receive the `Put` based on the rowkey and makes the RPC call. The RegionServer receives the `Put` and delegates it to the appropriate region. The region handles the

---

[1] The HBase blog has an excellent overview of coprocessors that is appended periodically with new details of current and future work: Mingjie Lai, Eugene Koontz, and Andrew Purtell, "Coprocessor Introduction," http://mng.bz/TzuY.

[2] Jeff Dean, "Designs, Lessons and Advice from Building Large Distributed Systems," LADIS '09, http://mng.bz/U2DB, pages 66-67.

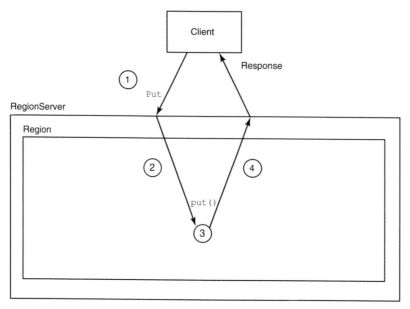

1   Client sends Put request.

2   Request is dispatched to appropriate RegionServer and region.

3   The region receives the put(), processes it, and constructs a response.

4   The final result is returned to the client.

Figure 5.1   The lifecycle of a request. A Put request dispatched from the client results directly in a put() call on the region.

request and constructs a response, which is passed back to the client. Figure 5.1 illustrates this path.

Observers sit between the client and HBase, modifying data access as it happens. You can run an observer after every Get command, modifying the result returned to the client. Or you can run an observer after a Put command, performing manipulation on the data that a client writes to HBase before it's persisted. You can think of observer coprocessors as analogous to *triggers* from a relational database or to *advice* from aspect-oriented programming (AOP). Multiple observers can be registered simultaneously; they're executed in priority order. The CoprocessorHost class manages observer registration and execution on behalf of the region. Figure 5.2 illustrates a RegionObserver intercepting a Put command.

A word of caution

Bear in mind that coprocessors are executed in the same process space as the RegionServer. This means code in a coprocessor has full rights and privileges of the HBase user process on the server. It also means a buggy coprocessor can potentially crash the process. No isolation guarantees are in place at this point. You can follow along with the efforts to resolve this potential issue by tracking the JIRA ticket.[3]

---

[3]   "[Coprocessors] Generic external process host," Apache Software Foundation, http://mng.bz/9uOy.

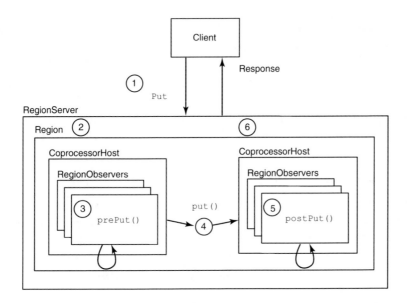

1   Client sends `Put` request.

2   Request is dispatched to appropriate RegionServer and region.

3   CoprocessorHost intercepts the request and invoices `prePut()` on each RegionObserver
    registered on the table.

4   Unless interrupted by a `prePut()`, the request continues to region and is processed normally.

5   The result produced by the region is once again intercepted by the CoprocessorHost.
    This time `postPut()` is called on each registered RegionObserver.

6   Assuming no `postPut()` interrupts the response, the final result is returned to
    the client.

**Figure 5.2   A RegionObserver in the wild. Instead of calling `put()` directly, the region calls
`prePut()` and `postPut()` on all registered RegionObservers, one after the next. Each has
a chance to modify or interrupt the operation before a response is returned to the client.**

As of HBase version 0.92, three kinds of observers are available:

- RegionObserver—This observer hooks into the stages of data access and manipulation. All of the standard data-manipulation commands can be intercepted with both pre- and post-hooks. It also exposes pre- and post-hooks for internal region operations such as flushing the MemStore and splitting the region. The RegionObserver runs on the region; thus there can be multiple RegionObservers running on the same RegionServer. Register RegionObservers through either schema updates or the `hbase.coprocessor.region.classes` configuration property.

- WALObserver—The write-ahead log (WAL) also supports an observer coprocessor. The only available hooks are pre- and post-WAL write events. Unlike the RegionObserver, WALObservers run in the context of a RegionServer. Register

WALObservers through either schema updates or the `hbase.coprocessor`
`.wal.classes` configuration property.

- MasterObserver—For hooking into DDL events, such as table creation or
schema modifications, HBase provides the MasterObserver. For example, you
can use the `postDeleteTable()` hook to also delete secondary indexes when
the primary table is deleted. This observer runs on the Master node. Register
MasterObservers through the `hbase.coprocessor.master.classes` configuration property.

5.1.2   Endpoint Coprocessors

Endpoints are a generic extension to HBase. When an endpoint is installed on your cluster, it extends the HBase RPC protocol, exposing new methods to client applications. Just
like observers, endpoints execute on the RegionServers, right next to your data.

Endpoint coprocessors are similar to stored procedures in other database engines.
From the client's perspective, invoking an endpoint coprocessor is similar to invoking
any other HBase command, except that the functionality is based on the custom code
that defines the coprocessor. The request object is created, it's passed to the `HTab-`
`leInterface` to execute on the cluster, and the results are collected. This arbitrary
code can do anything for which you can write code in Java.

At their most basic, endpoints can be used to implement *scatter-gather algorithms*.
HBase ships with an Aggregate example: an endpoint that computes simple aggregates like sum and average. `AggregateImplementation` instances calculate partial
results on the nodes hosting data, and the `AggregationClient` computes the final
result in the client process. Figure 5.3 illustrates the Aggregation example in action.

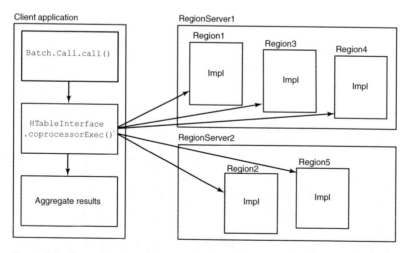

**Figure 5.3   An endpoint coprocessor at work. The regions deploy an implementation of
the interface consumed by the client. An instance of `Batch.Call` encapsulates method
invocation, and the `coprocessorExec()` method handles distributed invocation. After
each request completes, results are returned to the client and aggregated.**

We'll show you how to implement both kinds of coprocessors and demonstrate activation of these implementations on your HBase installation.

5.2 Implementing an observer

You can use coprocessors as part of TwitBase. Think back to the `follows` relationship table you created in the last chapter. Instead of manually maintaining the secondary index in `followedBy`, let's write an observer to maintain that relationship.

> ### Caveat emptor
>
> This example shows how you might maintain a secondary index using coprocessors. In practice, we don't recommend this approach when throughput is a consideration. Updating a secondary index likely requires communication with a region hosted on a different RegionServer. That communication is additional networking overhead and will impact cluster performance.
>
> That said, if your application doesn't require maximum throughput, this is a pretty simple way to offload that work. Under such a scenario, you can reduce client latency by making the `postPut` operation asynchronous, removing it from the critical path of the write. Then you can use a MapReduce job to rebuild the index periodically, catching records that fell through the cracks.

5.2.1 Modifying the schema

To accomplish this goal, you'll implement a RegionObserver and override its `post-Put()` method. Inside of `postPut()`, the only relevant context you'll have is the `Put` instance sent by the client. That means you need to slightly modify the `follows` and `followedBy` schema you defined in the previous chapter. Why's that? Start by studying the entity diagram of the `follows` and `followedBy` tables, illustrated in figure 5.4.

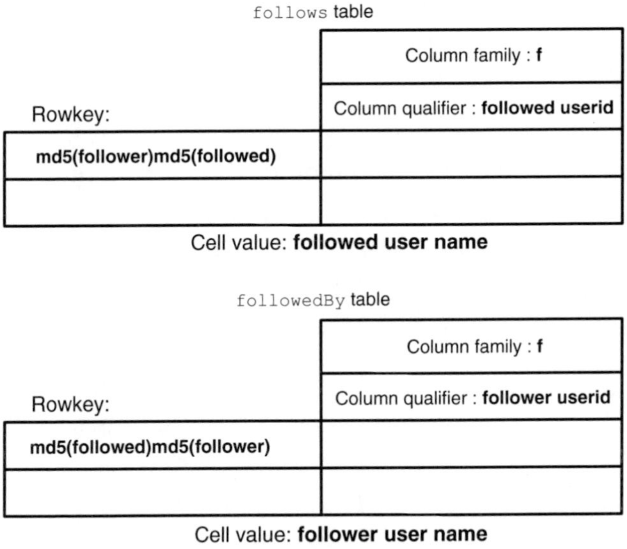

Figure 5.4 Schema for `follows` and `followedBy` tables as optimized for space and I/O efficiency. The `follows` table stores half of a `relation` entity indexed according to the `follower` participant. The `followedBy` table stores the other half of the same `relation` entity indexed according to the `followed` participant.

follows table

Rowkey:	Column family : **f**			
	to: **followed userid**	to_name: **followed user name**	from: **follower userid**	from_name: **follower user name**
md5(follower)md5(followed)				

followedBy table

Rowkey:	Column family : **f**			
	to: **followed userid**	to_name: **followed user name**	from: **follower userid**	from_name: **follower user name**
md5(followed)md5(follower)				

Figure 5.5   Schema for the updated `follows` and `followedBy` tables. Now both tables store a full relation entity in each row.

Writing a new record to the `follows` table requires the cell {id_followed:name _followed}. That's the only information contained in the `Put` instance available to the observer. Writing to the `followedBy` table requires the cell {id_follower:name _follower}. This portion of the relation isn't available. In order to implement the observer, a single `Put` instance to the `follows` table must contain the entire relation.

Because a `Put` to the `follows` table now must contain the entire relation entity, you can store the same entity in the `followedBy` table. That way both tables have a complete entity stored per row. The updated entity diagram is illustrated in figure 5.5.

With the full context available in the `Put`, you can go about implementing the observer.

5.2.2   *Starting with the Base*

You'll implement your own `FollowsObserver` to maintain these relationships. Doing so requires extending `BaseRegionObserver` and overriding the `postPut()` method:

```
public class FollowsObserver extends BaseRegionObserver {

    @Override
    public void postPut(
        final ObserverContext<RegionCoprocessorEnvironment> e,
        final Put put,
        final WALEdit edit,
        final boolean writeToWAL)
      throws IOException {
      ... // implementation
    }
}
```

The `FollowsObserver` keeps track of `Put`s against the `follows` table, watching for new follower relationship entries. When a new entry is found, it constructs the inversion of that relationship and writes it back to the `followedBy` table. The first step is detecting the correct context. Check the column family name used in the incoming `Put` request:

```
if (!put.getFamilyMap().containsKey("follows"))
  return;
```

This check is necessary because coprocessors installed via configuration in hbase-site.xml are applied to all tables. For your purpose, you only want to operate on the `follows` table. This check verifies that you're not operating on some other table. Find out which table context the observer is executing under by inspecting the `RegionCoprocessorEnvironment` object. It holds a reference to `HRegion` and associated `HRegionInfo`:

```
byte[] table
  = e.getEnvironment().getRegion().getRegionInfo().getTableName();
if (!Bytes.equals(table, Bytes.toBytes("follows")))
  return;
```

Exit early and exit often!
If this isn't a `Put` you're interested in, be sure to return right away. The coprocessor is executing as part of the path of data flow. Time spent here is time the client spends waiting for a response!

With the correct condition detected, it's time to do some work. Step two is extracting the relevant components from the incoming `Put` command. You'll use these components as parameters to creating the inverted relation. To do that, reach into the `Put` instance and retrieve the parameters you need using the method `Put.get(byte[] family, byte[] qualifier)`. It returns a list of `KeyValues` matching the parameters requested. You know the first `KeyValue` is the one you're interested in because the `Put` contains only a single version for this cell:

```
KeyValue kv = put.get(Bytes.toBytes('f'), Bytes.toBytes("from")).get(0);
String from = Bytes.toString(kv.getValue());
kv = put.get(Bytes.toBytes('f'), Bytes.toBytes("to")).get(0);
String to = Bytes.toString(kv.getValue());
```

The final step is writing the new relation back to HBase. You can reuse the connection information to operate on the same table as the original. Remember, the new row is likely hosted on a different RegionServer, so a network operation is often required:

```
RelationsDAO relations = new RelationsDAO(pool);     │ Invert
relations.addFollowedBy(to, from);               ◁───┘ relation
```

Normally you wouldn't want to mix client and server code as you've done here. You reuse the `RelationsDAO` to keep the focus on adding a followed relation rather than constructing that `Put`.

Smells like recursion

In this example, you're spinning up a new HBase client and interacting with the cluster—from within the cluster! That is to say, a client `Put` against the `follows` table results in a client `Put` against the followed table. An observer implemented thoughtlessly could result in yet another client `Put` against the followed table, and so on. Such code would wreak havoc on a perfectly innocent HBase cluster. In this case, the *base case* is verified by checking the direction of the relationship. Be mindful of these kinds of scenarios when implementing your own observers.

Writing back to HBase using the `RelationsDAO` requires an `HTablePool` instance. You can use an instance variable to manage it by hooking into the coprocessor lifecycle. The `start()` and `stop()` methods are provided for this purpose, although their documentation isn't terribly verbose:

```
@Override
public void start(CoprocessorEnvironment env) throws IOException {
  pool = new HTablePool(env.getConfiguration(), Integer.MAX_VALUE);
}

@Override
public void stop(CoprocessorEnvironment env) throws IOException {
  pool.close();
}
```

The complete `FollowsObserver` is shown in the following listing.

Listing 5.1   `FollowsObserver`

```
package HBaseIA.TwitBase.coprocessors;
                                            ┐ Imports
// ...                                   ◁──┘ omitted

public class FollowsObserver extends BaseRegionObserver {

  private HTablePool pool = null;

  @Override
  public void start(CoprocessorEnvironment env) throws IOException {
    pool = new HTablePool(env.getConfiguration(), Integer.MAX_VALUE);
  }

  @Override
  public void stop(CoprocessorEnvironment env) throws IOException {
    pool.close();
  }

  @Override
  public void postPut(
      final ObserverContext<RegionCoprocessorEnvironment> e,
      final Put put,
      final WALEdit edit,
      final boolean writeToWAL)
    throws IOException {
```

```
    byte[] table
      = e.getEnvironment().getRegion().getRegionInfo().getTableName();
    if (!Bytes.equals(table, FOLLOWS_TABLE_NAME))
      return;                                              This isn't the table
                                                           you're looking for
    KeyValue kv = put.get(RELATION_FAM, FROM).get(0);
    String from = Bytes.toString(kv.getValue());
    kv = put.get(RELATION_FAM, TO).get(0);
    String to = Bytes.toString(kv.getValue());

    RelationsDAO relations = new RelationsDAO(pool);
    relations.addFollowedBy(to, from);                     Invert
  }                                                        relation
}
```

5.2.3 Installing your observer

It's time to test it. There are two methods of installing an observer coprocessor: a table schema change or through configuration in hbase-site.xml. Unlike the configuration method, installation via schema change can be done without restarting HBase, but it does require taking the table offline temporarily.

Let's try the schema update method first. To install FollowsObserver, you need to package it in a JAR. Do so the same way you did before:

```
$ mvn package
...
[INFO] -----------------------------------------------------------------
[INFO] BUILD SUCCESS
[INFO] -----------------------------------------------------------------
...
```

Now open the HBase shell and install the observer:

```
$ hbase shell

HBase Shell; enter 'help<RETURN>' for list of supported commands.
Type "exit<RETURN>" to leave the HBase Shell
Version 0.92.0, r1231986, Mon Jan 16 13:16:35 UTC 2012

hbase(main):001:0> disable 'follows'
0 row(s) in 7.0560 seconds

hbase(main):002:0> alter 'follows', METHOD => 'table_att',
'coprocessor'=>'file:///Users/ndimiduk/repos/hbaseia-
twitbase/target/twitbase-1.0.0.jar
|HBaseIA.TwitBase.coprocessors.FollowsObserver|1001|'
Updating all regions with the new schema...
1/1 regions updated.
Done.
0 row(s) in 1.0770 seconds

hbase(main):003:0> enable 'follows'
0 row(s) in 2.0760 seconds
```

Disabling the table take all of its regions offline. This allows the process classpath to be updated, a requirement of the installation process. The alter command updates the table schema to be aware of the new coprocessor. This online installation is only available to observer coprocessors. The `coprocessor` attribute parameters are delimited by the | character. The first parameter is the path to the JAR containing your coprocessor implementation. The second parameter is the coprocessor implementation class. The third parameter is the coprocessor priority. When you load multiple observers, they're executed in priority order. For any given invocation, a previous coprocessor has the opportunity to interrupt the execution chain, preventing later coprocessors from executing. The final parameter, omitted in this example, is a list of arguments passed to the coprocessor implementation's constructor.

If all went well, you can describe the `follows` table and confirm the presence of your new coprocessor:

```
hbase(main):004:0> describe 'follows'
DESCRIPTION                                          ENABLED
{NAME => 'follows', coprocessor$1 => 'file:///U    true
 sers/ndimiduk/repos/hbaseia-twitbase/target/twi
 tbase-1.0.0.jar|HBaseIA.TwitBase.coprocessors.F
 ollowsObserver|1001|', FAMILIES => [{NAME => 'f
 ', BLOOMFILTER => 'NONE', REPLICATION_SCOPE =>
 '0', VERSIONS => '1', COMPRESSION => 'NONE', MI
 N_VERSIONS => '0', TTL => '2147483647', BLOCKSI
 ZE => '65536', IN_MEMORY => 'false', BLOCKCACHE
  => 'true'}]}
1 row(s) in 0.0330 seconds
```

The next time you add a new record to the `follows` table, the `FollowsObserver` coprocessor will kick in, updating the inverted index for you. Verify by inserting a relationship:

```
$ java -cp target/twitbase-1.0.0.jar \
  HBaseIA.TwitBase.RelationsTool follows TheRealMT SirDoyle
Successfully added relationship
$ java -cp target/twitbase-1.0.0.jar \
  HBaseIA.TwitBase.RelationsTool list follows TheRealMT
<Relation: TheRealMT -> SirDoyle>
$ java -cp target/twitbase-1.0.0.jar \
  HBaseIA.TwitBase.RelationsTool list followedBy SirDoyle
<Relation: SirDoyle <- TheRealMT>
```

> **Picky, picky!**
>
> When installing coprocessors into a schema, be careful. The coprocessor specification isn't validated until runtime. HBase won't notice any errors, such as extra whitespace or an invalid JAR path. You won't know the installation failed until the next client operation when your observer doesn't run. We suggest you smoke-test your coprocessor deployment before you assume everything is in place.

In this example, you've installed the coprocessor JAR from a path on the local file system. This may be simple if your cluster is managed with a tool like Chef (www.opscode.com/chef/) or Puppet (http://puppetlabs.com). HBase can also load

JARs from the HDFS. In practice, the HDFS deployment model is much easier than dealing with copying your application JARs to the individual nodes.

5.2.4 *Other installation options*

Observer coprocessors can also be installed via configuration. Doing so requires that the observer classes be available in the HBase classpath. In this case, the observer is registered for all tables, so you must take care in intercepting operations within the intended context. Configuration is the primary mechanism for registering instances of the MasterObserver coprocessor.

> **Stealth mode**
>
> Observers registered via the hbase-site.xml file won't show up when you describe a table in the shell, as you did previously. The only method available to validate that the observer is registered is to exercise it, preferably via an automated post-deploy test of some kind. Don't say we didn't warn you.

If you want to register two MasterObserver coprocessors, you can do so by adding this property to your hbase-site.xml file:

```
<property>
  <name>hbase.coprocessor.master.classes</name>
  <value>foo.TableCreationObserver,foo.RegionMoverObserver</value>
</property>
```

This snippet registers the class `TableCreationObserver` as the highest priority observer, followed by `RegionMoverObserver`.

5.3 *Implementing an endpoint*

Tracking these relationships is important for maintaining the connected network of people using TwitBase. We hope this digital connectivity between people allows for real human relationships to flourish. Realistically, though, the only reason to keep track of such things is to see if you have more followers than the other guy. A TwitBase user wants to know exactly how many followers they have *right now*. In this case, waiting for a MapReduce job to complete is unacceptable. Even the overhead of all the data moving over the wire during a standard scan won't do. You'll build this feature into TwitBase using an endpoint coprocessor.

For an individual user, you can implement an on-demand follower count feature using a `Scan`. Doing so is simple enough. Define the scan range, and count the results:

```
final byte[] startKey = Md5Utils.md5sum(user);          ⟵┐ Construct
final byte[] endKey = Arrays.copyOf(startKey, startKey.length);  │ start key ...
endKey[endKey.length-1]++;               ⟵┐ ... and
Scan scan = new Scan(startKey, endKey);   │ end key
scan.setMaxVersions(1);     ⟵┐ Limit
                            │ KeyValues returned
long sum = 0;
```

```
ResultScanner rs = followed.getScanner(scan);
for(Result r : rs) {
  sum++;                          ◁──┐  Count
}                                      │  results
```

The scan approach works just fine. Why would you want to make this any more compli-cated? It could be that every millisecond matters. This scan may be in your application's critical path. Every `Result` returned is taking up bytes over the wire—even if you omit all data, you still have rowkeys to transmit. By implementing this scan as an endpoint, you keep all that data on the HBase nodes. The only data transmitted is the sum.

5.3.1   *Defining an interface for the endpoint*

To implement followers count as an endpoint, you'll start with a new interface. The interface serves as the contract for extending the RPC protocol and must match on both client and server:

```
public interface RelationCountProtocol extends CoprocessorProtocol {
  public long followedByCount(String userId) throws IOException;
}
```

Here you define the `RelationCountProtocol`, which exposes the single method `followedByCount()`. This is the building block on which both the client and server code can be written. Let's start with the server.

5.3.2   *Implementing the endpoint server*

Creating a scanner in the region looks a little different from the client API. Unlike a scan executed via the client API, this scan is reading over data on the machine execut-ing the scan. This object is called the `InternalScanner`. `InternalScanner`s are identi-cal in concept to `Scanner`s in the client API. The difference is that they reside in the RegionServer and interact with the storage and caching layers directly. Remember, implementing an endpoint is programming the RegionServer directly.

Create an instance of `InternalScanner` like this:

```
byte[] startkey = Md5Utils.md5sum(userId);
Scan scan = new Scan(startkey);
scan.setFilter(new PrefixFilter(startkey));
scan.addColumn(Bytes.toBytes('f'), Bytes.toBytes("from"));
scan.setMaxVersions(1);

RegionCoprocessorEnvironment env
  = (RegionCoprocessorEnvironment)getEnvironment();
InternalScanner scanner = env.getRegion().getScanner(scan);
```

`InternalScanner`s are specific to the region where the coprocessor is running. Access that region via the `getRegion()` helper method provided by the calling environment. That environment is exposed via `getEnvironment()` on `BaseEndpointCoprocessor`. In this case, you can use local buffers instead of copying bytes over the wire. It's much faster, but the interface is a little different. Read the scan results:

```
long sum = 0;
List<KeyValue> results = new ArrayList<KeyValue>();
boolean hasMore = false;
do {
  hasMore = scanner.next(results);
  sum += results.size();
  results.clear();
} while (hasMore);
scanner.close();
return sum;
```

do-while, don't while

Unfortunately, InternalScanner doesn't implement the usual java.util.Itera-
tor interface. To make sure you receive all batches of results, use a do-while form
as you see here, rather than a standard while loop. The alternative is to duplicate
the logic within your loop: once to read the first page, and again in the normal while
form. This style of iteration is more common in C programs.

The results returned by InternalScanner are raw KeyValue objects. This is a notable
difference from scanners in the client API. Those scanners return Result instances
that represent an entire row. InternalScanners iterate over KeyValue instances corresponding to individual cells. By carefully limiting the data returned by the scan, you
guarantee that a single KeyValue represents a single row in the desired result set. It
also limits the amount of data that must be read off disk.

Putting it all together, the complete RelationCountImpl is shown next.

Listing 5.2 RelationCountImpl.java: server half of implementing an endpoint

```
package HBaseIA.TwitBase.coprocessors;          Imports
//...                                           omitted

public class RelationCountImpl
  extends BaseEndpointCoprocessor implements RelationCountProtocol {

  @Override
  public long followedByCount(String userId) throws IOException {
    byte[] startkey = Md5Utils.md5sum(userId);
    Scan scan = new Scan(startkey);
    scan.setFilter(new PrefixFilter(startkey));
    scan.addColumn(RELATION_FAM, FROM);
    scan.setMaxVersions(1);

    RegionCoprocessorEnvironment env
      = (RegionCoprocessorEnvironment)getEnvironment();       Open local
    InternalScanner scanner = env.getRegion().getScanner(scan);   scanner

    long sum = 0;
    List<KeyValue> results = new ArrayList<KeyValue>();
    boolean hasMore = false;
    do {
```

```
    hasMore = scanner.next(results);        ◁┐   Iterate over
    sum += results.size();                   │   scan results
    results.clear();                ◁┐
  } while (hasMore);                 │
  scanner.close();                   └─  Don't forget to clear
  return sum;                            local results buffer
}                                        between iterations
}
```

5.3.3 Implement the endpoint client

With the server portion of your custom endpoint in place, it's time to build the client. You'll put this code in the existing `RelationsDAO` you built previously. As is clear by the interface definition, the server portion expects a `userId` to query. But the table still needs to know a key range over which the coprocessor will be invoked. This range is translated into a set of regions to call it against and calculated on the client side. As it happens, that code is identical to the client-side scanner range calculation:

```
final byte[] startKey = Md5Utils.md5sum(userId);            ◁┐  Construct
final byte[] endKey = Arrays.copyOf(startKey, startKey.length);   └  start key ...
endKey[endKey.length-1]++;            ◁┐
                                       └   ... and
                                           end key
```

The fun begins in aggregating results. Executing the endpoint is a three-step process. Step one is to define a `Call` object. This instance does the work of invoking your specific endpoint; the details of your `RelationCountProtocol` are contained entirely within. You can define an anonymous `Call` instance inline:

```
Batch.Call<RelationCountProtocol, Long> callable =
  new Batch.Call<RelationCountProtocol, Long>() {
    @Override
    public Long call(RelationCountProtocol instance)
        throws IOException {
      return instance.followedByCount(userId);
    }
};
```

The second step is to call the endpoint. This is done directly from the `HTableInterface`:

```
HTableInterface followers = pool.getTable(TABLE_NAME);
Map<byte[], Long> results =
  followers.coprocessorExec(
    RelationCountProtocol.class,
    startKey,
    endKey,
    callable);
```

When the client code executes the `coprocessorExec()` method, the HBase client sends the invocation to the appropriate RegionServers based on the `startKey` and `endKey`. In this case, it's splitting the scan range according to region assignments and sending the invocation only to the relevant nodes.

The final step in executing an endpoint is aggregating the results. Your client receives a response for each invoked RegionServer and must sum the results. Loop over the region name to value pairs and sum the results:

```
long sum = 0;
for(Map.Entry<byte[], Long> e : results.entrySet()) {
  sum += e.getValue().longValue();
}
```

Thus you have a simple scatter-gather approach to computing. For this example, the client-side scan is about as fast as implementing the scan in an endpoint because you're working with a small amount of data. But the network I/O consumed by the client-side scan increases linearly with the number of rows scanned. When the scan is pushed to the endpoint, you save on the network I/O by not having to return the scan results to the client. The other thing is that the endpoint coprocessor executes in parallel on all regions that contain the relevant rows. A client-side scan is likely a single-threaded scan. Making it multithreaded and distributed over regions brings in the complexity of managing a distributed application, which we talked about earlier.

In the long run, pushing the scan down into the RegionServers with an endpoint introduces a little deployment complexity but is far faster than a traditional client-side scan.

The client code in its entirety is shown in this listing.

Listing 5.3 Client portion of the endpoint; snippet from RelationsDAO.java

```
public long followedByCount (final String userId) throws Throwable {
  HTableInterface followed = pool.getTable(FOLLOWED_TABLE_NAME);      Construct
                                                                      start key ...
  final byte[] startKey = Md5Utils.md5sum(userId);
  final byte[] endKey = Arrays.copyOf(startKey, startKey.length);
  endKey[endKey.length-1]++;                                          ... and
                                                                      end key
  Batch.Call<RelationCountProtocol, Long> callable =
    new Batch.Call<RelationCountProtocol, Long>() {
      @Override
      public Long call(RelationCountProtocol instance)
          throws IOException {                                  Step I: define
        return instance.followedByCount(userId);                Call instance
      }
  };

  Map<byte[], Long> results =
    followed.coprocessorExec(                            Step 2: invoke
      RelationCountProtocol.class,                       endpoint
      startKey,
      endKey,
      callable);

  long sum = 0;
  for(Map.Entry<byte[], Long> e : results.entrySet()) {
    sum += e.getValue().longValue();                     Step 3: aggregate results
  }                                                       from each RegionServer
  return sum;
}
```

5.3.4   *Deploying the endpoint server*

Now that the server portion is ready, let's deploy it. Unlike the observer example, endpoints must be deployed via configuration only. You need to edit two files, both of which are found in the $HBASE_HOME/conf directory. The first is hbase-site.xml. Add `RelationCountImpl` to the `hbase.coprocessor.region.classes` property:

```
<property>
  <name>hbase.coprocessor.region.classes</name>
  <value>HBaseIA.TwitBase.coprocessors.RelationCountImpl</value>
</property>
```

You also need to ensure that HBase can find your new class. That means updating hbase-env.sh as well. Add your application JAR to the HBase classpath:

```
export HBASE_CLASSPATH=/path/to/hbaseia-twitbase/target/twitbase-1.0.0.jar
```

5.3.5   *Try it!*

Does it work? Let's find out. Rebuild the code, and restart HBase so your new configuration will take effect. You already had one relationship stored; add another. You only need to define it in one direction; your observer is still registered and handles updating the index:

```
$ java -cp target/twitbase-1.0.0.jar \
  HBaseIA.TwitBase.RelationsTool follows GrandpaD SirDoyle
Successfully added relationship
```

Now verify that the relationships are in place, and hit your endpoint:

```
$ java -cp target/twitbase-1.0.0.jar \
  HBaseIA.TwitBase.RelationsTool list followedBy SirDoyle
<Relation: SirDoyle <- TheRealMT>
<Relation: SirDoyle <- GrandpaD>
$ java -cp target/twitbase-1.0.0.jar \
  HBaseIA.TwitBase.RelationsTool followedByCoproc SirDoyle
SirDoyle has 2 followers.
```

It works! Not only is your observer updating the inversion view of the followers relationship, but you can have follower counts in record time.

5.4   *Summary*

The coprocessor API provides a powerful extension point for HBase. Observers give you fine-grained control over the data pipeline. Endpoints allow you to build custom APIs into HBase. Coprocessors are relatively young, and users are still figuring out how to use the feature. They're also no substitute for a well-designed table schema. Still, coprocessors are a flexible tool for your toolbox and may be just what the doctor ordered to get you out of a bind. The only way to find out is to build an application!

Alternative HBase clients

All interaction with HBase we've covered thus far has focused on using the Java client API and the library that comes bundled with HBase. Java is a core part of the Hadoop stack's DNA, and you can't decouple the two easily. Hadoop is written in Java; HBase is written in Java; the stock HBase client is written in Java. There's only one problem: you may not use Java. You might not even like the JVM. You still want to use HBase. Now what? HBase provides you with alternate clients (both JVM-based as well as those that don't require the JVM) that you can use when Java isn't an option.

In this chapter, you'll see how to interact with HBase in other ways. Each section presents a miniature, self-contained application built using the client that is being explained. Each of these toy applications communicates with HBase using a different type of client. Each section follows the same structure: introduce the context, install any necessary support libraries, build out the application step-by-step, and summarize the results. Each application is independent of the others, so feel free to skip around to what you find useful. No new theory or HBase internals are covered here, just simple recipes for using HBase from non-Java and non-JVM languages.

This chapter starts by exploring alternative online access methods. First you'll see how to script HBase externally via UNIX shell scripts. Next you'll see how to use the JRuby interface on top of which the HBase shell is implemented. After that, you'll explore asynchbase, an alternative Java client library that is designed for asynchronous interaction. Finally, as promised, you'll move beyond Java and the JVM and explore both the REST and Thrift gateways to HBase, using Curl and Python, respectively.

6.1   *Scripting the HBase shell from UNIX*

The simplest way to program HBase is by scripting the HBase shell. You've had a brief introduction to how to use the shell in the earlier chapters. Now you'll take that knowledge and build a useful tool. Every database installation needs to maintain its schema, and HBase is no different.

In the relational world, management of schema migrations is a prevalent source of headache. Broadly speaking, this headache comes from two sources. The first is the tight coupling between schema and application. If you want to add a new attribute to a persisted entity, it usually means adding a new column to a table somewhere. When you're working on a young product, especially in a young company, rapid iteration is crucial to your application's success. Using a relational database, adding a new column requires a schema change. Over time, your database schema becomes the sum total of the original design plus each of these incremental changes. The core relational system isn't well suited for managing these changes, and thus they become an effort of software engineering. Some RDBMSs ship powerful tools for managing these kinds of issues, but many don't. This brings us to the second headache.

The changes themselves often take the form of SQL scripts called *migrations*. These scripts must be run in order because each builds on the last. For long-lived, successful data-driven applications, it's common to find a schema folder containing tens or even hundreds of these files. Each file name starts with a number indicating its position in the migration sequence. Slightly more sophisticated versions of migration management exist, but they're ultimately tools to support the execution of these migration scripts in the proper order.

HBase also has a schema that must be managed. The first problem is less an issue with HBase. Within a column family, columns need not be predefined. The application can change incrementally without a change to the HBase schema in such a case. But introducing a new column family, changing attributes of an existing column family, or adding a new table does require a schema change. You could create a custom application for each migration, but that would be terrible. Instead, you can replicate the same migration-management scheme used for relational systems by scripting the HBase shell. This section will show you how to create these scripts.

You can find the completed init_twitbase.sh script from this section in the Twit-Base project source at https://github.com/hbaseinaction/twitbase/blob/master/bin/init_twitbase.sh.

6.1.1   *Preparing the HBase shell*

The HBase shell comes as part of the default HBase installation. It's launched via the $HBASE_HOME/bin/hbase script. Depending on how you installed HBase, that script may also be on your $PATH. As you saw in chapter 1, launch the shell like this:

```
$ $HBASE_HOME/bin/hbase shell
```

You'll enter the shell application and receive a greeting:

```
HBase Shell; enter 'help<RETURN>' for list of supported commands.
Type "exit<RETURN>" to leave the HBase Shell
Version 0.92.1, r1298924, Fri Mar  9 16:58:34 UTC 2012

hbase(main):001:0>
```

Now that you've verified your shell installation, you can get down to scripting it.

6.1.2   *Script table schema from the UNIX shell*

Way back when learning HBase, you started development on the TwitBase application. One of the first things you did with TwitBase was to create a users table using the HBase shell. As TwitBase grew, so did your schema. Tables for Twits and Followers soon emerged. All management code for those tables accumulated in the InitTables class. Java isn't a convenient language for schema management because it's verbose and requires building a custom application for each migration. Let's reimagine that code as HBase shell commands.

The main body of code for creating a table in InitTables looks mostly the same for each table:

```
System.out.println("Creating Twits table...");
HTableDescriptor desc = new HTableDescriptor(TwitsDAO.TABLE_NAME);
HColumnDescriptor c = new HColumnDescriptor(TwitsDAO.INFO_FAM);
c.setMaxVersions(1);
desc.addFamily(c);
admin.createTable(desc);
System.out.println("Twits table created.");
```

You can achieve the same effect using the shell:

```
hbase(main):001:0> create 'twits', {NAME => 't', VERSIONS => 1}
0 row(s) in 1.0500 seconds
```

> ### A brush with JRuby
>
> If you're familiar with the Ruby programming language, the create command may look conspicuously like a function invocation. That's because it is. The HBase shell is implemented in JRuby. We'll look more at this link to JRuby later in this chapter.

Five lines of Java reduced to a single shell command? Not bad. Now you can take that HBase shell command and wrap it in a UNIX shell script. Note that the line `exec hbase shell` may be slightly different for you if the `hbase` command isn't on your path. You handle that scenario in the final script, shown in listing 6.1:

```
#!/bin/sh

exec $HBASE_HOME/bin/hbase shell <<EOF
create 'twits', {NAME => 't', VERSIONS => 1}
EOF
```

Adding the other tables to your script is easy:

```
exec $HBASE_HOME/bin/hbase shell <<EOF
create 'twits', {NAME => 't', VERSIONS => 1}
create 'users', {NAME => 'info'}
create 'followes', {NAME => 'f', VERSIONS => 1}
create 'followedBy', {NAME => 'f', VERSIONS => 1}
EOF
```

At this point, you've moved your table and column family names out of Java. Overriding them on the command line is now much easier:

```
#!/bin/sh

TWITS_TABLE=${TWITS_TABLE-'twits'}
TWITS_FAM=${TWITS_FAM-'t'}

exec $HBASE_HOME/bin/hbase shell <<EOF
create '$TWITS_TABLE', {NAME => '$TWITS_FAM', VERSIONS => 1}
create 'users', {NAME => 'info'}
create 'followes', {NAME => 'f', VERSIONS => 1}
create 'followedBy', {NAME => 'f', VERSIONS => 1}
EOF
```

If you update your application code to read those same constants from a configuration file, you can move your schema definition completely out of the Java code. Now you can easily test different versions of TwitBase against different tables on the same HBase cluster. That flexibility will simplify the process of bringing TwitBase to production. The complete script is shown next.

> **Listing 6.1   UNIX shell replacement for InitTables.java**

```
#!/bin/sh

HBASE_CLI="$HBASE_HOME/bin/hbase"

test -n "$HBASE_HOME" || {                          ◁── Find hbase
  echo >&2 'HBASE_HOME not set. using hbase on $PATH'     command
  HBASE_CLI=$(which hbase)
}

TWITS_TABLE=${TWITS_TABLE-'twits'}                  ◁── Determine table and
TWITS_FAM=${TWITS_FAM-'t'}                               column family names
USERS_TABLE=${USERS_TABLE-'users'}
USERS_FAM=${USERS_FAM-'info'}
FOLLOWS_TABLE=${FOLLOWS_TABLE-'follows'}
```

```
FOLLOWS_FAM=${FOLLOWS_FAM-'f'}
FOLLOWEDBY_TABLE=${FOLLOWED_TABLE-'followedBy'}
FOLLOWEDBY_FAM=${FOLLOWED_FAM-'f'}

exec "$HBASE_CLI" shell <<EOF                          ◁─┐ Run shell
create '$TWITS_TABLE',                                   └ commands
  {NAME => '$TWITS_FAM', VERSIONS => 1}

create '$USERS_TABLE',
  {NAME => '$USERS_FAM'}

create '$FOLLOWS_TABLE',
  {NAME => '$FOLLOWS_FAM', VERSIONS => 1}

create '$FOLLOWEDBY_TABLE',
  {NAME => '$FOLLOWEDBY_FAM', VERSIONS => 1}
EOF
```

This was a primer on how you can use the HBase shell to create scripts that make it easy to do janitorial tasks on your HBase deployment. The HBase shell isn't something you'll use as your primary access method to HBase; it's not meant to have an entire application built on top of it. It's an application itself that has been built on top of JRuby, which we study next.

6.2 Programming the HBase shell using JRuby

The HBase shell provides a convenient interactive environment and is sufficient for many simple administrative tasks. But it can become tedious for more complex operations. As we mentioned in the previous section, the HBase shell is implemented in JRuby.[1] Behind the scenes is a nice library exposing the HBase client to JRuby. You can access that library in your own scripts to create increasingly complex automation over HBase. In this example, you'll build a tool for interacting with the TwitBase `users` table, similar to the `UsersTool` you wrote in Java. This will give you a feel for interacting with HBase from JRuby.

Programming HBase via this JRuby interface is one step above the shell in terms of sophistication. If you find yourself writing complex shell scripts, a JRuby application may be a preferable approach. If for whatever reason you need to use the C implementation of Ruby instead of JRuby, you'll want to explore Thrift. We demonstrate using Thrift from Python later in this chapter; using it from Ruby is similar.

You can find the completed `TwitBase.jrb` script from this section in the TwitBase project source at https://github.com/hbaseinaction/twitbase/blob/master/bin/TwitBase.jrb.

6.2.1 Preparing the HBase shell

The easiest way to launch your own JRuby applications is through the existing HBase shell. If you haven't already done so, locate the shell by following the instructions at the beginning of the previous section.

---

[1] JRuby is the Ruby programming language implemented on top of the JVM. Learn more at http://jruby.org/.

Once you've found the `hbase` command, you can use that as the interpreter for your own scripts. This is particularly useful because it handles importing the necessary libraries and instantiates all the classes you'll need. To get started, create a script to list the tables. Call it `TwitBase.jrb`:

```
def list_tables()
  @hbase.admin(@formatter).list.each do |t|
    puts t
  end
end

list_tables
exit
```

The variables `@hbase` and `@formatter` are two instances created for you by the shell. They're part of that JRuby API you're about to take advantage of. Now give the script a try:

```
$ $HBASE_HOME/bin/hbase shell ./TwitBase.jrb
followers
twits
users
```

With everything in place, let's start working with TwitBase.

6.2.2 *Interacting with the TwitBase users table*

A great thing about writing code for the shell is that it's easy to try out. Launch the shell, and explore the API. Scanning over the `users` table requires a handle to the table and a scanner. Start by acquiring your handle:

```
$ hbase shell
...
hbase(main):001:0> users_table = @hbase.table('users', @formatter)
=> #<Hbase::Table:0x57cae5b7 @table=...>>
```

From the table, create a scanner. Specify the scanner options using a regular hash. The scanner constructor looks for a few specific keys in that hash, including `"START-ROW"`, `"STOPROW"`, and `"COLUMNS"`. Scan over all users, returning only their username, name, and email address:

```
hbase(main):002:0> scan = {"COLUMNS" => ['info:user', 'info:name',
'info:email']}
=> {"COLUMNS"=>["info:user", "info:name", "info:email"]}
hbase(main):003:0> users_table.scan(scan)
=> {"GrandpaD"=>
    {"info:email"=>"timestamp=1338961216314, value=fyodor@brothers.net",
     "info:name"=>"timestamp=1338961216314, value=Fyodor Dostoyevsky",
     "info:user"=>"timestamp=1338961216314, value=GrandpaD"},
   "HMS_Surprise"=>
    {"info:email"=>"timestamp=1338961187869, value=aubrey@sea.com",
     "info:name"=>"timestamp=1338961187869, value=Patrick O'Brian",
     "info:user"=>"timestamp=1338961187869, value=HMS_Surprise"},
   "SirDoyle"=>
    {"info:email"=>"timestamp=1338961221470,
```

```
value=art@TheQueensMen.co.uk",
    "info:name"=>"timestamp=1338961221470, value=Sir Arthur Conan Doyle",
    "info:user"=>"timestamp=1338961221470, value=SirDoyle"},
  "TheRealMT"=>
    {"info:email"=>"timestamp=1338961231471, value=samuel@clemens.org",
     "info:name"=>"timestamp=1338961231471, value=Mark Twain",
     "info:user"=>"timestamp=1338961231471, value=TheRealMT"}}
```

Now you have everything you need to iterate over the keypairs produced by the scanner. It's time to start building the script.

A slight diversion in the API, the block version of `scan()` condenses each column into a string of the format `"column=..., timestamp=..., value=..."`. Parse out the data you're interested in, and accumulate the results:

```
scan = {"COLUMNS" => ['info:user', 'info:name', 'info:email']}
results = {}
users_table.scan(scan) do |row,col|
  unless results[row]
    results[row] = {}
  end
  m = /^.*info:(.*), t.*value=(.*)$/.match(col)    ⟵┤ Parse KeyValue
  results[row][m[1]] = m[2] if m                        results
end
```

The regular expression extracts just the qualifier and cell value from the scan result. It accumulates that data in the results hash. The last step is to format the results:

```
results.each do |row,vals|
  puts "<User %s, %s, %s>" % [vals['user'], vals['name'], vals['email']]
end
```

Now you have everything you need to complete the example. Wrap it up in a `main()`, and ship it! The final `TwitBase.jrb` script is shown in the following listing.

Listing 6.2 TwitBase.jrb: programming the HBase shell

```
def list_users()
  users_table = @hbase.table('users', @formatter)           Connect to table ⟵
  scan = {"COLUMNS" => ['info:user', 'info:name', 'info:email']}    Scan
  results = {}                                                      columns
  users_table.scan(scan) do |row,col|              ⟵           of interest
    results[row] ||= {}
    m = /^.*info:(.*), t.*value=(.*)$/.match(col)    ⟵┐ Parse KeyValue
    results[row][m[1]] = m[2] if m                       results
  end

  results.each do |row,vals|                                      ⟵
    puts "<User %s, %s, %s>" % [vals['user'], vals['name'], vals['email']]
  end
end                                                          Print user
                                                                  rows
def main(args)
  if args.length == 0 || args[0] == 'help'
    puts <<EOM
TwitBase.jrb action ...
  help - print this message and exit
```

```
   list - list all installed users.
EOM
    exit
  end

  if args[0] == 'list'
    list_users
  end

  exit
end

main(ARGV)
```

With your script in order, set it to executable and give it a try:

```
$ chmod a+x TwitBase.jrb
$ ./TwitBase.jrb list
<User GrandpaD, Fyodor Dostoyevsky, fyodor@brothers.net>
<User HMS_Surprise, Patrick O'Brian, aubrey@sea.com>
<User SirDoyle, Sir Arthur Conan Doyle, art@TheQueensMen.co.uk>
<User TheRealMT, Mark Twain, samuel@clemens.org>
```

That's all there is to it. Programming the JRuby interface is an easy way to explore prototypes on top of HBase or automate common tasks. It's all built on the same HBase Java client you've used in previous chapters. For the next sample application, we'll move off the JVM entirely. HBase provides a REST interface, and we'll demonstrate that interface using Curl on the command line.

6.3   *HBase over REST*

One of the factors that prevents people from experimenting with HBase is its close relationship with Java. There are a couple of alternatives for people who are willing to run HBase but want nothing to do with Java for their applications. Whether you're exploring HBase or you want to put an HBase cluster directly in the hands of your application developers, the REST interface may be appropriate. For the uninitiated,[2] REST is a convention for interacting with objects over the web. HBase ships with a REST service that you can use to access HBase, no Java required.

The REST service runs as a separate process and communicates with HBase using the same client API we explored earlier. It can run on any machine configured to communicate with HBase. That means you can spin up a cluster of REST service

> ### REST? Really?
> You refuse Java and reject REST? You're incorrigible! Never fear, HBase has a solution for you as well: Thrift. In practice, the REST service is rarely used for critical application paths. Instead, you'll want to use the Thrift bindings. The next section covers exactly this: communicating with HBase from a Python application over Thrift.

---

[2] Just in case you've never encountered REST, here's a nice introduction: Stefan Tilkov, "A Brief Introduction to REST," InfoQ, www.infoq.com/articles/rest-introduction.

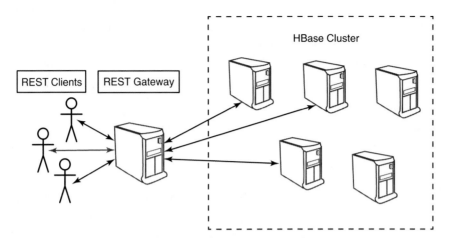

Figure 6.1 A REST gateway deployment. All client activity is funneled through the gateway, greatly reducing client throughput. Clustering the REST gateway machines can mitigate some of this limitation. Clustering introduces a new limitation, however, forcing the client to only use the stateless portions of the API.

machines to host your cluster. Well, almost. The Scanner API is stateful and requires resource allocation, which happens only on the machine that receives the request. That means a client using the scanner must always return to the same REST host while performing that scan. Figure 6.1 loosely illustrates the network topology of a REST gateway deployment.

The REST service also supports a number of response formats, controlled by the `Content-Type` request header. All endpoints support XML, JSON, and Protobufs. Many of the status and administrative endpoints also support plain text. The appropriate header values are `text/plain`, `text/xml`, `application/json`, `application/x-protobuf`, and `application/octet-stream`.

6.3.1 Launching the HBase REST service

Get started by launching the REST service. You'll need HBase installed and configured correctly. Running the service as an active process is done using the same `hbase` base command used to launch the shell:

```
$ hbase rest
...
usage: bin/hbase rest start [-p <arg>] [-ro]
 -p,--port <arg>    Port to bind to [default: 8080]
 -ro,--readonly     Respond only to GET HTTP method requests [default:
                    false]
```

Launch the REST service, listening on port 9999, like this:

```
$ hbase rest start -p 9999
...
INFO mortbay.log: jetty-6.1.26
INFO mortbay.log: Started SocketConnector@0.0.0.0:9999
```

Verify that your service is up and running by launching a new terminal and issuing a simple curl command. All the cool kids these days are using JSON, so you will too. We've even taken the liberty of cleaning up the output for your enjoyment:

```
$ curl -H "Accept: application/json" http://localhost:9999/version
 {
    "JVM": "Apple Inc. 1.6.0_31-20.6-b01-415",
    "Jersey": "1.4",
    "OS": "Mac OS X 10.7.4 x86_64",
    "REST": "0.0.2",
    "Server": "jetty/6.1.26"
}
```

That's the short version about the REST service. If you want info about the underlying cluster, you'll need to ask for that separately:

```
$ curl -H ... http://localhost:9999/version/cluster
"0.92.1"
```

> ### Pretty-printing JSON
> The actual command used to generate that snippet is `curl -H "Accept: application/json" http://localhost:9999/version 2>/dev/null | python -mjson.tool`. We'll continue to gloss over the headers and show beautified output, even though the full command isn't explicitly shown.

Notice in the first terminal window that the service is logging the requests it received. This is handy for debugging.

Running the REST service as a daemon is almost as easy. Depending on your installation, the hbase-daemon.sh script may not be on your PATH. If not, look in your HBase installation directory, HBASE_HOME/bin. Once you've found it, launch the daemon:

```
$ hbase-daemon.sh start rest -p 9999
starting rest, logging to logs/hbase-hbase-rest-ubuntu.out
```

Again, prove to yourself the service is running. This time request a list of tables:

```
$ curl -H ... http://localhost:9999/
{
    "table": [
        {
            "name": "followers"
        },
        {
            "name": "twits"
        },
        {
            "name": "users"
        }
    ]
}
```

Now you're in business. Time to explore HBase over HTTP.

6.3.2 *Interacting with the TwitBase users table*

With your service running, it's time to reach right into HBase. Want to find out Mark Twain's password? You just need his rowkey and the column. Thinking about the logical HBase data model, a map of maps, it's easy to guess what the RESTful URI will be. Construct the request:

```
$ curl -H ... http://localhost:9999/users/TheRealMT/info:password
{
    "Row": [
        {
            "Cell": [
                {
                    "$": "YWJjMTIz",
                    "column": "aW5mbzpwYXNzd29yZA==",
                    "timestamp": 1338701491422
                }
            ],
            "key": "VGhlUmVhbE1U"
        }
    ]
}
```

You wanted a single cell from a single row in a single table, and that's what you received. The Cell object has three fields. column and timestamp should be self-evident; $ is the cell's value.

> **XML in JSON's clothes**
>
> This output format is indeed JSON. It differs from idiomatic JSON in a couple of key ways, because it's generated using the same library and with the same rules used to generate XML. The $ field is an example artifact of this implementation detail. Another is experienced when PUTting new values: attribute order matters.
>
> When in doubt, check the source code. The classes used to render data from the REST service are well documented[3] and clearly describe the schema they expect to produce and consume.

Rowkeys, columns, and values are all bytes to HBase, so they're returned as Base64-encoded Strings. Because you've stored the passwords as simple Strings, you can decode them enough to find the value using the base64 utility:

```
$ echo "YWJjMTIz" | base64 --decode
abc123
```

Let's give Mark a better password. The simplest way to write data is to send raw bytes. This time, you'll specify the Content-Type header to indicate how you're sending the data. In this case the value you want to write is an ASCII string, so there's no complication:

---

[3] Find the REST service's model documentation at http://mng.bz/PyHp.

```
$ curl -XPUT \
  -H "Content-Type: application/octet-stream" \
  http://localhost:9999/users/TheRealMT/info:password \
  -d '70N@rI NO 70t0R0'
```

To continue using JSON, you'll also need to Base64-encode the data before you send it. Start by encoding the new value. Be sure to include the -n option to echo, or you'll introduce an unintentional newline character at the end of the new password:

```
$ echo -n "70N@rI NO 70t0R0" | base64
NzBOQHJJIE4wIDcwdDBSMA==
```

Now send the message body. This is a case where attribute order matters. Be sure to place the $ last in the Cell object map. Don't forget to specify the Content-Type header to indicate you're sending JSON. The full command is as follows:

```
$ curl -XPUT \
  -H "Content-Type: application/json" \
  http://localhost:9999/users/TheRealMT/info:password \
  -d '{
    "Row": [
      {
        "Cell": [
          {
            "column": "aW5mbzpwYXNzd29yZA==",
            "$": "NzBOQHJJIE4wIDcwdDBSMA=="
          }
        ],
        "key": "VGhlUmVhbE1U"
      }
    ]
}'
```

The REST service log will confirm data was received. The (truncated) log line will look something like this:

```
rest.RowResource: PUT http://localhost:9999/users/TheRealMT/info:password
rest.RowResource: PUT {"totalColumns":1...[{... "vlen":16}]...}
```

The REST service also exposes a simple table listing. A GET sent to the table will provide a listing of the *entire* table. The same endpoint exposes basic filter scanning using an asterisk (*) for prefix matching. To find all users whose username starts with the letter *T*, use the following:

```
$ curl -H ... http://localhost:9999/users/T*
{
    "Row": [
      {
        "Cell": [
          ...
        ],
        "key": "VGhlUmVhbE1U"
      },
      ...
    ]
}
```

For a slightly more granular scan, you can instantiate a scanner on the server and ask it to page through results. Create a scanner over all users whose username is less than *I*, paging one cell at a time. The REST service will return an HTTP 201 Created response code with the URI of your scanner instance. Use the -v option on curl to see the response code:

```
$ echo -n "A" | base64
QQ==

$ echo -n "I" | base64
SQ==

$ curl -v -XPUT \
  -H "Content-Type: application/json" \
  http://localhost:9999/users/scanner \
  -d '{
    "startRow": "QQ==",
    "endRow": "SQ==",
    "batch": 1
}'
...
< HTTP/1.1 201 Created
< Location: http://localhost:9999/users/scanner/133887004656926fc5b01
< Content-Length: 0
...
```

Use the location in the response to page through scan results:

```
$ curl -H ... http://localhost:9999/users/scanner/133887004656926fc5b01
{
    "Row": [
        {
            "Cell": [
                {
                    "$": "ZnlvZG9yQGJyb3RoZXJzLm5ldA==",
                    "column": "aW5mbzpibWFpbA==",
                    "timestamp": 1338867440053
                }
            ],
            "key": "R3JhbmRwYUQ="
        }
    ]
}
```

Repeated calls to this URI will return consecutive scan results. Once the row list is exhausted, further calls to the scanner instance will return the HTTP response code 204 No Content.

That's the gist of using the HBase REST gateway. When it comes to doing anything more than exploring a cluster, you'll want to use the Thrift gateway instead. We cover that in the next section.

6.4   *Using the HBase Thrift gateway from Python*

When you live in the world beyond Java, the most common way to interact with HBase is via Thrift.[4] Thrift is a language and set of tools for generating code. Thrift has an Interface Definition Language (IDL) for describing services and objects. It provides a networking protocol for communication between processes using those object and service definitions. Thrift uses the IDL you describe to generate code for you in your favorite languages. Using that code, you can write applications that communicate with each other using the lingua franca provided by Thrift.

HBase ships a Thrift IDL describing a service layer and set of objects. It also provides a service implementing that interface. In this section, you'll generate the Thrift client library for interacting with HBase. You'll use that client library to interact with HBase from Python, completely outside of Java and the JVM. We chose Python because its syntax is approachable to both novice and seasoned programmers. The same approach applies for interacting with HBase from your favorite language. At the time of this writing, Thrift supports 14 different languages.

This API is ... different

In part because of Thrift's ambitions to support so many languages, its IDL is relatively simple. It lacks features common in many languages, such as object inheritance. As a result, the HBase interface via Thrift is slightly different from the Java client API we've explored thus far.

An effort[5] is under way to bring the Thrift API closer to Java, but it remains a work in progress. An early version is available with HBase 0.94, but it lacks some key features like filters and access to coprocessor endpoints.[6] The API we're exploring here will be deprecated upon completion of this effort.

The beauty of using the Thrift API is that it's the same for all languages. Whether you're using PHP, Perl, or C#, the interface is always the same. Additional HBase feature support added to the Thrift API is additional feature support available everywhere.

The Thrift gateway isn't without limitations. Notably, it suffers the same throughput challenges as the REST gateway. All client connections are funneled through a single machine that communicates with the cluster on their behalf. Because the Thrift client opens a connection to a single instance for the duration of its session, clustering Thrift gateways is easier than with REST. Still, portions of the API are stateful, so a disconnected client will lose access to allocated resources when it opens a new connection. Figure 6.2 illustrates the network topology of a Thrift gateway deployment.

---

[4] Originally a project out of Facebook, Thrift is now an Apache project. Learn more at http://thrift.apache.org/.

[5] For more details, see the JIRA ticket "Thrift server to match the new Java API": https://issues.apache.org/jira/browse/HBASE-1744.

[6] Well, you can access them, but you have to modify the Hbase.thrift file for each endpoint you want to expose. For details, see "Make Endpoint Coprocessors Available from Thrift," https://issues.apache.org/jira/browse/HBASE-5600.

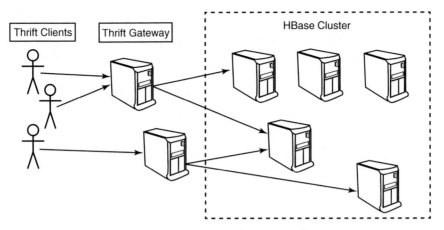

Figure 6.2 A Thrift gateway deployment. All clients are funneled through the gateway, greatly reducing client throughput. Clustering is easier because the Thrift protocol is session-based.

Python is the language for this exercise, so let's begin by creating a Python project, complete with an HBase client library. The final code for this project is available in the GitHub repository, https://github.com/hbaseinaction/twitbase.py.

6.4.1 Generating the HBase Thrift client library for Python

To build the Thrift client library, you need Thrift. Thrift isn't packaged yet, so you'll have to build it from source. On a Mac, that's easy because Thrift is available through Homebrew:[7]

```
$ brew install thrift
...
==> Summary
/usr/local/Cellar/thrift/0.8.0: 75 files, 5.4M, built in 2.4 minutes
```

Those running other platforms will need to build Thrift manually. See the Thrift Requirements[8] doc for details specific to your platform.

Once that's done, verify that your build is alive and well:

```
$ thrift -version
Thrift version 0.8.0
```

You thought you were going to get through this whole book without downloading the HBase source code, didn't you? Sorry to disappoint you. If you want a Thrift client, you'll need to grab the source:

```
$ wget http://www.apache.org/dist/hbase/hbase-0.92.1/hbase-0.92.1.tar.gz
...
Saving to: `hbase-0.92.1.tar.gz'
$ tar xzf hbase-0.92.1.tar.gz
```

---

[7] Homebrew is "The missing package manager for OS X." Find out more at http://mxcl.github.com/homebrew/.

[8] Apache Thrift Requirements: http://thrift.apache.org/docs/install/.

With the HBase source in hand and Thrift installed, you're interested in one file: src/
main/resources/org/apache/hadoop/hbase/thrift/Hbase.thrift. That's the IDL file
that describes the HBase service API and related objects. Skim through it—the Thrift
IDL is legible. Now you have everything you need to generate the Python client.

Start by creating a project directory for yourself and generating the HBase client
bindings:

```
$ mkdir twitbase.py
$ cd twitbase.py
$ thrift -gen py ../hbase-0.92.1/src/main/resources/org/apache/hadoop/hbase/
    thrift/Hbase.thrift
$ mv gen-py/* .
$ rm -r gen-py/
```

You've created a project called twitbase.py and generated the HBase Python library.
Thrift generated its code in a subdirectory called gen-py. By moving all that up into
your project, you can easily import the code into your application. Look at what was
generated:

```
$ find .
./__init__.py
./hbase
./hbase/__init__.py
./hbase/constants.py
./hbase/Hbase-remote
./hbase/Hbase.py
./hbase/ttypes.py
```

You also need to install the Thrift Python library. These are the core components common across all Thrift services used from Python, so you can install them globally:

```
$ sudo easy_install thrift==0.8.0
Searching for thrift==0.8.0
Best match: thrift 0.8.0
...
Finished processing dependencies for thrift
```

Alternately, this library is also part of the source you compiled. You can copy these
files into your project as you did with the HBase client. From within the twitbase.py
directory, you do so as follows:

```
$ mkdir thrift
$ cp -r ../thrift-0.8.0/lib/py/src/* ./thrift/
```

Verify that everything worked as expected. Launch Python, and import both the
Thrift and HBase libraries. No output means everything is as it should be:

```
$ python
Python 2.7.1 (r271:86832, Jul 31 2011, 19:30:53)
...
>>> import thrift
>>> import hbase
```

Be sure to run these commands from within the twitbase.py directory, or the import
statements will fail. With the client library ready to go, let's start the server component.

6.4.2   Launching the HBase Thrift service

The server component ships with HBase, so it doesn't involve all the setup required by the client library. Launch the Thrift service the same way you launch the shell, using the hbase command:

```
$ hbase thrift
...
usage: Thrift [-b <arg>] [-c] [-f] [-h] [-hsha | -nonblocking |
       -threadpool]  [-p <arg>]
 -b,--bind <arg>     Address to bind the Thrift server to. Not supported by
                     the Nonblocking and HsHa server [default: 0.0.0.0]
 -c,--compact        Use the compact protocol
 -f,--framed         Use framed transport
 -h,--help           Print help information
 -hsha               Use the THsHaServer. This implies the framed transport.
 -nonblocking        Use the TNonblockingServer. This implies the framed
                     transport.
 -p,--port <arg>     Port to bind to [default: 9090]
 -threadpool         Use the TThreadPoolServer. This is the default.
```

Make sure HBase is up and running, then launch the Thrift service. The default settings should be fine:

```
$ hbase thrift start
...
ThriftServer: starting HBase ThreadPool Thrift server on /0.0.0.0:9090
```

With both the client and server ready, it's time to test them. Open a terminal window in your twitbase.py project directory, and once again launch Python:

```
$ python
Python 2.7.1 (r271:86832, Jul 31 2011, 19:30:53)
...
>>> from thrift.transport import TSocket
>>> from thrift.protocol import TBinaryProtocol
>>> from hbase import Hbase
>>> transport = TSocket.TSocket('localhost', 9090)
>>> protocol = TBinaryProtocol.TBinaryProtocol(transport)
>>> client = Hbase.Client(protocol)
>>> transport.open()
>>> client.getTableNames()
['followers', 'twits', 'users']
```

It took you a little while to get here, but it all works! Now you can get down to business.

6.4.3   Scanning the TwitBase users table

Before you start writing code, let's explore at the interpreter a little more to get a feel for the API. You're interested in scanning the users table, so let's start with a scanner. Examining the Hbase.IFace class in Hbase.py, it looks like scannerOpen() is the simplest method. It returns a scanner ID you can call on the Thrift server. Let's try it:

```
>>> columns = ['info:user','info:name','info:email']
>>> scanner = client.scannerOpen('users', '', columns)
>>> scanner
14
```

Here you've asked for an unbounded scanner over the users table, returning only three qualifiers from the info column. It happens to have the ID 14. Let's take the first row and see what you get:

```
>>> row = client.scannerGet(scanner)
>>> row
[TRowResult(
   columns={'info:email': TCell(timestamp=1338530917411,
                                value='samuel@clemens.org'),
            'info:name': TCell(timestamp=1338530917411,
                               value='Mark Twain'),
            'info:user': TCell(timestamp=1338530917411,
                               value='TheRealMT')},
   row='TheRealMT')]
```

scannerGet() returns a list with a single TRowResult. That row has a columns field that is a dictionary from column qualifier to a TCell instance.

Now that you know what you're working with, let's build out a class to wrap up all these details. Call that helper class TwitBaseConn and give it a constructor to hide all these Thrift connection details. Also, be sure to close() anything you open():

```
class TwitBaseConn(object):
    def __init__(self, host="localhost", port=9090):
        transport = TSocket.TSocket(host, port)
        self.transport = TTransport.TBufferedTransport(transport)
        self.protocol = TBinaryProtocol.TBinaryProtocol(self.transport)
        self.client = Hbase.Client(self.protocol)
        self.transport.open()

    def close(self):
        self.transport.close()
```

This defines a default constructor that will connect to the Thrift service running locally. It also adds an extra layer to the networking stack, wrapping the socket in a buffer. Now add a method to handle scanning rows from the users table:

```
def scan_users(self):
    columns = ['info:user','info:name','info:email']
    scanner = self.client.scannerOpen('users', '', columns)
    row = self.client.scannerGet(scanner)
    while row:
        yield row[0]
        row = self.client.scannerGet(scanner)
    self.client.scannerClose(scanner)
```

That takes care of reading rows and cleaning up after the scanner. Those rows are full of Thrift library details, though, so let's add another method to pull out the data you want:

```
def _user_from_row(self, row):
    user = {}
    for col,cell in row.columns.items():
        user[col[5:]] = cell.value
    return "<User: {user}, {name}, {email}>".format(**user)
```

This method loops through the TCells and creates a string from their contents.
Update scan_users() to call this method instead of returning the raw rows:

```python
def scan_users(self):
    columns = ['info:user','info:name','info:email']
    scanner = self.client.scannerOpen('users', '', columns)
    row = self.client.scannerGet(scanner)
    while row:
        yield self._user_from_row(row[0])
        row = self.client.scannerGet(scanner)
    self.client.scannerClose(scanner)
```

Great! All that's left is to wrap it up in a main(), and you can give it a spin. The final
TwitBase.py script is shown next.

Listing 6.3   TwitBase.py: connecting to TwitBase from Python via Thrift

```python
#! /usr/bin/env python

import sys

from thrift.transport import TSocket, TTransport
from thrift.protocol import TBinaryProtocol

from hbase import Hbase
from hbase.ttypes import *

usage = """TwitBase.py action ...
  help - print this messsage and exit
  list - list all installed users."""

class TwitBaseConn(object):
    def __init__(self, host="localhost", port=9090):
        transport = TSocket.TSocket(host, port)
        self.transport = TTransport.TBufferedTransport(transport)
        self.protocol = TBinaryProtocol.TBinaryProtocol(self.transport)
        self.client = Hbase.Client(self.protocol)
        self.transport.open()

    def close(self):
        self.transport.close()

    def _user_from_row(self, row):
        user = {}
        for col,cell in row.columns.items():
            user[col[5:]] = cell.value
        return "<User: {user}, {name}, {email}>".format(**user)

    def scan_users(self):
        columns = ['info:user','info:name','info:email']
        scanner = self.client.scannerOpen('users', '', columns)
        row = self.client.scannerGet(scanner)
        while row:
            yield self._user_from_row(row[0])
            row = self.client.scannerGet(scanner)
        self.client.scannerClose(scanner)

def main(args=None):
```

```
        if args is None:
            args = sys.argv[1:]

        if len(args) == 0 or 'help' == args[0]:
            print usage
            raise SystemExit()

        twitBase = TwitBaseConn()

        if args[0] == 'list':
            for user in twitBase.scan_users():
                print user

        twitBase.close()

if __name__ == '__main__':
    main()
```

The `main()` is super simple. It opens the connection, calls the scan, prints the results, and closes the connection again. With Python, there's nothing to compile. You do need to make the file executable, though, which is a one-liner:

```
$ chmod a+x TwitBase.py
```

Now you're ready to try it:

```
$ ./TwitBase.py list
<User: TheRealMT, Mark Twain, samuel@clemens.org>
<User: GrandpaD, Fyodor Dostoyevsky, fyodor@brothers.net>
<User: SirDoyle, Sir Arthur Conan Doyle, art@TheQueensMen.co.uk>
<User: HMS_Surprise, Patrick O'Brian, aubrey@sea.com>
```

Nicely done! You have everything you need to start building HBase applications in Python. Next up, we'll explore an entirely new Java language client, asynchbase.

6.5   *Asynchbase: an alternative Java HBase client*

The HBase Java client is completely synchronous. When your application interacts with HBase through the `HTableInterface`, every action blocks your application thread while HBase can respond to the request. This behavior isn't always desirable. Some applications don't need to wait on the server to respond before continuing with the execution path. In fact, the synchronous dependency on the server is detrimental to many user-facing applications.

Asynchbase[9] is an alternative HBase client, also written in Java. It's fully asynchronous, which means it doesn't block the thread of the calling application. It makes thread safety a priority, and its client API is designed for use in multithreaded applications. The author of asynchbase strives for maximal client performance and maintains a set of benchmarks[10] comparing asynchbase to the stock HBase client.

---

[9] Learn more about asynchbase at https://github.com/stumbleupon/asynchbase.

[10] Benchmarks, including reproduction instructions and results, can be found attached to this HBase JIRA ticket: "Asynchbase PerformanceEvaluation," https://issues.apache.org/jira/browse/HBASE-5539.

Asynchbase is built on an asynchronous library called async.[11] It's modeled after the asynchronous processing component of the Python Twisted[12] library. Async allows you to build parallel data-processing pipelines by *chaining successive actions* onto asynchronous computations. An explanation of the concepts core to these projects is beyond the scope of this section. We provide you with some of the basics but recommend that you explore these related projects and concepts on your own if you're serious about using asynchbase. Asynchronous programming is relatively uncommon and can be unintuitive. It's a different way of thinking, albeit an important one, when considering a user-facing application dealing with large amounts of data at the back end.

The primary notable deployment of asynchbase is OpenTSDB, an application covered in detail in a later chapter. Both asynchbase and OpenTSDB are written and maintained by the same community of users. That community is relatively small in comparison to the wider HBase community. As with any open source project, caution is advised when approaching a project that has not yet achieved critical mass. That said, the popularity of asynchbase is growing.

Another serious consideration for choosing asynchbase is multiversion support. HBase releases are labeled with a version number of the form major.minor.patch. This book tracks HBase version 0.92.x, or major version 0, minor version 92, and an unspecified patch level. When using the stock client, your client major and minor versions must match the cluster major and minor versions.[13] You can use a 0.90.3 client with any 0.90.x cluster, but it isn't compatible with a 0.92.x cluster. The asynchbase client, on the other hand, supports all HBase releases since version 0.20.4 (released mid-2010). That means your client code is entirely decoupled from your cluster deployment. This can be a huge win when considering client code that can't be upgraded as frequently as the cluster.

In this example, you'll build an alternative client to the TwitBase users table using the asynchbase client. The final code for this project is available in the GitHub repository, https://github.com/hbaseinaction/twitbase-async.

6.5.1 Creating an asynchbase project

To get started, you'll need a new Java project. The simplest way to create one is using Maven archetypes. Maven archetypes are prebuilt project templates that provide basic Maven project scaffolding. For this you'll use the simplest, the quickstart archetype. You can follow along here to create the project.

Create the project structure using the archetype:generate command:

```
$ mvn archetype:generate \
    -DarchetypeGroupId=org.apache.maven.archetypes \
    -DarchetypeArtifactId=maven-archetype-quickstart \
    -DgroupId=HBaseIA \
    -DartifactId=twitbase-async \
    -Dversion=1.0.0
```

---

[11] Async provides asynchronous event processing in Java: https://github.com/stumbleupon/async.
[12] Twisted provides a Deferred object for building chains of nonblocking event handlers. The Deferred documentation is available at http://twistedmatrix.com/documents/current/core/howto/defer.html.
[13] This versioning scheme is roughly outlined in the Apache Release Management guide: http://mng.bz/6uvM.

After Maven downloads any missing dependencies, it will prompt you to confirm the parameters. Press Enter and let it do its thing. This will create a directory called twit-base-async in the current directory. It's populated with a basic "hello world" command-line application.

The next thing to do is add asynchbase to the project as a dependency. A file called pom.xml in the top-level project directory manages the Maven project. Edit the generated pom.xml, and add a couple of new `<dependency>` entries to the `<dependencies>` block:

```xml
<dependencies>
  <dependency>
    <groupId>org.hbase</groupId>
    <artifactId>asynchbase</artifactId>
    <version>1.3.1</version>
  </dependency>
  <dependency>
    <groupId>org.slf4j</groupId>
    <artifactId>slf4j-api</artifactId>
    <version>1.6.6</version>
  </dependency>
  <dependency>
    <groupId>org.slf4j</groupId>
    <artifactId>slf4j-simple</artifactId>
    <version>1.6.6</version>
  </dependency>
  ...
</dependencies>
```

Let's also add `maven-assembly-plugin` to the pom.xml file. This will allow you to create a JAR containing all of the project's dependencies and simplify launching the AsyncTwitBase application. Add a new `<build>` block to the `<project>`:

```xml
<project ...>
  ...
  <build>
    <plugins>
      <plugin>
        <artifactId>maven-assembly-plugin</artifactId>
        <version>2.3</version>
        <executions>
          <execution>
            <id>jar-with-dependencies</id>
            <phase>package</phase>
            <goals>
              <goal>single</goal>
            </goals>
            <configuration>
              <descriptorRefs>
                <descriptorRef>jar-with-dependencies</descriptorRef>
              </descriptorRefs>
              <appendAssemblyId>false</appendAssemblyId>
```

```
            </configuration>
          </execution>
        </executions>
      </plugin>
    </plugins>
  </build>
</project>
```

Now is a good time to make sure everything works. Go ahead and build and run your application with the following commands. You should see the following output:

```
$ mvn package
[INFO] Scanning for projects...
[INFO]
[INFO] ------------------------------------------------------------
[INFO] Building twitbase-async 1.0.0
[INFO] ------------------------------------------------------------
...
[INFO] ------------------------------------------------------------
[INFO] BUILD SUCCESS
[INFO] ------------------------------------------------------------
[INFO] Total time: 12.191s

$ java -cp target/twitbase-async-1.0.0.jar HBaseIA.App
Hello World!
```

Now your project is ready to start using asynchbase.

6.5.2 *Changing TwitBase passwords*

Let's create an application to randomize the passwords of all users in the system. This kind of thing would be useful if your TwitBase deployment suffered a security breach. You'd like your application to scan through all users in the users table, retrieve the user's password, and generate a new password based on the old one. You also want the application to notify the user of the security breach and inform them as to how they can retrieve their account. You'll do all this by chaining successive actions using async's Deferred and Callback objects. The workflow as a Callback chain is illustrated in figure 6.3.

Wiring a Callback instance onto a Deferred instance chains successive steps together. This is done using the addCallback family of methods provided by the Deferred class. Callbacks can also be attached to handle error cases, as you see in step 4b. Async calls these Errbacks, a term consistent with the terminology used in Twisted Python. The final result of a Callback chain is retrieved by calling join() on the associated Deferred instance. If the Deferred is finished processing, calling join(long timeout) returns immediately with a result. If the Deferred's Callback chain is still processing, the current thread blocks until either the Deferred completes or the timeout, in milliseconds, expires.

With your newfound understanding of the async data-processing pipeline and a rough idea of the pipeline you want to build, let's start building it.

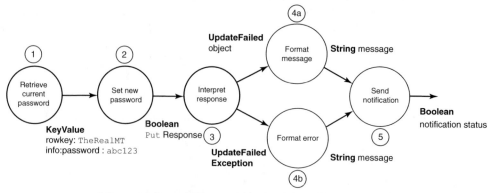

1 Scan over all rows in the users table. A `KeyValue` is produced for each user.
2 Calculate a new password based on the old and send a `Put` to HBase.
3 Interpret the `Put` response as either a success or failure.
4 Format a message to send based on response result.
5 Send the notification message and return true.

Figure 6.3   Building a data-processing pipeline with `Callbacks`. Each step takes output from the previous one, processes it, and sends it to the next, until a final result is reached.

THE ASYNCHRONOUS HBASE CLIENT

Your primary entry point into asynchbase is the `HBaseClient` class. It manages your interactions with the HBase cluster. Its responsibility is something of a combination of both `HTablePool` and `HTableInterface` from the stock client.

Your application needs only a single instance of `HBaseClient`. Much like an `HTable-Interface`, you need to make sure you close it after you're finished using it. Using the stock client, you would do this:

```
HTablePool pool = new HTablePool(...);
HTableInterface myTable = pool.getTable("myTable");
// application code
myTable.close();
pool.closeTablePool("myTable");
```

In asynchbase, you have the following:

```
final HBaseClient client = new HBaseClient("localhost");
// application code
client.shutdown().joinUninterruptibly();
```

This snippet creates an instance of `HBaseClient` that talks to an HBase managed by localhost. It then closes that instance and blocks the current thread until the `shutdown()` method completes. Waiting on `shutdown()` to complete is necessary to ensure that all pending RPC requests are completed and the thread pool is properly disposed before the application exits. `shutdown()` returns an instance of the `Deferred` class, which represents an operation executing on another thread. Waiting is accomplished by calling one of the `join` family of methods on the `Deferred` instance. Here you call `joinUninterruptibly()` because you want to ensure that the client resources are cleaned when you're finished. Note that if your thread is interrupted while waiting on joinUninterruptibly(), it will still be marked as interrupted.

You'll use this client instance to create a Scanner. The asynchbase Scanner is similar to the ResultsScanner with which you're already familiar. Create a Scanner against the users table, and limit its results to the info:password column:

```
final Scanner scanner = client.newScanner("users");
scanner.setFamily("info");
scanner.setQualifier("password");
```

Use this Scanner instance to walk the rows in your table by calling nextRows(). Like the other asynchronous operations in this library, nextRows() returns a Deferred instance. Like the stock scanner, you can request specific number of results per page by passing a number to nextRows(). To help emphasize the asynchronous nature of the application, let's limit the scan results to a single row per page.

> **Don't do this in a real application!**
> Limiting your scanner to a single row per request will significantly hinder your application performance. The only reason we do so here is to maximize the opportunity for failure scenarios to trigger. You'll see what we're talking about later in the section.

Each returned row consists of a list of its cells. These cells are represented by instances of the KeyValue class. In order to walk the page of returned rows, you loop over a list of lists of KeyValue instances:

```
ArrayList<ArrayList<KeyValue>> rows = null;
while ((rows = scanner.nextRows(1).joinUninterruptibly()) != null) {
  for (ArrayList<KeyValue> row : rows) {
    // ...
  }
}
```

Like the call to shutdown(), this code blocks the current thread until all results are available before consuming them. Scanning rows asynchronously doesn't make a lot of sense when you're interested in maintaining row order. By joining on each Deferred instance, you realize the scan results into the rows variable. Parsing the results is similar to consuming KeyValue objects in the stock client. This is step 1 from the state diagram, illustrated in figure 6.4.

The code looks like this:

```
KeyValue kv = row.get(0);
byte[] expected = kv.value();
String userId = new String(kv.key());
```

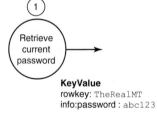

Figure 6.4   Step 1 is to scan over all rows in the users table. A KeyValue is produced for each user.

```
PutRequest put = new PutRequest(
  "users".getBytes(), kv.key(), kv.family(),
  kv.qualifier(), mkNewPassword(expected));
```

Store new password based on old

The scanner was limited to returning the `info:password` column, so you know there will be only a single `KeyValue` per result row. You take that `KeyValue` and pull out the bits relevant to you. For this example, the old password is used to seed the new password, so pass it into the `mkNewPassword()` method. Create a new `Put` instance, which asynchbase calls a `PutRequest`, to update the user's password. The last step is to construct a `Callback` chain and attach it to the `PutRequest` invocation.

Thus far you've implemented all of step 1 and most of step 2 from figure 6.3. Before you start chaining `Callbacks`, let's write a couple of methods to help you watch the asynchronous application at work.

DEVELOPING AN ASYNCHRONOUS APPLICATION

Developing and debugging asynchronous applications can be tricky, so you'll set yourself up for success. The first thing you want is to print debugging statements with their associated thread. For this, you'll use the logging library SLF4J, the same logging library used by asynchbase. The following line gives you what you need:

```
static final Logger LOG = LoggerFactory.getLogger(AsyncUsersTool.class);
```

To help explore the asynchronous nature of this code, it's useful to introduce simulated latency into the system. The method `latency()` will occasionally delay processing by forcing the thread to sleep:

```
static void latency() throws Exception {
  if (System.currentTimeMillis() % 2 == 0) {
    LOG.info("a thread is napping...");
    Thread.sleep(1000);
  }
}
```

You can do the same by introducing occasional failures, slightly less frequently, with the `entropy()` method:

```
static boolean entropy(Boolean val) {
  if (System.currentTimeMillis() % 3 == 0) {
    LOG.info("entropy strikes!");
    return false;
  }
  return (val == null) ? Boolean.TRUE : val;
}
```

You'll call `latency()` at the beginning and end of each `Callback` to slow things down a little. Call `entropy()` on the result produced by step 2 so you can exercise the error handling provided by step 4b. Now it's time to implement `Callbacks` for each of the remaining steps.

CHAINING SUCCESSIVE ACTIONS USING CALLBACKS

Step 3 in the data pipeline is to interpret the response generated by the `PutRequest` sent to HBase. This step is summarized in figure 6.5.

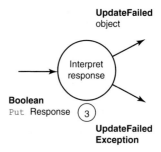

You'll do this by implementing async's `Callback` interface. The implementation receives a `Boolean` from the HBase response and generates an `UpdateResult` instance, an object specific to your application. The `UpdateResult` class is simple, just a package for data:

```
static final class UpdateResult {
  public String userId;
  public boolean success;
}
```

Figure 6.5   Step 3 is to interpret the Put response as either a success or a failure.

Step 3 can also throw an `UpdateFailedException` when the `PutRequest` fails or when `entropy()` strikes. Async looks for `Exceptions`, either thrown by or returned by `Deferred` and `Callback` instances, to trigger the error-handling callback chain. You implement your own exception so you can package a little context along with the exception. It looks like this:

```
static final class UpdateFailedException extends Exception {
  public UpdateResult result;

  public UpdateFailedException(UpdateResult r) {
    this.result = r;
  }
}
```

Now you can implement your `Callback` to handle step 3. The responsibility of this class is to translate the asynchbase response into an application-specific datatype. You'll call it `InterpretResponse`. It has a constructor to pass in the user ID; that way you know which user you were processing when you received this response. The meat of the code is in the `UpdateResult call(Boolean response)` method. This method starts and ends by calling `latency()`. It also takes the `response` received from HBase and subjects it to `entropy()`. This is purely for the purposes of your understanding. The real work is in taking the response and either constructing an `UpdateResult` instance or throwing an `UpdateFailedException`. Either way, there's not much work involved. You can imagine performing an arbitrarily complex operation in your real working code:

```
static final class InterpretResponse
    implements Callback<UpdateResult, Boolean> {

  private String userId;

  InterpretResponse(String userId) {
    this.userId = userId;
  }

  public UpdateResult call(Boolean response) throws Exception {
```

```
      latency();

      UpdateResult r = new UpdateResult();
      r.userId = this.userId;
      r.success = entropy(response);
      if (!r.success)
        throw new UpdateFailedException(r);

      latency();
      return r;
    }
}
```

InterpretResponse is the most complex Callback in this example, so if you're still following, you should be in good shape. This Callback has either performed its transformation or detected an error and bailed. Either way, the decision of what Callback to invoke next is left up to async. This is an important concept when thinking about these data-processing pipelines. Each step in the chain is ignorant of the others. Notice that the type signature of InterpretResponse implements Callback<UpdateResult, Boolean>. Those generic types correspond to the signature of the call() method. The only thing that links step 3 to step 4 is the contract between them in the form of type signatures.

For the next step, you'll implement the successful case first: step 4a from the state diagram. For context, figure 6.6 illustrates both steps 4a and 4b.

This step takes the UpdateResult produced in step 3 and converts it into a String message, perhaps to send to the user via email or to update a log somewhere. Thus, step 4a is implemented by a Callback<String, UpdateResult>. Call this one ResultToMessage:

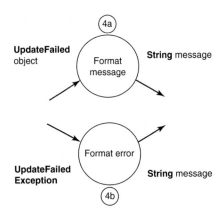

Figure 6.6   Steps 4a and 4b format a message to send based on response result.

```
static final class ResultToMessage
    implements Callback<String, UpdateResult> {

  public String call(UpdateResult r) throws Exception {
    latency();
    String fmt = "password change for user %s successful.";
    latency();
    return String.format(fmt, r.userId);
  }
}
```

Again, you're calling latency() at the beginning and end of the call() method. Otherwise, there's nothing fancy here. Construction of the message is simple, and it looks like it's appropriate for the user. There's also nothing going on to throw an Exception, so you won't consider an Errback chain for this step.

The Errback defining step 4b is similar to the Callback in 4a. It's also implemented as a Callback, this time parameterized on String and UpdateFailedException. The processing work is almost identical, except it retrieves the user ID context from the Exception instead of an UpdateResult:

```
static final class FailureToMessage
    implements Callback<String, UpdateFailedException> {

  public String call(UpdateFailedException e) throws Exception {
    latency();
    String fmt = "%s, your password is unchanged!";
    latency();
    return String.format(fmt, e.result.userId);
  }
}
```

Both ResultToMessage and FailureToMessage produce a String for their output. That means they can be chained to the same Callback instance for the final step, 5. Step 5 is handled by SendMessage and is an implementation of Callback<Object, String>; see figure 6.7.

SendMessage should either succeed, in which case it returns true, or throw a SendMessageFailed-Exception. There's nothing special about the failure Exception; it's application-specific for the sake of clarity in the example. SendMessage looks like this:

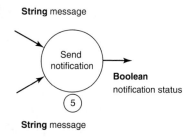

String message

Boolean
notification status

String message

Figure 6.7   Step 5 sends the notification message.

```
static final class SendMessage
    implements Callback<Boolean, String> {

  public Boolean call(String s) throws Exception {
    latency();
    if (entropy(null))
      throw new SendMessageFailedException();
    LOG.info(s);
    latency();
    return Boolean.TRUE;
  }
}
```

Again, you have a little latency() and entropy() to keep things interesting. Either the message is delivered or an Exception is thrown. In this case, there is no Errback to chain into the data pipeline, so that error needs to be handled in client code. With the processing pipeline implemented, let's return to the code consuming the scanner.

WIRING UP THE DATA PIPELINE

When you last saw your user application, it was reading rows off the scanner and building PutRequest objects to initiate the processing pipeline, essentially step 1 from the state diagram. The last thing to do is to send those Puts off to HBase and pass the response down the Callback chain, as shown in figure 6.8.

This is where you finally get your hands on a `Deferred` instance! For this example, you use the method `Deferred<Boolean> HBaseClient.compareAndSet(PutRequest put, byte[] expected)` instead of `put()` to simplify explanation of the `Callback` chain. This is the atomic version of `put()`. `compareAndSet()` returns a `Deferred` instance that, once `join()`ed, will return a `Boolean`. That's the entry point for chaining `Callbacks`. The chaining looks like this:

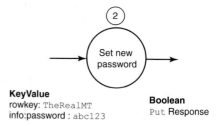

KeyValue
rowkey: `TheRealMT`
info:password : `abc123`

Boolean
`Put` Response

Figure 6.8   Step 2 calculates a new password based on the old and sends a `Put` to HBase.

Execute step 2

```
Deferred<Boolean> d = client.compareAndSet(put, expected)     ← | Append step 3
  .addCallback(new InterpretResponse(userId))                 ←
  .addCallbacks(new ResultToMessage(), new FailureToMessage()) ← Append steps
  .addCallback(new SendMessage());   ←                            4a and 4b
```
Append step 5

Each consecutive call to `addCallback()` returns the same `Deferred` instance but with its type updated to correspond to the return type of the attached `Callback`. So, executing step 2 returns a `Deferred<Boolean>`, and after chaining the `Callback` for step 3 it becomes a `Deferred<UpdateResult>`. Chaining on steps 4a and 4b is done using `addCallbacks()`, with an *s*. This returns a `Deferred<String>`, which is typed by the return type of the success case. The error case in async is always typed by an `Exception`, so it need not be specified in the `Deferred`. Step 5 turns it into a `Deferred<Boolean>`, the type ultimately consumed by the application.

Each row in the scan result has a corresponding `Deferred<Boolean>` whose execution you want to see completed. The only way to see the results of the full `Callback` chain for each row is to collect the final `Deferred<Boolean>` instances and `join()` on them. This is the same code as before, just with the extra bookkeeping of collecting the `Deferred<Boolean>` instances:

```
ArrayList<Deferred<Boolean>> workers
  = new ArrayList<Deferred<Boolean>>();
while ((rows = scanner.nextRows(1).joinUninterruptibly()) != null) {
  for (ArrayList<KeyValue> row : rows) {
    // ...
    Deferred<Boolean> d = ...;
    workers.add(d);
  }
}
```

Notice that your list of `workers` preserves the order in which the rows were produced. This isn't particularly useful for this example because you've been careful to keep track of necessary context as you go using the custom `UpdateResult` and `Update-FailedException` classes. You could as easily accumulate state out at this level, for instance, by creating a `Map` of user ID to `Deferred<Boolean>` results. Because you're not interested in any specific result, you can join on all the `Deferred` instances as a group. The last step is to invoke `join()` and accumulate the results of your processing:

```
Deferred<ArrayList<Object>> d = Deferred.group(workers);
try {
  d.join();
} catch (DeferredGroupException e) {
  LOG.info(e.getCause().getMessage());
}
```

Your machine is executing them all in the background simultaneously. When you call `join()`, async gives you back all the results of the processing chains for each worker. If any component of the chain threw or returned an instance of `Exception` along the way, it throws that `Exception` for you to catch here. The `Deferred` that encapsulates all of the individual `Deferred` instances wraps those exceptions in the `Deferred-GroupException`. Unpack it with a call to `getCause()` to see the underlying error.

To round it all out, let's give the command-line application a meaningful name. Rename the file src/main/java/HBaseIA/App.java something useful like AsyncUsers-Tool.java, move it into an appropriate package path, and update the class name and package as well. Your final `AsyncUsersTool` will look like this.

Listing 6.4 Complete asynchbase client to TwitBase: `AsyncUsersTool`

```
package HBaseIA.TwitBase;                     Imports
// ...                                        omitted

  static final byte[] TABLE_NAME    = "users".getBytes();
  static final byte[] INFO_FAM      = "info".getBytes();
  static final byte[] PASSWORD_COL = "password".getBytes();
  static final byte[] EMAIL_COL     = "email".getBytes();

  public static final String usage =
    "usertool action ...\n" +
    "  help - print this message and exit.\n" +
    "  update - update passwords for all installed users.\n";

  static final Object lock = new Object();

  static void println(String msg) {              Synchronize writing to
    synchronized (lock) {                        stdout among threads
      System.out.println(msg);
    }
  }

  static byte[] mkNewPassword(byte[] seed) {     Generate new password
    // ...                                       based on old
  }

  static void latency() throws Exception {       Add reality to
    if (System.currentTimeMillis() % 2 == 0) {   sample app
      println("a thread is napping...");
      Thread.sleep(1000);
    }
  }
```

```
static boolean entropy(Boolean val) {                    Add reality to
  if (System.currentTimeMillis() % 3 == 0) {             sample app
    println("entropy strikes!");
    return false;
  }
  return (val == null) ? Boolean.TRUE : val;
}

static final class UpdateResult {                                        ◁─┐
  public String userId;                                                    │
  public boolean success;                                                  │
}                                                                          │
                                                                           │
static final class UpdateFailedException extends Exception {      ◁──      │
  private static final long serialVersionUID = 1L;                         │
  public UpdateResult result;                                              │
                                           Application-specific            │
  public UpdateFailedException(UpdateResult r) {    container and          │
    this.result = r;                                    exceptions         │
  }                                                                        │
}                                                                          │
                                                                           │
static final class SendMessageFailedException extends Exception { ◁──────┘
  private static final long serialVersionUID = 1L;

  public SendMessageFailedException() {
    super("Failed to send message!");
  }
}                                             Convert
                                              Deferred<Boolean> into
static final class InterpretResponse          Deferred<UpdateResult>
    implements Callback<UpdateResult, Boolean> {  ◁──┘

  private String userId;

  InterpretResponse(String userId) {
    this.userId = userId;
  }

  public UpdateResult call(Boolean response) throws Exception {
    latency();

    UpdateResult r = new UpdateResult();
    r.userId = this.userId;
    r.success = entropy(response);         Throw during exceptional
    if (!r.success)                        cases; let async handle the
      throw new UpdateFailedException(r);  ◁── rest

    latency();
    return r;
  }

  @Override
  public String toString() {
    return String.format("InterpretResponse<%s>", userId);
  }
}
                                              Convert
                                              Deferred<UpdateResult>
static final class ResultToMessage            into a Deferred<String>
    implements Callback<String, UpdateResult> {  ◁──┘
```

```
  public String call(UpdateResult r) throws Exception {
    latency();
    String fmt = "password change for user %s successful.";
    latency();
    return String.format(fmt, r.userId);
  }

  @Override
  public String toString() {
    return "ResultToMessage";
  }
}
static final class FailureToMessage
    implements Callback<String, UpdateFailedException> {

  public String call(UpdateFailedException e) throws Exception {
    latency();
    String fmt = "%s, your password is unchanged!";
    latency();
    return String.format(fmt, e.result.userId);
  }

  @Override
  public String toString() {
    return "FailureToMessage";
  }
}

static final class SendMessage
    implements Callback<Boolean, String> {

  public Boolean call(String s) throws Exception {
    latency();
    if (entropy(null))
      throw new SendMessageFailedException();
    println(s);
    latency();
    return Boolean.TRUE;
  }

  @Override
  public String toString() {
    return "SendMessage";
  }
}

static List<Deferred<Boolean>> doList(HBaseClient client)
    throws Throwable {
  final Scanner scanner = client.newScanner(TABLE_NAME);
  scanner.setFamily(INFO_FAM);
  scanner.setQualifier(PASSWORD_COL);

  ArrayList<ArrayList<KeyValue>> rows = null;
  ArrayList<Deferred<Boolean>> workers
    = new ArrayList<Deferred<Boolean>>();
  while ((rows = scanner.nextRows(1).joinUninterruptibly()) != null) {
    println("received a page of users.");
```

Annotations:

- **Convert Deferred<UpdateFailedException> into Deferred<String>** (points to `static final class FailureToMessage`)
- **Convert Deferred<String> into Deferred<Boolean>** (points to `static final class SendMessage`)
- **Create scanner; restrict to info:password column** (points to `scanner.setQualifier(PASSWORD_COL);`)

```
      for (ArrayList<KeyValue> row : rows) {                    ◁─┐  Parse single row;
        KeyValue kv = row.get(0);                                 │  produce PutRequest
        byte[] expected = kv.value();
        String userId = new String(kv.key());
        PutRequest put = new PutRequest(
            TABLE_NAME, kv.key(), kv.family(),
            kv.qualifier(), mkNewPassword(expected));
        Deferred<Boolean> d = client.compareAndSet(put, expected) ◁─┐  Wire up
          .addCallback(new InterpretResponse(userId))               │  Callback
          .addCallbacks(new ResultToMessage(), new FailureToMessage())  │  chain
          .addCallback(new SendMessage());
        workers.add(d);                                      ◁─┐  Collect Deferred
      }                                                        │  instances as
    }                                                          │  produced
    return workers;
  }

  public static void main(String[] args) throws Throwable {
    if (args.length == 0 || "help".equals(args[0])) {
      System.out.println(usage);
      System.exit(0);
    }

    final HBaseClient client = new HBaseClient("localhost");

    if ("update".equals(args[0])) {
      for(Deferred<Boolean> d: doList(client)) {
        try {                                            ┐  join() on workers;
          d.join();                                   ◁─┘  handle result
        } catch (SendMessageFailedException e) {
          println(e.getMessage());
        }
      }
    }
    client.shutdown().joinUninterruptibly();    ┐  Clean up connection
  }                                          ◁─┘  resources
}
```

The final step is to configure the logger. You want to do this so you'll be able to see your log messages, and, in particular, so you can see which thread is doing what work. Create a new file at src/main/resources/simplelogger.properties with the following content:

```
org.slf4j.simplelogger.showdatetime = false
org.slf4j.simplelogger.showShortLogname = true

org.slf4j.simplelogger.log.org.hbase.async = warn
org.slf4j.simplelogger.log.org.apache.zookeeper = warn
org.slf4j.simplelogger.log.org.apache.zookeeper.client = error
```

You made it! Let's give it a whirl.

6.5.3   *Try it out*

Make sure you have HBase running and have populated the users table. Refer back to chapter 2 if need be. Build your asynchbase client application just like the TwitBase Java project:

```
$ mvn clean package
[INFO] Scanning for projects...
[INFO]
[INFO] ------------------------------------------------------------------
[INFO] Building twitbase-async 1.0.0
[INFO] ------------------------------------------------------------------
...
[INFO] ------------------------------------------------------------------
[INFO] BUILD SUCCESS
[INFO] ------------------------------------------------------------------
```

Now you can run it by invoking your new class:

```
$ java -cp target/twitbase-async-1.0.0.jar \
  HBaseIA.TwitBase.AsyncUsersTool update
196 [main] INFO AsyncUsersTool - received a page of users.
246 [client worker #1-1] INFO AsyncUsersTool - a thread is napping...
1251 [client worker #1-1] INFO AsyncUsersTool - a thread is napping...
2253 [main] INFO AsyncUsersTool - received a page of users.
2255 [main] INFO AsyncUsersTool - received a page of users.
2256 [client worker #1-1] INFO AsyncUsersTool - a thread is napping...
3258 [client worker #1-1] INFO AsyncUsersTool - a thread is napping...
3258 [main] INFO AsyncUsersTool - received a page of users.
4259 [client worker #1-1] INFO AsyncUsersTool - entropy strikes!
4259 [client worker #1-1] INFO AsyncUsersTool - entropy strikes!
4260 [client worker #1-1] INFO AsyncUsersTool -  Bertrand91, your password
is unchanged!
4260 [client worker #1-1] INFO AsyncUsersTool - a thread is napping...
...
```

It works! You now have a working baseline from which to build a suite of asynchronous applications around HBase.

6.6   *Summary*

The decision to deploy HBase ties you to the JVM, at least on the server side. But that decision doesn't restrict your client application options. For managing schema migrations, we recommend becoming comfortable with scripting the HBase shell. If your migrations are particularly complex, or if you feel like building an ActiveRecord[14] style migration tool, definitely explore the JRuby library on which the shell is built. If you're working with Java, we recommend that you give asynchbase serious consideration. Asynchronous programming can be a challenge, but you're already stepping up to learn HBase, so we think you can handle it.

Outside of the JVM, you have REST and Thrift. REST is easy to get started with because it doesn't require anything in your target language other than an HTTP client. Launching the REST gateway against your cluster is simple, and it even scales reasonably well. Although REST is convenient, Thrift is likely the way to go. Thrift provides some measure of language-agnostic API definition and has seen more usage in the community than REST. As always, such decisions are best made on a case-by-case basis.

---

[14] ActiveRecord is the database abstraction library commonly use in Ruby and famously used in Ruby on Rails. It defines a schema-migration pattern that is superior to other tools with which we're familiar. Check it out at http://ar.rubyonrails.org/.

Part 3

Example applications

Part 3 moves past toy example applications and gives you a taste of HBase in real applications. Chapter 7 is a deep-dive into OpenTSDB, an infrastructure-monitoring application designed for efficient storage and query of time-series data. In chapter 8, you get a glimpse at using HBase for geospatial data. You'll learn how to adapt an HBase schema for multidimensional spatial data as you implement multiple spatial queries. When you finish this part of the book, you'll be ready to architect your own distributed, fault-tolerant, HBase-backed data systems from the ground up.

HBase by example: OpenTSDB

In this chapter, we want to give you a sense of what it's like to build applications against HBase. What better way is there to learn a technology than to see first-hand how it can be used to solve a familiar problem? Rather than continuing on with our contrived example, we'll look at an existing application: OpenTSDB. Our goal is to show you what an application backed by HBase looks like, so we won't skimp on the gritty details.

How is building an application against HBase different than building for other databases? What are the primary concerns when designing an HBase schema? How can you take advantage of these designs when implementing your application code? These are the questions we'll answer throughout this chapter. By the time we're through, you'll have a good idea of what it takes to build an application on

HBase. Perhaps more important, you'll have insight into how to think like an HBase application designer.

To start, we'll give you some context. You'll gain an understanding of what OpenTSDB is and what challenge it solves. Then we'll peel back the layers, exploring the design of both the application and the database schema. After that, you'll see how OpenTSDB uses HBase. You'll see the application logic necessary for storing and retrieving data from HBase and how this data is used to build informative charts for the user.

7.1   An overview of OpenTSDB

What is OpenTSDB? Here's a description taken directly from the project homepage (www.opentsdb.net):

> OpenTSDB is a distributed, scalable Time Series Database (TSDB) written on top of HBase. OpenTSDB was written to address a common need: store, index, and serve metrics collected from computer systems (network gear, operating systems, applications) at a large scale, and make this data easily accessible and graphable.

OpenTSDB is a great project for a practical book because it solves the pervasive problem of infrastructure monitoring. If you've deployed a production system, you know the importance of infrastructure monitoring. Don't worry if you haven't; we'll fill you in. It's also interesting because the data OpenTSDB stores is *time series*. Efficient storage and querying of time-series data is something for which the standard relational model isn't well suited. Relational database vendors often look to nonstandard solutions for this problem, such as storing the time-series data as an opaque *blob* and providing proprietary query extensions for its introspection.

What is a blob?

As you'll learn later in the chapter, time-series data has distinct characteristics. These properties can be exploited by customized data structures for more efficient storage and queries. Relational systems don't natively support these kinds of specialized storage formats, so these structures are often serialized into a binary representation and stored as an unindexed byte array. Custom operators are then required to inspect this binary data. Data stored as a bundle like this is commonly called a blob.

OpenTSDB was built at StumbleUpon, a company highly experienced with HBase. It's a great example of how to build an application with HBase as its backing store. OpenTSDB is open source, so you have complete access to the code. The entire project is less than 15,000 lines of Java so it can easily be digested in its entirety. OpenTSDB is ultimately a tool for online data visualization. While studying the schema, keep this in mind. Every data point it stores in HBase must be made available to the user, on demand, in a chart like the one shown in figure 7.1.

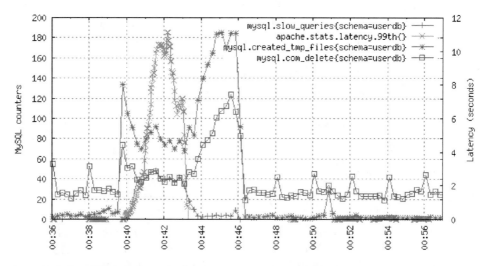

Figure 7.1   OpenTSDB graph output.[1] OpenTSDB is a tool for visualizing data. Ultimately it's about providing insight into the data it stores in graphs like this one.

That's OpenTSDB in a nutshell. Next we'll look more closely at the challenge OpenTSDB is designed to solve and the kinds of data it needs to store. After that, we'll consider why HBase is a good choice for an application like OpenTSDB. Let's look now at infrastructure monitoring so you can understand how the problem domain motivates the schema.

7.1.1   Challenge: infrastructure monitoring

Infrastructure monitoring is the term we use for keeping tabs on deployed systems. The vast majority of software projects are deployed as online systems and services communicating over a network. Odds are, you've deployed a system like this, which means odds are you've found it your professional responsibility to maintain that system. How did you know if the system was up or down? Did you keep track of how many requests it served every hour or what times of the day it sustained the most traffic? If you've been paged in the night because a service went down, you've worked with infrastructure-monitoring tools.

Infrastructure monitoring is much more than notification and alerting. The series of events that triggered your midnight alarm represent only a small amount of the total data those tools collect. Relevant data points include service requests per second, concurrent active user sessions, database reads and writes, average response latency, process memory consumption, and so on. Each of these is a time-series measurement associated with a specific metric and individually provides only a small snapshot of visibility into overall system operation. Take these measurements together along a common time window, and you begin to have an actionable view of the running system.

---

[1]   Graph reproduced directly from the OpenTSDB website.

Generating a graph like the one in figure 7.1 requires that data be accessible by metric as well as time interval. OpenTSDB must be able to collect a variety of metrics from a huge number of systems and yet support online queries against any of those metrics. You'll see in the next section how this requirement becomes a key consideration in the OpenTSDB schema design.

We've mentioned time series more than a few times because it also plays a critical role in the design of OpenTSDB's schema. Let's become more familiar with this kind of data.

7.1.2   Data: time series

Think of time-series data as a collection of data points or tuples. Each point has a timestamp and a measurement. This set of points ordered by time is the time-series. The measurements are usually collected at a regular interval. For instance, you might use OpenTSDB to collect bytes sent by the MySQL process every 15 seconds. In this case, you would have a series of points like those in figure 7.2. It's common for these data points to also carry metadata about the measurement, such as the fully qualified hostname generating the series.

Time-series data is commonly found in economics, finance, natural sciences, and signal processing. By attaching a timestamp to a measurement, we can understand differences between measurement values as time progresses and also understand patterns over time. For instance, the current temperature at a particular location can be measured

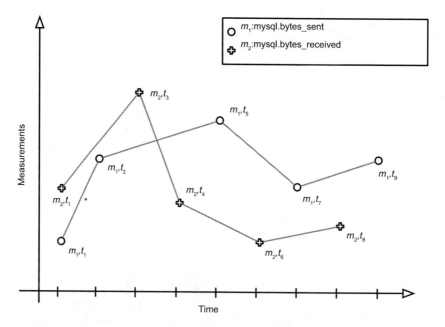

Figure 7.2 A time series is a sequence of time-ordered points. Here, two time series on the same scale are rendered on the same graph. They don't share a common interval. The timestamp is commonly used as an X-axis value when representing a time series visually.

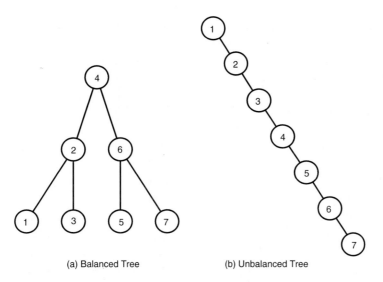

(a) Balanced Tree   (b) Unbalanced Tree

Figure 7.3   Balanced and unbalanced trees. Persisting data into structures that arrange themselves based on data values can result in worst-case data distribution.

every hour. It's natural to assume previous points can inform a future point. You could guess the next hour's temperature based on the last five hours' measurements.

Time-series data can be challenging from a data-management perspective. All data points in a system may share the same fields, for instance: date/time, location, and measurement. But two data points with different values for any one of these fields might be completely unrelated. If one point is the temperature in New York and another in San Francisco, they're likely not related even with a similar timestamp. How do we know how to store and order the data in a way that is relevant and efficient? Shouldn't we store all measurements for New York close together?

Another notable issue with time series is in recording this data. Trees are an efficient data structure for random access, but special care must be taken when building them in sorted order. A time series is naturally ordered by time and is often persisted according to that order. This can result in the storage structures being built in the worst possible way, as illustrated by (b) in figure 7.3.

Just like a tree, this ordering can also cause havoc on a distributed system. HBase is a distributed B-Tree, after all. When data is partitioned across nodes according to the timestamp, new data bottlenecks at a single node, causing a *hot spot*. As the number of clients writing data increases, that single node is easily overwhelmed.

That's time-series data in a nutshell. Now let's see what HBase can bring to the table for the OpenTSDB application.

7.1.3   *Storage: HBase*

HBase makes an excellent choice for applications such as OpenTSDB because it provides scalable data storage with support for low-latency queries. It's a general-purpose data store with a flexible data model, which allows OpenTSDB to craft an efficient and relatively customized schema for storing its data. In this case, that schema is customized for time-series measurements and their associated tags. HBase provides strong consistency, so reports generated by OpenTSDB can be used for real-time reporting. The view of collected data HBase provides is always as current as possible. The horizontal scalability of HBase is critical because of the data volume required of OpenTSDB.

Certainly other databases could be considered. You could back a system like OpenTSDB with MySQL, but what would that deployment look like after a month of collecting hundreds of millions of data points per day? After six months? After 18 months of your application infrastructure running in production, how will you have grown and extended that original MySQL machine to cope with the volume of monitoring data produced by your datacenter? Suppose you've grown this deployment with the data produced, and you're able to maintain your clustered deployment. Can you serve the ad-hoc queries required by your operational team for diagnosing a system outage?

All this is possible with a traditional relational database deployment. There's an impressive list of stories describing massive, successful deployments of these technologies. The question comes down to cost and complexity. Scaling a relational system to cope with this volume of data requires a partitioning strategy. Such an approach often places the burden of partitioning in the application code. Your application can't request a bit of data from *the database*. Instead, it's forced to resolve which database hosts the data in question based on its current knowledge of all available hosts and all ranges of data. Plus, in partitioning the data, you lose a primary advantage of relational systems: the powerful query language. Partitioned data is spread across multiple systems unaware of each other, which means queries are reduced to simple value lookups. Any further query complexity is again pressed to client code.

HBase hides the details of partitioning from the client applications. Partitions are allocated and managed by the cluster so your application code remains blissfully unaware. That means less complexity for you to manage in your code. Although HBase doesn't support a rich query language like SQL, you can design your HBase schema such that most of your online query complexity resides on the cluster. HBase coprocessors give you the freedom to embed arbitrary online code on the nodes hosting the data, as well. Plus, you have the power of MapReduce for offline queries, giving you a rich variety of tools for constructing your reports. For now, we'll focus on one specific example.

At this point you should have a feel for the goals of OpenTSDB and the technical challenges those goals present. Let's dig into the details of how to design an application to meet these challenges.

7.2   *Designing an HBase application*

Although OpenTSDB could have been built on a relational database, it's an HBase application. It's built by individuals who think about scalable data systems in the same way HBase does. This is different than the way we typically think about relational data systems. These differences can be seen in both the schema design and application architecture of OpenTSDB.

This section begins with a study of the OpenTSDB schema. For many of you, this will be your first glimpse of a nontrivial HBase schema. We hope this working example will provide useful insight into taking advantage of the HBase data model. After that, you'll see how to use the key features of HBase as a model for your own applications.

7.2.1 Schema design

OpenTSDB depends on HBase for two distinct functions. The `tsdb` table provides storage and query support over time-series data. The `tsdb-uid` table maintains an index of globally unique values for use as metric tags. We'll first look at the script used to generate these two tables and dive deeper into the usage and design of each one. First, let's look at the script.

> **Listing 7.1 Scripting the HBase shell to create the tables used by OpenTSDB**

```sh
#!/bin/sh
# Small script to setup the hbase table used by OpenTSDB.

test -n "$HBASE_HOME" || {                                        ◁——— From environment,
  echo >&2 'The environment variable HBASE_HOME must be set'            not parameter
  exit 1
}
test -d "$HBASE_HOME" || {
  echo >&2 "No such directory: HBASE_HOME=$HBASE_HOME"
  exit 1
}

TSDB_TABLE=${TSDB_TABLE-'tsdb'}
UID_TABLE=${UID_TABLE-'tsdb-uid'}
COMPRESSION=${COMPRESSION-'LZO'}

exec "$HBASE_HOME/bin/hbase" shell <<EOF
create '$UID_TABLE',                          Make tsdb-uid table
  {NAME => 'id', COMPRESSION => '$COMPRESSION'},     with column families
  {NAME => 'name', COMPRESSION => '$COMPRESSION'}     id and name

create '$TSDB_TABLE',
  {NAME => 't', COMPRESSION => '$COMPRESSION'}       Make tsdb table with
EOF                                                  t column family
```

The first thing to notice is how similar the script is to any script containing Data Definition Language (DDL) code for a relational database. The term *DDL* is often used to distinguish code that provides schema definition and modification from code performing data updates. A relational database uses SQL for schema modifications; HBase depends on the API. As you've seen, the most convenient way to access the API for this purpose is through the HBase shell.

DECLARING THE SCHEMA

The `tsdb-uid` table contains two column families: id and name. The `tsdb` table also specifies a column family, named t. Notice that the lengths of the column-family names are all pretty short. This is because of an implementation detail of the HFile storage format of the current version of HBase—shorter names mean less data to store per `KeyValue` instance. Notice, too, the lack of a higher-level abstraction. Unlike most popular relational databases, there is no concept of table groups. All table names in HBase exist in a common namespace managed by the HBase master.

Now that you've seen how these two tables are created in HBase, let's explore how they're used.

THE TSDB-UID TABLE

Although this table is ancillary to the `tsdb` table, we explore it first because understanding why it exists will provide insight into the overall design. The OpenTSDB schema design is optimized for the management of time-series measurements and their associated tags. By *tags*, we mean anything used to further identify a measurement recorded in the system. In OpenTSDB, this includes the observed metric, the metadata name, and the metadata value. It uses a single class, `UniqueId`, to manage all of these different tags, hence `uid` in the table name. Each metric in figure 7.2, `mysql.bytes_sent` and `mysql.bytes_received`, receives its own unique ID (UID) in this table.

The `tsdb-uid` table is for UID management. UIDs are of a fixed 3-byte width and used in a *foreign-key* relationship from the `tsdb` table; more on that later. Registering a new UID results in two rows in this table, one mapping tag name-to-UID, the other is UID-to-name. For instance, registering the `mysql.bytes_sent` metric generates a new UID used as the rowkey in the UID-to-name row. The `name` column family for that row stores the tag name. The column qualifier is used as a kind of namespace for UIDs, distinguishing this UID as a metric (as opposed to a metadata tag name or value). The name-to-UID row uses the name as the row key and stores the UID in the `id` column family, again qualified by the tag type. The following listing shows how to use the `tsdb` application to register two new metrics.

Listing 7.2   Registering metrics in the `tsdb-uid` table

```
hbase@ubuntu:~$ tsdb mkmetric mysql.bytes_sent mysql.bytes_received
metrics mysql.bytes_sent: [0, 0, 1]
metrics mysql.bytes_received: [0, 0, 2]

hbase@ubuntu:~$ hbase shell
hbase(main):001:0> scan 'tsdb-uid', {STARTROW => "\0\0\1"}
ROW                      COLUMN+CELL
 \x00\x00\x01            column=name:metrics, value=mysql.bytes_sent
 \x00\x00\x02            column=name:metrics, value=mysql.bytes_received
 mysql.bytes_received    column=id:metrics,    value=\x00\x00\x02
 mysql.bytes_sent        column=id:metrics,    value=\x00\x00\x01
4 row(s) in 0.0460 seconds
hbase(main):002:0>
```

The name-to-UID rows enable support for autocomplete of tag names. OpenTSDB's UI allows a user to start typing a UID name, and OpenTSDB populates a list of suggestions with UIDs from this table. It does this using an HBase row scan bounded by rowkey range. Later you'll see exactly how that code works. These rows are also used by the service that receives incoming data to map metric names to their associated UIDs when recording new values.

THE TSDB TABLE

This is the heart of the time-series database: the table that stores time series of measurements and metadata. This table is designed to support queries of this data filtered by date range and tag. This is accomplished through careful design of the rowkey. Figure 7.4 illustrates the rowkey for this table. Take a look and then we'll walk through it. Remember the UIDs generated by tag registration in the `tsdb-uid` table? They're used here in the rowkey of this table. OpenTSDB is optimized for metric-centric queries, so the metric UID comes first. HBase stores rows ordered by rowkey, so the entire history for a single metric is stored as contiguous rows. Within the run of rows for a metric, they're ordered by timestamp. The timestamp in the rowkey is rounded down to the nearest 60 minutes so a single row stores a bucket of measurements for the hour. The tag name and value UIDs come last in the rowkey. Storing all these attributes in the rowkey allows them to be considered while filtering search results. You'll see exactly how that's done shortly.

Now that we've covered rowkeys, let's look at how measurements are stored. Notice that the schema contains only a single column family, `t`. This is because HBase requires a table to contain at least one column family. This table doesn't use the column family to organize data, but HBase requires one all the same. OpenTSDB uses a 2-byte column qualifier consisting of two parts: the rounded seconds in the first 12 bits and a 4-bit bitmask. The measurement value is stored on 8 bytes in the cell. Figure 7.5 illustrates the column qualifier.

How about an example? Let's say you're storing a `mysql.bytes_sent` metric measurement of 476 observed on Sun, 12 Dec 2010 10:02:03 GMT for the `ubuntu` host. You previously stored this metric as UID `0x1`, the `host` tag name as `0x2`, and the `ubuntu` tag value as `0x3`. The timestamp is represented as a UNIX epoch value of 1292148123. This value is rounded down to the nearest hour and split into 1292148000 and 123. The rowkey and cell as inserted into the `tsdb` table are shown in figure 7.6. Other measurements collected during the same hour for the same metric on the same host are all stored in other cells in this row.

Metric UID (3 bytes)	Partial Timestamp (4 bytes)	Tag 1 Name UID (3 bytes)	Tag 1 Value UID (3 bytes)	...

Figure 7.4   The layout of an OpenTSDB rowkey consists of 3 bytes for the metric id, 4 bytes for the high-order timestamp bits, and 3 bytes each for the tag name ID and tag value ID, repeated

Lower Timestamp (12 bits)	Mask (4 bits)

Figure 7.5   Column qualifiers store the final precision of the timestamp as well as a bitmask. The first bit in that mask indicates whether the value in the cell is an integer or a float value.

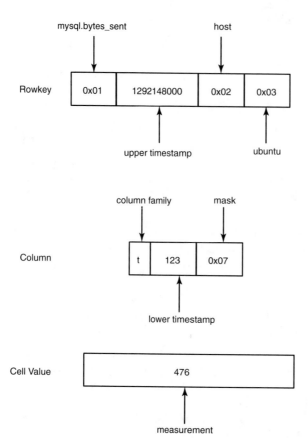

Figure 7.6 An example rowkey, column qualifier, and cell value storing 476 `mysql.bytes_sent` **at 1292148123 seconds in the** `tsdb` **table.**

It's not often we see this kind of bit-wise consideration in Java applications, is it? Much of this is done as a performance optimization. Storing multiple observations per row lets filtered scans disqualify more data in a single exclusion. It also drastically reduces the overall number of rows that must be tracked by the Bloom Filter on rowkey.

Now that you've seen the design of an HBase schema, let's look at how to build a reliable, scalable application using the same methods as those used for OpenTSDB.

7.2.2 Application architecture

While pursuing study of OpenTSDB, it's useful to keep these HBase design fundamentals in mind:

- *Linear scalability over multiple nodes*, not a single monolithic server
- *Automatic partitioning* of data and assignment of partitions
- *Strong consistency of data* across partitions
- *High availability* of data services

High availability and linear scalability are frequently primary motivators behind the decision to build on HBase. Often, the application relying on HBase is required to

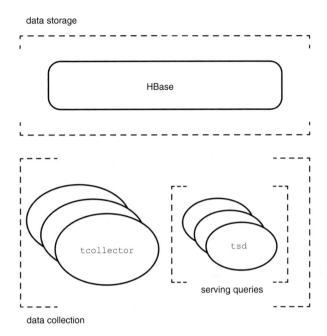

Figure 7.7 OpenTSDB architecture: separation of concerns. The three areas of concern are data collection, data storage, and serving queries.

meet these same requirements. Let's look at how OpenTSDB achieves these goals through its architectural choices. Figure 7.7 provides a view of that architecture.

Conceptually speaking, OpenTSDB has three responsibilities: data collection, data storage, and serving queries. As you might guess, data storage is provided by HBase, which already meets these requirements. How does OpenTSDB provide these features for the other responsibilities? Let's look at them individually, and you'll see how they're tied back together through HBase.

SERVING QUERIES

OpenTSDB includes a process called `tsd` for handling interactions with HBase. It exposes a simple HTTP interface[2] for serving queries against HBase. Requests can query for either metadata or an image representing the requested time series. All `tsd` processes are identical and stateless, so *high availability* is achieved by running multiple `tsd` machines. Traffic to these machines is routed using a load balancer, just like striping any other HTTP traffic. A client doesn't suffer from the outage of a single `tsd` machine because the request is routed to a different one.

Each query is self-contained and can be answered by a single `tsd` process independently. This allows OpenTSDB reads to achieve *linear scalability*. Support for an increasing number of client requests is handled by running more `tsd` machines. The self-contained nature of the OpenTSDB query has the added bonus of making the results served by `tsd` cacheable. Figure 7.8 illustrates the OpenTSDB read path.

---

[2] The `tsd` HTTP API is documented at http://opentsdb.net/http-api.html.

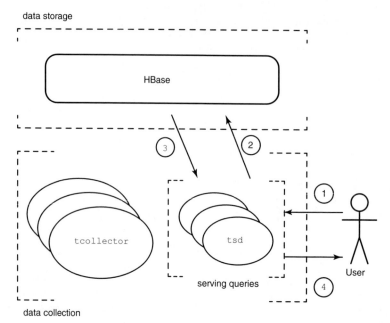

1 User specifies query parameters.

2 `tsd` constructs filter and requests range scan.

3 HBase scans key range, omitting filtered records, and returns results.

4 `tsd` renders time series.

Figure 7.8   OpenTSDB read path. Requests are routed to an available `tsd` process that queries HBase and serves the results in the appropriate format.

DATA COLLECTION

Data collection requires "boots on the ground," so to speak. Some process somewhere needs to gather data from the hosts being monitored and store it in HBase. OpenTSDB makes data collection *linearly scalable* by placing the burden of collection on the hosts being monitored. Each machine runs local processes that collect measurements, and each machine is responsible for sending this data off to OpenTSDB. Adding a new host to your infrastructure places no additional workload exclusively on any individual node in the OpenTSDB cluster.

Network connections time out. Collection services crash. How does OpenTSDB guarantee observation delivery? Attaining *high availability*, it turns out, is mundane. The `tcollector`[3] daemon, also running on each monitored host, takes care of these concerns by gathering measurements locally. It's responsible for ensuring that observations are delivered to OpenTSDB by waiting out such a network outage. It also manages collection scripts, running them on the appropriate interval or restarting them when they crash. As an added bonus, collection agents written for `tcollector` can be simple shell scripts.

---

[3] `tcollector` handles other matters as well. More information can be found at http://opentsdb.net/tcollector.html.

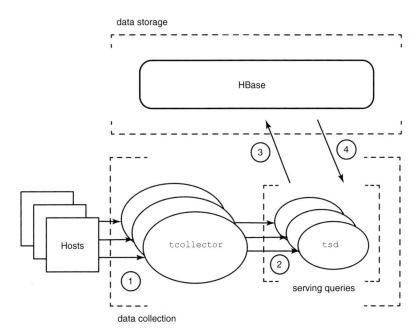

1 Hosts report measurements to local `collectd`.
2 `collectd` sends measurements to remote `tsd`.
3 `tsd` constructs record and `put`s data to HBase.
4 HBase stores data and acknowledges `put` request.

Figure 7.9   OpenTSDB write path. Collection scripts on monitored hosts report measurements to the local `tcollector` process. Measurements are then transmitted to a `tsd` process that handles writing observations to HBase.

Collector agents don't write to HBase directly. Doing so would require the `tcollector` installation to ship an HBase client library along with all its dependencies and configuration. It would also put an unnecessarily large load on HBase. Because the `tsd` is already deployed to support query load, it's also used for receiving data. The `tsd` process exposes a simple telnet-like protocol for receiving observations. It then handles interaction with HBase. The `tsd` does little work supporting writes, so a small number of `tsd` instances can handle many times their number in `tcollector` agents. The OpenTSDB write path is illustrated in figure 7.9.

You now have a complete view of OpenTSDB. More important, you've seen how an application can take advantage of HBase's strengths. Nothing here should be particularly surprising, especially if you've developed a highly available system before. It's worth noting how much simpler such an application can be when the data-storage system provides these features out of the box. Next, let's see some code!

7.3   *Implementing an HBase application*

HBase wants to be used! Notice these interface features directly listed on the HBase home page:

- Easy-to-use Java API for client access
- Thrift gateway and a REST-ful web service that supports XML, Protobuf, and binary data-encoding options
- Query predicate push-down via server-side filters

OpenTSDB's `tsd` is implemented in Java but uses an alternative client library called asynchbase[4] for all interaction, the same asynchbase we covered in depth in chapter 6. To keep the discussion as generally applicable as possible, we'll present first pseudo-code for HBase interactions and then show you the snippets from OpenTSDB. It's easier to understand how data is read if you know how it's written, so this time we'll begin with the write path.

7.3.1   *Storing data*

As you saw while studying the schema, OpenTSDB stores data in two tables. Before a row can be inserted into the `tsdb` table, all UIDs must first be generated. Let's start at the beginning.

CREATE A UID

Before a measurement can be written to the `tsdb` table, all of its tags must first be written to `tsdb-uid`. In pseudo-code, that process is handled by the `UniqueId.getOrCreateId()` method, which is shown here.

Listing 7.3   Pseudo-code for inserting a tag into the `tsdb-uid` table

```
class UniqueId:
  MAXID_ROW = 0x0
  ID_FAMILY = toBytes("id")
  NAME_FAMILY = toBytes("name")

  def UniqueId(this, table, kind):        Single UniqueId instance
    this.table = table                    instantiated for each
    this.kind = toBytes(kind)             kind of tag

  def getOrCreateId(this, name):          Kind can be metric, tag
    uid = HBase.get(this.table, toBytes(name),   name, or tag value
                ID_FAMILY, this.kind)
    if 0x0 != uid:                        Return UID for name
      return uid                          if it already exists

    uid = HBase.incrementColumnValue(MAXID_ROW,
                            ID_FAMILY,            Otherwise generate
                            this.kind)            and store new UID
    HBase.put(this.table, toBytes(uid),           Write UID =>
            NAME_FAMILY, this.kind, toBytes(name))   name mapping
```

[4] For more details, see https://github.com/stumbleupon/asynchbase.

```
HBase.put(this.table, toBytes(name), ID_FAMILY,          Write name =>
        this.kind, toBytes(uid))                          UID mapping
return uid
```

One `UniqueId` class is instantiated by a `tsd` process for each kind of UID stored in the table. In this case, `metric`, `tag name`, and `tag value` are the three kinds of UIDs in the system. The local variable `kind` will be set appropriately in the constructor, along with the variable `table` for the table name, `tsdb-uid` by default. The first thing the `UniqueId.getOrCreateId()` method does is look in the table to see if there's already a UID of this kind with this name. If it's there, you're done. Return it and move on. Otherwise, a new UID needs to be generated and registered for this mapping.

New UIDs are generated by way of a counter stored in this table, increased using the `Increment` command. A new UID is generated, and the two mappings are stored to the table. Once a mapping is written, it never changes. For this reason, the UID-to-name mapping is written before the name-to-UID mapping. A failure here results in a wasted UID but no further harm. A name-to-UID mapping without its reciprocal means the name is available in the system but can never be resolved from a measurement record. That's a bad thing because it can lead to orphaned data. Finally, having assigned the bidirectional mapping, the UID is returned.

The Java code for this method contains additional complexity due to error handling and a workaround for a feature not yet implemented in the client API. It's included here but with these additional concerns removed for the sake of brevity.

Listing 7.4   Reduced Java code for `UniqueId.getOrCreateId()`

```java
public byte[] getOrCreateId(String name) throws HBaseException {
  HBaseException hbe = null;

  try {
    return getId(name);              Error-handling
    ...                              omitted
  } catch (NoSuchUniqueName e) {
    ...
  }
  RowLock lock = ... getLock();      Rowlock used only to work
  try {                              around a feature lacking
    try {                            from RPC protocol
      final byte[] id = getId(name);           Verify that row still
      return id;                               doesn't exist, to avoid
                                               race condition
    ...
    } catch (NoSuchUniqueName e) {}  Error-handling
                                     omitted
    long id;
    byte[] row;                             Same as id but
    try {                                   as a byte array
      row = hbaseICV(MAXID_ROW, ID_FAMILY, lock)
      if (row == null) {
        id = 1;
        row = Bytes.fromLong(id);
      } else {
```

```
        id = Bytes.getLong(row);
    }                                        UID width
    ...                                      validation omitted

    row = Arrays.copyOfRange(row, row.length - idWidth, row.length);
} catch (...) {
    ...                                      Error-handling
}                                            omitted
try {
    final PutRequest reverse_mapping = new PutRequest(      Create
        table, row, NAME_FAMILY, kind, toBytes(name));      reverse
    hbasePutWithRetry(reverse_mapping, MAX_ATTEMPTS_PUT,     mapping
                INITIAL_EXP_BACKOFF_DELAY);
} catch (...) {
    ...                                      Error-handling
}                                            omitted
try {
    final PutRequest forward_mapping = new PutRequest(      Create
        table, toBytes(name), ID_FAMILY, kind, row);        forward
    hbasePutWithRetry(forward_mapping, MAX_ATTEMPTS_PUT,     mapping
                INITIAL_EXP_BACKOFF_DELAY);
} catch (...) {
    ...                                      Error-handling
}                                            omitted
addIdToCache(name, row);
addNameToCache(row, name);
return row;
} finally {
    unlock(lock);
}
}
```

Having registered the tags, you can move on to generating a rowkey for an entry in the tsdb table.

GENERATING A PARTIAL ROWKEY

Every rowkey in the tsdb table for the same metric and tag name value pairs looks the same except for the timestamp. OpenTSDB implements this functionality in a helper method for partial construction of these rowkeys in IncomingDataPoints.rowKeyTemplate(). That method implemented in pseudo-code looks like this.

Listing 7.5 Pseudo-code for generating a rowkey template

```
class IncomingDataPoints:
  TIMESTAMP_BYTES = 4

  def static getOrCreateTags(tsdb, tags):        tags is a map from
    tag_ids = []                                 tag name => tag
    for(name, value in tags.sort()):             value
      tag_ids += tsdb.tag_names.getOrCreateId(name)
      tag_ids += tsdb.tag_values.getOrCreateId(value)    tsdb.tag_names
    return ByteArray(tag_ids)                           is a UniqueID
                                          So is          instance
                                    tsdb.tag_values
```

```
def static rowKeyTemplate(tsdb, metric, tags):
  metric_width = tsdb.metrics.width()                      Requires tsdb
  tag_name_width = tsdb.tag_names.width()                  instance for
  tag_value_width = tsdb.tag_values.width()                relevant context
  num_tags = tags.size()

  row_size = (metric_width + TIMESTAMP_BYTES               Width of rowkey is
                + tag_name_width * num_tags                variable based on
                + tag_value_width * num_tags)              number of tags
  row = ByteArray(row_size)
                                                           tsdb.metrics is a
  row[0 .. metric_width] =                                 UniqueID instance
    tsdb.metrics.getOrCreateId(metric)              <──
  row[metric_width + TIMESTAMP_BYTES ..] =                 tag UIDs
    getOrCreateTags(tsdb, tags)                            come last

  return row
```

The primary concern of this method is correct placement of the rowkey components. As you saw earlier in figure 7.5, this order is metric UID, partial timestamp, and tag pair UIDs. Notice that the tags are sorted before insertion. This guarantees that the same metric and tags map to the same rowkey every time.

The Java implementation in the following listing is almost identical to the pseudocode in listing 7.5. The biggest difference is organization of helper methods.

Listing 7.6   Java code for `IncomingDataPoints.rowKeyTemplate()`

```java
static byte[] rowKeyTemplate(final TSDB tsdb,
                             final String metric,
                             final Map<String, String> tags) {
  final short metric_width = tsdb.metrics.width();
  final short tag_name_width = tsdb.tag_names.width();
  final short tag_value_width = tsdb.tag_values.width();
  final short num_tags = (short) tags.size();

  int row_size = (metric_width + Const.TIMESTAMP_BYTES
                + tag_name_width * num_tags
                + tag_value_width * num_tags);
  final byte[] row = new byte[row_size];

  short pos = 0;

  copyInRowKey(row, pos, (AUTO_METRIC ? tsdb.metrics.getOrCreateId(metric)
                  : tsdb.metrics.getId(metric)));
  pos += metric_width;

  pos += Const.TIMESTAMP_BYTES;

  for(final byte[] tag : Tags.resolveOrCreateAll(tsdb, tags)) {
    copyInRowKey(row, pos, tag);
    pos += tag.length;
  }
  return row;
}
```

That's all there is to it! You now have all the pieces.

WRITING A MEASUREMENT

With all the necessary helper methods in place, it's time to write a record to the `tsdb` table. The process looks like this:

1 Build the rowkey.
2 Decide on the column family and qualifier.
3 Identify the bytes to store in the cell.
4 Write the record.

This logic is encapsulated in the `TSDB.addPoint()` method. Those `tsdb` instances in the previous code listings are instances of this class. Let's start once more with pseudo-code before diving into the Java implementation.

Listing 7.7   Pseudo-code for inserting a `tsdb` record

```
class TSDB:
  FAMILY = toBytes("t")                    60 seconds * 60
  MAX_TIMESPAN = 3600                      minutes = I hour        4 bits of 2-byte
  FLAG_BITS    = 4                         resolution per row      column qualifier
  FLOAT_FLAGS  = 1011b                     Flag masks              reserved for mask
  LONG_FLAGS   = 0111b                     in binary

  def addPoint(this, metric, timestamp, value, tags):
    row =
      IncomingDataPoints.rowKeyTemplate(this, metric, tags)       Assemble
    base_time = (timestamp - (timestamp % MAX_TIMESPAN))          column
    row[metrics.width()..] = base_time                           qualifier

    flags = value.isFloat? ? FLOAT_FLAGS : LONG_FLAGS
    qualifier = (timestamp - basetime) << FLAG_BITS | flags       Assemble
    qualifier = toBytes(qualifier)                               rowkey

    HBase.put(this.table, row, FAMILY, qualifier, toBytes(value))
```

Writing the value is as simple as that! Now let's look at the same thing in Java. The code for writing `Long`s and `Float`s is almost identical. We'll look at writing `Long`s.

Listing 7.8   Java code for `TSDB.addPoint()`

```
public Deferred<Object> addPoint(final String metric,
                                 final long timestamp,
                                 final long value,
                                 final Map<String, String> tags) {
  final short flags = 0x7;
  return addPointInternal(metric, timestamp, Bytes.fromLong(value),
                          tags, flags);
}

private Deferred<Object> addPointInternal(final String metric,
                                          final long timestamp,
                                          final byte[] value,
                                          final Map<String, String> tags,
                                          final short flags) {
  if ((timestamp & 0xFFFFFFFF00000000L) != 0) {
    throw ...                                    Verify timestamp < 0 ||
  }                                              timestamp > Integer.MAX_VALUE
```

```
IncomingDataPoints.checkMetricAndTags(metric, tags);
final byte[] row = IncomingDataPoints.rowKeyTemplate(this, metric, tags);
final long base_time = (timestamp - (timestamp % Const.MAX_TIMESPAN));
Bytes.setInt(row, (int) base_time, metrics.width());
final short qualifier = (short) ((timestamp - base_time) <<
  Const.FLAG_BITS | flags);
final PutRequest point = new PutRequest(table, row, FAMILY,
                            Bytes.fromShort(qualifier), value);
return client.put(point);
}
```

Looking back over these listings, both pseudo-code and Java, there's not much inter-action with HBase going on. The most complicated part of writing a row to HBase is assembling the values you want to write. Writing the record is the easy part!

OpenTSDB goes to great lengths to assemble a rowkey. Those efforts are well rewarded at read time. The next section shows you how.

7.3.2 Querying data

With data stored in HBase, it's useful to pull it out again. OpenTSDB does this for two distinct use cases: UID name auto-completion and querying time series. In both cases, the sequence of steps is identical:

1 Identify a rowkey range.
2 Define applicable filter criteria.
3 Execute the scan.

Let's see what it takes to implement auto-complete for time-series metadata.

UID NAME AUTO-COMPLETION

Do you remember the bidirectional mapping in the `tsdb-uid` table? The reverse map-ping is used in support of the auto-completion UI feature shown in figure 7.10.

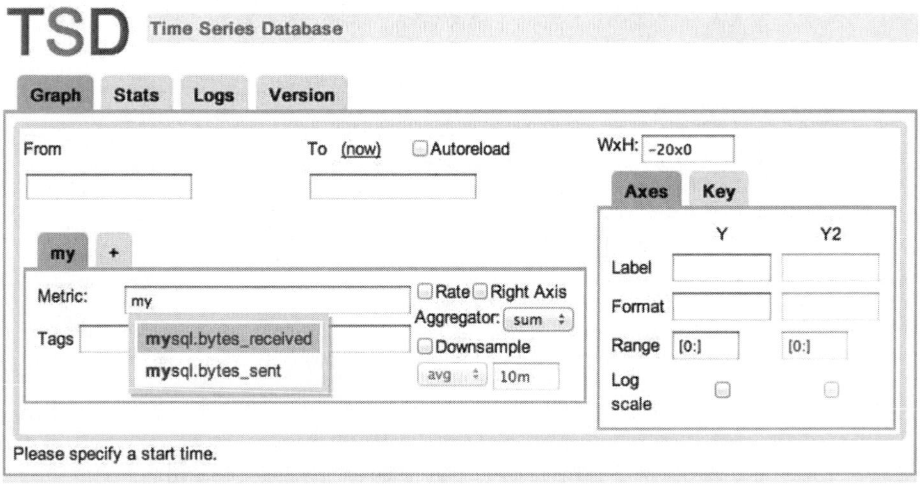

Figure 7.10 OpenTSDB metric auto-completion is supported by the name-to-UID mapping stored in the `tsdb-uid` table.

HBase supports this application feature with the *rowkey scan* pattern of data access. HBase keeps an index over the rowkeys in each table so locating the starting point is very fast. From there, the HBase BlockCache takes over, rapidly reading consecutive blocks from memory and off the HDFS when necessary. In this case, those consecutive blocks contain rows in the `tsdb-uid` table. In figure 7.10, the user entered `my` in the Metric field. These characters are taken as the start row of the scan. You want to display entries matching only this prefix, so the end row of the scan is calculated to be `mz`. You also only want records where the `id` column family is populated; otherwise you'll interpret UIDs as text. The Java code is readable, so we'll skip the pseudo-code.

Listing 7.9   Creating a scanner over `tsdb-uid` in `UniqueId.getSuggestScanner()`

```
private Scanner getSuggestScanner(final String search) {
  final byte[] start_row;
  final byte[] end_row;
  if (search.isEmpty()) {
    start_row = START_ROW;           │ Empty search scans
    end_row = END_ROW;               │ ASCII range, ! to ~
  } else {
    start_row = toBytes(search);     ◄─┐ 'my' becomes
    end_row = Arrays.copyOf(start_row, start_row.length);   byte[] ['m' 'y']
    end_row[start_row.length - 1]++;  ◄─┐ ['m' 'y'] becomes
  }                                     │ byte[] ['m' 'z']
  final Scanner scanner = client.newScanner(table);
  scanner.setStartKey(start_row);
  scanner.setStopKey(end_row);              │ Only include name-
  scanner.setFamily(ID_FAMILY);        ◄─── │ to-UID rows
  scanner.setQualifier(kind);          ◄───┐
  scanner.setMaxNumRows(MAX_SUGGESTIONS);  │ Only include relevant
  return scanner;                          │ type of UID: metrics
}
```

With a scanner constructed, consuming records out of HBase is like reading any other iterator. Reading suggestions off the scanner is a matter of extracting the byte array and interpreting it as a string. Lists are used to maintain the sorted order of returned results. Here's the Java code, again reduced of ancillary concerns.

Listing 7.10   Reduced Java code for `UniqueId.suggest()`

```
public List<String> suggest(final String search) throws HBaseException {
  final Scanner scanner = getSuggestScanner(search);
  final LinkedList<String> suggestions = new LinkedList<String>();
  try {
    ArrayList<ArrayList<KeyValue>> rows;
    while ((rows = scanner.nextRows().joinUninterruptibly()) != null) {
      for (final ArrayList<KeyValue> row : rows) {       ◄───┐
        ...                                        ◄───┐    │ Each cell in row
        final byte[] key = row.get(0).key();           │    │ is KeyValue
        final String name = fromBytes(key);            │
        ...                                        ◄───┐│ Validate row size;
        suggestions.add(name);   Caching logic omitted │ should be only one
                                                        │ cell per row
```

```
            if ((short) suggestions.size() > MAX_SUGGESTIONS) {
              break;
            }
          }
        }
      }
    } catch (...) {
      ...
    }
    return suggestions;
}
```

READING TIME SERIES

The same technique is used to read segments of time-series data from the tsdb table. The query is more complex because this table's rowkey is more complex than tsdb-uid. That complexity comes by way of the multifield filter. Against this table, metric, date range, and tags are all considered in the filter. That filter is applied *on the HBase servers*, not on the client. That detail is crucial because it drastically reduces the amount of data transferred to the tsd client. Keep in mind that this is a regex over the *un-interpreted bytes* in the rowkey.

The other primary difference between this scan and the previous example is time-series aggregation. The OpenTSDB UI allows multiple time series over common tags to be aggregated into a single time series for display. These groups of tags must also be considered while building the filter. TsdbQuery maintains private variables named group_bys and group_by_values for this purpose.

All this filter business is implemented through the TsdbQuery.run() method. This method works just like before, creating a filtered scanner, iterating over the returned rows, and gathering data to display. Helper methods TsdbQuery.getScanner() and TsdbQuery.findSpans() are almost identical to UniqueId.getSuggestScanner() and UniqueId.suggest(), respectively; their listings are omitted. Instead, look at Tsdb-Query.createAndSetFilter() in the following listing. It handles the interesting part of setting up a regular expression filter over the rowkeys.

Listing 7.11 Java code for `TsdbQuery.createAndSetFilter()`

```
void createAndSetFilter(final Scanner scanner) {
  ...
  final short name_width = tsdb.tag_names.width();
  final short value_width = tsdb.tag_values.width();
  final short tagsize = (short) (name_width + value_width);

  final StringBuilder buf = new StringBuilder(              Allocate StringBuffer
      15 + ((13 + tagsize)                                  long enough to hold
            * (tags.size() + (group_bys.size())))));         regex

  buf.append("(?s)"
            + "^.{")                                        Start by skipping
    .append(tsdb.metrics.width() + Const.TIMESTAMP_BYTES)   metric ID and
    .append("}");                                           timestamp
  final Iterator<byte[]> tags = this.tags.iterator();
  final Iterator<byte[]> group_bys = this.group_bys.iterator();
```

```
byte[] tag = tags.hasNext() ? tags.next() : null;
byte[] group_by = group_bys.hasNext() ? group_bys.next() : null;

do {
  buf.append("(?:.{").append(tagsize).append("})*\\Q");      ◄─┐  Tags and groups
  if (isTagNext(name_width, tag, group_by)) {          ◄──────┤  already sorted;
    addId(buf, tag);                                          │  merge by UID
    tag = tags.hasNext() ? tags.next() : null;
  } else {                                               isTagNext() is effectively
    addId(buf, group_by);                                a UID comparator
    final byte[][] value_ids = (group_by_values == null
                               ? null
                               : group_by_values.get(group_by));
    if (value_ids == null) {                            ◄─┐
      buf.append(".{").append(value_width).append('}');   │  If no tag values
    } else {                                              ─┤  considered in
      buf.append("(?:");                            ◄──────┘  grouping
      for (final byte[] value_id : value_ids) {
        buf.append("\\Q");
        addId(buf, value_id);                       ┌─ Join multiple tag
        buf.append('|');                            │  values with |
      }
      buf.setCharAt(buf.length() - 1, ')');       ◄─┐
    }                                               │  Don't leave
    group_by = group_bys.hasNext() ? group_bys.next() : null;  trailing |
  }
} while (tag != group_by);
buf.append("(?:.{").append(tagsize).append("})*$");
scanner.setKeyRegexp(buf.toString(), CHARSET);       ◄─┐ Apply
}                                                       filter
```

Building a byte-wise regular expression isn't as scary as it sounds. With this filter in place, OpenTSDB submits the query to HBase. Each node in the cluster hosting data between the start and end keys handles its portion of the scan, filtering relevant records. The resulting rows are sent back to tsd for rendering. Finally, you see your graph on the other end.

7.4   Summary

Earlier we said that HBase is a flexible, scalable, accessible database. You've just seen some of that in action. A flexible data model allows HBase to store all manner of data, time-series being just one example. HBase is designed for scale, and now you've seen how to design an application to scale right along with it. You also have some insight into how to use the API. We hope the idea of building against HBase is no longer so daunting. We'll continue exploring building real-world applications on HBase in the next chapter.

Scaling GIS on HBase

This chapter covers

- Adapting HBase to the challenge of indexing multidimensional data
- Applying domain knowledge in your schema design
- Real-world application of custom `Filters`

In this chapter, we'll use HBase to tackle a new domain: Geographic Information Systems (GIS). GIS is an interesting area of exploration because it poses two significant challenges: latency at scale and modeling spatial locality. We'll use the lens of GIS to demonstrate how to adapt HBase to tackle these challenges. To do so, you'll need to use domain-specific knowledge to your advantage.

8.1 Working with geographic data

Geographic systems are frequently used as the foundation of an online, interactive user experience. Consider a location-based service, such as Foursquare, Yelp, or Urban Spoon. These services strive to provide relevant information about hundreds of millions of locations all over the globe. Users of these applications depend on them to find, for instance, the nearest coffee shop in an unfamiliar neighborhood. They don't want a MapReduce job standing between them and their latte. We've already discussed HBase as a platform for online data access, so this first constraint seems a reasonable match for HBase. Still, as you've seen in previous chapters, HBase can only provide low request latency when your schema is designed to use the physical storage of data. This brings you conveniently to the second challenge: spatial locality.

Spatial locality in GIS data is tricky. We'll spend a major portion of this chapter explaining an algorithm called the geohash, which is a solution to this problem. The idea is to store data so that all the information about a place on Earth is stored close together. That way, when you want to investigate that location, you need to make as few data requests as possible. You also want the information about places that are close together on Earth to be stored close together on disk. If you're accessing information about Midtown Manhattan, it's likely you'll also want information about Chelsea and Greenwich Village. You want to store that data closer to the Midtown data than, say, data about Brooklyn or Queens. By storing information about these spatially similar places so that the information is physically close together, you can potentially achieve a faster user experience.

Spatial locality isn't Hadoop's data locality

This idea of *spatial locality* is similar to but not the same as Hadoop's concept of *data locality*. In both cases, we're considering the work of moving data. Spatial locality in GIS is about storing data with a similar spatial context in a similar place. Data locality in Hadoop is about performing the data access and computation on the machine in the cluster where that data is physically stored. Both cases are about minimizing the overhead of working with the data, but that's where the similarity ends.

The simplest form of geographic data, a single point on Earth, is composed of two equally relevant dimensions: longitude (X-axis) and latitude (Y-axis). Even this is a simplification. Many professional GIS systems must also consider a Z-axis, such as elevation or altitude, in addition to the X- and Y-axes. Many GIS applications also track position over time, which presents all the challenges of time-series data discussed in the previous chapter. Both kinds of data locality are critical when designing systems providing low-latency data access. HBase makes this clear through schema design and use of the rowkey. The sorted rowkey gives you direct control over the locality of storage of your data.

How do you guarantee data locality for your spatial data when both dimensions (or perhaps all four dimensions) are equally relevant? Building an index exclusively over longitude, for example, places New York City closer to Chicago than Seattle. But as figure 8.1 illustrates, it would also give you Bogotá, Columbia, before the District of Columbia. Considering only one dimension isn't sufficient for the needs of GIS.

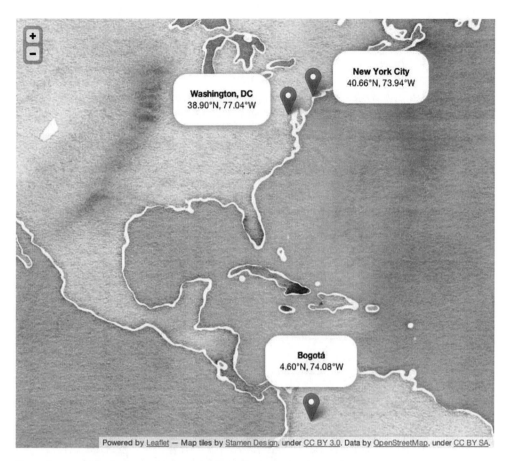

Figure 8.1 In GIS, all dimensions matter. Building an index of the world's cities over only longitude, the X-axis, would order data inaccurately for a certain set of queries.

NOTE This chapter explores spatial concepts that can be communicated effectively only via illustrations. Toward that end, we've employed a browser-based cartography library called Leaflet to build these illustrations with repeatable precision. GitHub claims this chapter's project is 95% JavaScript. The map tiles behind the figures are of the beautiful Watercolor tile set from Stamen Design and are built from completely open data. Learn more about Leaflet at http://leaflet.cloudmade.com. Watercolor lives at http://maps.stamen.com/#watercolor. The underlying data is from OpenStreetMap, a project like Wikipedia, but for geographic data. Find out more at www.openstreetmap.org.

How do you organize your data such that New York City (NYC) and Washington, D.C., are closer than NYC and Bogotá? You'll tackle this challenge over the course of this chapter in the form of a specialized *spatial index*. You'll use this index as the foundation of two kinds of spatial queries. The first query, "k nearest neighbors," is built directly on that index. The second query, "polygon within," is implemented twice. The first time, it's built against the spatial index alone. The second implementation moves as much work as possible to the server side, in the form of a *custom filter*. This will maximize the work performed in your HBase cluster and minimize the superfluous data returned to the client. Along the way, you'll learn enough of this new domain to turn HBase into a fully capable GIS machine. The devil, as they say, is in the details, so let's zoom in from this question of distance between international cities and solve a much more local problem.

The code and data used through the course of this chapter are available on our GitHub account. This project can be found at https://github.com/hbaseinaction/gis.

8.2   *Designing a spatial index*

Let's say you're visiting NYC and need an internet connection. "Where's the nearest wifi hotspot?" How might an HBase application help you answer that question? What kind of design decisions go into solving that problem, and how can it be solved in a scalable way?

You know you want fast access to a relevant subset of the data. To achieve that, let's start with two simple and related goals:

1 You want to store location points on disk such that *points close to each other in space are close to each other on disk.*

2 You want to *retrieve as few points as possible* when responding to a query.

Achieving these goals will allow you to build a highly responsive online application against a spatial dataset. The main tool HBase gives you for tackling both of these goals is the rowkey. You saw in previous chapters how to index multiple attributes in a compound rowkey. Based on the D.C. versus Bogotá example, we have a hunch it won't meet the first design goal. It doesn't hurt to try, especially if you can learn something along the way. It's easy to implement, so let's evaluate the basic compound rowkey before trying anything more elaborate.

Let's start by looking at the data. New York City has an open-data program and publishes many datasets.[1] One of those datasets[2] is a listing of all the city's wifi hotspots. We don't expect you to be familiar with GIS or GIS data, so we've preprocessed it a bit. Here's a sample of that data:

```
        X            Y         ID    NAME
1   -73.96974759   40.75890919   441   Fedex Kinko's
2   -73.96993203   40.75815170   442   Fedex Kinko's
3   -73.96873588   40.76107453   463   Smilers 707
4   -73.96880474   40.76048717   472   Juan Valdez NYC
5   -73.96974993   40.76170883   219   Startegy Atrium and Cafe
6   -73.96978387   40.75850573   388   Barnes & Noble
7   -73.96746533   40.76089302   525   McDonalds
8   -73.96910155   40.75873061   564   Public Telephone
9   -73.97000655   40.76098703   593   Starbucks
```

---

[1]   Some of those datasets are pretty cool, in particular the Street Tree Census data. Look for yourself at https://nycopendata.socrata.com/.

[2]   The raw dataset used in this chapter is available at https://nycopendata.socrata.com/d/ehc4-fktp

You've processed the data into a tab-separated text file. The first line contains the column names. The columns X and Y are the longitude and latitude values, respectively. Each record has an ID, a NAME, and a number of other columns.

A great thing about GIS data is that it lends itself nicely to pictures! Unlike other kinds of data, no aggregations are required to build a meaningful visualization—just throw points on a map and see what you have. This sample data looks like figure 8.2.

Based on the goals outlined earlier, you now have a pretty good spot-check for your schema designs. Remember goal ❶. Point 388 is close to point 441 on the map, so those records should be close to each other in the database. As goal ❷ states, if you want to retrieve those two points, you shouldn't have to retrieve point 219 as well.

Now you know the goals and you know the data. It's time to take a stab at the schema. As you learned in chapter 4, *design of the rowkey is the single most important thing you can do in your HBase schema*, so let's start there.

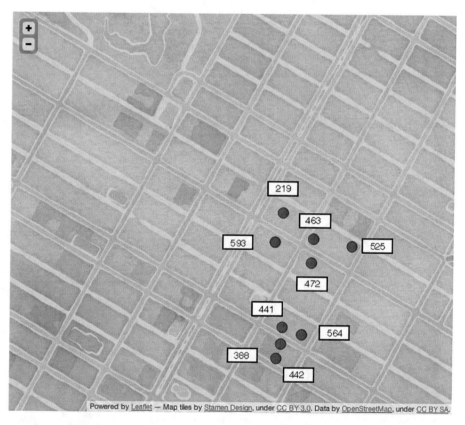

Figure 8.2   Find the wifi. Geographic data wants to be seen, so draw it on a map. Here's a sampling of the full dataset—a handful of places to find a wifi connection in Midtown Manhattan.

8.2.1 *Starting with a compound rowkey*

We claimed earlier that concatenating X- and Y-axis values as the rowkey won't cut it for an efficient schema. We cited the D.C. versus Bogotá example as proof. Let's see why. Sort the sample records first by longitude, then latitude, and connect the dots. Figure 8.3 does just that. When you store data this way, scanning returns results ordered from 1 to 9. Notice in particular the distance between steps 6 and 7, and steps 8 and 9. This sorting results in lots of hopping between the northern and southern clusters because of sorting first on longitude, then latitude.

This schema design does okay with goal ❶, but that's likely because the data sample is small. Goal ❷ is also poorly represented. Every jump from the northern cluster to the southern cluster represents retrieval of data you don't need. Remember the Bogotá versus D.C. example from figure 8.1? That's precisely the problem you see in this schema design. Points close to each other aren't necessarily close together as records in HBase. When you translate this to a rowkey scan, you have to retrieve every possible point along the latitude for the desired longitude range. Of course, you could work around this flaw in the design. Perhaps you could build a latitude filter,

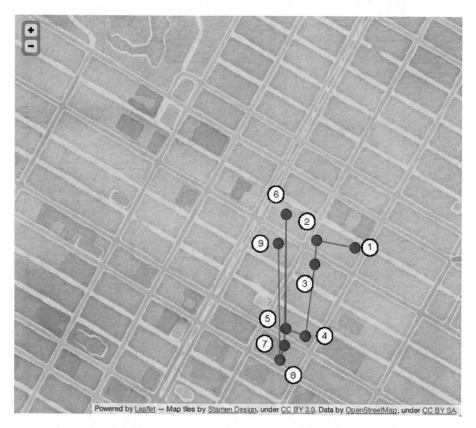

Figure 8.3 A naïve approach to spatial schema design: concatenated axes values. This schema fails the first objective of mapping spatial locality to record locality.

implemented as a `RegexStringComparator` attached to a `RowFilter`. At least that way you could keep all that extra data from hitting the client. That's not ideal, though. A filter is reading records out of the store in order to execute the filter logic. It would be better to never touch that data, if you can avoid it.

This schema design, placing one dimension ahead of the other in the rowkey, also implies an ordered relationship between dimensions that doesn't exist. You can do better. To do so, you need to learn about a trick the GIS community devised for solving these kinds of problems: the geohash.

8.2.2 Introducing the geohash

As the previous example shows, longitude and latitude are equally important in defining the location of a point. In order to use them as the basis for the spatial index, you need an algorithm to combine them. Such an algorithm will create a value based on the two dimensions. That way, two values produced by the algorithm are related to each other in a way that considers both dimensions equally. The geohash does exactly this.

A *geohash* is a function that turns some number of values into a single value. For it to work, each of those values must be from a dimension with a fixed domain. In this case, you want to turn both longitude and latitude into a single value. The longitude dimension is bounded by the range [-180.0, 180.0], and the latitude dimension is bounded by the range [-90.0, 90.0]. There are a number of ways to reduce multiple dimensions to a single one, but we're using the geohash here because its output preserves spatial locality.

A geohash isn't a flawless encoding of the input data. For you audiophiles, it's a bit like an MP3 of your source recording. The input data is mostly there, but only mostly. Like an MP3, you must specify a precision when calculating a geohash. You'll use 12 geohash characters for the precision because that's the highest precision you can fit in an 8-byte `Long` and still represent a meaningful character string. By truncating characters from the end of the hash, you get a less precise geohash and a correspondingly less precise selection of the map. Where full precision represents a point, partial precision gives you an area on the map, effectively a bounding box around an area in space. Figure 8.4 illustrates the decreasing precision of a truncated geohash.

For a given geohash prefix, all points within that space match the common prefix. If you can fit your query inside a geohash prefix's bounding box, all matching points will share a common prefix. That means you can use HBase's prefix scan on the rowkeys to get back a set of points that are all relevant to the query. That accomplishes goal ❶. But as figure 8.4 illustrates, if you have to choose an overly generous precision, you'll end up with much more data than you need. That violates goal ❷. You need to work around these edge cases, but we'll cover that a little later. For now, let's look at some real points.

Consider these three locations: LaGuardia Airport (40.77° N, 73.87° W), JFK International Airport (40.64° N, 73.78° W), and Central Park (40.78° N, 73.97° W). Their coordinates geohash to the values `dr5rzjcw2nze`, `dr5x1n711mhd`, and `dr5ruzb8wnfr`,

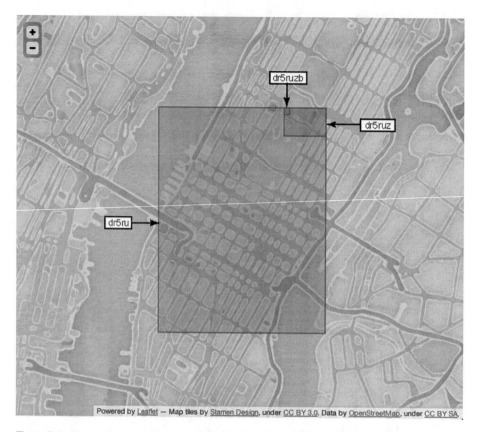

Figure 8.4 Truncating a geohash. By dropping characters from the end of a geohash, you drop precision from the space that hash represents. A single character goes a long way.

respectively. You can look at those points on the map in figure 8.5 and see that Central Park is closer to LaGuardia than JFK. In absolute terms, Central Park to LaGuardia is about 5 miles, whereas Central Park to JFK is about 14 miles.

Because they're closer to each other spatially, you expect Central Park and LaGuardia to share more common prefix characters than Central Park and JFK. Sure enough:

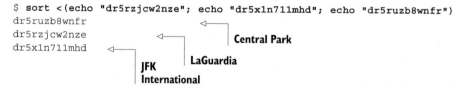

```
$ sort <(echo "dr5rzjcw2nze"; echo "dr5x1n711mhd"; echo "dr5ruzb8wnfr")
dr5ruzb8wnfr
dr5rzjcw2nze
dr5x1n711mhd
```
Central Park

LaGuardia

JFK
International

Now that you understand how a geohash can work for you, we'll show you how to calculate one. Don't worry; you won't be hashing all these points by hand. With HBase, it's useful to understand how it works in order to use it effectively. Likewise with the geohash, understanding how it's constructed will help you understand its edge cases.

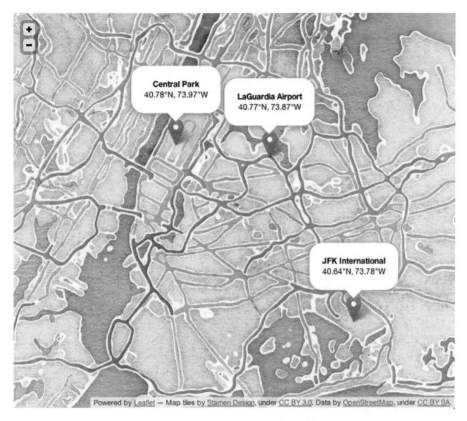

Figure 8.5 Relative distances. When viewed on a map, it's easy to see that the distance between Central Park and JFK is much farther than the distance between Central Park and LaGuardia. This is precisely the relationship you want to reproduce with your hashing algorithm.

8.2.3 Understand the geohash

The geohashes you've seen are all represented as character strings in the Base32 encoding alphabet.[3] In reality, the geohash is a sequence of bits representing an increasingly precise subdivision of longitude and latitude.

For instance, 40.78° N is a latitude. It falls in the upper half[4] of the range [-90.0, 90.0], so its first geohash bit is 1. Its second bit is 0 because 40.78 is in the lower half of the range [0.0, 90.0]. The third range is [0.0, 45.0], and 40.78 falls in the upper half, so the third bit is 1.

---

[3] Base32 is an encoding used to represent a binary value as a sequence of ASCII characters. Note that although geohash uses an alphabet of characters similar to that of Base32, the geohash spec doesn't follow the Base32 RFC. Learn more about Base32 at http://en.wikipedia.org/wiki/Base32.

[4] When including a direction, degrees of latitude are measured from 0.0 to 90.0 with the northern hemisphere corresponding to positive values and the southern hemisphere to negative values on the absolute latitude range. Likewise, degrees of longitude are measured from 0.0 to 180.0 with the eastern hemisphere indicating positive values and western hemisphere indicating negative values.

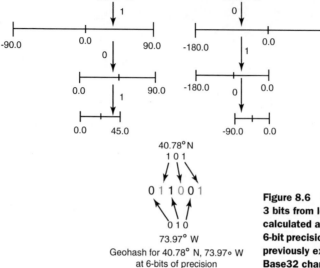

Figure 8.6   **Constructing a geohash. The first 3 bits from longitude and latitude are calculated and woven to produce a geohash of 6-bit precision. The example data we discussed previously executed this algorithm out to 7 Base32 characters, or 35-bit precision.**

The contribution provided by each dimension is calculated by halving the value range and determining which half the point resides in. If the point is greater than or equal to the midpoint, it's a 1-bit. Otherwise, it's a 0-bit. This process is repeated, again cutting the range in half and selecting a 1 or 0 based on where the target point lies. This binary partitioning is performed on both the longitude and latitude values. Rather than using the bit sequence from each dimension independently, the encoding weaves the bits together to create the hash. The spatial partitioning is why geohashes have the spatial locality property. The weaving of bits from each dimension is what allows for the prefix-match precision trickery.

Now that you understand how each component is encoded, let's calculate a full value. This process of bisecting the range and selecting a bit is repeated until the desired precision is achieved. A bit sequence is calculated for both longitude and latitude, and the bits are interwoven, longitude first, then latitude, out to the target precision. Figure 8.6 illustrates the process. Once the bit sequence is calculated, it's encoded to produce the final hash value.

Now that you understand why the geohash is useful to you and how it works, let's plug it in for your rowkey.

8.2.4   *Using the geohash as a spatially aware rowkey*

The geohash makes a great choice for the rowkey because it's inexpensive to calculate and the prefix gets you a long way toward finding nearest neighbors. Let's apply it to the sample data, sort by geohash, and see how you're doing on prefixes. We've calculated the geohash for each point using a library[5] and added it to the data. All of the

---

[5] We're using Silvio Heuberger's Java implementation at https://github.com/kungfoo/geohash-java. We've made it available in Maven for easy distribution.

data in the sample is relatively close together, so you expect a good deal of prefix overlap across the points:

```
    GEOHASH        X            Y           ID   NAME
1   dr5rugb9rwjj  -73.96993203  40.75815170  442  Fedex Kinko's
2   dr5rugbge05m  -73.96978387  40.75850573  388  Barnes & Noble
3   dr5rugbvggqe  -73.96974759  40.75890919  441  Fedex Kinko's
4   dr5rugckg406  -73.96910155  40.75873061  564  Public Telephone
5   dr5ruu1x1ct8  -73.96880474  40.76048717  472  Juan Valdez NYC
6   dr5ruu29vytq  -73.97000655  40.76098703  593  Starbucks
7   dr5ruu2y5vkb  -73.96974993  40.76170883  219  Startegy Atrium and Cafe
8   dr5ruu3d7x0b  -73.96873588  40.76107453  463  Smilers 707
9   dr5ruu693jhm  -73.96746533  40.76089302  525  McDonalds
```

Sure enough, you get five characters of common prefix. That's not bad at all! This means you're a long way toward the distance query and goal ❶ with a simple range scan. For context, figure 8.7 puts this data on a map.

This is much better than the compound rowkey approach, but it's by no means perfect. All these points are close together, within a couple blocks of each other. Why are

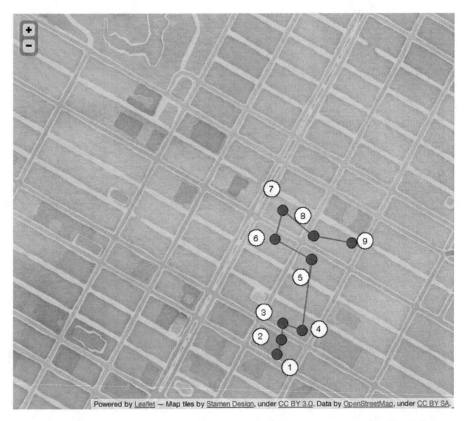

Figure 8.7 Seeing prefix matches in action. If the target search is in this area, a simple rowkey scan will get the data you need. Not only that, but the order of results makes a lot more sense than the order in figure 8.3.

you only matching on 5 of 12 characters? We would hope data this spatially close would be stored much closer together. Thinking back to figure 8.4, the difference in size of the spatial area covered by a prefix scan of five versus six versus seven characters is significant—far more than a couple of blocks. You'd make strides toward goal ❷ if you could make two scans of prefix six rather than a single scan of prefix five. Or better still, how about five or six scans of prefix seven? Let's look at figure 8.8, this time with more perspective. The geohash boxes for both the six-character and seven-character geohash prefixes are overlaid.

Compared to the target query area, the six-character prefix match areas are huge. Worse still, the query spans two of those larger prefixes. Seen in this context, those five characters of common prefix include far more data than you need. Relying on prefix match results in scanning a huge amount of extra area. Of course, there's a trade-off. If your data isn't dense at this precision level, executing fewer, longer scans isn't such a big deal. The scans don't return too much superfluous data, and you can minimize the remote procedure call (RPC) overhead. If your data is dense, running

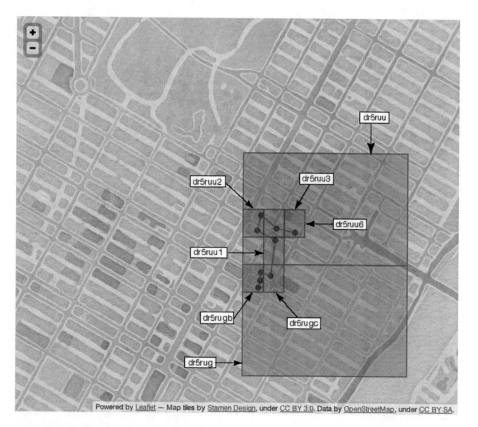

Figure 8.8 Prefix matches with geohash overlay. Lots of additional, unnecessary area is introduced into the query result by using the 6-character prefix. An ideal implementation would use only 7-character prefixes to minimize the amount of extra data transmitted over the wire.

more, shorter scans will reduce the number of excess points transported over the wire. Plus, if there's one thing that computers are getting good at these days, it's parallelism. Execute each of those shorter scans on its own CPU core, and the query is still as fast as the slowest scan.

Let's scroll the map over to a different part of Manhattan, not far from the space we've explored thus far. Look at figure 8.9. Notice that the geohash of the center box has six characters (dr5ruz) of prefix in common with the boxes to its east, southeast, and south. But there are only five characters (dr5ru) in common with the west and southwest boxes. If five characters of common prefix is bad, then the prefix match with the entire northern row is abysmal, with only two characters (dr) in common! This doesn't happen every time, but it does happen with a surprisingly high frequency. As a counterexample, all eight neighbors of the southeast box (dr5ruz9) share a common six-character prefix.

The geohash is effective, but you can't use a simple naïve prefix match either. Based on these figures, it looks like the optimal approach for the data is to scan the center tile and its eight neighbors. This approach will guarantee correct results while minimizing

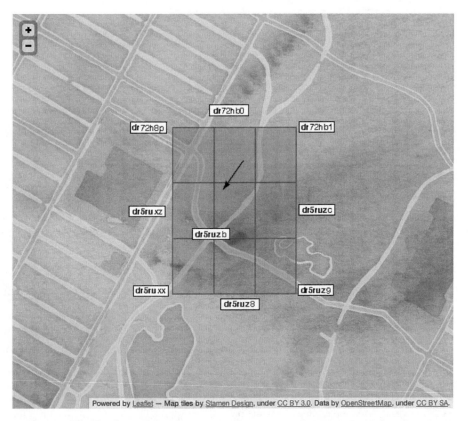

Figure 8.9 Visualizing the geohash edge case. The encoding isn't perfect; this is one such case. Imagine a nearest-neighbor search falling on the point under the arrow in this illustration. It's possible you'll find a neighbor in a tile with only two characters of common prefix.

the amount of unnecessary network IO. Luckily, calculating those neighbors is a simple bit-manipulation away. Explaining the details of that manipulation is beyond the scope of our interest, so we'll trust the geohash library to provide that feature.

> **Not all linearization techniques are created equal**
>
> The geohash is approximating the data space. That is, it's a function that computes a value on a single output dimension based on input from multiple dimensions. In this case, the dimensionality of the input is only 2, but you can imagine how this could work for more. This is a form of linearization, and it's not the only one. Other techniques such as the Z-order curve[1] and the Hilbert curve[2] are also common. These are both classes of space-filling curves:[3] curves defined by a single, uninterrupted line that touches all partitions of a space. None of these techniques can perfectly model a two-dimensional plane on a one-dimensional line and maintain the relative characteristics of objects in those spaces. We choose the geohash because, for our purposes, its error cases are less bad than the others.

8.3 *Implementing the nearest-neighbors query*

Now it's time to put your newfound geohash knowledge into practice by implementing the query. Remember the question you're trying to answer: "Where are the five nearest wifi hotspots?" That sounds like a function with three arguments: a target location, in the form of a latitude and longitude, and the maximum number of results, something along the lines of the following:

```
public Collection<QueryMatch> queryKNN(double lat, double lon, int n) {
    ...
}
```

QueryMatch is a data class you'll use to keep track of, well, a query result. Here are the steps involved:

1 Construct the target GeoHash.
2 Iterate through it and its eight neighbors to find candidate results. The results from each scan are ranked according to distance from the target point and limited to only the n closest results.
3 Rank and limit the results of the nine scans to compute the final n results returned to the caller.

You'll implement this in two functions: one to handle the HBase scan and the other to handle the geohash and aggregation. In pseudo-code, the first function looks like this:

---

[6] The Z-order curve is extremely similar to the geohash, involving the interleaving of bits. Read more at http://en.wikipedia.org/wiki/Z-order_curve.
[7] The Hilbert curve is similar to a Z-order curve. Learn more at http://en.wikipedia.org/wiki/Hilbert_curve.
[8] Read more about space-filling curves at http://en.wikipedia.org/wiki/Space-filling_curves.

```
takeN(origin, prefix, n):
  table = HBase.table('wifi')
  scanner = table.scan(prefix)
  results = []
  for result in scanner:
    results.add(result)
  comp = distance_from(origin)
  results = sort(comp, results)
  return limit(n, results)
```

Read records from wifi table matching prefix ← (points to `scanner = table.scan(prefix)`)

Sort results by distance from query origin (points to `comp` / `results = sort` lines)

Return closest n results ← (points to `return limit(n, results)`)

There's nothing particularly special here; you're interacting with HBase as you've done before. You don't need to hang onto all the query results from each scan, only the closest n. That cuts down on the memory usage of the query process, especially if you're forced to use a shorter prefix than desired.

The main query function builds on the takeN helper function. Again, here it is in pseudo-code:

```
queryKNN(lat, lon, n):
  origin = [lat, lon]
  target = geohash(lat, lon)
  results = []
  results.addAll(takeN(origin, target, n)
  for neighbor in target.neighbors:
    results.addAll(takeN(origin, neighbor, n)
  comp = distance_from(origin)
  results = sort(comp, results)
  return limit(n, results)
```

Geohash target ← (points to `target = geohash(lat, lon)`)

Call takeN on target hash ... ← (points to `results.addAll(takeN(origin, target, n)`)

... and on all neighbors (points to `results.addAll(takeN(origin, neighbor, n)`)

Use same distance function as before (points to `comp` / `results = sort` lines)

Return closest n results ← (points to `return limit(n, results)`)

The queryKNN function handles generating the geohash from the query target, calculating the nine prefixes to scan, and consolidating the results. As you saw in figure 8.9, all nine prefixes must be scanned to guarantee correct results. The same technique used to limit memory usage in takeN is used to pare down the final results. This is also where you'd want to put any concurrency code, if you're so inclined.

Now let's translate the pseudo-code into the Java implementation. Google's Guava[9] library provides a handy class to manage the sorted, size-limited bucket of results via the MinMaxPriorityQueue. It accepts a custom Comparator for order maintenance and enforcing the eviction policy; you'll need to build one for your QueryMatch class. The Comparator is based on distance from the origin of the query target. The java.awt.geom.Point2D class gives you a simple distance function that's good enough[10] for your needs. Let's start with the helpers, QueryMatch and DistanceComparator:

---

[9] Guava is the missing utils library for Java. If you're a professional Java developer and you've never explored it, you're missing out. There's a nice overview on the wiki: http://mng.bz/ApbT.

[10] We're being pretty flippant with the domain specifics here. Realistically, you don't want to use a simple distance function, especially if you're calculating distances spanning a large area. Remember, the Earth is roundish, not flat. Simple things like Euclidean geometry need not apply. In general, take extra care when calculating nonrelative values, especially when you want to think in uniform geometries like circles and squares or return human-meaningful units like miles or kilometers.

```
public class QueryMatch {
  public String id;
  public String hash;                    Nothing
  public double lon, lat;                but data
  public double distance = Double.NaN;

  public QueryMatch(String id, String hash, double lon, double lat) {
    this.id = id;
    this.hash = hash;
    this.lon = lon;
    this.lat = lat;
  }
}

public class DistanceComparator implements Comparator<QueryMatch> {
  Point2D origin;

  public DistanceComparator(double lon, double lat) {
    this.origin = new Point2D.Double(lon, lat);
  }

  public int compare(QueryMatch o1, QueryMatch o2) {
    if(Double.isNaN(o1.distance)) {
      o1.distance = origin.distance(o1.lon, o1.lat);
    }
    if (Double.isNaN(o2.distance)) {
      o2.distance = origin.distance(o2.lon, o2.lat);     Defer to Point2D
    }                                                      implementation
    return Double.compare(o1.distance, o2.distance);  ◄─┘ of distance
  }
}
```

> **It's not customary to modify an object from within a Comparator**
> Normally you wouldn't write Comparators the way we did in the code example. Don't do this in your normal code! We've done so here to make it easier to inspect the results from within the text. It's only to help explain what's happening here. Really, please, don't do this!

With the result sorting in place, you need a Java version of takeN, the method to perform the HBase scan. Each prefix needs to sort and limit the set of partial results returned, so it takes a Comparator in addition to the prefix and n. That's instead of receiving the origin point as you did in pseudo-code:

```
Collection<QueryMatch> takeN(Comparator<QueryMatch> comp,
                             String prefix,
                             int n) throws IOException {
  Collection<QueryMatch> candidates
    = MinMaxPriorityQueue.orderedBy(comp)          Limit results to only n
                    .maximumSize(n)                nearest, sorted by distance
                    .create();

  Scan scan = new Scan(prefix.getBytes());
  scan.setFilter(new PrefixFilter(prefix.getBytes()));
```

```
scan.addFamily(FAMILY);
scan.setMaxVersions(1);
scan.setCaching(50);

HTableInterface table = pool.getTable("wifi");

ResultScanner scanner = table.getScanner(scan);
for (Result r : scanner) {
  String hash = new String(r.getRow());
  String id = new String(r.getValue(FAMILY, ID));
  double lon = Bytes.toDouble(r.getValue(FAMILY, X_COL));
  double lat = Bytes.toDouble(r.getValue(FAMILY, Y_COL));
  candidates.add(new QueryMatch(id, hash, lon, lat));
}
table.close();
return candidates;
}
```

Setting scan cache higher than I dramatically cuts down RPC calls

Read records from wifi table matching prefix

Collect candidates

This is the same kind of table scan used when you learned about scans in chapter 2. The only new thing to point out here is the call to Scan.setCaching(). That method call sets the number of records returned per RPC call the scanner makes to 50—a somewhat arbitrary number, based on the number of records traversed by the scan and the size of each record. For this dataset, the records are small and the idea is to restrict the number of records scanned via the geohash. Fifty should be far more data than you expect to pull from a single scan at this precision. You'll want to play with that number to determine an optimal setting for your use case. There's a useful post[11] on the hbase-user[12] mailing list describing in detail the kinds of trade-offs you're balancing with this setting. Be sure to play with it, because anything is likely better than the default of 1.

Finally, fill out the stub you defined earlier. It computes a GeoHash from the target query point and calls takeN over that prefix as well as the eight surrounding neighbors. Results are aggregated using the same limiting MinMaxPriorityQueue class used in takeN:

```
public Collection<QueryMatch> query(double lat, double lon, int n)
  throws IOException {
  DistanceComparator comp = new DistanceComparator(lon, lat);
  Collection<QueryMatch> ret
    = MinMaxPriorityQueue.orderedBy(comp)
                         .maximumSize(n)
                         .create();

  GeoHash target = GeoHash.withCharacterPrecision(lat, lon, 7);
  ret.addAll(takeN(comp, target.toBase32(), n));
  for (GeoHash h : target.getAdjacent()) {
    ret.addAll(takeN(comp, h.toBase32(), n));
  }

  return ret;
}
```

Geohash the target

Call takeN on target hash ...

... and on all neighbors

---

[11] http://mng.bz/5UY5.

[12] You mean you've not subscribed to hbase-user yet? Get on it! Subscribe and browse the archives from http://mail-archives.apache.org/mod_mbox/hbase-user/.

Instantiating a `Comparator` is simple, instantiating the queue is simple, and the `for` loop over the geohash neighbors is simple. The only odd thing here is the construction of the `GeoHash`. This library allows you to specify a character precision. Earlier in the chapter, you wanted to hash a point in space, so you used the maximum precision you could get: 12 characters. Here the situation is different. You're not after a single point, but a bounding box. Choose a precision that's too high, and you won't query over enough space to find n matches, particularly when n is small. Choose a precision that's too low, and your scans will traverse orders of magnitude more data than you need. Using seven characters of precision makes sense for this dataset and this query. Different data or different values of n will require a different precision. Striking that balance can be tricky, so our best advice is to profile your queries and experiment. If all the queries look roughly the same, perhaps you can decide on a value. Otherwise, you'll want to build a heuristic to decide on a precision based on the query parameters. In either case, you need to get to know your data and your application!

> ## Design your scans according to the query, not the data
> Notice that we said to choose your geohash prefix precision based on the application-level query. You always want to design your HBase scans according to the query instead of designing them based on the data. Your data will change over time, long after your application is "finished." If you tie your queries to the data, your query performance will change along with the data. That means a fast query today may become a slow query tomorrow. Building scans based on the application-level query means a "fast query" will always be fast relative to a "slow query." If you couple the scans to the application-level query, users of your application will enjoy a more consistent experience.

Toss together a simple `main()`, and then you can see if it all works. Well, almost. You need to load the data too. The details of parsing a tab-separated values (TSV) file aren't terribly interesting. The part you care about is using the `GeoHash` library to construct the hash you use for a rowkey. That code is simple enough. These are points, so you use 12 characters of precision. Again, that's the longest printable geohash you can construct and still fit in a Java `long`:

```
double lat = Double.parseDouble(row.get("lat"));
double lon = Double.parseDouble(row.get("lon"));
String rowkey = GeoHash.withCharacterPrecision(lat, lon, 12).toBase32();
```

Now you have everything you need. Start by opening the shell and creating a table. The column family isn't particularly important here, so let's choose something short:

```
$ echo "create 'wifi', 'a'" | hbase shell
HBase Shell; enter 'help<RETURN>' for list of supported commands.
Type "exit<RETURN>" to leave the HBase Shell
Version 0.92.1, r1298924, Fri Mar  9 16:58:34 UTC 2012

create 'wifi', 'a'
0 row(s) in 6.5610 seconds
```

The test data is packaged in the project, so you have everything you need. Build the application, and run the `Ingest` tool against the full dataset:

```
$ mvn clean package
...
[INFO] ---------------------------------------------------------
[INFO] BUILD SUCCESS
[INFO] ---------------------------------------------------------
$ java -cp target/hbaseia-gis-1.0.0.jar \
  HBaseIA.GIS.Ingest \
  wifi data/wifi_4326.txt
Geohashed 1250 records in 354ms.
```

Looks good! It's time to run a query. For the target point, let's cheat a little and choose the coordinates of one of the existing data points. If the distance algorithm isn't completely broken, that point should be the first result. Let's center the query on ID 593:

```
$ java -cp target/hbaseia-gis-1.0.0.jar \
  HBaseIA.GIS.KNNQuery -73.97000655 40.76098703 5
Scan over 'dr5ruu2' returned 2 candidates.
Scan over 'dr5ruu8' returned 0 candidates.
Scan over 'dr5ruu9' returned 1 candidates.
Scan over 'dr5ruu3' returned 2 candidates.
Scan over 'dr5ruu1' returned 1 candidates.
Scan over 'dr5ruu0' returned 1 candidates.
Scan over 'dr5rusp' returned 0 candidates.
Scan over 'dr5rusr' returned 1 candidates.
Scan over 'dr5rusx' returned 0 candidates.
<QueryMatch:  593, dr5ruu29vytq, -73.9700, 40.7610, 0.00000 >
<QueryMatch:  219, dr5ruu2y5vkb, -73.9697, 40.7617, 0.00077 >
<QueryMatch: 1132, dr5ruu3d9tn9, -73.9688, 40.7611, 0.00120 >
<QueryMatch:  463, dr5ruu3d7x0b, -73.9687, 40.7611, 0.00127 >
<QueryMatch:  472, dr5ruu1x1ct8, -73.9688, 40.7605, 0.00130 >
```

Excellent! ID 593, the point that matched the query target, comes up first! We've added a bit of debugging information to help understand these results. The first set of output is the contributions from each of the prefix scans. The second set of output is the match results. The fields printed are ID, geohash, longitude, latitude, and distance from the query target. Figure 8.10 illustrates how the query comes together spatially.

That's pretty cool, right? As you likely noticed, all the comparison work happened on the client side of the operation. The scans pulled down all the data, and postprocessing happened in the client. You have a cluster of machines in your HBase deployment, so let's see if you can put them to work. Perhaps you can use some other features to extend HBase into a full-fledged distributed geographic query engine.

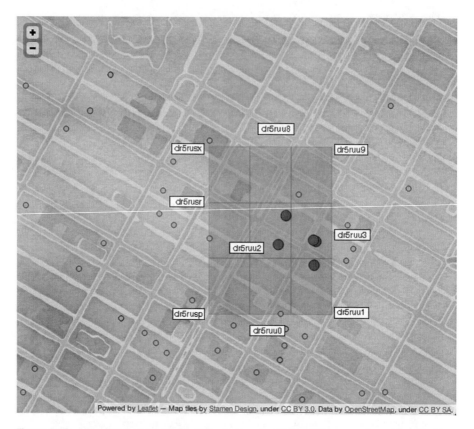

Figure 8.10   Visualizing query results. This simple spiraling technique searches out around the query coordinate looking for matches. A smarter implementation would take into account the query coordinate's position within the central spatial extent. Once the minimum number of matches had been found, it would skip any neighbors that are too far away to contribute.

8.4   *Pushing work server-side*

The sample dataset is pretty small, only 1,200 points and not too many attributes per point. Still, your data will grow, and your users will always demand a faster experience. It's generally a good idea to push as much work server-side as you can. As you know, HBase gives you two mechanisms for pushing work into the RegionServers: filters and coprocessors. In this section, you'll extend the wifi example you've started. You'll implement a new kind of geographic query, and you'll do so using a custom filter. Implementing a custom filter has some operational overhead, so before you do that you'll make an improvement on the way you use the geohash.

You'll start by changing the query. Instead of looking for wifi hotspots near a particular location, let's look for all hotspots in a requested space. Specifically, you'll answer the query, "What are all wifi hotspots within a block of Times Square?" That space containing Times Square is a relatively simple shape to draw by hand: just four corners. You'll use the points (40.758703° N, 73.980844° W), (40.761369° N, 73.987214° W), (40.756400° N, 73.990839° W), (40.753642° N, 73.984422° W). The

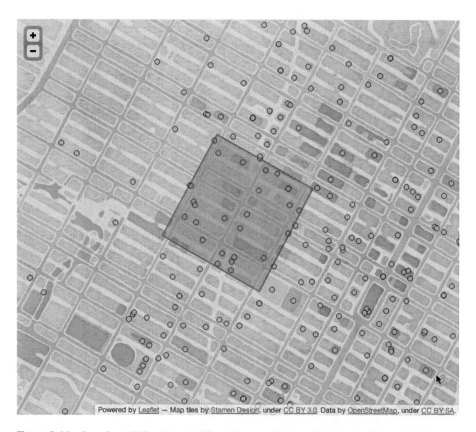

Figure 8.11 Querying within a block of Times Square. We used Google Earth to eyeball the four corners of the query space. It looks like all those flashy sign boards sucked up the wifi; it's not very dense compared to other parts of the city. You can expect about 25 points to match your query.

query region, along with the data, is illustrated in figure 8.11. As you can see, you expect to receive about 25 points in the query results.

This is a pretty simple shape, drawn by hand and overlaid on the map. What you have here is a simple polygon. There are plenty of sources for polygons you might use in your query. For instance, a service like Yelp might provide a user with predefined polygons describing local neighborhood boundaries. You could even allow the user of your application to sketch their query polygon by hand. The approach you're going to take works as well with this simple rectangle as with a more complex shape.

With the query shape defined, it's time to devise a plan for implementing the query. Like the *k*-nearest-neighbors query, you want the implementation to minimize the number of candidate points read out of HBase. You have the geohash index, which takes you fairly far along. The first step is to translate the query polygon into a set of geohash scans. As you know from the previous query, that will give you all candidate points without too many extra. The second step is to pull out only the points that are contained by the query polygon. Both of these will require help from a geometry library. Luckily, you have such a companion in the JTS Topology Suite (JTS).[13] You'll use that library to bridge the gap between the geohash and the query polygon.

8.4.1 Creating a geohash scan from a query polygon

For this step of query building, you need to work out exactly which prefixes you want to scan. As before, you want to minimize both the number of scans made and the spatial extent covered by the scans. The `GeoHash.getAdjacent()` method gave you a cheap way to extend the query area before stepping up to a less precise geohash. Let's use that to find a suitable set of scans—a minimal bounding set of prefixes. Before we describe the algorithm, it's helpful to know a couple of geometry tricks.

The first trick you want to use is the *centroid*,[14] a point at the geometric center of a polygon. The query parameter is a polygon, and every polygon has a centroid. You'll use the centroid to start your search for a minimum bounding prefix scan. JTS can calculate this for you using the `Geometry.getCentroid()` method, assuming you have a `Geometry` instance. Thus you need a way to make `Geometry` an object from your query argument. There's a simple text format for describing geometries called well-known text (WKT).[15] The query around Times Square translated into WKT looks like this:

```
POLYGON ((-73.980844 40.758703,
          -73.987214 40.761369,
          -73.990839 40.756400,
          -73.984422 40.753642,
          -73.980844 40.758703))
```

That's Times Square in data. Technically speaking, a polygon is a closed shape, so the first and last point must match. The application accepts WKT as the input query. JTS provides a parser for WKT, which you can use to create a `Geometry` from the query input. Once you have that, the centroid is just a method call away:

```
String wkt = ...
WKTReader reader = new WKTReader();
Geometry query = reader.read(wkt);
Point queryCenter = query.getCentroid();
```

Figure 8.12 illustrates the query polygon with its centroid.

Now that you know the query polygon's centroid, you have a place to begin calculating the geohash. The problem is, you don't know how large a geohash is required to fully contain the query polygon. You need a way to compute a geohash and see if it fully contains the user's query. The `Geometry` class in JTS has a `contains()` method that does just that. You also don't want to step down the precision level if you don't

---

[13] JTS is a full-featured library for computational geometry in Java. Check it out at http://tsusiatsoftware.net/jts/main.html.

[14] *Centroid* is a mathematical term with a strict meaning in formal geometry. One point of note is that the centroid of a polygon isn't always contained by it. That isn't the case with the query example; but in real life data is messy, and this does happen. The Wikipedia article provides many useful example illustrations: http://en.wikipedia.org/wiki/Centroid.

[15] More examples of well-known text can be found at http://en.wikipedia.org/wiki/Well-known_text.

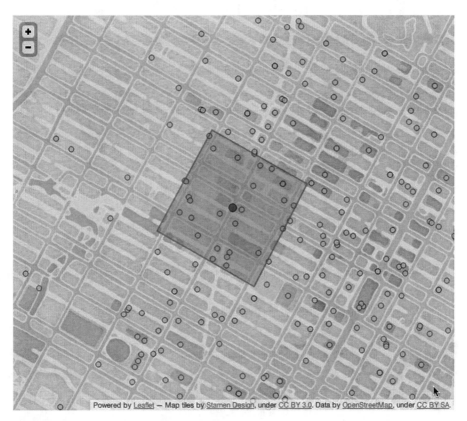

Figure 8.12   Query polygon with centroid. The centroid point is where you'll begin with the calculation for a minimum bounding set of geohashes.

have to. If the geohash at the current precision doesn't contain the query geometry, you should try the geohash plus all its immediate neighbors. Thus, you need a way to convert a `GeoHash` or a group of `GeoHashes` into a `Geometry`. This brings you to our second geometry trick: the convex hull.

The *convex hull* is formally defined in terms of the intersections of sets of geometries. The Wikipedia page[16] has a simpler description that is adequate for your needs. It says you can think of the convex hull of a collection of geometries as the shape a rubber band makes when you stretch it over the geometries. These geometric concepts are easily explained in pictures, so figure 8.13[17] shows the convex hull over a random scattering of points.

The convex hull is useful for the case when you want to know if the query polygon falls inside the full set of geohash neighbors. In this case, that means whether you have a single geohash or a group of them, you can create your containment-testing

---

[16] You can find the formal definition of the convex hull at http://en.wikipedia.org/wiki/Convex_hull.

[17] JTS comes with an application for exploring the interactions between geometries, called the JTSTestBuilder. This figure was created in part using that tool.

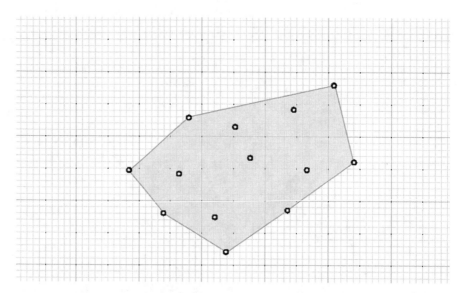

Figure 8.13 The convex hull is the shape made by fully containing a collection of geometries. In this case, the geometries are simple points. You'll use this to test query containment of the full set of neighbors of a geohash.

polygon by taking the convex hull over the corner points from all the hashes. Every GeoHash has a BoundingBox that describes its corners. Let's wrap that up in a method:

```
Set<Coordinate> getCoords(GeoHash hash) {
  BoundingBox bbox = hash.getBoundingBox();
  Set<Coordinate> coords = new HashSet<Coordinate>(4);
  coords.add(new Coordinate(bbox.getMinLon(), bbox.getMinLat()));
  coords.add(new Coordinate(bbox.getMinLon(), bbox.getMaxLat()));
  coords.add(new Coordinate(bbox.getMaxLon(), bbox.getMaxLat()));
  coords.add(new Coordinate(bbox.getMaxLon(), bbox.getMinLat()));
  return coords;
}
```

Southwest corner · Northwest corner · Northeast corner · Southeast corner

In the case of the full set of neighbors, you loop though all of them, calling get-Coords() on each one, and collect their corners. Using the Coordinates, you can create a simple kind of Geometry instance, the MultiPoint. MultiPoint extends Geometry and is a group of points. You're using this instead of something like a Polygon because the Multipoint doesn't impose additional geometric restrictions. Create the MultiPoint and then take its convexHull(). You can put all this together in another helper method:

```
Geometry convexHull(GeoHash[] hashes) {
  Set<Coordinate> coords = new HashSet<Coordinate>();
  for (GeoHash hash : hashes) {
    coords.addAll(getCoords(hash));
  }
```

Collect all corners for all hashes

```
GeometryFactory factory = new GeometryFactory();
Geometry geom
  = factory.createMultiPoint(coords.toArray(new Coordinate[0]));
return geom.convexHull();
}
```

Take that Geometry's convex hull

Create simple Geometry from corner coordinates

Now you have everything you need to calculate the minimum bounding set of geohash prefixes from the query polygon. Thus far, you've used a geohash precision of seven characters with reasonable success on this dataset, so you'll start there. For this algorithm, you'll begin by calculating the geohash at seven characters from the query polygon's centroid. You'll check that hash for containment. If it's not big enough, you'll perform the same calculation over the complete set of the geohash and its neighbors. If that set of prefixes still isn't large enough, you'll step the precision level back to six and try the whole thing again.

Code speaks louder than words. The `minimumBoundingPrefixes()` method looks like this:

```
GeoHash[] minimumBoundingPrefixes(Geometry query) {
  GeoHash candidate;
  Geometry candidateGeom;
  Point queryCenter = query.getCentroid();
  for (int precision = 7; precision > 0; precision--) {
    candidate
      = GeoHash.withCharacterPrecision(queryCenter.getY(),
                                       queryCenter.getX(),
                                       precision);
    candidateGeom = convexHull(new GeoHash[]{ candidate });
    if (candidateGeom.contains(query)) {
      return new GeoHash[]{ candidate };
    }
    candidateGeom = convexHull(candidate.getAdjacent());
    if (candidateGeom.contains(query)) {
      GeoHash[] ret = Arrays.copyOf(candidate.getAdjacent(), 9);
      ret[8] = candidate;
      return ret;
    }
  }
  throw new IllegalArgumentException(
    "Geometry cannot be contained by GeoHashs");
}
```

Start with centroid …

… and geohash at 7-character precision

Check hash for containment

Failing that, check entire block for containment

Don't forget to include center hash

Failing that, drop level of precision and try again

Of course, pictures speak louder than code. Figure 8.14 illustrates the attempt to bind the query with geohashes at seven and six characters of precision. Seven characters is insufficient, so a level of precision must be dropped.

Figure 8.14 also emphasizes the imperfection in the current approach. At six-character precision, you do cover the entire query extent, but the entire western set of panels isn't contributing any data that falls inside the query. You could be smarter in choosing your prefix panels, but that involves much more complex logic. We'll call this good enough for now and move on to continue implementing the query.

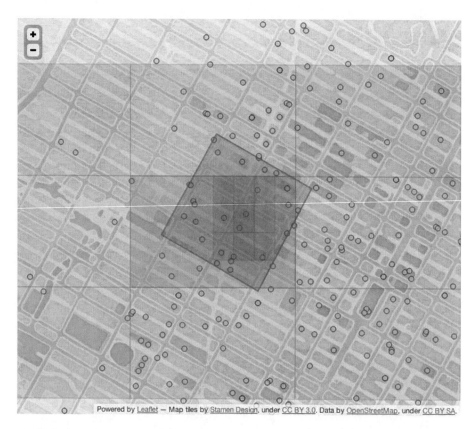

Powered by Leaflet — Map tiles by Stamen Design, under CC BY 3.0. Data by OpenStreetMap, under CC BY SA.

Figure 8.14 Checking for containment at seven and six characters of precision. At seven characters, both the central geohash and the combined set of all its neighbors aren't sufficiently large to cover the entire query extent. Moving up to six characters gets the job done.

8.4.2 *Within query take 1: client side*

Before building out the server-side filter, let's finish building and testing the query logic on the client side. Deploying, testing, and redeploying any server-side component can be annoying, even when running locally, so let's build and test the core logic client-side first. Not only that, but you'll build it in a way that's reusable for other kinds of queries.

The main body of client-side logic is nearly identical to that of KNNQuery. In both cases, you're building a list of geohash prefixes to scan, running the scan, and collecting results. Because it's largely identical, we'll skip the scanner code. What you're interested in is checking to see if a returned point is inside of the query polygon. To do that, you'll need to create a Geometry instance from each QueryMatch instance. From there, the same contains() call you used earlier will do the trick:

```
GeoHash[] prefixes = minimumBoundingPrefixes(query);
Set<QueryMatch> ret = new HashSet<QueryMatch>();
HTableInterface table = pool.getTable("wifi");
for (GeoHash prefix : prefixes) {
```

Get prefixes
to scan

```
      ...
  }                                 ◄─┐  Perform scan, creating          Iterate through
  table.close();                       QueryMatch instances               candidates
  for (Iterator<QueryMatch> iter = ret.iterator(); iter.hasNext();) {
    QueryMatch candidate = iter.next();                            ◄─────────────┘
    Coordinate coord = new Coordinate(candidate.lon, candidate.lat);
    Geometry point = factory.createPoint(coord);                              Create
    if (!query.contains(point))          ◄─┐  Test for               Geometry from
       iter.remove();        ◄─┐             containment            each candidate
  }                            │  Toss losers
```

The `QueryMatch` results contain latitude and longitude values, so you turn those into a
`Coordinate` instance. That `Coordinate` is translated into a `Point`, a subclass of `Geome-`
`try`, using the same `GeometryFactory` class you used earlier. `contains()` is just one of
many spatial predicates[18] available to you via the `Geometry` class. That's good news,
because it means the harness you've built to support this within query will work for
many other kinds of spatial operations.

Let's package up the code and try the query. Again, the `main()` method isn't terribly interesting, just parsing arguments and dispatching the query, so you'll skip listing
it. The data is already loaded so you can get right to running the code. Rebuild and
then run a query over the target area around Times Square:

```
$ mvn clean package
...
[INFO] ------------------------------------------------------------
[INFO] BUILD SUCCESS
[INFO] ------------------------------------------------------------
$ java -cp target/hbaseia-gis-1.0.0.jar \
  HBaseIA.GIS.WithinQuery local \
  "POLYGON ((-73.980844 40.758703, \
             -73.987214 40.761369, \
             -73.990839 40.756400, \
             -73.984422 40.753642, \
             -73.980844 40.758703))"
Geometry predicate filtered 155 points.
Query matched 26 points.
<QueryMatch:  644, dr5ru7tt72wm, -73.9852, 40.7574, NaN >
<QueryMatch:  634, dr5rukjkhsd0, -73.9855, 40.7600, NaN >
<QueryMatch:  847, dr5ru7q2tn3k, -73.9841, 40.7553, NaN >
<QueryMatch: 1294, dr5ru7hpn094, -73.9872, 40.7550, NaN >
<QueryMatch:  569, dr5ru7rxeqn2, -73.9825, 40.7565, NaN >
<QueryMatch:  732, dr5ru7fvm5jh, -73.9889, 40.7588, NaN >
<QueryMatch:  580, dr5rukn9brrk, -73.9840, 40.7596, NaN >
<QueryMatch:  445, dr5ru7zsemkp, -73.9825, 40.7587, NaN >
<QueryMatch:  517, dr5ru7yhj0n3, -73.9845, 40.7586, NaN >
<QueryMatch:  372, dr5ru7m0bm8m, -73.9860, 40.7553, NaN >
<QueryMatch:  516, dr5rue8nk1y4, -73.9818, 40.7576, NaN >
<QueryMatch:  514, dr5ru77myu3f, -73.9882, 40.7562, NaN >
<QueryMatch:  566, dr5rukk42vj7, -73.9874, 40.7611, NaN >
```

---

[18] If you're curious about the full breadth of spatial predicates, check out slide 5 in this deck: Martin Davis, "JTS
Topology Suite: A Library for Geometry Processing," March 2011, http://mng.bz/ofve.

```
<QueryMatch:  656, dr5ru7e5hcp5, -73.9886, 40.7571, NaN >
<QueryMatch:  640, dr5rukhnyc3x, -73.9871, 40.7604, NaN >
<QueryMatch:  653, dr5ru7epfg17, -73.9887, 40.7579, NaN >
<QueryMatch:  570, dr5ru7fvdecd, -73.9890, 40.7589, NaN >
<QueryMatch: 1313, dr5ru7k6h9ub, -73.9869, 40.7555, NaN >
<QueryMatch:  403, dr5ru7hv4vyw, -73.9863, 40.7547, NaN >
<QueryMatch:  750, dr5ru7ss0bu1, -73.9867, 40.7572, NaN >
<QueryMatch:  515, dr5ru7g0bgy5, -73.9888, 40.7581, NaN >
<QueryMatch:  669, dr5ru7hzsnz1, -73.9862, 40.7551, NaN >
<QueryMatch:  631, dr5ru7t33776, -73.9857, 40.7568, NaN >
<QueryMatch:  637, dr5ru7xxuccw, -73.9824, 40.7579, NaN >
<QueryMatch: 1337, dr5ru7dsdf6g, -73.9894, 40.7573, NaN >
<QueryMatch:  565, dr5rukp0fp9v, -73.9832, 40.7594, NaN >
```

You get 26 results. That's pretty close to our guess earlier. For a taste of things to come, notice how many points were excluded by the contains() predicate. By pushing the filter logic into the cluster, you can reduce the amount of data transmitted over the network by about 500%! First, though, let's double-check that the results are correct. QueryMatch lines are interesting, but it'll be easier to notice a bug if you can see the results. Figure 8.15 illustrates the query results in context of the query.

Figure 8.15 Within query results. The containment filter appears to work as expected. It's also good to know that the geometry library appears to agree with the cartography library.

That looks pretty good. It also looks like you might want to expand the borders of the query a little. That way, it will catch the handful of locations that sit just outside the line. Now that you know the logic works, let's push the work out to those lazy RegionServers.

8.4.3 *Within query take 2: WithinFilter*

Now that you have a working implementation, let's move the predicate logic into a filter. That way you can keep all the extra data on the cluster. You have everything in place to verify the implementation via the client-side version. The only difference you should see is that the filtered version will have drastically reduced network overhead and thus, ideally, run faster. Unless, that is, you're running against a dataset on a standalone HBase.

The WithinFilter is similar to the PasswordStrengthFilter you saw in chapter 4. Just like PasswordStrengthFilter, you're filtering based on data stored in the cells within the row, so you need to maintain some state. In this case, you need to override the void filterRow(List<KeyValue>) method in order to access both the X- and Y-coordinates at the same time. That's where you'll move the logic from the client-side implementation. That method will update the state variable in the cases when you want to exclude a row. Minus a little error-checking, the filterRow() method looks like this:

```
public void filterRow(List<KeyValue> kvs) {
  double lon = Double.NaN;
  double lat = Double.NaN;

  for (KeyValue kv : kvs) {
    if (Bytes.equals(kv.getQualifier(), X_COL))          ← Find X-coordinate
      lon = Double.parseDouble(new String(kv.getQualifier()));
    if (Bytes.equals(kv.getQualifier(), Y_COL))          ← Find Y-coordinate
        lat = Double.parseDouble(new String(kv.getQualifier()));
  }
  Coordinate coord = new Coordinate(lon, lat);           ← Create Point
  Geometry point = factory.createPoint(coord);
  if (!query.contains(point))                            ← Test for containment
    this.exclude = true;
}
```

Methods that iterate over every KeyValue in every column family in every row can be slow. HBase will optimize away calls to filterRow() if it can; you must explicitly enable it in your extension to FilterBase. Tell the filter to tell HBase to call this method by providing one more override:

```
public boolean hasFilterRow() { return true; }
```

When you want to exclude a row because it doesn't fall within the query bounds, you set the exclude flag. That flag is used in boolean filterRow() as the condition for exclusion:

```
public boolean filterRow() {
  return this.exclude;
}
```

You'll construct your filter from the query `Geometry` parsed from `main()`'s arguments. Constructing the filter on the client looks like this:

```
Filter withinFilter = new WithinFilter(query);
```

Other than moving the exclusion logic out to the `Filter` implementation, the updated method doesn't look very different. In your own filters, don't forget to include a default constructor with no arguments. That's necessary for the serialization API. Now it's time to install the filter and give it a go.

A road less traveled

At the time of this writing, there aren't many examples of custom `Filter` implementations. We have the list of filters that ship with HBase (an impressive list) but not much beyond that. Thus if you choose to implement your own filters, you may find yourself scratching your head. But never fear! HBase is open, and you have the source!

If you think HBase isn't respecting a contract between the interface and its calling context, you can always fall back to the source. A handy trick for such things is to create and log an exception. There's no need to throw it; just create it and log it. `LOG.info("", new Exception());` should do the trick. The stack trace will show up in your application logs, and you'll know exactly where to dive into the upstream code. Sprinkle exceptions throughout to get a nice sampling of what is (or isn't) calling your custom filter.

If you're debugging a misbehaving filter, you'll have to stop and start HBase with each iteration so it picks up the changes to your JAR. That's why in the example, you tested the logic on the client side first.

The filter must be installed on the HBase cluster in order for your RegionServers to be able to instantiate it. Add the JAR to the classpath, and bounce the process. If your JAR includes dependencies as this one does, be sure to register those classes as well. You can add those JARs to the classpath, or you can create an uber-JAR, exploding all of those JARs' classes inside your own. That's what you do here, for simplicity. In practice, we recommend that you keep your JAR lean and ship the dependencies just as you do your own. It will simplify debugging the version conflicts that will inevitably pop up later down the line. Your future self will thank you. The same applies to custom `Coprocessor` deployments.

To find out exactly which external JARs your `Filter` or `Coprocessor` depends on, and which JARs those dependencies depend on, Maven can help. It has a *goal* for determining exactly that. In this case, it shows only two dependencies not already provided by Hadoop and HBase:

```
$ mvn dependency:tree
...
[INFO] --- maven-dependency-plugin:2.1:tree (default-cli) @ hbaseia-gis ---
[INFO] HBaseIA:hbaseia-gis:jar:1.0.0-SNAPSHOT
[INFO] +- org.apache.hadoop:hadoop-core:jar:1.0.3:compile
```

```
[INFO] |   +- commons-cli:commons-cli:jar:1.2:compile
...
[INFO] +- org.apache.hbase:hbase:jar:0.92.1:compile
[INFO] |   +- com.google.guava:guava:jar:r09:compile
...
[INFO] +- org.clojars.ndimiduk:geohash-java:jar:1.0.6:compile
[INFO] \- com.vividsolutions:jts:jar:1.12:compile
[INFO] ------------------------------------------------------------
[INFO] BUILD SUCCESS
[INFO] ------------------------------------------------------------
```

You're lucky: the dependencies don't pull any dependencies of their own—at least, no JARs not already provided. Were there any, they'd show up in the tree view.

You install the JAR and any dependencies by editing the file hbase-env.sh in $HBASE_HOME/conf. Uncomment the line that starts with export HBASE_CLASSPATH, and add your JAR. You can add multiple JARs by separating them with a colon (:). It looks something like this:

```
# Extra Java CLASSPATH elements.  Optional.
export HBASE_CLASSPATH=/path/to/hbaseia-gis-1.0.0.jar
```

Now you can rebuild, restart, and try it. Notice that you change the first parameter of the query tool's launch command from local to remote:

```
$ mvn clean package
...
[INFO] ------------------------------------------------------------
[INFO] BUILD SUCCESS
[INFO] ------------------------------------------------------------
$ $HBASE_HOME/bin/stop-hbase.sh
stopping hbase.....
$ $HBASE_HOME/bin/start-hbase.sh
starting master, logging to …
$ java -cp target/hbaseia-gis-1.0.0.jar \                    ◁── remote rather
  HBaseIA.GIS.WithinQuery remote \                                than local
  "POLYGON ((-73.980844 40.758703, \
            -73.987214 40.761369, \
            -73.990839 40.756400, \
            -73.984422 40.753642, \
            -73.980844 40.758703))"
Query matched 26 points.
<QueryMatch:  644, dr5ru7tt72wm, -73.9852, 40.7574, NaN >
<QueryMatch: 1313, dr5ru7k6h9ub, -73.9869, 40.7555, NaN >
<QueryMatch:  403, dr5ru7hv4vyw, -73.9863, 40.7547, NaN >
<QueryMatch:  565, dr5rukp0fp9v, -73.9832, 40.7594, NaN >
<QueryMatch:  516, dr5rue8nk1y4, -73.9818, 40.7576, NaN >
<QueryMatch:  669, dr5ru7hzsnz1, -73.9862, 40.7551, NaN >
<QueryMatch:  445, dr5ru7zsemkp, -73.9825, 40.7587, NaN >
<QueryMatch:  580, dr5rukn9brrk, -73.9840, 40.7596, NaN >
<QueryMatch:  732, dr5ru7fvm5jh, -73.9889, 40.7588, NaN >
<QueryMatch:  637, dr5ru7xxuccw, -73.9824, 40.7579, NaN >
<QueryMatch:  566, dr5rukk42vj7, -73.9874, 40.7611, NaN >
<QueryMatch:  569, dr5ru7rxeqn2, -73.9825, 40.7565, NaN >
<QueryMatch:  515, dr5ru7g0bgy5, -73.9888, 40.7581, NaN >
<QueryMatch:  514, dr5ru77myu3f, -73.9882, 40.7562, NaN >
```

```
<QueryMatch:    634,  dr5rukjkhsd0,  -73.9855,  40.7600,  NaN >
<QueryMatch:    640,  dr5rukhnyc3x,  -73.9871,  40.7604,  NaN >
<QueryMatch:    372,  dr5ru7m0bm8m,  -73.9860,  40.7553,  NaN >
<QueryMatch:    517,  dr5ru7yhj0n3,  -73.9845,  40.7586,  NaN >
<QueryMatch:    656,  dr5ru7e5hcp5,  -73.9886,  40.7571,  NaN >
<QueryMatch:   1294,  dr5ru7hpn094,  -73.9872,  40.7550,  NaN >
<QueryMatch:    653,  dr5ru7epfg17,  -73.9887,  40.7579,  NaN >
<QueryMatch:    570,  dr5ru7fvdecd,  -73.9890,  40.7589,  NaN >
<QueryMatch:    847,  dr5ru7q2tn3k,  -73.9841,  40.7553,  NaN >
<QueryMatch:   1337,  dr5ru7dsdf6g,  -73.9894,  40.7573,  NaN >
<QueryMatch:    750,  dr5ru7ss0bu1,  -73.9867,  40.7572,  NaN >
<QueryMatch:    631,  dr5ru7t33776,  -73.9857,  40.7568,  NaN >
```

The same number of points are returned. A quick `cat`, `cut`, `sort`, `diff` will prove the output is identical. Visual inspection via figure 8.16 confirms this.

The final test would be to load lots of data on a distributed cluster and time the two implementations. Queries over a large area will show significant performance gains. Be careful, though. If your queries are *really* big, or you build up a complex filter hierarchy, you may run into RPC timeouts and the like. Refer to our previous comments about setting scanner caching (section 8.3) to help mitigate that.

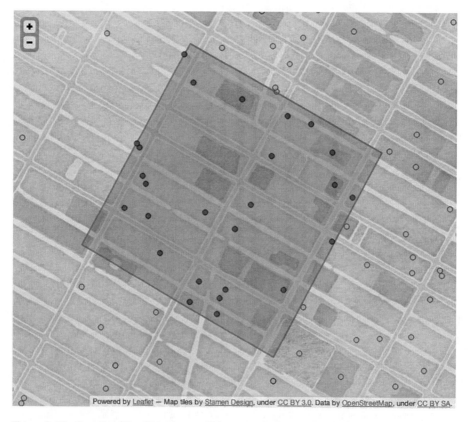

Figure 8.16   Results of the filtered scan. This should look an awful lot like figure 8.15.

8.5 *Summary*

This chapter was as much about GIS as about HBase. Remember, HBase is just a tool. To use it effectively, you need to know both the tool and the domain in which you want to apply it. The geohash trick proves that point. A little domain knowledge can go a long way. This chapter showed you how to combine that domain knowledge with your understanding of HBase to create an efficient tool for churning through mounds of GIS data efficiently and in parallel. It also showed you how to push application logic server-side and provided advice on when and why that might be a good idea.

It's also worth noting that these queries are only the beginning. The same techniques can be used to implement a number of other spatial predicates. It's no replacement for PostGIS,[19] but it's a start. It's also only the beginning of exploring how to implement these kinds of multidimensional queries on top of HBase. As an interesting follow-up, a paper was published in 2011[20] that explores methods for porting traditional data structures like quad-trees and kd-trees to HBase in the form of a secondary index.

This chapter concludes the portion of this book dedicated to building applications on HBase. Don't think the book is over, though. Once your code is written and your JARs ship, the fun has only begun. From here on out, you'll get a sense of what it takes to plan an HBase deployment and how to run HBase in production. Whether you're working on the project plan as a project manager or a network administrator, we hope you'll find what you need to get started. Application developers will find the material useful as well. Your application's performance depends quite a bit on configuring the client to match your cluster configuration. And of course, the more you know about how the cluster works, the better equipped you are to solve production bugs in your application.

---

[19] PostGIS is a set of extensions to the PostgreSQL database and is the canonical open source GIS database in the open source world. If you thought the geohash algorithm was clever, peek under the hood of this system: http://postgis.refractions.net/.

[20] Shoji Nishimura, Sudipto Das, Divyakant Agrawal, and Amr El Abbadi, "MD-HBase: A Scalable Multi-dimensional Data Infrastructure for Location Aware Services," 2011, www.cs.ucsb.edu/~sudipto/papers/md-hbase.pdf.

Part 4

Operationalizing HBase

The two chapters in this part of the book are geared to help you take your HBase application from a development prototype to a full-fledged production system.

You can provision and prepare the hardware for your HBase cluster using the guidance provided by chapter 9. Use that advice to deploy and configure HBase specifically for your application.

Chapter 10 explains how to set up your HBase cluster for success in production. From hard-earned performance configuration strategies to health monitoring and data-preservation techniques, chapter 10 will guide you through the tough scenarios that pop up in a production HBase cluster.

Deploying HBase

This chapter covers

- Choosing hardware for your HBase deployment
- Installing, configuring, and starting HBase
- Deploying HBase in the cloud
- Understanding the important configuration parameters

By now, you've learned a lot about HBase as a system and how to use it. As you've read the chapters, we hope you've set up HBase in standalone mode and played around with client code. A single-node standalone HBase install is only meant for basic access, which you typically do either while learning how to use the system or while developing an application. It can't handle any real workload or scale.

When planning a fully distributed HBase setup, you have to think about all the individual components: HBase Master, ZooKeeper, RegionServers, and HDFS DataNodes. Sometimes this list also includes the MapReduce framework. Each of these has different requirements in terms of hardware resources. This chapter will teach you in detail about the requirements for all the components and how you should choose hardware for a fully distributed HBase install. We'll then talk about the different HBase distributions available and considerations you should take into account when choosing one over the other. We'll also discuss deployment strategies and what you should consider when architecting your deployment system.

Remember the cloud? We shied away from talking about it in the preceding chapters, but we'll discuss it now. Once you have everything set up and the HBase components deployed, you have to configure the system too. We'll cover the important configuration parameters and what each means.

NOTE If you're looking to build out a production system, you'll most likely have to work with your system administrator and involve them in the deployment process.

9.1   Planning your cluster

Planning an HBase cluster includes planning the underlying Hadoop cluster. This section will highlight the considerations to keep in mind when choosing hardware and how the roles (HBase Master, RegionServers, ZooKeeper, and so on) should be deployed on the cluster. Choosing the right hardware for your deployment is crucial. Hardware will probably be your single largest investment in your Hadoop and HBase deployment, outside of hiring engineers to build the application that will use the systems. Hadoop and HBase run on commodity hardware. *Commodity doesn't mean low-end configuration.* It means nonexotic parts that are easily available from several manufacturers. In other words, you don't need to buy top-of-the-line, enterprise-grade servers to have a successful deployment.

When choosing hardware for any application, you have to make choices such as the number of CPUs, the amount of RAM, the number and size of disks, and so on. For an HBase deployment, it's important to have the right ratio of all these resources in order to maximize the performance and minimize costs. You don't want to have a cluster with lots of CPU but not enough RAM to hold the cache or the MemStore. A slightly lower CPU but more RAM would probably be a better choice, but the cost would remain the same.

As you've learned by now, there are multiple roles in an HBase deployment. Each has specific hardware requirements, some more extensive than others.

The hardware selection and what is deployed to which location is governed by the size of the cluster. In clusters up to 25 nodes, having a single node running the Hadoop JobTracker and NameNode isn't uncommon. You can put the Secondary NameNode there too, but it's generally recommended that you keep it separate. Clusters larger than 25 nodes typically have dedicated hardware for each of the Hadoop NameNode, JobTracker, and Secondary NameNode. Don't think that 25 is a magic number; it's a general guideline to give you an idea about the direction to consider when planning your cluster.

Let's add HBase to the picture now. The HBase RegionServers are almost always collocated with the Hadoop DataNodes. When planning a cluster, SLAs come into the picture, and planning carefully becomes crucial. As a blanket rule, don't collocate HBase RegionServers with the Hadoop TaskTrackers if HBase is being used for low-latency workloads. If your use case doesn't contain any MapReduce jobs, it's a good idea to not set up the MapReduce framework at all—that is, don't install the JobTracker and the TaskTrackers. If you have MapReduce as well as real-time workloads, use two separate clusters—one for MapReduce and one for HBase. Your MapReduce jobs can read from the remote HBase cluster. Yes, you do lose data locality and will be transferring data over the network for every job, but that's the only way to reliably guarantee SLAs for the real-time workloads.

We typically don't recommend serving MapReduce and real-time workloads at the same time from the same HBase cluster. If you absolutely have to, make sure you tune the number of tasks way down so as to not overwhelm the HBase RegionServers. Having a higher number of disks also helps alleviate I/O contention issues by distributing the load across the disks. Get more RAM, because your tasks will need resources too.

If the primary use case is doing MapReduce jobs over the data in HBase, collocating RegionServers and TaskTrackers is fine.

Now, let's look at some common deployment scenarios and how you should plan them. It generally helps to think in terms of the kind of cluster you're looking to deploy. Some of the common kinds of cluster types are listed next.

9.1.1 Prototype cluster

If you're building a simple prototype cluster, you can collocate the HBase Master with the Hadoop NameNode and JobTracker on the same node. If those already reside on separate nodes, you can collocate the HBase Master with either of them and call it a day. ZooKeeper can be hosted on any of these nodes too.

Given that you'll have the Hadoop NameNode, JobTracker, HBase Master, and ZooKeeper on the same node, it helps to have a node with sufficient memory and disks to sustain this load. A prototype cluster would most likely be less than 10 nodes, which limits the capacity of your HDFS. Having a machine with 4–6 cores, 24–32 GB RAM, and 4 SATA disks should be okay. There is no need to get redundant power supplies, SAS disks, and so on; you don't need a lot of high availability in a prototype cluster, so save yourself some money that you can invest in the production cluster when your application becomes a hit!

Tl;dr:[1]

- A prototype cluster is one that doesn't have strict SLAs, and it's okay for it to go down.
- It typically has fewer than 10 nodes.
- It's okay to collocate multiple services on a single node in a prototype cluster.
- 4–6 cores, 24–32 GB RAM, and 4 disks per node should be a good place to start. This assumes you aren't collocating MapReduce with HBase, which is the recommended way of running HBase if you're using it for low-latency access. Collocating the two would require more cores, RAM, and spindles.

---

[1] Tl;dr (too long; didn't read). We know that some readers jump straight to the bullet points!

9.1.2   *Small production cluster (10–20 servers)*

Generally, you shouldn't have fewer than 10 nodes in a production HBase cluster. Again, 10 isn't a magic number. It's hard to operate a small cluster with performance guarantees and tight SLAs (this statement is more anecdotal than logic based).

In a small production cluster, the Hadoop NameNode and JobTracker can remain collocated. There isn't enough load on either of them to warrant extra hardware. But given that you need a reliable system, you want to consider better quality hardware than you did for a prototype cluster. We cover typical hardware for each of the role types later.

The HBase Master should be on its own hardware, but not because it's doing a lot of work. The reason to separate it from the NameNode and JobTracker is to reduce the load on the node hosting those roles. The HBase Master node can have a lower-grade hardware profile than the other two. You can get by with a single Master, but given that it's a production system, it's a good idea to have redundancy. Thus you should have multiple HBase Masters, each deployed on dedicated hardware.

A single ZooKeeper instance is usually enough in a small production cluster. Zoo-Keeper doesn't do resource-intensive work and can be hosted on modest hardware as well. You can also consider hosting ZooKeeper and HBase Master together on the same host, as long as you give ZooKeeper a dedicated disk to write its data to. Having multiple ZooKeeper nodes increases availability; but on a small cluster, you most likely won't expect high traffic, and maintaining availability with a single ZooKeeper instance is doable. Also, having the NameNode act as a single point of failure is a problem even if you have multiple ZooKeepers.

The downside of having a single ZooKeeper and HBase Master instance hosted on the same node is that it limits serviceability. Things like kernel upgrades, minor reboots, and so on become impossible to do without downtime. But in a small cluster, having more than one ZooKeeper and HBase Master means the cost goes up. You need to make an informed choice.

Tl;dr:

- Fewer than 10 slave nodes is hard to make operationalize.
- Consider relatively better hardware for the Master nodes if you're deploying a production cluster. Dual power supplies and perhaps RAID are the order of the day.
- Small production clusters with not much traffic/workload can have services collocated.
- A single HBase Master is okay for small clusters.
- A single ZooKeeper is okay for small clusters and can be collocated with the HBase Master. If the host running the NameNode and JobTracker is beefy enough, put ZooKeeper and HBase Master on it too. This will save you having to buy an extra machine.
- A single HBase Master and ZooKeeper limits serviceability.

9.1.3 Medium production cluster (up to ~50 servers)

Things change as you scale up to a greater number of servers than in a small deployment. The cluster has more data, more servers doing work, and more processes to manage. Separate out the NameNode and JobTracker, and give them dedicated hardware. Keep the HBase Masters and ZooKeeper on the same hardware, as in a small deployment. The work the Master will do doesn't scale up linearly with the size of the cluster; in fact, the Master's load doesn't increase much.

You could get by with a single ZooKeeper instance in a small deployment. As the deployment scales, you'll probably have more client threads as well. Increase the number of ZooKeeper instances to three. Why not two? Because ZooKeeper needs an odd number of instances in order to have a quorum of servers to make decisions.

Tl;dr:

- Up to 50 nodes, possibly in production, would fall in this category.
- We recommend that you not collocate HBase and MapReduce for performance reasons. If you do collocate, deploy NameNode and JobTracker on separate hardware.
- Three ZooKeeper and three HBase Master nodes should be deployed, especially if this is a production system. You don't need three HBase Masters and can do with two; but given that you already have three ZooKeeper nodes and are sharing ZooKeeper and HBase Master, it doesn't hurt to have a third Master.
- Don't cheap out on the hardware for the NameNode and Secondary NameNodes.

9.1.4 Large production cluster (>~50 servers)

A large cluster can be approached almost like a medium-sized cluster, except that we recommend increasing the number of ZooKeeper instances to five. Collocate the HBase Masters with ZooKeeper. This gives you five HBase Masters, too. Make sure you give ZooKeeper a dedicated disk for it to write its data to.

The hardware profiles of the Hadoop NameNode and Secondary NameNode change as you look at larger-scale deployments; we'll talk about that shortly.

Tl;dr:

- Everything for the medium-sized cluster holds true, except that you may need five ZooKeeper instances that can also collocate with HBase Masters.
- Make sure NameNode and Secondary NameNode have enough memory, depending on the storage capacity of the cluster.

9.1.5 Hadoop Master nodes

The Hadoop NameNode, Secondary NameNode, and JobTracker are typically referred to as the Hadoop Master processes. As you read earlier, depending on the size of the cluster, these are either deployed together or on separate nodes of similar hardware configuration. All of these are single processes and don't have any failover strategy built in. Because of this, you need to ensure that the hardware you deploy is as highly available as possible. Of course, you don't want to go overboard and get the most expensive system. But don't be cheap either!

For the nodes hosting these processes, it's recommended that you have redundancy at the hardware level for the various components: dual power supplies, bonded network interface cards (NICs), and possibly RAID disks. It's not uncommon to find RAID 1 disks on the NameNode and Secondary NameNode for metadata storage, although JBODs[2] serve the purpose because the NameNode can write metadata to multiple locations. If the disks holding the metadata on the NameNode go down and you don't have redundancy or backups built into your deployment, you'll lose the data in the cluster, and that's something you don't want to experience when running in production. Either get RAID 1 and write to a single location, or get multiple disks and configure the NameNode to write to multiple locations. It's also not uncommon to use an NFS mount as one of the metadata directories for the NameNode in order to write the metadata to storage outside of the NameNode server. The OS on any of these nodes needs to be highly available too. Configure RAID 1 for the disk hosting the OS.

The NameNode serves all the metadata from main memory, and, therefore, you need to ensure that there is enough RAM to be able to address the entire namespace.[3] A server with 8 cores, at least 16 GB DDR3 RAM, dual 1 GB Ethernet NICs, and SATA drives should be enough for small clusters. Medium and large clusters can benefit from additional RAM, with the rest of the hardware configuration remaining the same. Typically, add another 16 GB RAM for the medium clusters and another 16 GB RAM for the large clusters to accommodate more metadata owing to a higher capacity.

The Secondary NameNode should have the same hardware as the NameNode. Apart from doing its job of checkpointing and backing up the metadata, it's also typically the server you fall back on if the NameNode server goes to lunch and doesn't come back.

9.1.6 HBase Master

The HBase Master doesn't do much heavy-duty work, and you can have multiple Masters for failover purposes. Because of these two factors, having expensive hardware with redundancy built in is overkill for the HBase Master. You won't gain much.

A typical hardware configuration for the HBase Master nodes is 4 cores, 8–16 GB DDR3 RAM, 2 SATA disks (one for the OS and the other for the HBase Master logs), and a 1 GbE NIC. Build redundancy into the system by having multiple HBase Masters, and you should be good to go.

---

[2] JBOD stands for Just a Bunch of Disks. You can read more about non-RAID drive architectures at http://mng.bz/Ta1c.

[3] Here's a great article on NameNode scalability and how much RAM you need by Konstantin Shvachko, an HDFS committer: "HDFS scalability: the limits to growth," April 2010, http://mng.bz/A5Ey.

Tl;dr:

- HBase Master is a lightweight process and doesn't need a lot of resources, but it's wise to keep it on independent hardware if possible.
- Have multiple HBase Masters for redundancy.
- 4 cores, 8–16 GB RAM, and 2 disks are more than enough for the HBase Master nodes.

9.1.7 *Hadoop DataNodes and HBase RegionServers*

The Hadoop DataNodes and HBase RegionServers are typically referred to as the *slave nodes* in the system. They don't have fancy hardware requirements like the Master nodes because of the built-in redundancy in the architecture. All slave nodes are alike, and any one of them can replace the function of any other. The job of the slave nodes is to store the HDFS data, do MapReduce computation, and serve requests from the HBase RegionServer. To do all that work well, they need ample RAM, disk storage, and CPU cores. Remember, *commodity* doesn't mean a low-end configuration but instead modest-quality hardware. No single hardware configuration is optimal for all workloads; some workloads can be more memory intensive and others can be more CPU intensive. And then there are archival storage workloads, which don't need a lot of CPU resources.

HBase RegionServers are memory hogs and will happily consume all the RAM you give them. That doesn't mean you should allocate 30 GB of heap to the RegionServer process. You'll run into stop-the-world garbage collectors (GCs), and that will bring down your system in no time. Remember, HBase is latency sensitive, and stop-the-world garbage collection is the bane of its existence. Anecdotally, a 10–15 GB heap for the RegionServer performs well, but you should test it against your workload to find the optimal number. If all you're running is HBase (and of course HDFS), the slave nodes need a total of 8–12 cores for the DataNode, RegionServer, OS, and other processes (monitoring agents and so on). Add to that 24–32 GB RAM and 12x 1 TB drives, and you should be good to go. Extra RAM on the box never hurts and can be used up by the file-system cache.

Note that no MapReduce is running here. If you choose to run MapReduce as well on the same cluster,[4] add another 6–8 cores and 24 GB to that configuration. Generally, each MapReduce task needs about 2–3 GB memory and at least 1 CPU core. Having a high storage density per node (like 12x 2 TB disks) leads to suboptimal behavior such as too much data to replicate if a node fails.

Tl;dr:

- DataNodes and RegionServers are always collocated. They serve the traffic. Avoid running MapReduce on the same nodes.
- 8–12 cores, 24–32 GB RAM, 12x 1 TB disks is a good place to start.
- You can increase the number of disks for higher storage density, but don't go too high or replication will take time in the face of node or disk failure.

TIP Get a larger number of reasonably sized boxes instead of fewer beefy ones.

---

[4] We generally recommend keeping TaskTrackers and HBase RegionServers separate unless your primary workload is MapReduce over HBase tables and you don't expect a guaranteed low-latency response from HBase all the time.

9.1.8   ZooKeeper(s)

Like the HBase Master, ZooKeeper is a relatively lightweight process. But ZooKeeper is more latency sensitive than the HBase Master. Because of that, we recommend giving ZooKeeper a dedicated spindle to write its data to. ZooKeeper serves everything out of memory, but it persists its data onto the disk as well; and if that is slow (because of I/O contention), it can degrade ZooKeeper's functioning.

Other than that, ZooKeepers don't need many hardware resources. You can easily have the same hardware configuration as the HBase Master and call it a day.

Tl;dr:

- ZooKeepers are lightweight but latency sensitive.
- Hardware similar to that of the HBase Master works fine if you're looking to deploy them separately.
- HBase Master and ZooKeeper can be collocated safely as long as you make sure ZooKeeper gets a dedicated spindle for its data persistence. Add a disk (for the ZooKeeper data to be persisted on) to the configuration mentioned in the HBase Master section if you're collocating.

9.1.9   What about the cloud?

We've talked about the various components of HBase and what kind of hardware you need to provision for them to function optimally. Recently, the *cloud* is becoming popular because of the flexibility it offers users. In the context of HBase, we consider the cloud to be just another set of hardware choices with a different cost model. This may be a restrictive view, but let's start with that. It's important to understand the various properties the cloud has to offer and what the implications are from the perspective of deploying a production-quality HBase instance.

The biggest (and oldest) player right now in the cloud infrastructure space is Amazon Web Services (AWS). Some of the other players are Rackspace and Microsoft. AWS is the most popular, and several people have deployed HBase instances in AWS. We haven't come across many instances deployed in Rackspace or in Microsoft. It's possible that those deployments are just top-secret ones and haven't been shared openly, but we'll never know! For this section, we'll focus more on what AWS has to offer, and most of what we talk about will hold true for other providers as well.

From the context of planning your HBase deployment, AWS offers three services that are relevant: Elastic Compute Cloud (EC2), Simple Storage Service (S3), and Elastic Block Store (EBS; http://aws.amazon.com/ebs/). As you've probably realized by now, you need plain servers for an HBase deployment, and EC2 is the service that provides virtual servers to work with. Configuration options (called instance types: http://aws.amazon.com/ec2/#instance) are available, and AWS keeps adding to the list. We recommend using instances with at least 16 GB RAM and ample compute and storage. That's keeping it a little vague, but given the dynamic nature of the landscape, chances are that by the time you get your hands on this book to read this section, there will be something new out there that's better than the best we mention here.

In general, adhere to the following recommendations:

- At least 16 GB RAM. HBase RegionServers are RAM hungry. But don't give them too much, or you'll run into Java GC issues. We'll talk about tuning GC later in this chapter.
- Have as many disks as possible. Most EC2 instances at the time of writing don't provide a high number of disks.
- A fatter network is always better.
- Get ample compute based on your individual use case. MapReduce jobs need more compute power than a simple website-serving database.

Some EC2 instances are full machines, and the physical server isn't shared by multiple instance types. Those are better fits for HBase and even Hadoop for the most part. When a single physical server is being shared by multiple instances, chatty neighbors can cause a significant performance impact. If your neighbor is doing heavy I/O, you'll be seeking more and possibly getting much lower I/O performance in your instance than you would with a quieter neighbor instance.

You'll often hear people talk about S3 and EBS when discussing Hadoop or HBase in the cloud. Let's put those in context too. S3 is a highly durable and reliable file store. It can be used to back up your HBase instance by running export jobs on your table and writing the output to S3. EBS, on the other hand, can be attached as remote disk volumes onto your EC2 instances and provides storage that persists outside of your EC2 instances. This can come in handy if you want to look at starting and stopping your HBase cluster pretty often. You could possibly store your HDFS purely in EBS and shut down the EC2 instances when you want to stop the HBase instances and save some money. To resume the HBase instances, provision new EC2 instances and mount the same EBS volumes to them, and start Hadoop and HBase. This will involve complicated automation scripting.

Now that you know about your options in the cloud and how to think about them, it's important that you're aware of the arguments in favor of and against deploying HBase in the cloud. You'll hear strong opinions from people, and we'll try to limit this discussion to pure facts and their implications:

- *Cost*—The cloud offers a pay-as-you-use cost model. This can be good and bad. You don't have to invest a bunch of money and buy the hardware up front before you can start using HBase. You can provision a few instances, pay per hour, and deploy the software on them. If you're running 24x7 clusters, do the math on the cost. Chances are that the instances in the cloud will work out to be more expensive than having hardware in your own data center or even a shared data center.
- *Ease of use*—Provisioning instances in the cloud can be done with just a couple of API calls. You don't need to go through a hardware-provisioning cycle that your company most likely adheres to in order to get those first few instances on which to deploy HBase. If nodes go down, spin up some more. It's as simple as that.

- *Operations*—If you have to buy your own hardware, you also have to buy racks, power, and network equipment. Operating this equipment will require some human resources, and you'll need to hire for that purpose. Operating servers, racks, and data centers might not be your core competency and might not be something you want to invest in. If you're using AWS, Amazon does that for you, and the company has a proven track record.

- *Reliability*—EC2 instances aren't as reliable as dedicated hardware you'll buy. We have personally seen instances go down randomly without any degradation in performance that could have hinted at an issue. Reliability has increased over time, but it isn't comparable to the dedicated boxes you'll buy.

- *Lack of customization*—You have to choose from the instance types that AWS provides and can't customize for your use case. If you're buying your own hardware, you can customize it. For instance, you need denser storage but not much compute power if you're only storing large amounts of data in an archival manner. But if you want to do a lot of computation, you need to flip it around and get more compute with less storage density per node.

- *Performance*—Virtualization doesn't come free. You pay with a hit in performance. Some virtualization types are better than others, but none come without an impact on performance. The impact is more on I/O than other factors, and that hurts HBase most.

- *Security*—Look into the security guarantees that the cloud provider has in place. Sometimes this can be an issue for sensitive data, and you may want to get hardware that you manage and can guarantee security on.

Make your hardware decisions keeping all this in mind. At the end of the day, it's all about the cost of ownership, and we recommend looking at the cost in terms of dollars per amount of data stored or dollars per read/write operation. Those are difficult numbers to calculate, but they will give you the insight you need if you're trying to choose between dedicated on-premises hardware and the public cloud. Once you've made up your mind, bought the hardware, or provisioned the instances, it's time to deploy the software.

9.2   *Deploying software*

Managing and deploying on a cluster of machines, especially in production, is non-trivial and needs careful work. There are numerous challenges in doing so, and we'll list a few of the major ones here. It's not an unsolvable problem or one that people haven't already solved, but it's one that shouldn't be ignored.

When deploying to a large number of machines, we recommend that you automate the process as much as possible. There are multiple reasons for this. First, you don't want to repeat the same process on all the machines that need to be set up. Second, when you add nodes to the cluster, you don't want to have to manually ensure that the new node is set up correctly. Having an automated system that does all this for you is desirable, and most companies have it in some form or other. Some companies have homegrown scripts, whereas others have adopted an open source solution such as Puppet (http://puppetlabs.com/) or Chef (www.opscode.com/chef/). There are some proprietary tools as well, such as HP Opsware. If you're deploying in the cloud, Apache Whirr (http://whirr.apache.org) is a framework that can come to your rescue and make spinning up and configuring instances easy. With any of these frameworks, you can create custom manifests/recipes/configurations that the frameworks can use to configure and deploy on the servers you run them on. They'll set up the OS and install and manage various packages, including Hadoop and HBase. They can also help manage configurations from a centralized place, which is what you want.

Specialized tools like Cloudera Manager are specifically designed to manage Hadoop and HBase clusters. These tools have a bunch of Hadoop-specific management features that are otherwise not available in general package-management frameworks.

Going into the details of all these options is beyond the scope of this book; our intent is to introduce you to all the ways you can think about deployments. Invest up front in one of these frameworks, and operating your cluster over time will be much easier.

9.2.1 Whirr: deploying in the cloud

If you're looking to deploy HBase in the cloud, you should get Apache Whirr to make your life easier. Whirr 0.7.1 doesn't support HBase 0.92, but you can spin up clusters with CDH3 using the recipe shown in the following listing. The recipe shown is for clusters in AWS EC2 and assumes that you set your access key and secret key as environment variables (`AWS_ACCESS_KEY_ID` and `AWS_SECRET_ACCESS_KEY`). Put this recipe into a file that you can pass as a configuration to the Whirr script, such as my_cdh_recipe.

Listing 9.1 Whirr recipe (file named my_cdh_recipe) to spin up a CDH3 cluster

```
$ cat my_cdh_recipe

whirr.cluster-name=ak-cdh-hbase
whirr.instance-templates=1 zookeeper+hadoop-namenode+hadoop-jobtracker+hbase-
    master,
5 hadoop-datanode+hadoop-tasktracker+hbase-regionserver
hbase-site.dfs.replication=3
whirr.zookeeper.install-function=install_cdh_zookeeper
whirr.zookeeper.configure-function=configure_cdh_zookeeper
whirr.hadoop.install-function=install_cdh_hadoop
whirr.hadoop.configure-function=configure_cdh_hadoop
whirr.hbase.install-function=install_cdh_hbase
whirr.hbase.configure-function=configure_cdh_hbase
whirr.provider=aws-ec2
whirr.identity=${env:AWS_ACCESS_KEY_ID}
whirr.credential=${env:AWS_SECRET_ACCESS_KEY}
whirr.hardware-id=m1.xlarge
# Ubuntu 10.04 LTS Lucid. See http://cloud.ubuntu.com/ami/
whirr.image-id=us-east-1/ami-04c9306d
whirr.location-id=us-east-1
```

You can use these recipes and spin up the cluster like this:

```
bin/whirr launch-cluster --config my_cdh_recipe
```

Once you've spun up a cluster, you can use the list command to list the nodes that form the cluster:

```
bin/whirr list-cluster --config my_cdh_recipe
us-east-1/i-48c4e62c      us-east-1/ami-04c9306d  23.20.55.128    10.188.69.151
RUNNING us-east-1a        zookeeper,hadoop-namenode,
hadoop-jobtracker,hbase-master
us-east-1/i-4ac4e62e      us-east-1/ami-04c9306d  50.17.58.44
    10.188.214.223
RUNNING us-east-1a        hadoop-datanode,
hadoop-tasktracker,hbase-regionserver
us-east-1/i-54c4e630      us-east-1/ami-04c9306d  107.21.147.166  10.4.189.107
RUNNING us-east-1a        hadoop-datanode,
hadoop-tasktracker,hbase-regionserver
us-east-1/i-56c4e632      us-east-1/ami-04c9306d  107.21.77.75
    10.188.108.229
RUNNING us-east-1a        hadoop-datanode,
hadoop-tasktracker,hbase-regionserver
us-east-1/i-50c4e634      us-east-1/ami-04c9306d  184.72.159.27   10.4.229.190
RUNNING us-east-1a        hadoop-datanode,
hadoop-tasktracker,hbase-regionserver
us-east-1/i-52c4e636      us-east-1/ami-04c9306d  50.16.129.84    10.4.198.173
RUNNING us-east-1a        hadoop-datanode,
hadoop-tasktracker,hbase-regionserver
```

When you're done with your cluster and want to kill it, use the destroy-cluster command like this:

```
bin/whirr destroy-cluster --config my_cdh_recipe
```

9.3   *Distributions*

This section will cover installing HBase on your cluster. This isn't a reference guide to building out a full-fledged production deployment but is instead a starting point for setting up a fully distributed install that you can use for your application. Making HBase operational requires a little more work than that, and we cover various aspects in the next chapter.

Numerous distributions (or packages) of HBase are available, and each has multiple releases. The most notable distributions currently are the stock Apache distribution and Cloudera's CDH:

- *Apache*—The Apache HBase project is the parent project where all the development for HBase happens. All the code goes there, and developers across multiple companies contribute to it. As with any other open source project, the release cycle depends on the stakeholders (that is, the companies that hire the developers who work on the project) and what features they want to put into a particular release. The HBase community in general has been consistent with their releases. Some of the notable releases are 0.20.x, 0.90.x, 0.92.x and 0.94.x. This book is written with a focus on 0.92.x.

- *Cloudera's CDH*—Cloudera is a company that has its own distribution containing Hadoop and other components in the ecosystem, including HBase. This distribution is called CDH (Cloudera's distribution including Apache Hadoop). CDH builds off the Apache code base by taking a particular release and adding patches to it that haven't yet been included in any official Apache release. Cloudera does this to put extra features into CDH that customers demand. All the patches are in the Apache code base but not necessarily in the same base branch that CDH is based on.

We recommend using Cloudera's CDH distribution. It typically includes more patches than the stock releases to add stability, performance improvements, and sometimes features. CDH is also better tested than the Apache releases and is running in production in more clusters than stock Apache. These are points we recommend thinking about before you choose the distribution for your cluster.

The installation steps provided assume that you have Java, Hadoop, and Zoo-Keeper already installed. For instructions on setting up Hadoop and ZooKeeper, refer to their documentation for the distribution you're choosing.

9.3.1 *Using the stock Apache distribution*

To install the stock Apache distribution, you need to download the tarballs and install those into a directory of your choice. Many people create a special user that runs all the daemons and put the directory into the home directory of that user. We generally recommend installing into /usr/local/lib/hbase and keeping that as your HBase home so all users can access the files.

Detailed installation instructions are available on the HBase home page and sometimes change with different releases. In general, the steps to follow are listed next. These are specific to the 0.92.1 release, but you can adapt them to whatever release you're working with:

1 Download the tarball from one of the Apache mirrors. For 0.92.1, the name of the tarball is hbase-0.92.1.tar.gz:

```
cd /tmp
wget http://mirrors.axint.net/apache/hbase/hbase-0.92.1/
hbase-0.92.1.tar.gz
mv /tmp/hbase-0.92.1.tar.gz /usr/local/lib
```

2 As root, untar the tarball into /usr/local/lib and create a symlink from /usr/local/hbase to the newly created directory. This way, you can define the $HBASE_HOME variable as /usr/local/lib/hbase, and it will point to the current install:

```
tar xvfz hbase-0.92.1.tar.gz
cd /usr/local/lib
ln -s hbase-0.92.1 hbase
```

That's all. Now you need to do the various configurations, and you're good to go!

9.3.2   *Using Cloudera's CDH distribution*

The current release for CDH is CDH4u0 which is based on the 0.92.1 Apache release. The installation instructions are environment specific; the fundamental steps are as follows:

1   Add the CDH repository to your system. If you're using a Red Hat-based system, you use the yum package-management tool:

```
cd /etc/yum.repos.d
wget http://archive.cloudera.com/cdh4/redhat/6/x86_64/cdh/
cloudera-cdh4.repo
```

If you're using a Debian/Ubuntu-based system, you use the apt package-management tool:

```
wget http://archive.cloudera.com/cdh4/one-click-install/precise/amd64/
cdh4-repository_1.0_all.deb
sudo dpkg -i cdh4-repository_1.0_all.deb
```

You can find detailed environment-specific instructions on Cloudera's documentation site at http://mng.bz/ukS3.

2   Install the HBase packages. The names of the packages in CDH4 are hbase, hbase-master, and hbase-regionserver. The hbase package contains the binaries for HBase. The other two packages contain init scripts that help you start and stop the Master and RegionServer processes, respectively.

   The following commands install the HBase binaries on Red Hat-based systems:

```
sudo yum install hbase
sudo yum install hbase-master
sudo yum install hbase-regionserver
```

And these commands install the HBase binaries on ebian/Ubuntu-based systems:

```
sudo apt-get install hbase
sudo apt-get install hbase-master
sudo apt-get install hbase-regionserver
```

Installing these packages lays down the libraries in /usr/lib/hbase/ and the configuration files in /etc/hbase/conf/. The init scripts to start and stop the Master and RegionServer processes are /etc/init.d/hbase-master and /etc/init.d/hbase-regionserver, respectively.

Note that you won't be installing the Master and RegionServer scripts on all the nodes. Install the hbase-regionserver package on the slave nodes and the hbase-master package on the nodes that will run the HBase Master process. The hbase package needs to be installed on all the nodes because it contains the actual binaries.

9.4   Configuration

Deploying HBase requires configuring Linux, Hadoop, and, of course, HBase. Some of the configurations are straightforward, and recommendations are available based on experience from multiple production deployments. Some configurations are more iterative and depend on the use case and SLAs the HBase deployment will be serving. No single set of configurations will work for everyone, and chances are you'll make several configuration changes before you finalize what you'll run in production serving your application.

In order to configure the system in the most optimal manner, it's important that you understand the parameters and the implications of tuning them one way or another. This section gives you some insight into the important configuration parameters you'll most likely be working with while deploying your HBase instance. It covers the HBase-specific configurations first and then goes into the relevant Hadoop and Linux configurations that impact the HBase installation.

9.4.1   HBase configurations

Like Hadoop, there are two aspects of HBase configurations. One is the Linux-specific configuration (or environment configurations), which is different from the OS-level configuration we'll explain later. The other set is the configuration for the HBase daemons, which are read by them at start time.

On the HBase cluster, the location of the configuration files depends on the installation path you followed. If you used the Apache distribution, the configuration files reside in $HBASE_HOME/conf/; and if you used CDH, they reside in /etc/hbase/conf/. In general, we recommend that you keep permissions and file locations consistent with the best practices at your company. CDH follows the standard Linux directory architecture and lays out configuration files accordingly. This is acceptable to most system administrators and IT departments.

ENVIRONMENT CONFIGURATIONS

The environment configuration is put into the file hbase-env.sh. This file is sourced by the script running the HBase processes (Master and RegionServer), and therefore things like the Java heap size, garbage-collection parameters, and other environment variables are set here. A sample file is shown next.

> **Listing 9.2   A sample hbase-env.sh file**

```
export JAVA_HOME=/my/java/installation          ◁─┐ Set location of your
                                                    Java installation.

export HBASE_HOME=/my/hbase/installation    ◁─┐ Set location
                                                of your HBase installation.

export HBASE_MASTER_OPTS="-Xmx1000m"    ◁─┐
                                           Set Java options for Master
                                           process. GC settings go here.

export HBASE_REGIONSERVER_OPTS="-Xmx10000m -XX:+UseConcMarkSweepGC    ◁─┐
-XX:+CMSIncrementalMode"                            Set Java properties for
                                           RegionServer process. GC settings go here.
```

```
#export HBASE_REGIONSERVERS=${HBASE_HOME}/conf/regionservers
```

Set name of file containing list of RegionServers. Needed only if you're using start and stop scripts in $HBASE_HOME/bin.

```
export HBASE_LOG_DIR=${HBASE_HOME}/logs
```

Where HBase daemon logs go. Optionally, you can configure logs to go to /var/logs/hbase/. Automatically configured in CDH; you need to do it manually if using Apache distro.

```
export HBASE_MANAGES_ZK=false
```

HBase can manage ZooKeeper for you, but recommended that you manage it in production environments.

This isn't a complete file. You can set other parameters here, such as the niceness of the HBase processes. You can look at the default hbase-env.sh file from your installation to see the other available options. Listed here are the ones you'll work with 95% of the time. You won't need to configure the others in most cases.

Two of the important things configured here are the memory allocation and GC. It's critical to pay attention to these if you want to extract decent performance from your HBase deployment. HBase is a database and needs lots of memory to provide low-latency reads and writes. The word *real-time* is commonly used as well—the idea is that it doesn't take on the order of minutes to find the contents of the one row you want to read. Indexing, albeit by rowkey only, enables you to quickly find the location where the row should be read from or written to. Indexes are held in memory, and so are the write buffers. Remember the read and write paths we described in chapter 2? To provide this functionality and performance, HBase needs RAM—a lot of it! But you don't want to give it too much, either.

> **TIP**   Too much of anything isn't good, even if it's RAM for your new large-scale database deployment.

We don't recommend that you give the RegionServers more than 15 GB of heap in a production HBase deployment. The reason for not going over the top and allocating larger heaps than that is that GC starts to become too expensive. It will happen less frequently because you won't hit memory limits soon enough, and every time it happens, it will last for a longer period of time because it will be working through a much larger amount of memory. That doesn't mean 15 GB is a magic number and the maximum you should configure your RegionServer heap to; it's just a good place to start. We recommend that you experiment with heap sizes in your environment and see what works best for you and delivers performance that enables your application to meet its SLAs.

Allocating an optimal amount of heap doesn't solve all problems. You need to tune the GC as well. That's a little trickier than coming up with a number for your heap allocation to the RegionServers.

The HBase RegionServers don't perform well with the default Java GC configuration and need careful tuning on many occasions if you want to serve much load off

> ### Java GC
> In Java programs, you create new objects mostly by using the `new` operator. These objects are created in the JVM's heap. When these objects are freed up, the Java GC clears up the memory they were occupying by removing the unreferenced objects. The default configuration with which the GC runs makes certain assumptions about what your program is doing in terms of creating and deleting objects, which isn't necessarily optimal for all use cases.

them. This configuration goes into the hbase-env.sh file on all the nodes in the cluster. A good place to start is setting the HBase Java options to the following:

```
-Xmx8g -Xms8g -Xmn128m -XX:+UseParNewGC -XX:+UseConcMarkSweepGC
-XX:CMSInitiatingOccupancyFraction=70
```

Let's look at what the various options mean:

- `-Xmx8g`—Sets the maximum heap for the process. 8 GB is a decent place to start. We don't recommend going beyond 15 GB.
- `-Xms8g`—Sets the starting heap size to 8 GB. It's a good idea to allocate the maximum amount of heap when the process starts up. This avoids the extra overhead of increasing the heap as the RegionServers want more.
- `-Xmn128m`—Sets the young/new generation to 128 MB. Again, it's not a magic number that is always correct but a good place to start. The default new generation size is too small, and the RegionServer will start to GC aggressively as you put load on it. This will increase your CPU utilization. Setting the new generation to be much bigger puts you at risk of not GCing enough and thereby moving objects into the old/tenured generation as well as causing much larger pauses when the GC happens. Once the MemStore is flushed, which happens frequently when you insert data into an HBase table, the objects will be dereferenced and need to be GCed. Letting them move to the old generation causes the heap to become fragmented when objects are cleared out.
- `-XX:+UseParNewGC`—Sets the GC for the new generation to use the Parallel New Collector. This collector pauses the Java process and does the GC. This mode of working is acceptable for the new generation because it's small and the process isn't stopped for a long period (usually a few milliseconds). The pauses are sometimes also referred to as *stop-the-world* GC pauses, and they can be lethal if they're too long. If the GC pause exceeds the ZooKeeper-RegionServer session timeout, ZooKeeper will consider the RegionServer lost and will remove it from the cluster because ZooKeeper didn't get a heartbeat from it.
- `-XX:+UseConcMarkSweepGC`—The Parallel New Collector is okay for the new generation but doesn't work well for the old generation because of the larger size of the old generation. A stop-the-world GC for the old generation would last seconds and cause timeouts. Enabling the concurrent-mark-and-sweep (CMS)

GC mitigates this issue. The CMS garbage-collects in parallel with other things happening in the JVM and doesn't pause the process until it fails to do its job and gives a promotion error. At that point, the process needs to be paused and GC has to be performed. The CMS incurs a load on the CPU because it's doing GC in parallel while the process is still running.

- -XX:CMSInitiatingOccupancyFraction—The CMS collector can be configured to start when a certain percent of the heap is utilized. This parameter is used to set that. Setting the percentage too low causes the CMS to kick in often, and setting it too high causes the CMS to kick in late, leading to more promotion errors. A good place to start is 70%; you can increase/decrease this value as required once you do benchmarking on your system. The RegionServer heap consists of the block cache (20% of total heap by default) and the MemStore (40% of the heap by default), and setting the occupancy fraction to 70% keeps you just slightly above the total of those two.

Logging the GC activity can be useful in debugging issues when they happen. You can enable logging by adding the following to the GC configs:

```
-verbose:gc -XX:+PrintGCDetails -XX:+PrintGCTimeStamps
-Xloggc:$HBASE_HOME/logs/gc-$(hostname)-hbase.log
```

HBase heap and GC tuning are critical to the performance of the system, and we encourage that you test your setting heavily while planning a production system. The tuning can vary based on the kind of hardware on which you're running HBase and the kind of workload you're looking to run. For instance, a write-heavy workload needs a slightly larger new generation size than a read-heavy workload.

HBASE CONFIGURATIONS

The configuration parameters for HBase daemons are put in an XML file called hbase-site.xml. The XML configuration file can also be used by your client application. You keep it in the classpath of the application; when the `HBaseConfiguration` object is instantiated, it reads through the XML config file and picks up the relevant bits.

Now that you know where the configuration file is, let's look at its contents and how the parameters are specified. A sample configuration XML file is shown in the next listing. This isn't a complete file and contains only a single parameter to show you the format. We'll list the parameters and their meanings later.

Listing 9.3   Format of the hbase-site.xml configuration file

```
<?xml version="1.0"?>
<?xml-stylesheet type="text/xsl" href="configuration.xsl"?>

<configuration>
  <property>
    <name>hbase.rootdir</name>
    <value>file:///tmp/hbase-${user.name}/hbase</value>
```

```
      <description>The directory shared by region servers and into
      which HBase persists.
      </description>
    </property>
</configuration>
```

The configuration file is a standard XML file with each `<property>` tag representing a configuration parameter. You'll likely work with several parameters. The most important ones to configure are as follows:

- `hbase.zookeeper.quorum`—All the components in your HBase cluster need to know the servers that form the ZooKeeper quorum. This is the configuration parameter where you put that information. The XML tag looks like this:

```
<property>
  <name>hbase.zookeeper.quorum</name>
  <value>server1ip,server2ip,server3ip</value>
</property>
```

- `hbase.rootdir`—HBase persists its data in HDFS, and the location is explicitly configured using this property. The XML tag looks like this:

```
<property>
  <name>hbase.rootdir</name>
  <value>hdfs://namenode.yourcompany.com:5200/hbase</value>
</property>
```

5200 is the port on which your NameNode is configured to listen. It's configured in hdfs-site.xml while setting up Hadoop.

- `hbase.cluster.distributed`—HBase can be run in standalone mode, pseudo-distributed mode, or fully distributed mode. Standalone and pseudo-distributed modes are only for testing and playing around; they aren't intended for use in a production environment. Fully distributed mode is designed for production use; the `hbase.cluster.distributed` property must be set to true for HBase to run in fully distributed mode. Here's the XML tag:

```
<property>
  <name>hbase.cluster.distributed</name>
  <value>true</value>
</property>
```

These three configuration parameters in the hbase-site.xml file absolutely have to be set to run HBase in a distributed fashion. Other configuration parameters are generally used to optimize the cluster's performance; you'll probably tackle them while tuning the system based on your use case and SLA definitions. These are shown in table 9.1. This isn't a complete list of all the configurations you can put in hbase-site.xml; these are the configurations you're likely to want to tweak. If you want to see the whole list, we recommend looking at the hbase-default.xml file in the source code.

Table 9.1   HBase configuration parameters

Configuration parameter	Description
`hbase.client.scanner.caching`	Defines the number of rows that will be fetched when the next method is called on a scanner. The higher the number, the fewer remote calls the client needs to make to the RegionServer during scans. A higher number also means more memory consumption at the client side. This can be set on a per-client basis in the configuration object as well.
`hbase.balancer.period`	The region balancer runs periodically in the HBase Master. This property defines the time interval at which you want it to run. The default is 5 minutes set in milliseconds (300,000).
`hbase.client.write.buffer`	The write buffer in the `HTable` instance on the client side, configured in bytes. A larger buffer means fewer RPCs during writes but higher memory consumption.
`hbase.hregion.majorcompaction`	Major compactions can be configured to take place periodically. This configuration parameter specifies that time period in milliseconds. The default value is 1 day (86,400,000 milliseconds).
`hbase.hregion.max.filesize`	Maximum size of the underlying store files (`HStoreFile`). The region size is defined by this parameter. If any store file of any column family exceeds this size, the region is split.
`hbase.hregion.memstore.flush.size`	Maximum size of the MemStore, configured in bytes. The MemStore is flushed to disk when it exceeds this size. A thread that runs periodically checks the size of the MemStore. The frequency with which that thread runs is defined by `hbase.server.thread.wakefrequency`.
`hbase.hregion.memstore.mslab.enabled`	MemStore-Local Allocation Buffer is a feature in HBase that helps prevent heap fragmentation when there are heavy writes going on. In some cases, enabling this feature can help alleviate issues of long GC pauses if the heaps are too large. The default value is `true`.
`hbase.hstore.blockingStoreFiles`	If the number of store files in a particular column family in a region exceeds this number, the writes are blocked until a compaction is completed or the blocking times out. The timeout is configured using `hbase.hstore.blockingWaitTime` in milliseconds.
`hbase.hstore.compaction.max`	Maximum number of files to compact in a single minor compaction. The default value is 7.
`hbase.hstore.compactionThreshold`	HBase runs compactions on a particular region when the number of store files in a particular column family reaches this number. Setting a high value for this parameter results in infrequent compactions that take longer when they do occur.

Table 9.1   HBase configuration parameters *(continued)*

Configuration parameter	Description
`hbase.mapreduce.hfileoutputformat.blocksize`	The HFile block size is set at a per-column-family level for each table. This dictates the granularity at which the HFile is indexed. A smaller block size results in better random reads but a larger block index, which means more memory consumption. When you use the `HFileOutputFormat` in a MapReduce job to write directly into HFiles, the block size must be defined using this property so the MapReduce code doesn't have access to the table definition and doesn't know how the column families are configured.
`hbase.master.info.port`	The HBase UI, which we'll talk about shortly, is exposed on this port. The address of the web UI is http://master.yourcompany.com:<hbase.master.info.port>. The default value is 60010.
`hbase.master.port`	This is the port at which the Master process listens. The default value is 60000. For the most part, you don't need to change the default ports unless you need to close certain ports, including the default HBase port.
`hbase.regionserver.port`	This is the port that the RegionServer listens on.
`hbase.regionserver.global.memstore.lowerLimit` `hbase.regionserver.global.memstore.upperLimit`	upperLimit defines the maximum percentage of the heap on a RegionServer that the MemStores combined can use up. The moment the upperLimit is hit, MemStores are flushed until the lowerLimit is hit. Setting these values equal to each other means the minimum amount of flushing happens when writes are blocked due to the upperLimit being hit. This minimizes the pauses during writes but also causes more frequent flushing.
`hbase.regionserver.handler.count`	Number of RPC listeners that are spun up on RegionServer and Master processes.
`hbase.regionserver.optionallogflushinterval`	How often the HLog must be flushed to the file system, regardless of the number of edits in it. The parameter is configured in milliseconds. The default value is 1 second (1,000 ms).
`hbase.regionserver.regionSplitLimit`	Maximum number of regions that a system should have. The default value is `MAX_INT` (2,147,483,647).
`hbase.tmp.dir`	Temporary directory that HBase uses on the local file system.
`hfile.block.cache.size`	Maximum percentage of heap that the block cache can use. The block cache is the read cache (LRU).
`zookeeper.session.timeout`	HBase daemons/clients are clients to ZooKeeper. This is the session timeout for their sessions with ZooKeeper. The parameter is configured in milliseconds.
`zookeeper.znode.parent`	Root znode for HBase in ZooKeeper. The default is /hbase. All of HBase's ZooKeeper files are configured keeping this as the parent path.

9.4.2 *Hadoop configuration parameters relevant to HBase*

As you're aware, Hadoop and HBase are tightly coupled. HBase uses the HDFS, and the way Hadoop is configured impacts HBase. Tuning HDFS well can significantly improve the performance you can extract from HBase. Some of the important configuration parameters are described in table 9.2.

Table 9.2   Important HDFS configuration parameters from HBase's perspective

Configuration parameter	Description
`dfs.support.append`	HBase needs durable sync on HDFS so the write-ahead log is persisted when edits are written. Without durable sync, HBase can lose data if RegionServers go down without the data being persisted to disk. This configuration parameter has to be explicitly set to `true` to enable syncs on HDFS. This feature is available in Hadoop 0.20.205 and later versions. With HBase 0.92, you're most likely using Hadoop 1.0.x or later versions, and they support sync.
`dfs.datanode.max.xcievers`[a]	The max xcievers on DataNodes is an important configuration parameter and often not understood well by Hadoop administrators. It defines the maximum number of sockets/threads per DataNode that HDFS clients can use to read/write data. Lars George wrote one of the most comprehensive descriptions,[b] and we recommend reading it to get a good understanding of what's going on. For the most part, you're okay setting this number to 4,096. The default of 256 is low, and you'll see `IOExceptions` in the RegionServer logs if you have even slightly heavy I/O.

a. Yup, this is how it's spelled. Not xceivers.
b. Lars George, "HBase + Hadoop + Xceivers," March 14, 2012, http://mng.bz/Fcd4.

Not only the HDFS configurations but also MapReduce framework configurations have an impact on HBase if you're doing MapReduce jobs over HBase tables. If your use case doesn't include running MapReduce jobs against HBase tables, you can safely turn off the MapReduce framework: that is, stop the JobTracker and TaskTracker processes, and give more resources to HBase. If you're planning to run MapReduce jobs with HBase tables as the source or sink, tune the number of tasks per node to a lower number than you would on a standard MapReduce cluster. The idea is to give ample resources to HBase. Cutting down on the heap you allocate to the RegionServer processes will impact the performance you'll extract from HBase during those MapReduce jobs.

In general, mixing workloads that involve running MapReduce jobs with workloads that have relatively low-latency random reads and writes isn't recommended. You won't be able to extract good performance in either of those. If you're running MapReduce against HBase, the random read/write performance will be impacted, and the latencies will go up. The total throughput you can extract from a single HBase instance remains constant. You'll end up sharing that among the two workloads. Also, it's relatively more difficult to run HBase stably if you mix it with heavy MapReduce on the same cluster. It's not impossible, but it requires a little more careful resource allocation (heap to RegionServers, number of tasks per node, heap to tasks, and so on) than if you kept them separate.

9.4.3   Operating system configurations

In most production systems running HBase and Hadoop, Linux is the underlying OS. You don't need to tune much except the `ulimits` for the number of open files. HBase is a database and needs to keep files open so you can read from and write to them without incurring the overhead of opening and closing them on each operation. In a system under any real load, you can quickly hit the limits on the number of open files. We recommend that you increase this limit, especially if you're deploying in production. You don't have to increase it as a system-wide setting and can only do it for the DataNode and RegionServer processes. To keep it simple, you can increase it for the user under which you'll be running these processes.

To increase the open-file limit for the user, put the following statements in your /etc/ security/limits.conf file for the user that will run the Hadoop and HBase daemons. CDH does this for you as a part of the package installation:

```
hadoopuser                  nofile       32768
hbaseuser                   nofile       32768
hadoopuser    soft/hard     nproc        32000
hbaseuser     soft/hard     nproc        32000
```

You'll need to log out and log back in to your box for these to take effect. These configuration parameters increase the limit on the number of open files and the number of processes that the `hadoopuser` and `hbaseuser` can run.

Another important configuration parameter to tune is the swap behavior. Swapping on HBase RegionServers is lethal and will degrade performance drastically, if not entirely kill the RegionServer process because of ZooKeeper timeouts. Ideally, you should disable swap on the RegionServer nodes. If you haven't done that, you can use the kernel tunable parameter vm.swappiness (/proc/sys/vm/swappiness) to define how aggressively memory pages are swapped to disk. The higher the value, the more aggressive the swapping. Tune this parameter down to 0 like this:

```
$ sysctl -w vm.swappiness=0
```

9.5   Managing the daemons

There's a fair bit to operating a production HBase deployment, and the next chapter will focus on the details. Successfully deploying and bringing up the various services is one of the first steps in making a system operational. Until now, we've been talking about deploying the right components, configuring the OS, configuring Hadoop, and configuring HBase. Now that all that is done, you'll start the system and get the machine ready to take some writes and reads. The HBase distribution you installed comes bundled with scripts that can handle the starting and stopping of services. The Apache distribution uses the `hbase-daemon.sh` script from the $HBASE_HOME/bin/ directory, whereas CDH comes bundled with `init` scripts.

The relevant services need to be started on each node of the cluster. You probably already have a scheme for doing that, because you had Hadoop installed prior to HBase. If you don't have a method yet, here are some of the options:

- Use the bundled `start` and `stop` scripts. Both Hadoop and HBase come bundled with `start` and `stop` scripts that can remotely log in to all the machines in the cluster and start the correct processes. The downside is that they need passwordless SSH, which some IT departments don't allow because of security concerns. You may argue that you can enter the password every time the script is logging on to a node to start/stop a process. Sure, but think of entering the password over and over again for each start/stop action across hundreds of nodes. Sometimes you don't even have the password to the accounts—you can only `su` into it from your own account. That's more common than you may think.

- Cluster SSH (http://sourceforge.net/projects/clusterssh) is a useful tool if you're dealing with a cluster of machines. It allows you to simultaneously run the same shell commands on a cluster of machines that you're logged in to in separate windows. You can start the daemons on all the slave nodes by running the same command simultaneously on all the nodes. This is neat, but it's hairy to manage on a large number of machines.

- Homegrown scripts are always an option. Combine them with Chef/Puppet or your favorite deployment system, and you can put a script onto each host that starts the appropriate services.

- Use management software like Cloudera Manager that allows you to manage all the services on the cluster from a single web-based UI.

The basic idea is to start the appropriate daemons on each node. You can start an HBase daemon on a node by using the $HBASE_HOME/bin/hbase-daemon.sh script, as follows:

```
$HBASE_HOME/bin/hbase-daemon.sh --config $HBASE_HOME/conf/ start master
$HBASE_HOME/bin/hbase-daemon.sh --config $HBASE_HOME/conf/ start regionserver
$HBASE_HOME/bin/hbase-daemon.sh --config $HBASE_HOME/conf/ start master-
    backup

$HBASE_HOME/bin/hbase-daemon.sh --config $HBASE_HOME/conf/ stop master
$HBASE_HOME/bin/hbase-daemon.sh --config $HBASE_HOME/conf/ stop regionserver
$HBASE_HOME/bin/hbase-daemon.sh --config $HBASE_HOME/conf/ stop master-backup
```

Not all daemons are started everywhere. As we discussed earlier in this chapter, they're all on separate servers.

Once you've started the RegionServer processes on all the slaves and the Master process on the Master nodes, you can see the status of the system using the HBase shell and also the HBase Master web UI. A sample UI is shown in figure 9.1.

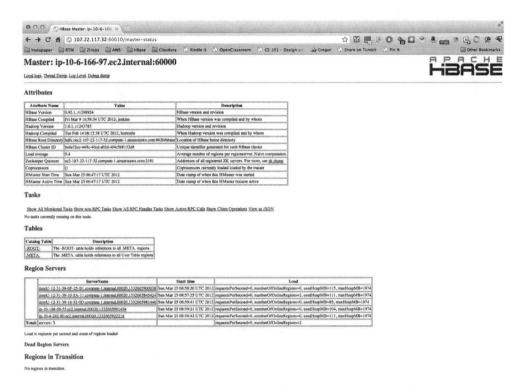

Figure 9.1 HBase Master UI of a working HBase instance

9.6   *Summary*

In this chapter, we covered the various aspects of deploying HBase in a fully distributed environment for your production application. We talked about the considerations to take into account when choosing hardware for your cluster, including whether to deploy on your own hardware or in the cloud. We next discussed installing and configuring the various distributions, followed by managing your cluster.

This chapter gets you ready to think about putting HBase in production. There is a lot more to it in terms of monitoring the system, and that's what the next chapter is all about.

10

Operations

This chapter covers

- Monitoring and metrics
- Performance testing and tuning
- Common management and operations tasks
- Backup and replication strategies

You've covered a lot of ground in understanding HBase and how to build applications effectively. We also looked at how to deploy HBase clusters in a fully distributed fashion, what kind of hardware to choose, the various distribution options, and how to configure the cluster. All this information is useful in enabling you to take your application and HBase into production. But there is one last piece of the puzzle left to be covered—operations. As a developer of the application, you wouldn't be expected to operate the underlying HBase cluster when everything is in production and the machines are churning full speed. But in the initial part of your project's HBase adoption, chances are that you'll be playing an integral role in the operations and helping the ops team get up to speed with all the aspects of operating an HBase cluster in production successfully.

Operations is a broad topic. Our goal for this chapter is to touch on the basic operational concepts pertaining to HBase. This will enable you to successfully operate your cluster and have your application serve the end users that it was built to serve. To do this, we'll start with covering the concepts of monitoring and metrics as they pertain to HBase. This will consist of the different ways you can monitor your HBase deployment and the metrics you need to monitor.

Monitoring is an important step, and once you have that in place, you'll be in a good place to start thinking about performance testing your HBase cluster and your application. There's no point making all that effort and taking a system to production if it can't sustain the load of all the users who want to use it!

We'll then cover common management and operations tasks that you'll need during the course of operating a cluster. These include things like starting and stopping services, upgrades, and detecting and fixing inconsistencies. The last topic in the chapter pertains to backup and replication of HBase clusters. This is important for business-continuity purposes when disaster strikes.

> **NOTE** This chapter covers topics that are relevant to the 0.92 release. Some of the recommendations may change with future releases, and we encourage you to look into those if you're using a later release.

Without further ado, let's jump right in.

10.1 *Monitoring your cluster*

A critical aspect of any production system is the ability of its operators to monitor its state and behavior. When issues happen, the last thing an operator wants to do is to sift through GBs and TBs of logs to make sense of the state of the system and the root cause of the issue. Not many people are champions at reading thousands of log lines across multiple servers to make sense of what's going on. That's where recording detailed metrics comes into play. Many things are happening in a production-quality database like HBase, and each of them can be measured in different ways. These measurements are exposed by the system and can be captured by external frameworks that are designed to record them and make them available to operators in a consumable fashion.

> **NOTE** Operations is particularly hard in distributed systems because many more components are involved, in terms of both the different pieces that make up the system and the scale at which they operate.

Collecting and graphing metrics isn't unique to HBase and can be found in any successful system, large or small scale. The way different systems implement this may differ, though. In this section, we'll talk about how HBase exposes metrics and the frameworks that are available to you to capture these metrics and use them to make sense of how your cluster is performing. We'll also talk about the metrics HBase exposes, what they mean, and how you can use them to alert you about issues when they happen.

TIP   We recommend that you set up your full metrics collection, graphing, and monitoring stack even in the prototyping stage of your HBase adoption. This will enable you to become familiar with the various aspects of operating HBase and will make the transition to production much smoother. Plus, it's fun to see pretty graphs showing requests hitting the system when they do. It will also help you in the process of building your application because you'll know more about what's going on in the underlying system when your application interacts with it.

10.1.1   *How HBase exposes metrics*

The metrics framework is another of the many ways that HBase depends on Hadoop. HBase is tightly integrated with Hadoop and uses Hadoop's underlying metrics framework to expose its metrics. At the time of writing this manuscript, HBase was still using the metrics framework v1.[1] Efforts are underway to have HBase use the latest and greatest,[2] but that hasn't been implemented yet.

It isn't necessary to delve deeply into how the metrics frameworks are implemented unless you want to get involved in the development of these frameworks. If that's your intention, by all means dive right into the code. If you're just interested in getting metrics out of HBase that you can use for your application, all you need to know is how to configure the framework and the ways it will expose the metrics, which we'll talk about next.

The metrics framework works by outputting metrics based on a context implementation that implements the `MetricsContext` interface. A couple of implementations come out of the box that you can use: Ganglia context and File context. In addition to these contexts, HBase also exposes metrics using Java Management Extensions (JMX).[3]

10.1.2   *Collecting and graphing the metrics*

Metrics solutions involve two aspects: *collection* and *graphing*. Typically these are both built into the same framework, but that's not a requirement. Collection frameworks collect the metrics being generated by the system that is being monitored and store them efficiently so they can be used later. These frameworks also do things like rollups on a daily, monthly, or yearly basis. For the most part, granular metrics that are a year old aren't as useful as a yearly summary of the same metrics.

Graphing tools use the data captured and stored by collection frameworks and make it easily consumable for the end user in the form of graphs and pretty pictures. These graphs are what the operator looks at to quickly get insight into the status of the system. Add to these graphs things like thresholds, and you can easily find out if the system isn't performing in the expected range of operation. And based on

[1] Hadoop metrics framework v1, Apache Software Foundation, http://mng.bz/J92f.
[2] Hadoop metrics framework v2, Apache Software Foundation, http://mng.bz/aOEI.
[3] Qusay H. Mahmoud, "Getting Started with Java Management Extensions (JMX): Developing Management and Monitoring Solutions," Oracle Sun Developer Network, January 6, 2004, http://mng.bz/619L.

these, you can take actions to prevent the end application from being impacted when Murphy strikes.[4]

Numerous collection and graphing tools are available. But not all of them are tightly integrated with how Hadoop and HBase expose metrics. You're limited to Ganglia (which has native support from the Hadoop metrics framework) or to frameworks that can collect metrics via JMX.

GANGLIA

Ganglia (http://ganglia.sourceforge.net/)[5] is a distributed monitoring framework designed to monitor clusters. It was developed at UC Berkeley and open-sourced. The Hadoop and HBase communities have been using it as the de facto solution to monitor clusters.

To configure HBase to output metrics to Ganglia, you have to set the parameters in the hadoop-metrics.properties file, which resides in the $HBASE_HOME/conf/ directory. The context you'll configure depends on the version of Ganglia you choose to use. For versions older than 3.1, the GangliaContext should be used. For 3.1 and newer, GangliaContext31 should be used. The hadoop-metrics.properties file configured for Ganglia 3.1 or later looks like the following:

```
hbase.class=org.apache.hadoop.metrics.ganglia.GangliaContext31
hbase.period=10
hbase.servers=GMETADHOST_IP:PORT
jvm.class=org.apache.hadoop.metrics.ganglia.GangliaContext31
jvm.period=10
jvm.servers=GMETADHOST_IP:PORT
rpc.class=org.apache.hadoop.metrics.ganglia.GangliaContext31
rpc.period=10
rpc.servers=GMETADHOST_IP:PORT
```

Once you have Ganglia set up and the HBase daemons started with these configuration properties, the metrics list in Ganglia will show metrics being spewed out by HBase, as shown in figure 10.1.

JMX

Apart from exposing metrics using the Hadoop metrics framework, HBase also exposes metrics via JMX. Several open source tools such as Cacti and OpenTSDB can be used to collect metrics via JMX. JMX metrics can also be viewed as JSON from the Master and RegionServer web UI:

- JMX metrics from the Master: http://master_ip_address:port/jmx
- JMX metrics from a particular RegionServer: http://region_server_ip _address:port/jmx

The default port for the Master is 60010 and for the RegionServer is 60030.

---

[4] You've certainly heard of Murphy's law: http://en.wikipedia.org/wiki/Murphy's_law.
[5] *Monitoring with Ganglia*, by Matt Massie et al., is expected to release in November 2012 and will be a handy resource for all things monitoring and Ganglia. See http://mng.bz/Pzw8.

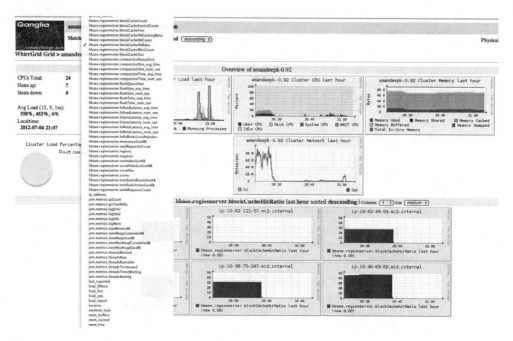

Figure 10.1   Ganglia, set up to take metrics from HBase. Notice the list of HBase and JVM metrics in the drop-down Metrics list.

FILE BASED

HBase can also be configured to output metrics into a flat file. Every time a metric is to be output, it's appended to that file. This can be done with or without timestamps, depending on the context. File-based metrics aren't a useful way of recording metrics because they're hard to consume thereafter. Although we haven't come across any production system where metrics are recorded into files for active monitoring purposes, it's still an option for recording metrics for later analysis:

To enable metrics logging to files, the hadoop-metrics.properties file looks like this:

```
hbase.class=org.apache.hadoop.hbase.metrics.file.TimeStampingFileContext
hbase.period=10
hbase.fileName=/tmp/metrics_hbase.log
jvm.class=org.apache.hadoop.hbase.metrics.file.TimeStampingFileContext
jvm.period=10
jvm.fileName=/tmp/metrics_jvm.log
rpc.class=org.apache.hadoop.hbase.metrics.file.TimeStampingFileContext
rpc.period=10
rpc.fileName=/tmp/metrics_rpc.log
```

Let's look at the metrics that HBase exposes that you can use to get insights into the health and performance of your cluster.

10.1.3   *The metrics HBase exposes*

The Master and RegionServers expose metrics. You don't need to look at the HBase code to understand these, but if you're curious and want to learn about how they're reported and the inner workings of the metrics framework, we encourage you to browse through the code. Getting your hands dirty with the code never hurts.

The metrics of interest depend on the workload the cluster is sustaining, and we'll categorize them accordingly. First we'll cover the general metrics that are relevant regardless of the workload, and then we'll look at metrics that are relevant to writes and reads independently.

GENERAL METRICS

Metrics related to the system load, network statistics, RPCs, alive regions, JVM heap, and JVM threads are of interest regardless of the kind of workload being run; they can be used to explain the system's behavior. The Master UI shows the heap usage and the requests per second being served by the RegionServers (figure 10.2).

HBase metrics are important, but so are the metrics from dependency systems—HDFS, underlying OS, hardware, and the network. Often the root cause for behavior that is out of the normal range lies in the way the underlying systems are functioning. Issues there typically result in a cascading effect on the rest of the stack and end up impacting the client. The client either doesn't perform properly or fails due to unexpected behavior. This is even more pronounced in distributed systems that have more components that can fail and more dependencies. Covering detailed metrics and monitoring for all dependencies is beyond the scope of this book, but plenty of resources exist that you can use to study those.[6]

The important bits that you absolutely need to monitor are as follows:

- HDFS throughput and latency
- HDFS usage
- Underlying disk throughput
- Network throughput and latency from each node

System- and network-level information can be seen from Ganglia (figure 10.3) and from several Linux tools such as `lsof`, `top`, `iostat`, `netstat`, and so on. These are handy tools to learn if you're administering HBase.

Region Servers

ServerName	Start time	Load
ip-10-38-75-247.ec2.internal,60020,1341378826878	Wed Jul 04 05:13:46 UTC 2012	requestsPerSecond=2161, numberOfOnlineRegions=43, usedHeapMB=1529, maxHeapMB=1974
ip-10-40-83-62.ec2.internal,60020,1341378826769	Wed Jul 04 05:13:46 UTC 2012	requestsPerSecond=3887, numberOfOnlineRegions=35, usedHeapMB=1051, maxHeapMB=1974
ip-10-60-29-145.ec2.internal,60020,1341378826834	Wed Jul 04 05:13:46 UTC 2012	requestsPerSecond=2211, numberOfOnlineRegions=41, usedHeapMB=1439, maxHeapMB=1974
ip-10-62-117-182.ec2.internal,60020,1341378826720	Wed Jul 04 05:13:46 UTC 2012	requestsPerSecond=2184, numberOfOnlineRegions=42, usedHeapMB=1318, maxHeapMB=1974
ip-10-62-121-57.ec2.internal,60020,1341378826656	Wed Jul 04 05:13:46 UTC 2012	requestsPerSecond=5635, numberOfOnlineRegions=35, usedHeapMB=1078, maxHeapMB=1974
ip-10-62-94-63.ec2.internal,60020,1341378826755	Wed Jul 04 05:13:46 UTC 2012	requestsPerSecond=2667, numberOfOnlineRegions=36, usedHeapMB=1012, maxHeapMB=1974
Total: servers: 6		requestsPerSecond=18745, numberOfOnlineRegions=232

Figure 10.2   The HBase Master web UI shows the number of requests per second being served by each of the RegionServers, the number of regions that are online on the RegionServers, and the used and max heap. This is a useful place to start when you're trying to find out the state of the system. Often, you can find issues here when RegionServers have fallen over, aren't balanced in terms of the regions and requests they're serving, or are misconfigured to use less heap than you had planned to give them.

---

[6]   *Hadoop Operations*, by Eric Sammer, is a good resource for all things related to operating Hadoop in production. It's expected to release in fall 2012. See http://mng.bz/iO24.

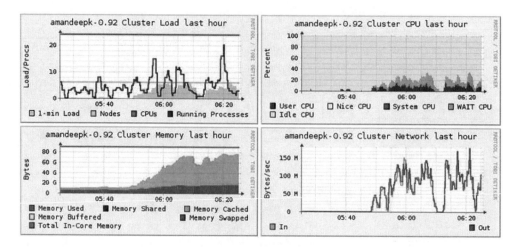

Figure 10.3   Ganglia graphs showing a summary of the entire cluster for load, CPU, memory, and network metrics

One interesting metric to keep an eye on is the CPU I/O wait percentage. This indicates the amount of time the CPU spends waiting for disk I/O and is a good indicator of whether your system is I/O bound. If it is I/O bound, you need more disks in almost all cases. Ganglia graphs for CPU I/O wait percentage from a cluster running a heavy write workload are shown in figure 10.4. This metric is useful when the read I/O is high as well.

We've talked about some of the generic metrics that are of interest in a running cluster. We'll now go into write- and read-specific metrics.

WRITE-RELATED METRICS

To understand the system state during writes, the metrics of interest are the ones that are collected as data is written into the system. This translates into metrics related to MemStore, flushes, compactions, garbage collection, and HDFS I/O.

During writes, the ideal MemStore metrics graph should look like saw teeth. That indicates smooth flushing of the MemStore and predictable garbage collection

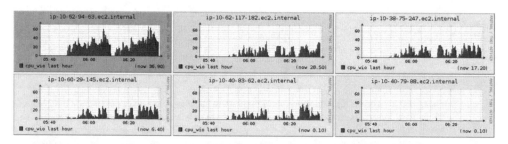

Figure 10.4   CPU I/O wait percentage is a useful metric to use to understand whether your system is I/O bound. These Ganglia graphs show significant I/O load on five out of the six boxes. This was during a heavy write workload. More disks on the boxes would speed up the writes by distributing the load.

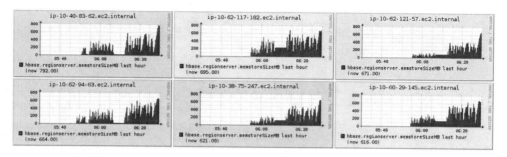

Figure 10.5 MemStore size metrics from Ganglia. This isn't an ideal graph: it indicates that tuning garbage collection and other HBase configs might help improve performance.

overhead. Figure 10.5 shows the MemStore size metrics from Ganglia during heavy writes.

To understand HDFS write latencies, the `fsWriteLatency` and `fsSyncLatency` metrics are useful. The write-latency metric includes the latency while writing HFiles as well as the WAL. The sync-latency metrics are only for the WALs.

Write latencies going up typically also causes the compaction queues to increase (figure 10.6).

Garbage-collection metrics are exposed by the JVM through the metric context; you can find them in Ganglia as `jvm.metrics.gc*`. Another useful way of finding out what's going on with garbage collection is to enable garbage-collection logging by putting the `-Xloggc:/my/logs/directory/hbase-regionserver-gc.log` flag in the Java options (in hbase-env.sh) for the RegionServers. This is useful information when dealing with unresponsive RegionServer processes during heavy writes. A common cause for that is long garbage-collection pauses, which typically means garbage collection isn't tuned properly.

READ-RELATED METRICS

Reads are different than writes, and so are the metrics you should monitor to understand them. During reads, the metrics of interest relate to the block cache primarily,

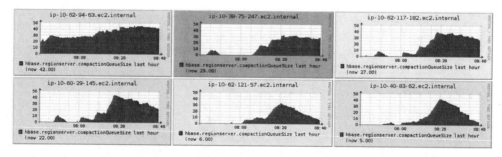

Figure 10.6 The compaction queues going up during heavy writes. Notice that the queue is higher in some boxes than the others. This likely indicates that the write load on those RegionServers is higher than on the others.

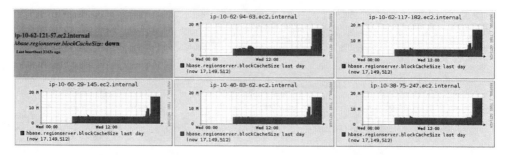

Figure 10.7   Block-cache-size metrics captured during a read-heavy workload. It turns out that the load was too heavy and brought down one of the RegionServers—that's the box in the upper-left corner. If this happens, you should configure your ops systems to alert you. It's not critical enough that you should be paged in the middle of the night if only one box goes down. If many go down, you should be worried.

apart from the general metrics that we covered initially. The block-cache metrics for cache hits, evictions, and cache size are useful in understanding the read performance; you can tune your cache and table properties accordingly. Figure 10.7 shows cache-size metrics during a read-heavy workload.

10.1.4   *Application-side monitoring*

Tools monitoring HBase may be giving you great-looking graphs, and everything at the system level may be running stably. But that doesn't mean your entire application stack is running well. In a production environment, we recommend that you add to the system-level monitoring that Ganglia and other tools provide and also monitor how HBase looks from your application's perspective. This is likely to be a custom implementation based on how your application is using HBase. The HBase community has not yet come up with templates for doing this, but that may change over time. You could well contribute to that initiative.

The following can be useful while monitoring HBase as seen by the application:

- Put performance as seen by the client (the application) for every RegionServer
- Get performance as seen by the client for every RegionServer
- Scan performance as seen by the client for every RegionServer
- Connectivity to all RegionServers
- Network latencies between the application tier and the HBase cluster
- Number of concurrent clients opening to HBase at any point in time
- Connectivity to ZooKeeper

Checks like these enable you to keep track of your application's view of HBase, and you can correlate that with HBase-level metrics to better understand the application's behavior. This is a solution for which you'll have to work with your system administrators and operations team. Invest time and effort in it. It will benefit you in the long run when operating your application in production.

10.2   Performance of your HBase cluster

Performance of any database is measured in terms of the response times of the operations that it supports. This is important to measure in the context of your application so you can set the right expectations for users. For instance, a user of an application backed by an HBase cluster shouldn't have to wait for tens of seconds to get a response when they click a button. Ideally, it should happen in milliseconds. Of course, this isn't a general rule and will depend a lot on the type of interaction the user is engaged in.

To make sure your HBase cluster is performing within the expected SLAs, you must test performance thoroughly and tune the cluster to extract the maximum performance you can get out of it. This section will cover the various ways you can test the performance of your cluster and then will look at what impacts the performance. From there, we'll cover the various knobs that are available to you to tune the system.

10.2.1   Performance testing

There are different ways you can test the performance of your HBase cluster. The best way is to put it under a real workload that emulates what your application is likely to see in production. But it's not always possible to test with real workloads without launching a beta version of the application where a select few users interact with it. Ideally, you'll want to do some level of testing before that so you can be confident of the performance to some degree. You can use a couple of options to achieve that.

> **NOTE**   Having a monitoring framework in place before testing the performance of your cluster is useful. Install it! You'll be able to get much more insight into the system's behavior with it than without it.

PERFORMANCEEVALUATION TOOL—BUNDLED WITH HBASE

HBase ships with a tool called `PerformanceEvaluation`, which you can use to evaluate the performance of your HBase cluster in terms of various operations. It's based on the performance-evaluation tool described in the original Bigtable paper by Google. To get its usage details, you can run the tool without any arguments:

```
$ $HBASE_HOME/bin/hbase org.apache.hadoop.hbase.PerformanceEvaluation

Usage: java org.apache.hadoop.hbase.PerformanceEvaluation \
   [--miniCluster] [--nomapred] [--rows=ROWS] <command> <nclients>

Options:
 miniCluster     Run the test on an HBaseMiniCluster
 nomapred        Run multiple clients using threads
                    (rather than use mapreduce)
 rows            Rows each client runs. Default: One million
 flushCommits    Used to determine if the test should
                    flush the table.  Default: false
 writeToWAL      Set writeToWAL on puts. Default: True

Command:
 filterScan      Run scan test using a filter to find
                    a specific row based on its value
                    (make sure to use --rows=20)
```

```
randomRead        Run random read test
randomSeekScan    Run random seek and scan 100 test
randomWrite       Run random write test
scan              Run scan test (read every row)
scanRange10       Run random seek scan with both start
                     and stop row (max 10 rows)
scanRange100      Run random seek scan with both start
                     and stop row (max 100 rows)
scanRange1000     Run random seek scan with both start
                     and stop row (max 1000 rows)
scanRange10000    Run random seek scan with both start
                     and stop row (max 10000 rows)
sequentialRead    Run sequential read test
sequentialWrite   Run sequential write test

Args:
 nclients          Integer. Required. Total number
                      of clients (and HRegionServers)
                      running: 1 <= value <= 500
Examples:
 To run a single evaluation client:
 $ bin/hbase org.apache.hadoop.hbase.PerformanceEvaluation sequentialWrite 1
```

As you can see from the usage details, you can run all kinds of tests using this tool. They all run as MapReduce jobs unless you set the number of clients as 1, in which case they run as a single-threaded client. You can configure the number of rows to be written/read per client and the number of clients. Run the `sequentialWrite` or the `randomWrite` commands first so they create a table and put some data in it. That table and data can thereafter be used for read tests like `randomRead`, `scan`, and `sequential-Read`. The tool doesn't need you to create a table manually; it does that on its own when you run the commands to write data into HBase.

If you care about random reads and writes only, you can run this tool from anywhere outside the cluster as long as the HBase JARs and configs are deployed there. MapReduce jobs will run from wherever the MapReduce framework is installed, which ideally shouldn't be collocated with the HBase cluster (as we talked about previously).

A sample run of this tool looks like this:

```
$ hbase org.apache.hadoop.hbase.PerformanceEvaluation --rows=10
    sequentialWrite 1
12/06/18 15:59:29 WARN conf.Configuration: hadoop.native.lib is deprecated.
    Instead, use io.native.lib.available
12/06/18 15:59:29 INFO zookeeper.ZooKeeper: Client
    environment:zookeeper.version=3.4.3-cdh4.0.0--1, built on 06/04/2012
    23:16 GMT
...
...
...
12/06/18 15:59:29 INFO hbase.PerformanceEvaluation: 0/9/10
12/06/18 15:59:29 INFO hbase.PerformanceEvaluation: Finished class
 org.apache.hadoop.hbase.PerformanceEvaluation$SequentialWriteTest
 in 14ms at offset 0 for 10 rows
```

This run wrote 10 rows sequentially from a single thread and took 14 ms to do so.

The limitation of this testing utility is that you can't run mixed workloads without coding it up yourself. The test has to be one of the bundled ones, and they have to be run individually as separate runs. If your workload consists of Scans and Gets and Puts happening at the same time, this tool doesn't give you the ability to truly test your cluster by mixing it all up. That brings us to our next testing utility.

YCSB—YAHOO! CLOUD SERVING BENCHMARK[7]

In chapter 1, we talked about NoSQL systems that were developed at various companies to solve their data-management problems. This led to flame wars and bake-offs about who was better than whom. Although it was fun to watch, it also made things unclear when it came to comparing the performance of the different systems. That's a hard task to do in general because these systems are designed for different use cases and with different trade-offs. But we need a standardized way of comparing them, and the industry still lacks that.

Yahoo! funded research to come up with a standard performance-testing tool that could be used to compare different databases. The company called it Yahoo! Cloud Serving Benchmark (YCSB). YCSB is the closest we have come to having a standard benchmarking tool that can be used to measure and compare the performance of different distributed databases. Although YCSB is built for comparing systems, you can use it to test the performance of any of the databases it supports, including HBase. YCSB consists of the YCSB client, which is an extensible workload generator, and the core workloads, which are a set of workloads that comes prepackaged and can be generated by the YCSB client.

YCSB is available from the project's GitHub repository (http://github.com/brianfrankcooper/YCSB/). You have to compile it using Maven.

To start, clone the Git repository:

```
$ git clone git://github.com/brianfrankcooper/YCSB.git
Cloning into YCSB...
...
...
Resolving deltas: 100% (906/906), done.
```

Once cloned, compile the code:

```
$ cd YCSB
$ mvn -DskipTests package
```

Once YCSB is compiled, put your HBase cluster's configuration in hbase/src/main/conf/hbase-site.xml. You only need to put the hbase.zookeeper.quorum property in the config file so YCSB can use it as the entry point for the cluster. Now you're ready to run workloads to test your cluster. YCSB comes with a few sample workloads that you can find in the workloads directory. We'll use one of those for this example, but you can create your own workloads based on what you want to test from your cluster.

---

[7] Yahoo! Cloud Serving Benchmark, Yahoo! Research, http://mng.bz/9U3c.

Before running the workload, you need to create the HBase table YCSB will write to. You can do that from the shell:

```
hbase(main):002:0> create 'mytable', 'myfamily'
```

After that, you're ready to test your cluster:

```
$ bin/ycsb load hbase -P workloads/workloada -p columnfamily=myfamily \
-p table=mytable
```

You can do all sorts of fancy stuff with YCSB workloads, including configuring multiple clients, configuring multiple threads, and running mixed workloads with different statistical distributions of the data.

You now know a couple of ways to test the performance of your HBase cluster; you'll likely do this testing before taking the cluster to production. There may be areas in which you can improve the performance of the cluster. To understand that, it's important to be familiar with all the factors that impact HBase's performance. [8]

10.2.2   *What impacts HBase's performance?*

HBase is a *distributed database* and is *tightly coupled* with Hadoop. That makes it susceptible to the entire stack under it (figure 10.8) when it comes to performance.

Performance is affected by everything from the underlying hardware that makes up the boxes in the cluster to the network connecting them to the OS (specifically the file system) to the JVM to HDFS. The state of the HBase system matters too. For

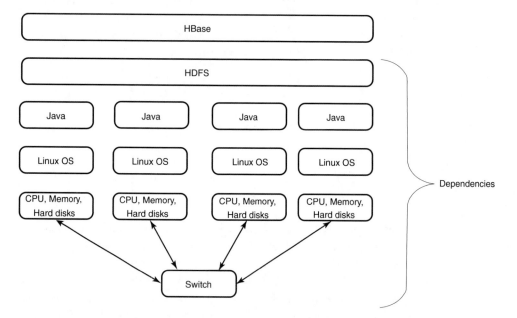

Figure 10.8   HBase and its dependencies. Every dependency affects the performance of HBase.

---

[8] Yahoo! Cloud Serving Benchmark: http://research.yahoo.com/Web_Information_Management/YCSB.

instance, performance is different during a compaction or during MemStore flushes compared to when nothing is going on in the cluster. Your application's performance depends on how it interacts with HBase, and your schema design plays an integral role as much as anything else.

When looking at HBase performance, all of these factors matter; and when you tune your cluster, you need to look into all of them. Going into tuning each of those layers is beyond the scope of this text. We covered JVM tuning (garbage collection specifically) in chapter 9. We'll discuss some key aspects of tuning your HBase cluster next.

10.2.3 Tuning dependency systems

Tuning an HBase cluster to extract maximum performance involves tuning all dependencies. There's not a lot you need to do with things like the hardware and OS if you choose them wisely and install them correctly, based on the best practices outlined by the HBase community and highlighted by us in chapter 9. We'll touch on them here as well. We recommend working with your system administrators on these to make sure you get them right.

HARDWARE CHOICES

We'll start with the most basic building block of your HBase cluster—the hardware. Make sure to choose the hardware based on the recommendations we provided in chapter 9. We won't repeat all the recommendations here. But to sum it up, get enough disks and RAM, but don't go overboard shopping for the state of the art. Buy commodity, but choose quantity over quality. Scaling out pays off much better in the case of Hadoop and HBase clusters.

NETWORK CONFIGURATION

Any self-respecting distributed system based on current-generation hardware is network bound. HBase is no different. 10GbE networks between the nodes and the TOR switches are recommended. Don't oversubscribe the network a lot, or you'll see performance impact during high load.

OPERATING SYSTEM

Linux has been the choice of OS as far as Hadoop and HBase systems go. There have been successful deployments on both Red Hat-based (Red Hat Enterprise Linux [RHEL], CentOS) and Debian-based (Ubuntu and so on) flavors of Linux. Choose the one that you have good support for.

LOCAL FILE SYSTEM

Local Linux file systems play an important role in the stack and impact the performance of HBase significantly. Although Ext4 is the recommended file system, Ext3 and XFS have been successfully used in production systems as well. Tune the file systems based on our recommendations in chapter 9.

HDFS

HDFS performance is key for a well-performing HBase cluster. There's not a lot to tune if you have the underlying network, disks, and local file system configured correctly.

The one additional configuration you may consider is short-circuiting local client reads. This feature is new with Hadoop 1.0 and allows an HDFS client to read blocks directly from the local file system when possible. This feature is particularly relevant to both read-heavy and mixed workloads. Enable it by setting `dfs.client.read.short-circuit` to `true` in hdfs-site.xml. All you need beyond that is to tune the data xcievers, which we highlighted in chapter 9.

10.2.4 Tuning HBase

Tuning an HBase cluster typically involves tuning multiple different configuration parameters to suit the workload that you plan to put on the cluster. Do this as you do performance testing on the cluster, and use the configurations mentioned in chapter 9 to get your combination right. No out-of-the-box recipes are available to configure HBase for certain workloads, but you can attempt to categorize them as one of the following:

- Random-read-heavy
- Sequential-read-heavy
- Write-heavy
- Mixed

Each of these workloads demands a different kind of configuration tuning, and we recommend that you experiment to figure out the best combination for you. Here are a few guidelines for you to work with when trying to tune your cluster based on the categories mentioned.

RANDOM-READ-HEAVY

For random-read-heavy workloads, effective use of the cache and better indexing will get you higher performance. Pay attention to the configuration parameters listing in table 10.1.

Table 10.1 Tuning tips for a random-read-heavy workload

Configuration parameter	Description	Recommendation
`hfile.block.cache.size`	The block cache is the read cache (LRU). This property defines the maximum percentage of heap that the block cache can use.	For random-read workloads, increase the percentage of heap that the cache uses.

Table 10.1 Tuning tips for a random-read-heavy workload *(continued)*

Configuration parameter	Description	Recommendation
`hbase.regionserver.global` `.memstore.lowerLimit` and `hbase.regionserver.global` `.memstore.upperLimit`	`upperLimit` defines the maximum percentage of the heap on a RegionServer that the MemStores combined can use. The moment `upperLimit` is hit, MemStores are flushed until `lowerLimit` is hit. Setting these values equal to each other means the minimum amount of flushing happens when writes are blocked because of `upperLimit` being hit. This minimizes the pauses during writes but also causes more frequent flushing.	For random-read-heavy workloads, where you increase the amount of heap that the block cache takes up, you need to reduce the percentage taken up by the MemStore using these parameters.
HFile block size	This is the parameter you set as a part of the column-family configuration for a given table, like this: `hbase(main):002:0>` `create 'mytable',` `{NAME => 'colfam1',` `BLOCKSIZE => '65536'}`	Lower block size gives you more granular indexing. 64 KB is a good place to start, but you should test with lower values to see if performance improves.
Bloom filters	You can enable bloom filters at a column-family level like this: `hbase(main):007:0>` `create 'mytable',` `{NAME => 'colfam1',` `BLOOMFILTER =>` `'ROWCOL'}`	Enabling bloom filters can reduce the number of HFiles that need to be read to find the `KeyValue` objects for a given row.
Aggressive caching	Column families can be configured so that they cache more aggressively than others. You do so like this: `hbase(main):002:0>` `create 'mytable',` `{NAME => 'colfam1',` `IN_MEMORY => 'true'}`	This can help random read performance. Enable this, and test to see how much it helps in your use case.
Disable caching for other tables and families	Column families can be configured to not be cached into the block cache at read time like this: `hbase(main):002:0>` `create 'mytable',` `{NAME => 'colfam1',` `BLOCKCACHE => 'false'}`	If some of your column families are used for random reads and others aren't, the ones that aren't used could be polluting the cache. Disable them from being cached, and it will improve your cache hits.

SEQUENTIAL-READ-HEAVY

For sequential-read-heavy workloads, the read cache doesn't buy you a lot; chances are you'll be hitting the disk more often than not unless the sequential reads are small in size and are limited to a particular key range. Pay attention to the configuration parameters in table 10.2.

Table 10.2   Tuning tips for a sequential-read-heavy workload

Configuration parameter	Description	Recommendation

HFile block size	This is the parameter you set as a part of the column family configuration for a given table like this:
	
	`hbase(main):002:0>`
	`create 'mytable',`
	`{NAME => 'colfam1',`
	`BLOCKSIZE =>`
	`'65536'}`
		Higher block size gives you more data read per disk seek. 64 KB is a good place to start, but you should test with higher values to see if performance improves. Very high values compromise performance in finding the start key for your scans.

`hbase.client.scanner.caching`	This defines the number of rows that will be fetched when the next method is called on a scanner. The higher the number, the fewer remote calls the client needs to make to the RegionServer during scans. A higher number also means more memory consumption at the client side. This can be set on a per-client basis in the configuration object as well.	Set a higher scanner-caching value so the scanner gets more rows back per RPC request while doing large sequential reads. The default value is 1. Increase it to a slightly higher number than what you expect to read in every scan iteration. Depending on your application logic and the size of the rows returned over the wire, potential values could be 50 or 1000. You can also set this on a per-`Scan` instance basis using the `Scan.setCaching(int)` method.
Disable caching blocks through scanner API `Scan.setCacheBlocks(..)`	This setting defines whether the blocks being scanned should be put into the BlockCache.	Loading all blocks read by a scanner into the BlockCache causes a lot of cache churn. For large scans, you can disable the caching of blocks by setting this value to `false`.

Disable caching on table	Column families can be configured to not be cached into the block cache at read time like this:
	
	`hbase(main):002:0>`
	`create 'mytable',`
	`{NAME => 'colfam1',`
	`BLOCKCACHE =>`
	`'false'}`
		If the table is primarily accessed using large scans, the cache most likely won't buy you much performance. Instead you'll be churning the cache and impacting other tables that are being accessed for smaller random reads. You can disable the BlockCache so it doesn't churn the cache on every scan.

WRITE-HEAVY

Write-heavy workloads need different tuning than read-heavy ones. The cache doesn't play an important role anymore. Writes always go into the MemStore and are flushed to form new HFiles, which later are compacted. The way to get good write performance is by not flushing, compacting, or splitting too often because the I/O load goes up during that time, slowing the system. The configuration parameters in table 10.3 are of interest while tuning for a write-heavy workload.

Table 10.3 Tuning tips for a write-heavy workload

Configuration parameter	Description	Recommendation
`hbase.hregion.max.filesize`	This determines the maximum size of the underlying store files (`HStoreFile`). The region size is defined by this parameter. If any store file of any column family exceeds this size, the region is split.	Larger regions mean fewer splits at write time. Increase this number, and see where you get optimal performance for your use case. We have come across region sizes ranging from 256 MB to 4 GB. 1 GB is a good place to begin experimenting.
`hbase.hregion.memstore.flush.size`	This parameter defines the size of the MemStore and is configured in bytes. The MemStore is flushed to disk when it exceeds this size. A thread that runs periodically checks the size of the MemStore.	Flushing more data to HDFS and creating larger HFiles reduce the number of compactions required by reducing the number of files created during writes.
`hbase.regionserver.global.memstore.lowerLimit` and `hbase.regionserver.global.memstore.upperLimit`	upperLimit defines the maximum percentage of the heap on a RegionServer that the MemStores combined can use. The moment `upper-Limit` is hit, MemStores are flushed until `lowerLimit` is hit. Setting these values equal to each other means that a minimum amount of flushing happens when writes are blocked because of `upperLimit` being hit. This minimizes pauses during writes but also causes more frequent flushing.	You can increase the percentage of heap allocated to the MemStore on every Region-Server. Don't go overboard with this because it can cause garbage-collection issues. Configure `upperLimit` such that it can accommodate the Mem-Store per region multiplied by the number of expected regions per RegionServer.

Table 10.3   Tuning tips for a write-heavy workload *(continued)*

Configuration parameter	Description	Recommendation
Garbage collection tuning		Java garbage collection plays an important role when it comes to the write performance of an HBase cluster. See the recommendations provided in chapter 9, and tune based on them.
`hbase.hregion.memstore .mslab.enabled`	MemStore-Local Allocation Buffer is a feature in HBase that helps prevent heap fragmentation when there are heavy writes going on. In some cases, enabling this feature can help alleviate issues of long garbage-collection pauses if the heaps are too large. The default value of this parameter is `true`.	Enabling this feature can give you better write performance and more stable operations.

MIXED

With completely mixed workloads, tuning becomes slightly trickier. You have to tweak a mix of the parameters described earlier to achieve the optimal combination. Iterate over various combinations, and run performance tests to see where you get the best results.

Outside of the previously mentioned configuration, the following impact performance in general:

- *Compression*—Enable compression to reduce the I/O load on the cluster. Compression can be enabled at a column-family level as described in chapter 4. This is done at table-instantiation time or by altering the table schema.

- *Rowkey design*—The performance you extract out of your HBase cluster isn't limited to how well the cluster is performing. A big part of it is how you use the cluster. All the previous chapters were geared toward equipping you with information so you can design your application optimally. A big part of this is optimal rowkey design based on your access patterns. Pay attention to that. If you think you've designed the best rowkey possible, look again. You might come up with something even better. We can't stress enough the importance of good rowkey design.

- *Major compactions*—Major compaction entails all RegionServers compacting all HFiles they're serving. We recommend that this be made a manual process that is carried out at the time the cluster is expected to have minimal load. This can be configured using the `hbase.hregion.majorcompaction` parameter in the hbase-site.xml configuration file.

- *RegionServer handler count*—Handlers are the threads receiving RPC requests on the RegionServers. If you keep the number of handlers too low, you can't get enough work out of the RegionServers. If you keep it too high, you expose yourself to the risk of oversubscribing the resources. This configuration can be tuned in hbase-site.xml using the `hbase.regionserver.handler.count` parameter. Tweak this configuration to see where you get optimal performance. Chances are, you'll be able to go much higher than the default value for this parameter.

10.3 Cluster management

During the course of running a production system, management tasks need to be performed at different stages. Even though HBase is a distributed system with various failure-resistance techniques and high availability built into it, it still needs a moderate amount of care on a daily basis. Things like starting or stopping the cluster, upgrading the OS on the nodes, replacing bad hardware, and backing up data are important tasks and need to be done right to keep the cluster running smoothly. Sometimes these tasks are in response to events like hardware going bad, and other times they're purely to stay up to date with the latest and greatest releases.

This section highlights some of the important tasks you may need to perform and teaches how to do them. HBase is a fast-evolving system, and not all problems are solved. Until recently, it was operated mostly by people intimately familiar with the internals, including some of the committers. There wasn't a lot of focus on making automated management tools that simplify life on the operations side. Therefore, some things that we'll cover in this section require more manual intervention than others. These will likely go into an operations manual that cluster administrators can refer to when required. Get ready to get your hands dirty.

10.3.1 Starting and stopping HBase

Starting and stopping the HBase daemons will probably be more common than you expect, especially in the early stages of setting up the cluster and getting things going. Configuration changes are the most common reason for this activity. You can do this different ways, but the underlying principles are the same. The order in which the HBase daemons are stopped and started matters only to the extent that the dependency systems (HDFS and ZooKeeper) need to be up before HBase is started and should be shut down only after HBase has shut down.

SCRIPTS

Different distributions come with different scripts to start/stop daemons. The stock Apache distribution has the following scripts (in the $HBASE_HOME/bin directory) available that you can use:

- *hbase-daemon.sh*—Starts/stops individual processes. It has to be run on every box where any HBase daemon needs to be run, which means you need to manually log in to all boxes in the cluster. Here's the syntax:

```
$HBASE_HOME/bin/hbase-daemon.sh [start/stop/restart] [regionserver/
    master]
```

- *hbase-daemons.sh*—Wrapper around the hbase-daemon.sh script that will SSH into hosts that are to run a particular daemon and execute hbase-daemon.sh. This can be used to spin up the HBase Masters, RegionServers, and ZooKeepers (if they're managed by HBase). It requires passwordless SSH between the host where you run this script and all the hosts where the script needs to log in and do remote execution.
- *start-hbase.sh*—Wrapper around hbase-daemons.sh and hbase-daemon.sh that can be used to start the entire HBase cluster from a single point. Requires passwordless SSH like hbase-daemons.sh. Typically, this script is run on the HBase Master node. It runs the HBase Master on the local node and backup masters on the nodes specified in the backup-masters file in the configuration directory. The list of RegionServers is compiled by this script from the RegionServers file in the configuration directory.
- *stop-hbase.sh*—Stops the HBase cluster. Similar to the start-hbase.sh script in the way it's implemented.

CDH comes with init scripts and doesn't use the scripts that come with the stock Apache release. These scripts are located in /etc/init.d/hbase-<daemon>.sh and can be used to start, stop, or restart the daemon process.

CENTRALIZED MANAGEMENT
Cluster-management frameworks like Puppet and Chef can be used to manage the starting and stopping of daemons from a central location. Proprietary tools like Cloudera Manager can also be used for this purpose. Typically, there are security concerns associated with passwordless SSH, and many system administrators try to find alternate solutions.

10.3.2 *Graceful stop and decommissioning nodes*

When you need to shut down daemons on individual servers for any management purpose (upgrading, replacing hardware, and so on), you need to ensure that the rest of the cluster keeps working fine and there is minimal outage as seen by client applications. This entails moving the regions being served by that RegionServer to some other RegionServer proactively rather than having HBase react to a RegionServer going down. HBase will recover from a RegionServer going down, but it will wait for the RegionServer to be detected as down and then start reassigning the regions elsewhere. Meanwhile, the application may possibly experience a slightly degraded availability. Moving the regions proactively to other RegionServers and then killing the RegionServer makes the process safer.

To do this, HBase comes with the graceful-stop.sh script. Like the other scripts we've talked about, this script is also located in the $HBASE_HOME/bin directory:

```
$ bin/graceful_stop.sh
Usage: graceful_stop.sh [--config <conf-dir>] [--restart] [--reload]
[--thrift] [--rest] <hostname>
 thrift      If we should stop/start thrift before/after the
```

```
                    hbase stop/start
rest        If we should stop/start rest before/after the hbase stop/start
restart     If we should restart after graceful stop
reload      Move offloaded regions back on to the stopped server
debug       Move offloaded regions back on to the stopped server
hostname    Hostname of server we are to stop
```

The script follows these steps (in order) to gracefully stop a RegionServer:

1 Disable the region balancer.

2 Move the regions off the RegionServer, and randomly assign them to other servers in the cluster.

3 Stop the REST and Thrift services if they're active.

4 Stop the RegionServer process.

This script also needs passwordless SSH from the node you're running it on to the Region-Server node you're trying to stop. If passwordless SSH isn't an option, you can look at the source code of the script and implement one that works for your environment.

Decommissioning nodes is an important management task, and using the graceful-shutdown mechanism to cleanly shut down the RegionServer is the first part. Thereafter, you need to remove the node from the list of nodes where the RegionServer process is expected to run so your scripts and automated-management software don't start the process again.

10.3.3 *Adding nodes*

As your application gets more successful or more use cases crop up, chances are you'll need to scale up your HBase cluster. It could also be that you're replacing a node for some reason. The process to add a node to the HBase cluster is the same in both cases.

Presumably, you're running the HDFS DataNode on the same physical node. The first part of adding a RegionServer to the cluster is to add the DataNode to HDFS. Depending on how you're managing your cluster (using the provided start/stop scripts or using centralized management software), start the DataNode process and wait for it to join the HDFS cluster. Once that is done, start the HBase RegionServer process. You'll see the node be added to the list of nodes in the Master UI. After this, if you want to balance out the regions being served by each node and move some load onto the newly added RegionServer, run the balancer using the following:

```
echo "balancer" | hbase shell
```

This will move some regions from all RegionServers to the new RegionServer and balance the load across the cluster. The downside of running the balancer is that you'll likely lose data locality for the regions that are moved. But this will be taken care of during the next round of major compactions.

10.3.4 *Rolling restarts and upgrading*

It's not rare to patch or upgrade Hadoop and HBase releases in running clusters—especially if you want to incorporate the latest and greatest features and performance improvements. In production systems, upgrades can be tricky. Often, it isn't possible to take downtime on the cluster to do upgrades. In some cases, the only option is to take downtime. This generally happens when you're looking to upgrade between major releases where the RPC protocol doesn't match the older releases, or other changes aren't backward compatible. When this happens, you have no choice but to plan a scheduled downtime and do the upgrade.

But not all upgrades are between major releases and require downtime. When the upgrade doesn't have backward-incompatible changes, you can do *rolling upgrades*. This means you upgrade one node at a time without bringing down the cluster. The idea is to shut down one node cleanly, upgrade it, and then bring it back up to join the cluster. This way, your application SLAs aren't impacted, assuming you have ample spare capacity to serve the same traffic when one node is taken down for the upgrade. In an ideal world, there would be scripts you could run for this purpose. HBase does ship with some scripts that can help, but they're naïve implementations of the concept[9] and we recommend you implement custom scripts based on your environment's requirements. To do upgrades without taking a downtime, follow these steps:

1 Deploy the new HBase version to all nodes in the cluster, including the new ZooKeeper if that needs an update as well.
2 Turn off the balancer process. One by one, gracefully stop the RegionServers and bring them back up. Because this graceful stop isn't meant for decommissioning nodes, the regions that the RegionServer was serving at the time it was brought down should be moved back to it when it comes back up. The graceful-stop.sh script can be run with the `--reload` argument to do this. Once all the RegionServers have been restarted, turn the balancer back on.
3 Restart the HBase Masters one by one.
4 If ZooKeeper requires a restart, restart all the nodes in the quorum one by one.
5 Upgrade the clients.

When these steps are finished, your cluster is running with the upgraded HBase version. These steps assume that you've taken care of upgrading the underlying HDFS.

You can use the same steps to do a rolling restart for any other purpose as well.

10.3.5 *bin/hbase and the HBase shell*

Throughout the book, you have used the shell to interact with HBase. Chapter 6 also covered scripting of the shell commands and extending the shell using JRuby. These are useful tools to have for managing your cluster on an everyday basis. The shell exposes several commands that come in handy to perform simple operations on the cluster or find out the cluster's health. Before we go into that, let's see the options that the bin/hbase script provides, which you use to start the shell. The script basically runs the Java class associated with the command you choose to pass it:

---

[9] This is true as of the 0.92.1 release. There may be more sophisticated implementations in future releases.

```
$ $HBASE_HOME/bin/hbase
Usage: hbase <command>
where <command> an option from one of these categories:

DBA TOOLS
  shell          run the HBase shell
  hbck           run the hbase 'fsck' tool
  hlog           write-ahead-log analyzer
  hfile          store file analyzer
  zkcli          run the ZooKeeper shell

PROCESS MANAGEMENT
  master         run an HBase HMaster node
  regionserver   run an HBase HRegionServer node
  zookeeper      run a Zookeeper server
  rest           run an HBase REST server
  thrift         run an HBase Thrift server
  avro           run an HBase Avro server

PACKAGE MANAGEMENT
  classpath      dump hbase CLASSPATH
  version        print the version

 or
  CLASSNAME       run the class named CLASSNAME
Most commands print help when invoked w/o parameters.
```

We'll cover the hbck, hlog, and hfile commands in future sections. For now, let's start with the shell command. To get a list of commands that the shell has to offer, type help in the shell, and here's what you'll see:

```
hbase(main):001:0> help
HBase Shell, version 0.92.1,
    r039a26b3c8b023cf2e1e5f57ebcd0fde510d74f2,
    Thu May 31 13:15:39 PDT 2012
Type 'help "COMMAND"', (e.g., 'help "get"' --
    the quotes are necessary) for help on a specific command.
Commands are grouped. Type 'help "COMMAND_GROUP"',
    (e.g., 'help "general"') for help on a command group.

COMMAND GROUPS:
  Group name: general
  Commands: status, version

  Group name: ddl
  Commands: alter, alter_async, alter_status, create,
    describe, disable, disable_all, drop, drop_all, enable,
    enable_all, exists, is_disabled, is_enabled, list, show_filters

  Group name: dml
  Commands: count, delete, deleteall, get, get_counter,
    incr, put, scan, truncate

  Group name: tools
  Commands: assign, balance_switch, balancer, close_region,
    compact, flush, hlog_roll, major_compact, move, split,
    unassign, zk_dump
```

```
Group name: replication
Commands: add_peer, disable_peer, enable_peer, list_peers,
   remove_peer, start_replication, stop_replication

Group name: security
Commands: grant, revoke, user_permission
```

```
SHELL USAGE:
Quote all names in HBase Shell such as table and column names.
   Commas delimit
command parameters.  Type <RETURN> after entering a command to run it.
Dictionaries of configuration used in the creation and
   alteration of tables are
Ruby Hashes. They look like this:

  {'key1' => 'value1', 'key2' => 'value2', ...}

and are opened and closed with curly-braces.
Key/values are delimited by the '=>' character combination.
Usually keys are predefined constants such as
NAME, VERSIONS, COMPRESSION, etc.
Constants do not need to be quoted.  Type
'Object.constants' to see a (messy) list of all constants in the environment.

If you are using binary keys or values and need
to enter them in the shell, use double-quote'd
hexadecimal representation. For example:

  hbase> get 't1', "key\x03\x3f\xcd"
  hbase> get 't1', "key\003\023\011"
  hbase> put 't1', "test\xef\xff", 'f1:', "\x01\x33\x40"

The HBase shell is the (J)Ruby IRB with the
above HBase-specific commands added.
For more on the HBase Shell, see http://hbase.apache.org/docs/current/
   book.html
```

We'll focus on the tools group of commands (shown in bold). To get a description for any command, you can run help 'command_name' in the shell like this:

```
hbase(main):003:0> help 'status'
Show cluster status. Can be 'summary', 'simple', or 'detailed'. The
default is 'summary'. Examples:

  hbase> status
  hbase> status 'simple'
  hbase> status 'summary'
  hbase> status 'detailed'
```

ZK_DUMP

You can use the zk_dump command to find out the current state of ZooKeeper:

```
hbase(main):030:0> > zk_dump
HBase is rooted at /hbase
Master address: 01.mydomain.com:60000
Region server holding ROOT: 06.mydomain.com:60020
Region servers:
 06.mydomain.com:60020
 04.mydomain.com:60020
```

```
 02.mydomain.com:60020
 05.mydomain.com:60020
 03.mydomain.com:60020
Quorum Server Statistics:
 03.mydomain.com:2181
  Zookeeper version: 3.3.4-cdh3u3--1, built on 01/26/2012 20:09 GMT
  Clients:
...
 02.mydomain.com:2181
  Zookeeper version: 3.3.4-cdh3u3--1, built on 01/26/2012 20:09 GMT
  Clients:
   ...
 01.mydomain.com:2181
  Zookeeper version: 3.3.4-cdh3u3--1, built on 01/26/2012 20:09 GMT
  Clients:
   ...
```

This tells you the current active HBase Master, the list of RegionServers that form the
cluster, the location of the -ROOT- table, and the list of servers that form the ZooKeeper
quorum. ZooKeeper is the starting point of the HBase cluster and the source of truth
when it comes to the membership in the cluster. The information spewed out by
zk_dump can come in handy while trying to debug issues about the cluster such as finding
out which server is the active Master Server or which RegionServer is hosting -ROOT-.

STATUS COMMAND

You can use the status command to determine the status of the cluster. This command has three options: simple, summary, and detailed. The default is the summary
option. We show all three here, to give you an idea of the information included with
each of them:

```
hbase(main):010:0> status 'summary'
1 servers, 0 dead, 6.0000 average load

hbase(main):007:0> status 'simple'
1 live servers
    localhost:62064 1341201439634
        requestsPerSecond=0, numberOfOnlineRegions=6,
usedHeapMB=40, maxHeapMB=987
0 dead servers
Aggregate load: 0, regions: 6

hbase(main):009:0> status 'detailed'
version 0.92.1
0 regionsInTransition
master coprocessors: []
1 live servers
    localhost:62064 1341201439634
        requestsPerSecond=0, numberOfOnlineRegions=6,
          usedHeapMB=40, maxHeapMB=987
        -ROOT-,,0
            numberOfStores=1, numberOfStorefiles=2,
     storefileUncompressedSizeMB=0,
storefileSizeMB=0, memstoreSizeMB=0,
storefileIndexSizeMB=0, readRequestsCount=48,
```

```
writeRequestsCount=1, rootIndexSizeKB=0,
totalStaticIndexSizeKB=0, totalStaticBloomSizeKB=0,
totalCompactingKVs=0, currentCompactedKVs=0,
compactionProgressPct=NaN, coprocessors=[]
        .META.,,1
            numberOfStores=1, numberOfStorefiles=1,
        storefileUncompressedSizeMB=0, storefileSizeMB=0,
memstoreSizeMB=0, storefileIndexSizeMB=0,
readRequestsCount=36, writeRequestsCount=4,
rootIndexSizeKB=0, totalStaticIndexSizeKB=0,
totalStaticBloomSizeKB=0, totalCompactingKVs=28,
currentCompactedKVs=28, compactionProgressPct=1.0,
coprocessors=[]
        table,,1339354041685.42667e4f00adacec75559f28a5270a56.
            numberOfStores=1, numberOfStorefiles=1,
        storefileUncompressedSizeMB=0, storefileSizeMB=0,
memstoreSizeMB=0, storefileIndexSizeMB=0,
readRequestsCount=0, writeRequestsCount=0,
rootIndexSizeKB=0, totalStaticIndexSizeKB=0,
totalStaticBloomSizeKB=0, totalCompactingKVs=0,
currentCompactedKVs=0, compactionProgressPct=NaN,
coprocessors=[]
        t1,,1339354920986.fba20c93114a81cc72cc447707e6b9ac.
            numberOfStores=1, numberOfStorefiles=1,
        storefileUncompressedSizeMB=0, storefileSizeMB=0,
memstoreSizeMB=0, storefileIndexSizeMB=0,
readRequestsCount=0, writeRequestsCount=0,
rootIndexSizeKB=0, totalStaticIndexSizeKB=0,
totalStaticBloomSizeKB=0, totalCompactingKVs=0,
currentCompactedKVs=0, compactionProgressPct=NaN,
coprocessors=[]
        table1,,1340070923439.f1450e26b69c010ff23e14f83edd36b9.
            numberOfStores=1, numberOfStorefiles=1,
        storefileUncompressedSizeMB=0, storefileSizeMB=0,
memstoreSizeMB=0, storefileIndexSizeMB=0,
readRequestsCount=0, writeRequestsCount=0,
rootIndexSizeKB=0, totalStaticIndexSizeKB=0,
totalStaticBloomSizeKB=0, totalCompactingKVs=0,
currentCompactedKVs=0, compactionProgressPct=NaN,
coprocessors=[]
        ycsb,,1340070872892.2171dad81bfe65e6ac6fe081a66c8dfd.
            numberOfStores=1, numberOfStorefiles=0,
        storefileUncompressedSizeMB=0, storefileSizeMB=0,
memstoreSizeMB=0, storefileIndexSizeMB=0,
readRequestsCount=0, writeRequestsCount=0,
rootIndexSizeKB=0, totalStaticIndexSizeKB=0,
totalStaticBloomSizeKB=0, totalCompactingKVs=0,
currentCompactedKVs=0, compactionProgressPct=NaN,
coprocessors=[]
0 dead servers
```

As you can see, the detailed status command gives out a bunch of information about the RegionServers and the regions they're serving. This can come in handy when you're trying to diagnose problems where you need in-depth information about the regions and the servers that are serving them.

Otherwise, the `summary` option gives you the number of live and dead servers and the average load at that point. This is mostly useful as a sanity check to see if nodes are up and not overloaded.

COMPACTIONS

Triggering compactions from the shell isn't something you'll need to do often, but the shell does give you the option to do so if you need it. You can use the shell to trigger compactions, both minor and major, using the `compact` and `major_compact` commands, respectively:

```
hbase(main):011:0> help 'compact'
Compact all regions in passed table or pass a region row to
compact an individual region
```

Trigger minor compaction on a table like this:

```
hbase(main):014:0> compact 't'
0 row(s) in 5.1540 seconds
```

Trigger minor compaction on a particular region like this:

```
hbase(main):015:0> compact
    't,,1339354041685.42667e4f00adacec75559f28a5270a56.'
0 row(s) in 0.0600 seconds
```

If you disable automatic major compactions and make it a manual process, this comes in handy; you can script the major compaction and run it as a cron job at a time that's suitable (when the load on the cluster is low).

BALANCER

The balancer is responsible for making sure all RegionServers are serving an equivalent number of regions. The current implementation of the balancer takes into consideration the number of regions per RegionServer and attempts to redistribute them if the distribution isn't even. You can run the balancer through the shell like this:

```
hbase(main):011:0> balancer
true
0 row(s) in 0.0200 seconds
```

The returned value when you run the balancer is `true` or `false`, and this pertains to whether the balancer ran.

You can turn off the balancer by using the `balance_switch` command. When you run the command, it returns `true` or `false`. The value it returns represents the state of the balancer before the command is run. To enable the balancer to run automatically, pass `true` as the argument to `balance_switch`. To disable the balancer, pass `false`. For example:

```
hbase(main):014:0> balance_switch false
true
0 row(s) in 0.0200 seconds
```

This switches off the automatic balancer. It was turned on before the command was run, as shown by the value returned.

SPLITTING TABLES OR REGIONS

The shell gives you the ability to split existing tables. Ideally, this is something you shouldn't have to do. But there are cases like region hot-spotting where you may need to manually split the region that's being hot-spotted. Region hot-spotting typically points to another problem, though—bad key design leading to suboptimal load distribution.

The split command can be given a table name, and it will split all the regions in that table; or you can specify a particular region to be split. If you specify the split key, it splits only around that key:

```
hbase(main):019:0> help 'split'
```

You can split an entire table or pass a region to split an individual region. With the second parameter, you can specify an explicit split key for the region. Here are some examples:

```
split 'tableName'
split 'regionName' # format: 'tableName,startKey,id'
split 'tableName', 'splitKey'
split 'regionName', 'splitKey'
```

The following example splits mytable around the key G:

```
hbase(main):019:0> split 'mytable' , 'G'
```

Tables can also be presplit at the time of table creation. You can do this using the shell too. We cover this later in the chapter.

ALTERING TABLE SCHEMAS

Using the shell, you can alter properties of existing tables. For instance, suppose you want to add compression to some column families or increase the number of versions. For this, you have to disable the table, make the alterations, and re-enable the table, as shown here:

```
hbase(main):019:0> disable 't'
0 row(s) in 2.0590 seconds

hbase(main):020:0> alter 't', NAME => 'f', VERSIONS => 1
Updating all regions with the new schema...
1/1 regions updated.
Done.
0 row(s) in 6.3300 seconds

hbase(main):021:0> enable 't'
0 row(s) in 2.0550 seconds
```

You can check that the table properties changed by using the describe 'tablename' command in the shell.

TRUNCATING TABLES

Truncating tables means deleting all the data but preserving the table structure. The table still exists in the system, but it's empty after the truncate command is run on it. Truncating a table in HBase involves disabling it, dropping it, and re-creating it. The truncate command does all of this for you. On large tables, truncating can take time, because all regions have to be shut down and disabled before they can be deleted:

```
hbase(main):023:0> truncate 't'
Truncating 't' table (it may take a while):
 - Disabling table...
 - Dropping table...
 - Creating table...
0 row(s) in 14.3190 seconds
```

10.3.6 Maintaining consistency—hbck

File systems come with a file-system check utility like fsck that checks for the consistency of a file system. These are typically run periodically to keep track of the state of the file system or especially to check integrity when the system is behaving abnormally. HBase comes with a similar tool called *hbck* (or *HBaseFsck*) that checks for the consistency and integrity of the HBase cluster. Hbck recently underwent an overhaul, and the resulting tool was nicknamed *uberhbck*. This uber version of hbck is available in releases 0.90.7+, 0.92.2+ and 0.94.0+. We'll describe the functionality that this tool has to offer and where you'll find it useful.[10]

> ### Read the manual!
> Depending on the release of HBase you're using, the functionality that hbck provides may differ. We recommend that you read the documentation for your release and understand what the tool provides in your environment. If you're a savvy user and want more functionality than what's present in your release but is available in later releases, you could back-port the JIRAs!

Hbck is a tool that helps in checking for inconsistencies in HBase clusters. Inconsistencies can occur at two levels:

- *Region inconsistencies*—Region consistency in HBase is defined by the fact that every region is assigned and deployed to exactly one RegionServer, and all information about the state of the region reflects that correctly. If this property is violated, the cluster is considered to be in an inconsistent state.
- *Table inconsistencies*—Table integrity in HBase is defined by the fact that every possible rowkey has exactly one region of the table that it belongs to. Violation of this property renders the HBase cluster in an inconsistent state.

Hbck performs two primary functions: detect inconsistencies and fix inconsistencies.

DETECTING INCONSISTENCIES
Detecting inconsistencies in your cluster can be done proactively using hbck. You could wait for your application to start spewing exceptions about not finding regions

---

[10] We hope you don't run into issues that make you need to run this. But as we said earlier, Murphy strikes sometimes, and you have to troubleshoot.

or not knowing what region to write a particular rowkey to, but that costs a lot more than detecting such issues before the application is impacted by them.

You can run the hbck tool to detect inconsistencies as shown here:

```
$ $HBASE_HOME/bin/hbase hbck
```

When this command runs, it gives you a list of inconsistencies it found. If all is well, it says OK. Occasionally when you run hbck, it catches inconsistencies that are transient. For instance, during a region split, it looks like more than one region is serving the same rowkey range, which hbck detects as an inconsistency. But the RegionServers know that the daughter regions should get all the requests and the parent region is on its way out, so this isn't really an inconsistency. Run hbck a few times over a few minutes to see if the inconsistency remains and isn't just an apparent one caught during a transition in the system. To get more details about the inconsistencies reported, you can run hbck with the -details flag, as shown here:

```
$ $HBASE_HOME/bin/hbase hbck -details
```

You can also run hbck on a regular basis in an automated manner to monitor the health of your cluster over time and alert you if hbck is consistently reporting inconsistencies. Running it every 10–15 minutes or so should be sufficient unless you have a lot of load on your cluster that could cause excessive splitting, compactions, and regions moving around. In this case, running it more frequently might be worth considering.

FIXING INCONSISTENCIES

If you find inconsistencies in your HBase cluster, you need to fix them as soon as possible to avoid running into further issues and unexpected behavior. Until recently, there was no automated tool that helped with this. This changed in the newer hbck versions: hbck can now fix inconsistencies in your cluster.

Warnings

- Some inconsistencies, such as incorrect assignment in .META. or regions being assigned to multiple RegionServers, can be fixed while HBase is online. Other inconsistencies, such as regions with overlapping key ranges, are trickier; we advise you not to have any workload running on HBase while fixing those.
- Fixing inconsistencies in HBase tables is like performing surgery—often, advanced surgery. You don't want to perform it unless you know what you're doing and are comfortable. Before you start operating on a production cluster, try out the tool in dev/testing environments and get comfortable with it, understand the internals and what it's doing, and talk to the developers on the mailing lists to pick their brains. The fact that you're having to fix inconsistencies points at potential bugs in HBase or maybe even a suboptimal application design that is pushing HBase to its limits in ways it isn't designed to work. Be careful!

Next, we'll explain the various types of inconsistencies and how you can use hbck to fix them:

- *Incorrect assignments*—These are due to .META. having incorrect information about regions. There are three such cases: regions are assigned to multiple RegionServers, regions are incorrectly assigned to a RegionServer but are being served by some other RegionServer; and regions exist in .META. but haven't been assigned to any RegionServer. These kind of inconsistencies can be fixed by running hbck with the -fixAssignments flag. In the older hbck versions, the -fix flag did this job.

- *Missing or extra regions*—If HDFS has regions that .META. doesn't contain entries for, or .META. contains extra entries for regions that don't exist on HDFS, it's considered to be an inconsistency. These can be fixed by running hbck with the -fixMeta flag. If HDFS doesn't contain regions that .META. thinks should exist, empty regions can be created on HDFS corresponding to the entries in .META.. You can do this using the -fixHdfsHoles flag.

The previously mentioned fixes are low risk and typically run together. To perform them together, run hbck with the -repairHoles flag. That performs all three fixes:

```
$ $HBASE_HOME/bin/hbase hbck -repairHoles
```

Inconsistencies can be more complicated than those we have covered so far and may require careful fixing:

- *Missing region metadata on HDFS*—Every region has a .regioninfo file stored in HDFS that holds metadata for the region. If that is missing and the .META. table doesn't contain an entry about the region, the -fixAssignments flag won't cut it. Adopting a region that doesn't have the .regioninfo file present can be done by running hbck with the -fixHdfsOrphans flag.

- *Overlapping regions*—This is by far the trickiest of all inconsistencies to fix. Sometimes regions can have overlapping key ranges. For instance, suppose Region 1 is serving key range A–I, and Region 2 is serving key range F–N. The key range F–I overlaps in both regions (figure 10.9).

  You can fix this by running hbck with the -fixHdfsOverlaps flag. Hbck fixes these inconsistencies by merging the two regions. If the number of regions overlapping is large and the merge will result in a big region, it could cause heavy compactions and splitting later. To avoid that, the underlying HFiles in such cases can be sidelined into a separate directory and later bulk-imported

Figure 10.9 The key ranges F–I are being served by two regions. There is an overlap in the ranges for which the regions are responsible. You can use hbck to fix this inconsistency.

into the HBase table. To limit the number of merges, use the `-maxMerge <n>` flag. If the number of regions to merge is greater than *n*, they're sidelined rather than merged. Use the `-sidelineBigOverlaps` flag to enable sidelining of regions if the maximum merge size is reached. You can limit the maximum number of regions to sideline that are sidelined in a single pass by using the `-maxOverlapsToSideline <m>` flag.

Often, if you're willing to run through all these fixes, you can use the `-repair` flag rather than specify each of the previous flags individually. You can also limit the repair to particular tables by passing the table name to the repair flag (`-repair MyTable`).

> **WARNING**   Fixing inconsistencies in HBase tables is an advanced operational task. We encourage you to read the online manual and also try running hbck on a development environment before running it on your production cluster. Also, it never hurts to read the script's code.

10.3.7   *Viewing HFiles and HLogs*

HBase provides utilities to examine the HFiles and HLogs (WAL) that are being created at write time. The HLogs are located in the .logs directory in the HBase root directory on the file system. You can examine them by using the `hlog` command of the bin/hbase script, like this:

```
$ bin/hbase hlog /hbase/.logs/regionserverhostname,60020,1340983114841/
    regionserverhostname%2C60020%2C1340983114841.1340996727020

12/07/03 15:31:59 WARN conf.Configuration: fs.default.name
is deprecated. Instead, use fs.defaultFS
12/07/03 15:32:00 INFO util.NativeCodeLoader: Loaded the
native-hadoop librarySequence 650517 from region
    a89b462b3b0943daa3017866315b729e in table users
  Action:
    row: user8257982797137456856
    column: s:field0
    at time: Fri Jun 29 12:05:27 PDT 2012
  Action:
    row: user8258088969826208944
    column: s:field0
    at time: Fri Jun 29 12:05:27 PDT 2012
  Action:
    row: user8258268146936739228
    column: s:field0
    at time: Fri Jun 29 12:05:27 PDT 2012
  Action:
    row: user825878197280400817
    column: s:field0
    at time: Fri Jun 29 12:05:27 PDT 2012
...
...
...
```

The output is a list of edits that have been recorded in that particular HLog file.

The script has a similar utility for examining the HFiles. To print the help for the command, run the command without any arguments:

```
$ bin/hbase hfile
usage: HFile [-a] [-b] [-e] [-f <arg>] [-k] [-m] [-p] [-r <arg>] [-s] [-v]
 -a,--checkfamily    Enable family check
 -b,--printblocks    Print block index meta data
 -e,--printkey       Print keys
 -f,--file <arg>     File to scan. Pass full-path; e.g.,
                     hdfs://a:9000/hbase/.META./12/34
 -k,--checkrow       Enable row order check; looks for out-of-order keys
 -m,--printmeta      Print meta data of file
 -p,--printkv        Print key/value pairs
 -r,--region <arg>   Region to scan. Pass region name; e.g., '.META.,,1'
 -s,--stats          Print statistics
 -v,--verbose        Verbose output; emits file and meta data delimiters
```

Here is an example of examining the stats of a particular HFile:

```
$ bin/hbase hfile -s -f /hbase/users/0a2485f4febcf7a13913b8b040bcacc7/s/
    633132126d7e40b68ae1c12dead82898
Stats:
Key length: count: 1504206     min: 35 max: 42 mean: 41.88885963757624
Val length: count: 1504206     min: 90 max: 90 mean: 90.0
Row size (bytes): count: 1312480   min: 133
 max: 280  mean: 160.32370931366574
Row size (columns): count: 1312480 min: 1
 max: 2  mean: 1.1460791783493844
Key of biggest row: user8257556289221384421
```

You can see that there is a lot of information about the HFile. Other options can be used to get different bits of information. The ability to examine HLogs and HFiles can be handy if you're trying to understand the behavior of the system when you run into issues.

10.3.8 Presplitting tables

Table splitting during heavy write loads can result in increased latencies. Splitting is typically followed by regions moving around to balance the cluster, which adds to the overhead. Presplitting tables is also desirable for bulk loads, which we cover later in the chapter. If the key distribution is well known, you can split the table into the desired number of regions at the time of table creation.

It's advisable to start with fewer regions. A good place to start is the low tens of regions per RegionServer. That can inform your region size, which you can configure at a system level using the `hbase.hregion.max.filesize` configuration property. If you set that number to the size you want your regions to be, HBase will split them when they get to that size. But setting that number much higher than the desired region size gives you the ability to manually manage the region size and split it before HBase splits it. That means more work for the system administrator but finer-grained control over the region sizes. Managing table splitting manually is an advanced operations concept and should be done only once you've tried it on a development cluster and are comfortable with it. If you oversplit, you'll end up with lots of small regions. If

Table: mytable

Master, Local logs, Thread Dump, Log Level

Table Attributes

Attribute Name	Value	Description
Enabled	true	Is the table enabled

Table Regions

Name	Region Server	Start Key	End Key	Requests
mytable,,1341524474547.e077d3bf4b5be0f338ccef42172098a8.	172.21.0.251:60030		A	0
mytable,A,1341524474553.683db2969f1aef777323051340dc4666.	172.21.0.251:60030	A	B	0
mytable,B,1341524474553.68e7e32bd6aacd221b2e954d82124088.	172.21.0.251:60030	B	C	0
mytable,C,1341524474553.20fef704d9e342675761d4187a7af769.	172.21.0.251:60030	C	D	0
mytable,D,1341524474553.4249f13108ecfbff05b1d0d594624a1a.	172.21.0.251:60030	D		0

Figure 10.10   The HBase Master UI showing the presplit table that was created by providing the split keys at creation time. Notice the start and end keys of the regions.

you don't split in time, HBase splitting will kick in when your regions reach the configured region size, and that will lead to major compactions taking much longer because the regions would likely be big.

The HBase shell can be used to presplit regions at the time of table creation. The way to do that is to have a list of split keys in a file, with one key per line. Here's an example:

```
$ cat ~/splitkeylist
A
B
C
D
```

To create a table with the listed keys as the split boundary, run the following command in the shell:

```
hbase(main):019:0> create 'mytable' , 'family',
{SPLITS_FILE => '~/splitkeylist'}
```

This creates a table with presplit regions. You can confirm that from your Master web UI (figure 10.10).

Another way to create a table with presplit regions is to use the `HBaseAdmin.create-Table(...)` API like this:

```
String tableName = "mytable";
String startKey = "A";
String endKey = "D";
int numOfSplits = 5;
```

```
HBaseAdmin admin = new HBaseAdmin(conf);
HTableDescriptor desc = new HTableDescriptor(tableName);
HColumnDescriptor col = new HColumnDescriptor("family");
desc.addFamily(col);
admin.createTable(desc, startKey, endKey, numOfSplits);
```

We have an implementation available for you in the provided code under the utils package. It's called TablePreSplitter.

Another implementation of creating presplit tables and even splitting them later comes packaged with HBase in the org.apache.hadoop.hbase.util.RegionSplitter class.

We've covered a lot of operations and management tasks in this section and equipped you with enough information to run your HBase cluster. Successful operations of a system also include the ability to handle failure scenarios of different kinds and to keep running with minimal degradation when disaster strikes. The next section explores the concept of backups in the context of HBase and where these are important.

10.4 Backup and replication

Backups tend to be one of the favorite topics of system administrators and the people responsible for operations of a system. In the world of Hadoop and HBase, the conversation changes a little. In traditional systems, backups were done to achieve redundancy in order to safeguard against system failures (hardware and/or software). Failures were considered to be something outside the system, affecting the normal operations of the system. For instance, if a relational database system goes down because the memory on the host fails, the system is unavailable until you replace the memory. If the hard disk crashes, chances are you'll lose part or all of your data (depending on how the hard disks are configured and how many disks are being used).

Hadoop and HBase are built with failure as a first-class concern, and their design is such that they're resilient to individual nodes failing. If a DataNode or a RegionServer host falls off the cluster, it's no problem. Other hosts will take over the workload (stored data or regions being served), and the system will continue to function normally. The entire Hadoop stack as it exists today has high availability, which means that there is no single point of failure within the system that can bring it down or make it unavailable. Individual nodes failing isn't a problem, but the entire data center hosting your cluster going down will cause the system to go down because Hadoop and HBase don't span multiple data centers as of today.[11] But if your requirement is to safeguard against that kind of failure, you need some sort of a backup strategy in place.

Another reason to have a separate copy of the data available is to do offline processing. As we recommended in chapter 9, collocating real-time and batch-processing workloads on the same HBase cluster impacts the latencies and the performance of the cluster for both the access patterns (as compared to running them independently).

---

[11] The high network latency between data centers make it impractical. The alternative is to run a replica cluster in another data center. Replicas are covered in the following subsection.

By having a second copy of data in another cluster, you can segregate the online access pattern from the batch-processing access pattern and have both of them perform optimally.

There are various ways of achieving backups or second copies of the data, and each has different properties.

10.4.1 *Inter-cluster replication*

Replication as a feature has been in an experimental state until recently, and only savvy users have used it in production. Active development and more user demand are getting the feature to a more stable state. You don't necessarily have to understand the ins and outs of how replication works, but we recommend that you have a good understanding of it if you plan to use it in production.

One way to copy data from one cluster to another is by replicating the writes as they come into the first cluster. This is a common operating mechanism for relational database systems. Inter-cluster replication in HBase is achieved by log shipping and is done asynchronously. That means the replication is done by sending the edits (`Puts` and `Deletes`) that go into the HLog at the time of writes to the secondary cluster to which they have to be replicated. The write to the first cluster doesn't block on the edits being replicated. The replication happens asynchronously after the writes are done and therefore can be done across data centers because it doesn't affect the latencies of the writes when they take place.

> ### Current state of affairs
> The instructions and descriptions of replication in this section are true for the Apache HBase 0.92.1 or the CDH4u0 releases. Given that this is a relatively new feature that hasn't seen a lot of production usage until now, there will still be active development and the addition of new features in the near term. We encourage you to look at the release notes of the release you're using and not take our description as set in stone.

You configure replication at a column-family level by setting the replication scope to 1 at table-instantiation time or by altering the table:

```
hbase(main):002:0> create 'mytable', {NAME => 'colfam1',
REPLICATION_SCOPE => '1'}
```

This configures the column family `colfam1` to replicate to the secondary cluster when data is written to it. The same table name and column family must exist on the secondary cluster. HBase won't create it if it doesn't exist, and replication will fail.

Inter-cluster replication can be of three types:

- *Master-slave*—In this method of replication, all the writes go to only one primary cluster (master) and are replicated to the secondary cluster (slave), as shown in figure 10.11. Nothing is ever written to the replicated column family in the secondary cluster directly. HBase doesn't enforce this restriction against direct writes to the replicated slave; you need to ensure this at the application level. If you by mistake end up writing to the slave cluster, that data won't be replicated back to the master cluster. The slave cluster can have other tables and column families that aren't being replicated from the master cluster.

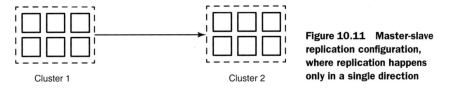

Figure 10.11 Master-slave replication configuration, where replication happens only in a single direction

- *Master-master*—In master-master replication, writes received by either cluster are replicated to the other, as shown in figure 10.12.

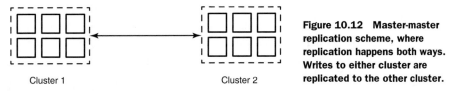

Figure 10.12 Master-master replication scheme, where replication happens both ways. Writes to either cluster are replicated to the other cluster.

- *Cyclic*—In cyclic replication, you can configure more than two clusters to replicate among themselves (see figure 10.13). The replication between any two clusters can be either in master-master mode or master-slave mode. The master-master replication scheme can be considered to be a cyclic replication with only two clusters involved.

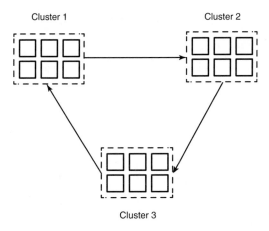

Figure 10.13 Cyclic replication scheme, where more than two clusters participate in the replication process and the relationship between any two clusters can be no replication, master-slave replication, or master-master replication

Depending on your application, you can choose which replication model will work best. If it's only for a backup purpose or for having a second copy over which to do batch processing, the master-slave model will work fine. Master-master and cyclic replication are useful in special cases where you either want a third cluster with the same data or have data coming in from different sources into different tables and the end goal is to have an identical state across both clusters.

CONFIGURING INTER-CLUSTER REPLICATION

To configure inter-cluster replication, follow these steps:

1   Put the following configuration parameter into the hbase-site.xml file of *both* clusters (the primary and the secondary):

```
<property>
  <name>hbase.replication</name>
  <value>true</value>
</property>
```

After you add this configuration on all the nodes in both clusters, you need to restart the HBase daemons (RegionServer as well as Master). Keep in mind that ZooKeeper needs to be self-managed for this to work. HBase-managed Zoo-Keeper hasn't been tested in a replication setup in HBase 0.92.1 or CDH4u0.

This setting enables the cluster to participate in the replication setup.

2   Add secondary clusters to the list of clusters where the logs will be shipped from the primary cluster. You do so using the `add_peer` command in the HBase shell. Here's the syntax:

```
add_peer '<n>',
    "slave.zookeeper.quorum:zookeeper.clientport:zookeeper.znode.parent"
```

For example:

```
hbase(main):002:0> add_peer '1',
    "secondary_cluster_zookeeper_quorum:2181:/hbase"
```

This registers the secondary cluster as the destination where the edits need to be sent for the purpose of replication.

3   Set up your tables for replication. You do so at the column-family level, as explained earlier. To enable replication on existing tables, disable them, modify the column-family description, and re-enable them. Replication will start happening immediately.

Ensure that the same table and column families exist on both clusters (the master and the destination slave cluster). Replication scope must be set to 1 only on the master cluster, though. Both clusters can have other tables and column families that aren't replicated.

After setting up replication, you should verify that it's working as desired before putting any load on the cluster.

TESTING THE REPLICATION SETUP

The easiest way to test that replication is working is to put a few rows into the table on the master cluster and check whether they exist on the Slave cluster. If the dataset is much larger, this may not be feasible, as can be the case if you enabled replication on a production cluster. HBase ships with a MapReduce job called `VerifyReplication` that you can run to compare the contents of the two tables:

```
$ $HBASE_HOME/bin/hbase
    org.apache.hadoop.hbase.mapreduce.replication.VerifyReplication
Usage: verifyrep [--starttime=X] [--stoptime=Y] [--families=A]
<peerid> <tablename>

Options:
  starttime    beginning of the time range
               without endtime means from starttime to forever
  stoptime     end of the time range
  families     comma-separated list of families to copy

Args:
  peerid       Id of the peer used for verification,
                  must match the one given for replication
  tablename    Name of the table to verify

Examples:
 To verify the data replicated from TestTable for a 1 hour window
    with peer #5
 $ bin/hbase org.apache.hadoop.hbase.mapreduce.replication.VerifyReplication
    --
     starttime=1265875194289 --stoptime=1265878794289 5 TestTable
```

But if you aren't running the MapReduce framework, that's not a choice. You'll need to manage with a manual scan of the tables on the two clusters to ensure that things are working fine.

MANAGING REPLICATION

There's not much you need to do to manage replication after it's enabled on a cluster. To stop replication in a running cluster where it's configured, you can run the `stop_replication` command in the HBase shell. To start it back up, run `start_replication`.

A few *gotchas* in the current implementation make some management tasks tricky. Replication is handled at the column-family level and is configured in the active HLog file. Thus if you stop replication and then start it again, and the HLogs haven't rolled, everything that was written between the time you stopped and restarted replication will also be replicated. This is a function of the current implementation of replication, and it may change in future releases.

To remove a peer cluster, you can use the `remove_peer` command with the peer ID:

```
hbase> remove_peer '1'
```

To see a list of the currently configured peers, you can use the `list_peers` command:

```
hbase> list_peers
```

Inter-cluster replication is an advanced feature and can make it easy to keep multiple copies of data. It's great for maintaining two hot copies of the data: your application can switch to the secondary cluster in case something goes wrong with the primary

> ### A note about time synchronization
>
> For replication to work properly, the time on the primary and secondary clusters needs to be in sync. As we described earlier, this can be achieved using NTP. Keeping time synchronized across all nodes running HBase is important in ensuring that the system operates reliably.

one. The hot-failover mechanism is something you need to build into your application. This can be done purely in the application logic, or you can use DNS tricks to get the application to talk to the secondary cluster if the primary one goes down. When the primary cluster is back up and running, you can use the same DNS trick and flip back to the primary cluster.

The issue now is to get the newly written data from the secondary cluster back to the primary one. This can be accomplished using the `CopyTable` or `Export/Import` job, which is what we talk about next.

10.4.2 *Backup using MapReduce jobs*

MapReduce jobs can be configured to use HBase tables as the source and sink, as we covered in chapter 3. This ability can come in handy to do point-in-time backups of tables by scanning through them and outputting the data into flat files or other HBase tables.

This is different from inter-cluster replication, which the last section described. Inter-cluster replication is a *push* mechanism: new edits are pushed to the replica cluster as they come in, albeit asynchronously. Running MapReduce jobs over tables is a *pull* mechanism: jobs are read from the HBase tables (that is, data is pulled out) and written to a sink of your choice.

There are a couple of ways you can use MapReduce over HBase for backups. HBase ships with prebundled jobs for this purpose, as we explain in detail in appendix B. We'll explain how you can use them for backups here.

EXPORT/IMPORT

The prebundled `Export` MapReduce job can be used to export data from HBase tables into flat files. That data can then later be imported into another HBase table on the same or a different cluster using the `Import` job.

The `Export` job takes the source table name and the output directory name as inputs. You can also give it the number of versions, start timestamp, end timestamp, and filters to have finer-grained control over what data it reads from the source table. Using the start and end timestamps can come in handy in doing incremental reads from the tables.

The data is written out efficiently in Hadoop SequenceFiles in the specified output directory, which can later be imported into another HBase table using the `Import` job. The SequenceFiles are keyed from rowkey to `Result` instances:

```
$ hbase org.apache.hadoop.hbase.mapreduce.Export
Usage: Export [-D<property=value>]* <tablename> <outputdir>
              [<versions> [<starttime> [<endtime>]]
                 [^[regex pattern] or [Prefix] to filter]]

  Note: -D properties will be applied to the conf used.
  For example:
   -Dmapred.output.compress=true
   -Dmapred.output.compression.codec=org.apache.hadoop.io.compress.GzipCodec
   -Dmapred.output.compression.type=BLOCK
  Additionally, the following SCAN properties can be specified
  to control/limit what is exported..
   -Dhbase.mapreduce.scan.column.family=<familyName>
```

Here's an example command to export table `mytable` to the directory export_out:

```
$ hbase org.apache.hadoop.hbase.mapreduce.Export mytable export_out
12/07/10 04:21:29 INFO mapred.JobClient: Default number of map tasks: null
12/07/10 04:21:29 INFO mapred.JobClient: Setting default number of map tasks
    based on cluster size to : 12
...
...
```

Let's examine the contents of the export_out directory. It should contain a bunch of output files from the map tasks:

```
$ hadoop fs -ls export_out
Found 132 items
-rw-r--r--   2 hadoop supergroup         0 2012-07-10 04:39 /user/hadoop/
    export_out/_SUCCESS
-rw-r--r--   2 hadoop supergroup 441328058 2012-07-10 04:21 /user/hadoop/
    export_out/part-m-00000
-rw-r--r--   2 hadoop supergroup 470805179 2012-07-10 04:22 /user/hadoop/
    export_out/part-m-00001
...
...
-rw-r--r--   2 hadoop supergroup 536946759 2012-07-10 04:27 /user/hadoop/
    export_out/part-m-00130
```

The `Import` job is the inverse of the `Export` job. It reads over the records in the source files, creating `Put` instances from the persisted `Result` instances. It then writes those `Put`s to the target table through the HTable API. `Import` doesn't provide any fancy filtering or manipulation of the data along the way. If you want to perform additional manipulation, you'll need to subclass its `Importer` implementation and override the map function. A simple tool has a simple invocation:

```
$ hbase org.apache.hadoop.hbase.mapreduce.Import
Usage: Import <tablename> <inputdir>
```

The command to import the table exported in the earlier example into another table named `myimporttable` is as follows:

```
$ hbase org.apache.hadoop.hbase.mapreduce.Import myimporttable export_out
```

Upon job completion, your target table contains the exported data.

ADVANCED IMPORT WITH IMPORTTSV

Although `Import` is a simple complement to `Export`, `ImportTsv` is more feature-rich. It allows you to load data from newline-terminated, delimited text files. Most commonly, this is a tab-separated format, but the delimiter is configurable (for loading comma-separated files). You specify a destination table and provide it with a mapping from columns in your data file(s) to columns in HBase:

```
$ hbase org.apache.hadoop.hbase.mapreduce.ImportTsv
Usage: importtsv -Dimporttsv.columns=a,b,c <tablename> <inputdir>

Imports the given input directory of TSV data into the specified table.

The column names of the TSV data must be specified using the
-Dimporttsv.columns option. This option takes the form of
comma-separated column names, where each column name is either a
simple column family, or a columnfamily:qualifier. The special column
name HBASE_ROW_KEY is used to designate that this column should be
used as the row key for each imported record. You must specify exactly
one column to be the row key, and you must specify a column name for
every column that exists in the input data.

By default importtsv will load data directly into HBase. To instead
generate HFiles of data to prepare for a bulk data load, pass the
option:
  -Dimporttsv.bulk.output=/path/for/output
  Note: if you do not use this option, then the target table must
already exist in HBase

Other options that may be specified with -D include:
  -Dimporttsv.skip.bad.lines=false - fail if encountering an invalid
  line '-Dimporttsv.separator=|' - eg separate on pipes instead of
  tabs
  -Dimporttsv.timestamp=currentTimeAsLong - use the specified
  timestamp for the import
  -Dimporttsv.mapper.class=my.Mapper - A user-defined Mapper to use
 instead of org.apache.hadoop.hbase.mapreduce.TsvImporterMapper
```

It's intended to be a flexible utility, allowing you even to override the `Mapper` class, which is used when parsing input files. You can also have `ImportTsv` create HFiles instead of executing `Put`s against the target deployment. This is called *bulk import*. It bypasses the HTable API, making it faster than the regular import. It does have a run-time requirement of access to the target table. `ImportTsv` inspects that table's region boundaries and uses those split delimiters to decide how many HFiles to create.

Once the HFiles are created, they have to be loaded into the table. The `LoadIncrementalHFiles` utility, also called `completebulkload`, handles the messy business of installing and activating new HFiles in a table in HBase. The operation is messy because careful consideration must be given to ensure that the new HFiles match the destination table's configuration. `LoadIncrementalHFiles` handles this for you by splitting any of the source HFiles so they each fit within the key-range of a single region. The HFiles are *moved* into place, not copied, so don't be surprised when your source data disappears after you run this command. With your HFiles staged on the HDFS, run the tool like this:

```
$ hbase org.apache.hadoop.hbase.mapreduce.LoadIncrementalHFiles
usage: completebulkload /path/to/hfileoutputformat-output tablename
```

Let's create a presplit table and bulk-load a tab-separated file into it:

1 Create a presplit table with 10 splits:

```
$ for i in {1..10}; do echo $i >> splits.txt ; done
$ cat splits.txt
1
2
3
4
5
6
7
8
9
10
$ hadoop fs -put splits.txt ./
$ echo "create 'bulk_import', 'a', {SPLITS_FILE => 'splits.txt'}" | \
hbase shell
0 row(s) in 2.3710 seconds
```

2 Import a tab-separated file into the table. You'll use the third column in the file as the rowkey for the HBase table. The input tab-separated file is my_input_file, and the HFiles created will be stored in the output path hfile_output:

```
$ hbase org.apache.hadoop.hbase.mapreduce.ImportTsv \
    -
    Dimporttsv.columns=a:lon,a:lat,HBASE_ROW_KEY,a:name,a:address,a:ci
    ty,a:url \
  -Dimporttsv.bulk.output=hfile_output bulk_import ./my_input_file
12/07/10 05:48:53 INFO util.NativeCodeLoader: Loaded the native-hadoop
    library
...
...
```

3 Complete the bulk load by moving the newly created HFiles into the presplit table:

```
$ hbase org.apache.hadoop.hbase.mapreduce.LoadIncrementalHFiles
  hfile_output my_bulk_import_table
```

COPYTABLE

You can use the CopyTable MapReduce job to scan through an HBase table and directly write to another table. It doesn't create flat files of any sort. The Puts are done directly into the sink table. The sink of the CopyTable job can be another table on the same cluster or a table on an entirely different cluster. The job can also be given start and end timestamps like the Export job, which allows finer-grained control over the data being read. It also supports scenarios where source and destination HBase deployments differ—that is, with different RegionServer implementations.

Executing `CopyTable` involves running a MapReduce job on the source deployment and populating the destination deployment. Invocation looks like this:

```
$ hbase org.apache.hadoop.hbase.mapreduce.CopyTable
Usage: CopyTable [--rs.class=CLASS] [--rs.impl=IMPL] [--starttime=X]
                 [--endtime=Y] [--new.name=NEW] [--peer.adr=ADR]
                 <tablename>

Options:
 rs.class     hbase.regionserver.class of the peer cluster
              specify if different from current cluster
 rs.impl      hbase.regionserver.impl of the peer cluster
 starttime    beginning of the time range
              without endtime means from starttime to forever
 endtime      end of the time range
 new.name     new table's name
 peer.adr     Address of the peer cluster given in the format
              zookeeer.quorum:zookeeper.client.port:zookeeper.znode.parent
 families     comma-separated list of families to copy
              To copy from cf1 to cf2, give sourceCfName:destCfName.
              To keep the same name, just give "cfName"

Args:
 tablename    Name of the table to copy
```

Here is an example command for copying table `mytable` from a cluster to a remote cluster where a table with the same name exists:

```
$ hbase org.apache.hadoop.hbase.mapreduce.CopyTable \
--peer.adr=destination-zk:2181:/hbase --families=a mytable
```

10.4.3 Backing up the root directory

HBase stores its data in the directory specified by the `hbase.rootdir` configuration property. This directory contains all the region information, all the HFiles for the tables, as well as the WALs for all RegionServers. In essence, this is where everything is persisted. But copying over this directory (using `distcp`) doesn't make for a great backup solution, especially in a running system.

When an HBase cluster is up and running, several things are going on: MemStore flushes, region splits, compactions, and so on. All of these cause changes in the underlying stored data, which makes copying the HBase root directory a futile effort. Another factor that plays in is the fact that in a running system, there is data in the MemStore that hasn't been flushed. Even if nothing else is going on, a copy of the HBase root directory doesn't necessarily completely represent the current state of the system.

But if you stop the HBase daemons cleanly, the MemStore is flushed and the root directory isn't altered by any process. At this moment, copying over the entire root directory could be a good point-in-time backup solution. But incremental backups still present challenges, which make this solution less viable. Restoring from the backed-up root directory is as simple as starting HBase when it's pointing to this new root directory.

10.5 *Summary*

Production-quality operations of any software system are learned over time. This chapter covered several aspects of operating HBase in production with the intention of getting you started on the path to understanding the concepts. New tools and scripts probably will be developed by HBase users and will benefit you. These basic concepts of HBase operations will enable you to understand when, where, and how to use them to your advantage.

The first aspect of operations is instrumenting and monitoring the system, and that's where we began this chapter. We covered the various monitoring systems and mechanisms and then went into the different metrics that are of interest. There are general metrics that you should monitor regardless of the workload being put on the system, and then there are metrics that are specific to the workload (read or write).

From monitoring, the chapter transitioned into talking about performance testing, measuring performance, and tuning HBase for different kinds of workloads. Performance testing is key to understanding how the cluster is tuned and what you can do to extract better performance from the cluster. Tuning HBase involves working with multiple different configuration parameters, and configurations depend on the kind of workload for which you're planning to use your cluster.

From there we covered a list of common management tasks and how and when to do them. Some of them are common tasks that you perform more often than others, which are more specific to certain situations. The chapter concluded with backup and replication strategies, talking about the common approaches to disaster recovery and what your options are currently.

Mastering HBase operations requires an understanding of the internals and experience gained by working with the system. As much as we'd wish for HBase to be a self-tuning and self-managing system, it isn't there yet. We hope it gets there soon, and your experience could certainly feed into that goal.

appendix A
Exploring the HBase system

Over the course of the book, you've learned a bit of theory about how HBase is designed and how it distributes the load across different servers. Let's poke around the system a little and get familiar with how these things work in practice. First, we'll look at what ZooKeeper says about your HBase instance. When running HBase in standalone mode, ZooKeeper runs in the same JVM as the HBase Master. In chapter 9, you learned about fully distributed deployments, where ZooKeeper runs as a separate service. For now, let's examine the commands and see what ZooKeeper has to tell you about your deployment.

A.1 *Exploring ZooKeeper*

Your main interface to interact directly with ZooKeeper is through the HBase shell. Launch the shell, and issue the zk_dump command.

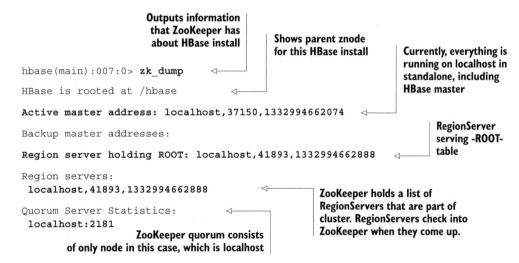

```
Zookeeper version: 3.4.3-1240972, built on 02/06/2012 10:48 GMT
Clients:
  ...
```

Let's look at a zk_dump from a fully distributed HBase instance. We've included the output from a running cluster and masked the server names. The portions in bold are analogous to the things we mentioned:

```
hbase(main):030:0> > zk_dump
HBase is rooted at /hbase
Master address: 01.mydomain.com:60000
Region server holding ROOT: 06.mydomain.com:60020
Region servers:
 06.mydomain.com:60020
 04.mydomain.com:60020
 02.mydomain.com:60020
 05.mydomain.com:60020
 03.mydomain.com:60020
Quorum Server Statistics:
 03.mydomain.com:2181
   Zookeeper version: 3.3.4-cdh3u3--1, built on 01/26/2012 20:09 GMT
   Clients:
     ...
 02.mydomain.com:2181
   Zookeeper version: 3.3.4-cdh3u3--1, built on 01/26/2012 20:09 GMT
   Clients:
     ...
 01.mydomain.com:2181
   Zookeeper version: 3.3.4-cdh3u3--1, built on 01/26/2012 20:09 GMT
   Clients:
     ...
```

If you have access to one, run the command on the shell and see what it tells you about the system. This is useful information when you're trying to understand the state of the system—what hosts are participating in the cluster, which host is playing what role, and, most important, which host is serving the -ROOT- table. The HBase client needs all this information to perform reads and writes on your application's behalf. Note that your application code isn't involved in this process; the client library handles all of this for you.

The client automatically handles communicating with ZooKeeper and finding the relevant RegionServer with which to interact. Let's still examine the -ROOT- and .META. tables to get a better understanding of what information they contain and how the client uses that information.

A.2   *Exploring -ROOT-*

Let's look at our standalone instance we've used so far for TwitBase. Here's -ROOT- for the standalone instance:

```
hbase(main):030:0> scan '-ROOT-'

 ROW            COLUMN+CELL

 .META.,,       column=info:regioninfo, timestamp=1335465653682,
 1              value={NAME => '.META.,,1', STARTKEY => '', ENDKEY
                => '', ENCODED => 1028785192,}

 .META.,,       column=info:server, timestamp=1335465662307,
 1              value=localhost:58269

 .META.,,       column=info:serverstartcode,
 1              timestamp=1335465662307, value=1335465653436

 .META.,,       column=info:v, timestamp=1335465653682,
 1              value=\x00\x00

1 row(s) in 5.4620 seconds
```

Let's examine the contents of the -ROOT- table. The -ROOT- table stores information about the .META. table. It's the first place a client application looks when it needs to locate data stored in HBase. In this example, there is only one row in -ROOT-, and it corresponds to the entire .META. table. Just like a user-defined table, .META. will split once it has more data to hold than can go into a single region. The difference between a user-defined table and .META. is that .META. stores information about the regions in HBase, which means it's managed entirely by the system. In the current example, a single region in .META. can hold everything. The corresponding entry in -ROOT- has the rowkey defined by the table name and the start key for that region. Because there is only one region, the start key and end key for that region are empty. This indicates the entire key range is hosted by that region.

A.3 Exploring .META.

The previous entry in the -ROOT- table also tells you which server the .META. region is hosted on. In this case, because it's a standalone instance and everything is on local-host, that column contains the value localhost:port. There is also a column for regioninfo that contains the name of the region, start key, end key, and encoded name. (The encoded name is used internally in the system and isn't of any consequence to you.) The HBase client library uses all this information to locate the correct region to talk to while performing the operations in your application code. When no other table exists in the system, .META. looks like the following:

```
hbase(main):030:0> scan '.META.'
ROW                COLUMN+CELL
0 row(s) in 5.4180 seconds
```

Notice that there are no entries in the .META. table. This is because there are no user-defined tables in this HBase instance. On instantiating the users table, .META. looks like the following:

```
hbase(main):030:0> scan '.META.'
```

```
ROW                             COLUMN+CELL

users,,1335466383956.4a1        column=info:regioninfo,
5eba38d58db711e1c7693581        timestamp=1335466384006, value={NAME =>
af7f1.                          'users,,1335466383956.4a15eba38d58
                                db711e1c7693581af7f1.', STARTKEY => '',
                                ENDKEY => '', ENCODED =>
                                4a15eba38d58db711e1c7693581af7f1,}

users,,1335466383956.4a1        column=info:server, timestamp=1335466384045,
5eba38d58db711e1c7693581        value=localhost:58269
af7f1.

users,,1335466383956.4a1        column=info:serverstartcode,
5eba38d58db711e1c7693581        timestamp=1335466384045, value=1335465653436
af7f1.
```

1 row(s) in 0.4540 seconds

In your current setup, that's probably what it looks like. If you want to play around a bit, you can disable and delete the users table, examine .META., and re-create and repopulate the users table. Disabling and deletion can be done in the HBase shell just like creating a table.

Similar to what you saw in -ROOT-, .META. contains information about the users table and other tables in your system. Information for all the tables you instantiate goes here. The structure of .META. is similar to that of -ROOT-.

Once you've examined the .META. table after instantiating the TwitBase users table, populate some users into the system using the LoadUsers command provided in the sample application code. When the users table outgrows a single region, that region will split. You can also split the table manually for experimentation right now:

```
hbase(main):030:0> split 'users'
0 row(s) in 6.1650 seconds
```

```
hbase(main):030:0> scan '.META.'
```

```
ROW                             COLUMN+CELL

users,,1335466383956.4a15eba    column=info:regioninfo,
38d58db711e1c7693581af7f1.      timestamp=1335466889942, value={NAME =>
                                'users,,1335466383956.4a15eba38d58db711e
                                1c7693581af7f1.', STARTKEY => '', ENDKEY
                                => '', ENCODED =>
                                4a15eba38d58db711e1c7693581af7f1,
                                OFFLINE => true, SPLIT => true,}

users,,1335466383956.4a15eba    column=info:server,
38d58db711e1c7693581af7f1.      timestamp=1335466384045,
                                value=localhost:58269
```

users,,1335466383956.4a15eba 38d58db711e1c7693581af7f1.	column=info:serverstartcode, timestamp=1335466384045, value=1335465653436
users,,1335466383956.4a15eba 38d58db711e1c7693581af7f1.	column=info:splitA, timestamp=1335466889942, value= {NAME => 'users,,1335466889926.9fd558ed44a63f016 c0a99c4cf141eb5.', STARTKEY => '', ENDKEY => '}7\ x8E\xC3\xD1\xE3\x0F\x0D\xE9\xFE'fIK\xB7\ xD6', ENCODED => 9fd558ed44a63f016c0a99c4cf141eb5,}
users,,1335466383956.4a15eba 38d58db711e1c7693581af7f1.	column=info:splitB, timestamp=1335466889942, value={NAME => 'users,}7\x8E\xC3\xD1\xE3\x0F\ x0D\xE9\xFE'fIK\xB7\xD6,1335466889926.a3 c3a9162eeeb8abc0358e9e31b892e6.', STARTKEY => '}7\x8E\ xC3\xD1\xE3\x0F\x0D\xE9\xFE'fIK\xB7\xD6' , ENDKEY => '', ENCODED => a3c3a9162eeeb8abc0358 e9e31b892e6,}
users,,1335466889926.9fd558e d44a63f016c0a99c4cf141eb5.	column=info:regioninfo, timestamp=1335466889968, value={NAME => 'users,,1335466889926.9fd558ed44a63f016c 0a99c4cf141eb5.', STARTKEY => '', ENDKEY => '}7\x8E\xC3\ xD1\xE3\x0F\x0D\xE9\xFE'fIK\xB7\xD6', ENCODED => 9fd558ed44a63f016c0a99c4cf141eb5,}
users,,1335466889926.9fd558e d44a63f016c0a99c4cf141eb5.	column=info:server, timestamp=1335466889968, value=localhost:58269
users,,1335466889926.9fd558e d44a63f016c0a99c4cf141eb5.	column=info:serverstartcode, timestamp=1335466889968, value=1335465653436
users,}7\x8E\xC3\xD1\xE3\x0F \x0D\xE9\xFE'fIK\xB7\xD6,133 5466889926.a3c3a9162eeeb8abc 0358e9e31b892e6.	column=info:regioninfo, timestamp=1335466889966, value={NAME => 'users,}7\x8E\xC3\xD1\xE3\x0F\x0D\xE9\xF E'fIK\xB7\xD6,1335466889926.a3c3a9162eee b8abc0358e9e31b892e6.', STARTKEY => '}7\x8E\xC3\xD1\xE3\x0F\ x0D\xE9\xFE'fIK\xB7\xD6', ENDKEY => '', ENCODED => a3c3a9162eeeb8abc0358e9e31b892e6,}

```
users,}7\x8E\xC3\xD1\xE3\x0F      column=info:server,
\x0D\xE9\xFE'fIK\xB7\xD6,133      timestamp=1335466889966,
5466889926.a3c3a9162eeeb8abc     value=localhost:58269
0358e9e31b892e6.

users,}7\x8E\xC3\xD1\xE3\x0F      column=info:serverstartcode,
\x0D\xE9\xFE'fIK\xB7\xD6,133      timestamp=1335466889966,
5466889926.a3c3a9162eeeb8abc     value=1335465653436
0358e9e31b892e6.
```

3 row(s) in 0.5660 seconds

After you split users, new entries are made in the .META. table for the daughter regions. These daughter regions replace the parent region that was split. The entry for the parent region contains the information about the splits, and requests are no longer served by the parent region. For a brief time, the information for the parent region remains in .META. Once the hosting RegionServer has completed the split and cleaned up the parent region, the entry is deleted from .META.. After the split is complete, .META. looks like this:

```
hbase(main):030:0> scan '.META.'

ROW                              COLUMN+CELL

users,,1335466889926.9fd558e     column=info:regioninfo,
d44a63f016c0a99c4cf141eb5.       timestamp=1335466889968, value={NAME =>
                                 'users,,1335466889926.9fd558ed44a63f016c
                                 0a99c4cf141eb5.', STARTKEY => '', ENDKEY
                                 => '}7\x8E\xC3\
                                 xD1\xE3\x0F\x0D\xE9\xFE'fIK\xB7\xD6',
                                 ENCODED =>
                                 9fd558ed44a63f016c0a99c4cf141eb5,}

users,,1335466889926.9fd558e     column=info:server,
d44a63f016c0a99c4cf141eb5.       timestamp=1335466889968,
                                 value=localhost:58269

users,,1335466889926.9fd558e     column=info:serverstartcode,
d44a63f016c0a99c4cf141eb5.       timestamp=1335466889968,
                                 value=1335465653436

users,}7\x8E\xC3\xD1\xE3\x0F     column=info:regioninfo,
\x0D\xE9\xFE'fIK\xB7\xD6,133     timestamp=1335466889966, value={NAME =>
5466889926.a3c3a9162eeeb8abc    'users,}7\x8E\xC3\xD1\xE3\x0F\x0D\xE9\xF
0358e9e31b892e6.                E'fIK\xB7\xD6,1335466889926.a3c3a9162eee
                                b8abc0358e9e31b892e6.', STARTKEY =>
                                '}7\x8E\xC3\xD1\xE3\
                                x0F\x0D\xE9\xFE'fIK\xB7\xD6', ENDKEY =>
                                '', ENCODED =>
                                a3c3a9162eeeb8abc0358e9e31b892e6,}
```

```
users,}7\x8E\xC3\xD1\xE3\x0F    column=info:server,
\x0D\xE9\xFE'fIK\xB7\xD6,133    timestamp=1335466889966,
5466889926.a3c3a9162eeeb8abc   value=localhost:58269
0358e9e31b892e6

users,}7\x8E\xC3\xD1\xE3\x0F    column=info:serverstartcode,
\x0D\xE9\xFE'fIK\xB7\xD6,133    timestamp=1335466889966,
5466889926.a3c3a9162eeeb8abc   value=1335465653436
0358e9e31b892e6.
```

2 row(s) in 0.4890 seconds

You may wonder why the start and end keys contain such long, funny values that don't look anything like the entries you put in. This is because the values you see are byte-encoded versions of the strings you entered.

Let's tie this back to how the client application interacts with an HBase instance. The client application does a get(), put(), or scan(). To perform any of these operations, the HBase client library that you're using has to find the correct region(s) that will serve these requests. It starts with ZooKeeper, from which it finds the location of -ROOT-. It contacts the server serving -ROOT- and reads the relevant records from the table that point to the .META. region that contains information about the particular region of the table that it has to finally interact with. Once the client library gets the server location and the name of the region, it contacts the RegionServer with the region information and asks it to serve the requests.

These are the various steps at play that allow HBase to distribute data across a cluster of machines and find the relevant portion of the system that serves the requests for any given client.

appendix B
More about the
workings of HDFS

Hadoop Distributed File System (HDFS) is the underlying distributed file system that is the most common choice for running HBase. Many HBase features depend on the semantics of the HDFS to function properly. For this reason, it's important to understand a little about how the HDFS works. In order to understand the inner working of HDFS, you first need to understand what a distributed file system is. Ordinarily, the concepts at play in the inner workings of a distributed file system can consume an entire semester's work for a graduate class. But in the context of this appendix, we'll briefly introduce the concept and then discuss the details you need to know about HDFS.

B.1   Distributed file systems

Traditionally, an individual computer could handle the amount of data that people wanted to store and process in the context of a given application. The computer might have multiple disks, and that sufficed for the most part—until the recent explosion of data. With more data to store and process than a single computer could handle, we somehow needed to combine the power of multiple computers to solve these new storage and compute problems. Such systems in which a network of computers (also sometimes referred to as a *cluster*) work together as a single system to solve a certain problem are called *distributed systems*. As the name suggests, the work is distributed across the participating computers.

Distributed file systems are a subset of distributed systems. The problem they solve is data storage. In other words, they're storage systems that span multiple computers.

TIP The data stored in these file systems is spread across the different nodes automatically: you don't have to worry about manually deciding which node to put what data on. If you're curious to know more about the placement strategy of HDFS, the best way to learn is to dive into the HDFS code.

Distributed file systems provide the scale required to store and process the vast amount of data that is being generated on the web and elsewhere. Providing such scale is challenging because the number of moving parts causes more susceptibility to failure. In large distributed systems, failure is a norm, and that must be taken into account while designing the systems.

In the sections that follow, we'll examine the challenges of designing a distributed file system and how HDFS addresses them. Specifically, you'll learn how HDFS achieves scale by separating metadata and the contents of files. Then, we'll explain the consistency model of HDFS by going into details of the HDFS read and write paths, followed by a discussion of how HDFS handles various failure scenarios. We'll then wrap up by examining how files are split and stored across multiple nodes that make up HDFS.

Let's get started with HDFS's primary components—NameNode and DataNode—and learn how scalability is achieved by separating metadata and data.

B.2 *Separating metadata and data: NameNode and DataNode*

Every file that you want to store on a file system has metadata attached to it. For instance, the logs coming in from your web servers are all individual files. The metadata includes things like filename, inode number, block location, and so on; the data is the actual content of the file.

In traditional file systems, metadata and data are stored together on the same machine because the file systems never span beyond that. When a client wants to perform any operation on the file and it needs the metadata, it interacts with that single machine and gives it the instructions to perform the operation. Everything happens at a single point. For instance, suppose you have a file Web01.log stored on the disk mounted at /mydisk on your *nix system. To access this file, the client application only needs to talk to the particular disk (through the operating system, of course) to get the metadata as well as the contents of the file. The only way this model can work with data that's more than a single system can handle is to make the client aware of how you distribute the data among the different disks, which makes the client stateful and difficult to maintain.

Stateful clients are even more complicated to manage as the number grows, because they have to share the state information with each other. For instance, one client may write a file on one machine. The other client needs the file location in order to access the file later, and has to get the information from the first client. As you can see, this can quickly become unwieldy in large systems and is hard to scale.

In order to build a distributed file system where the clients remain simple and ignorant of each other's activities, the metadata needs to be maintained outside of the clients. The easiest way to do this is to have the file system itself manage the metadata. But storing both metadata and data together at a single location doesn't work either, as we discussed earlier. One way to solve this is to dedicate one or more machines to hold the metadata and have the rest of the machines store the file contents. HDFS's design is based on this concept. It has two components: NameNode and DataNode. The metadata is stored in the NameNode. The data, on the other hand, is stored on a cluster of DataNodes. The NameNode not only manages the metadata for the content stored in HDFS but also keeps account of things like which nodes are part of the cluster and how many copies of a particular file exist. It also decides what needs to be done when nodes fall out of the cluster and replicas are lost.

This is the first time we've mentioned the word *replica*. We'll talk about it in detail later—for now, all you need to know is that every piece of data stored in HDFS has multiple copies residing on different servers. The NameNode essentially is the HDFS Master, and the DataNodes are the Slaves.

B.3   HDFS write path

Let's go back to the example with Web01.log stored on the disk mounted at /mydisk. Suppose you have a large distributed file system at your disposal, and you want to store that file on it. It's hard to justify the cost of all those machines otherwise, isn't it? To store data in HDFS, you have various options. The underlying operations that happen when you write data are the same regardless of what interface you use to write the data (Java API, Hadoop command-line client, and so on).

> **NOTE**   If you're like us and want to play with the system as you learn about the concepts, we encourage you to do so. But it's not required for this section, and you don't need to do so to understand the concepts.

Let's say you're using the Hadoop command-line client and you want to copy a file Web01.log to HDFS. You write the following command:

```
$ hadoop fs -copyFromLocal /home/me/Web01.log /MyFirstDirectory/
```

It's important that you understand what happens when you write this command. We'll go over the write process step by step while referring to figures B.1–B.4. Just to remind you, the client is simple and doesn't know anything about the internals of HDFS and how the data is distributed.

The client does, however, know from the configuration files which node is the NameNode. It sends a request to the NameNode saying that it wants to write a file Web01.log to HDFS (figure B.1). As you know, the NameNode is responsible for managing the metadata about everything stored in HDFS. The NameNode acknowledges the client's request and internally makes a note about the filename and a set of DataNodes that will store the file. It stores this information in a file-allocation table in its memory.

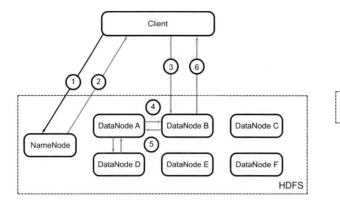

Client -> NameNode: "I want to write file
Web01.log."

**Figure B.1   Write operation:
client's communication with
the NameNode**

It then sends this information back to the client (figure B.2). The client is now aware
of the DataNodes to which it has to send the contents of Web01.log.

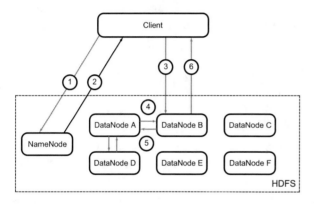

NameNode -> Client: "Absolutely, let's get
you started. You can write to DataNodes A, B,
and D. B will be the DataNode you should
contact directly."

**Figure B.2   Write operation: Name-
Node acknowledges the write operation and sends back a DataNode list**

The next step for it is to send the contents over to the DataNodes (figure B.3). The
primary DataNode streams the contents of the file synchronously to other DataNodes
that will hold the replicas of this particular file. Once all the DataNodes that have to

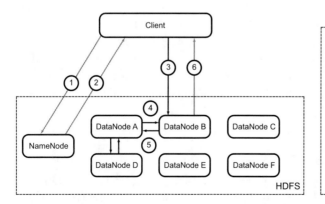

Client -> DataNode B: "Here is the content
of Web01.log. Please keep a copy and
send a copy each to DataNode A and D."

DataNode B -> DataNode A: "Here's file
Web01.log. Please keep a copy and send
a copy to DataNode D."

DataNode A -> DataNode D: "Here's file
Web01.log. Please keep a copy of it with
you."

DataNode D -> DataNode A: "Ack."

DataNode A -> DataNode B: "Ack."

Figure B.3   Write operation: client sends the file contents to the DataNodes

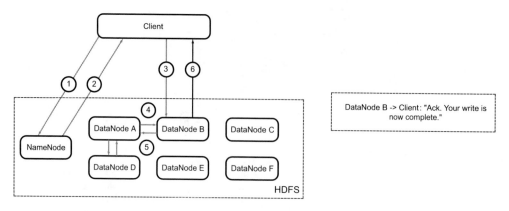

Figure B.4   Write operation: DataNode acknowledges completion of the write operation

hold replicas of the file have the contents in memory, they send an acknowledgement to the DataNode that the client connected to. The data is persisted onto disk asynchronously later. We'll cover the topic of replication in detail later in the appendix.

The primary DataNode sends a confirmation to the client that the file has been written to HDFS (figure B.4). At the end of this process, the file is considered written to HDFS and the write operation is complete.

Note that the file is still in the DataNodes' main memory and hasn't yet been persisted to disk. This is done for performance reasons: committing all replicas to disk would increase the time taken to complete a write operation. Once the data goes into the main memory, the DataNode persists it to disk as soon as it can. The write operation doesn't block on it.

In distributed file systems, one of the challenges is *consistency*. In other words, how do you make sure the view of the data residing on the system is consistent across all nodes? Because all nodes store data independently and don't typically communicate with each other, there has to be a way to make sure all nodes contain the same data. For example, when a client wants to read file Web01.log, it should be able to read exactly the same data from all the DataNodes. Looking back at the write path, notice that the data isn't considered written unless all DataNodes that will hold that data have acknowledged that they have a copy of it. This means all the DataNodes that are supposed to hold replicas of a given set of data have exactly the same contents before the write completes—in other words, consistency is accomplished during the write phase. A client attempting to read the data will get the same bytes back from whichever DataNode it chooses to read from.

B.4   HDFS read path

Now you know how a file is written into HDFS. It would be strange to have a system in which you could write all you want but not read anything back. Fortunately, HDFS isn't one of those. Reading a file from HDFS is as easy as writing a file. Let's see how the file you wrote earlier is read back when you want to see its contents.

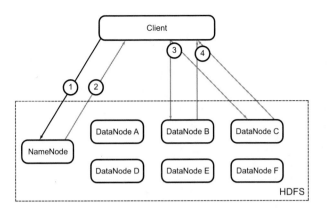

Client -> NameNode: "I want to read file Web01.log."

Figure B.5 Read operation: client's communication with the NameNode

Once again, the underlying process that takes place while reading a file is independent of the interface used. If you're using the command-line client, you write the following command to copy the file to your local file system so you can use your favorite editor to open it:

```
$ hadoop fs –copyToLocal /MyFirstDirectory/Web01.log /home/me/
```

Let's look at what happens when you run this command. The client asks the Name-Node where it should read the file from (figure B.5).

The NameNode sends back block information to the client (figure B.6).

The block information contains the IP addresses of the DataNodes that have copies of the file and the block ID that the DataNode needs to find the block on its local storage. These IDs are unique for all blocks, and this is the only information the DataNodes need in order to identify the block on their local storage. The client examines this information, approaches the relevant DataNodes, and asks for the blocks (figure B.7).

The DataNodes serve the contents back to the client (figure B.8), and the connection is closed. That completes the read step.

This is the first time we've mentioned the word *block* in the context of files in HDFS. In order to understand the read process, consider that a file is made up of blocks that are stored on the DataNodes. We'll dig deeper into this concept later in the appendix.

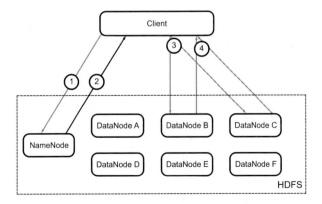

NameNode -> Client: "Absolutely, let's get you started. You can read block-1 from DataNode B and block-2 from DataNode C."

Figure B.6 Read operation: Name-Node acknowledges the read and sends back block information to the client

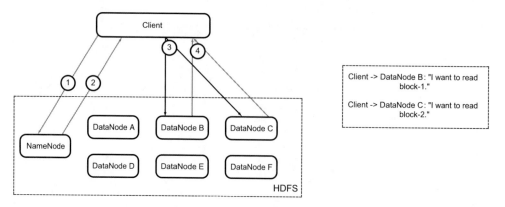

Figure B.7   Read operation: client contacts the relevant DataNodes and asks for the contents of the blocks

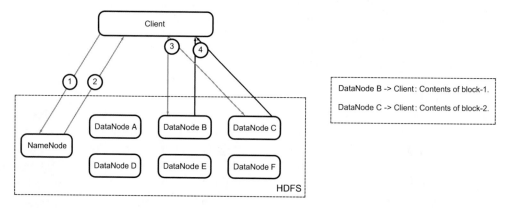

Figure B.8   Read operation: DataNodes serve the block contents to the client. This completes the read step.

Note that the client gets separate blocks for a file in parallel from different Data-Nodes. The client joins these blocks to make the full file. The logic for this is in the client library, and the user who's writing the code doesn't have to do anything manually. It's all handled under the hood. See how easy it is?

B.5   *Resilience to hardware failures via replication*

In large distributed systems, disk and network failures are commonplace. In case of a failure, the system is expected to function normally without losing data. Let's examine the importance of replication and how HDFS handles failure scenarios. (You may be thinking that we should have covered this earlier—hang on for a bit and it will make sense.)

When everything is working fine, DataNodes periodically send heartbeat messages to the NameNode (by default, every three seconds). If the NameNode doesn't receive a heartbeat for a predefined time period (by default, 10 minutes), it considers the DataNode to have failed, removes it from the cluster, and starts a process to recover from the failure. DataNodes can fall out of the cluster for various reasons—disk failures, motherboard failures, power outages, and network failures. The way HDFS recovers from each of these is the same.

For HDFS, losing a DataNode means losing replicas of the blocks stored on that disk. Given that there is always more than one replica at any point in time (the default is three), failures don't lead to data loss. When a disk fails, HDFS detects that the blocks that were stored on that disk are under-replicated and proactively creates the number of replicas required to reach a fully replicated state.

There could be a situation in which multiple disks failed together and all replicas of a block were lost, in which case HDFS would lose data. For instance, it's theoretically possible to lose all the nodes that are holding replicas of a given file because there is a network partition. It's also possible for a power outage to take down entire racks. But such situations are rare; and when systems are designed that have to store mission-critical data that absolutely can't be lost, measures are taken to safeguard against such failures—for instances, multiple clusters in different data centers for backups.

From the context of HBase as a system, this means HBase doesn't have to worry about replicating the data that is written to it. This is an important factor and affects the consistency that HBase offers to its clients.

B.6   *Splitting files across multiple DataNodes*

Earlier, we examined the HDFS write path. We said that files are replicated three ways before a write is committed, but there's a little more to that. Files in HDFS are broken into blocks, typically 64–128 MB each, and each block is written onto the file system. Different blocks belonging to the same file don't necessarily reside on the same DataNode. In fact, it's beneficial for different blocks to reside on different DataNodes. Why is that?

When you have a distributed file system that can store large amounts of data, you may want to put large files on it—for example, outputs of large simulations of sub-atomic particles, like those done by research labs. Sometimes, such files can be larger than the size of a single hard drive. Storing them on a distributed system by breaking them into blocks and spreading them across multiple nodes solves that problem.

There are other benefits of distributing blocks to multiple DataNodes. When you perform computations on these files, you can benefit from reading and processing different parts of the files in parallel.

You may wonder how the files are split into blocks and who determines which DataNodes the various blocks should go to. When the client is writing to HDFS and talks to the NameNode about where it should write the files, the NameNode tells it the DataNodes where it should write the blocks. After every few blocks, the client goes back to the NameNode to get a fresh list of DataNodes to which the next few blocks should be written.

Believe it or not, at this point, you know enough about HDFS to understand how it functions. You may not win an architectural argument with a distributed systems expert, but you'll be able to understand what they're talking about. Winning the argument wasn't the intention of the appendix anyway!

index